James Harrison Rigg

Oxford High Anglicanism

And its Chief Leaders

James Harrison Rigg

Oxford High Anglicanism
And its Chief Leaders

ISBN/EAN: 9783744764209

Printed in Europe, USA, Canada, Australia, Japan

Cover: Foto ©ninafisch / pixelio.de

More available books at **www.hansebooks.com**

OXFORD
HIGH ANGLICANISM

AND ITS CHIEF LEADERS.

BY THE

Rev. JAMES H. RIGG, D.D.,

PRINCIPAL OF WESTMINSTER TRAINING COLLEGE,
PRESIDENT OF THE WESLEYAN METHODIST CONFERENCE IN 1878 AND 1892.

SECOND EDITION, GREATLY ENLARGED,

AND INCLUDING

A SUPPLEMENTARY CHAPTER ON THE CHURCH CRISIS.

London:

CHARLES H. KELLY,

2, CASTLE ST., CITY RD., AND 26, PATERNOSTER ROW, E.C.

1899.

MORRISON AND GIBB LIMITED, PRINTERS, EDINBURGH

PREFACE.

THIS book is the result of many years' study. It is nearly forty years since I wrote a volume entitled *Modern Anglican Theology*, which is now in its third edition, and which dealt specially with the views of the "Broad Church," and particularly of the Coleridgean section of the clergy, at that time apparently on the ascendant scale in England. That volume contains evidence that I had already, at that date, begun the serious study of Oxford Anglicanism. During the years which have followed I have often been asked to write what my friends spoke of as a companion book to that volume, dealing dispassionately and thoroughly with modern Anglicanism of the Oxford school. Till lately, however, the materials for a thorough treatment of the subject historically did not exist, and therefore, though I followed closely the developments of the school, so far as I was able, and from time to time wrote articles on such phases of the history as could be best and most suggestively dealt with, I did not, till a few years ago, contemplate at all seriously the undertaking which was now and again still suggested to me; and I was the more indisposed to make any attempt in that direction, because my duties and engagements left me very little leisure for systematic special work. Within the last few years, however, the needful materials for a history of modern Oxford Anglicanism have rapidly accumulated. Mr. Wilfrid Ward's two volumes giving the history of his father's life; Dean Church's *History of the Oxford Movement*; and Dr. Pusey's Biography,—with the side-lights of Archbishop Tait's Life, the Letters of Mozley and Newman, and (though this, of course, was earlier), Bishop Wilberforce's Life,—added to the old basis of Newman's *Apologia*, and other publications of thirty years ago, have made it possible to gain an historical view which should not only be authentic and true, but living and complete, of the development of the Oxford High Anglican Movement from its earliest stirrings down to the present time. I have accordingly undertaken to write a history of that development, making it, as in the case of my volume on *Modern Anglican Theology*, a history woven in considerable part out of biographies, and in which what is living and personal is made the vehicle for conveying historical views of theological doctrines and principles, and of their influence and working.[1] I have written frankly as a liberal and yet evangelical Protestant; still, I hope it will be seen and felt that I have taken pains to understand and have not unfairly represented the ideas with which I do

---

[1] In the case of the two chief leaders of the distinctively Tractarian Movement, Newman and W. G. Ward, I have not limited my use of biographical material to the period during which they still remained ostensibly adherents of the Church of England, because the true meaning and force, the specific quality and influence, of their characteristic principles, ecclesiastical and theological, came fully out not before, nor in, but after their secession. The after period of their lives best illustrates the character of their Tractarian principles, and furnishes, in fact, the most powerful and convincing argument against them. The illustration, moreover, is such as to need little or no argumentative exposition; it suggests very plainly its own application.

not agree. I do not think I am a bitter Protestant; I shall hardly, I imagine, be regarded as a narrow Evangelical. I have written other books of argument and controversy, relating to ecclesiastical and theological questions, and have not been reproached with partisan bitterness or strong denominational prejudice. I hope my present book will not be held to discredit my record.

This volume is the only attempt to write anything like a history of Oxford High Anglicanism which as yet has been, so far as I know, made by a Nonconformist. It is indeed the only book which attempts to trace the history from its early origins more than sixty years ago, through its successive developments and phases down to the present time. These two points, it will be admitted, give a characteristic distinction to the present volume. It is, besides, the work of a septuagenarian, and the fruit of nearly fifty years of reading and observation on the part of one who has enjoyed special opportunities for gaining knowledge of different schools of Christian opinion, both theological and ecclesiastical. These considerations may perhaps be regarded as affording some warrant for a difficult undertaking and a venture which, if I were a young man, I might feel to be perilous. At my time of life risks to reputation are discounted. It is for truth on a great subject that I have to care.

I have described myself as a Nonconformist. As some passages, especially in the latter part of the volume, may seem to some readers to wear an aspect of unfriendliness to the modern Church of England, or at least to what seems at present to be the most active and influential section of that Church, it may not be improper, as a personal explanation, to add that I am, nevertheless, not a "political Dissenter." I am a Wesleyan Methodist of what may perhaps be regarded as the older school. While recognising the pressing need for reform in the Church of England, both as to its inner constitution and its administrative organisation, and also as to its relations with the State and the nation, I do not feel bound to dissent from it for conscience' sake, either on the ground that some thousand years ago it became the endowed national Church of England, or merely on the ground of its episcopal government. I can conceive circumstances in which I might thankfully accept the religious hospitality of its communion. I say as much as this, whilst disclaiming any sympathy with the utopian dream of organic union between my own world-wide Church and the great historic Church of England. I say it because I wish to be believed in affirming that, so far as I am competent to judge of my own feelings or motives, no partisan animosity or prejudice of education, whether sectarian or anti-sectarian, has lent bitterness or exaggeration to the objections expressed or implied throughout the volume to the principles of Oxford High Anglicanism, objections for which I would fain gain the candid consideration of High Churchmen no less than the approval of Nonconformists.

JAMES H. RIGG.

September 23, 1895.

PREFACE TO THE PRESENT EDITION.

THE later pages of this volume, as published a few years ago, contained warnings which have been more than justified by the deep national agitation and the violent Church conflict of the last two years. In the body of the book it was my aim to sketch the historical rise and development of the Oxford High Anglican party in the Church of England, and especially the personal character and influence of the leaders who in succession guided or inspired the movement, and at the same time to point out the fallacies which flawed it from stage to stage. Mr. Walsh's volume, laying bare the secret history of the same movement—by its revelation of the hidden counsels and special methods which, from underground, governed the sinuous course and covert schemes of the banded auxiliaries through whom the leaders of the party carried out their plans and purposes—has furnished a luminous commentary on the history with which my volume had to deal. The result is strongly to confirm the general view of that history unfolded in this book, and to confirm also some conjectures and intimations which for want of direct evidence I hesitated to affirm as matters of fact.

On the public mind the effect of Mr. Walsh's volume has been to excite a widespread feeling of alarm and indignation among all who value the principles of the Protestant Reformation, or care for civil liberty and the sanctities of family life. The warnings which were given in the last chapter of this book have been justified with terrible emphasis. The hour of visitation for the Church of England has come. Its future and the future of England depend very much on the spirit and conduct of its clergy and laity, and, above all, on the conduct of its bishops in the present crisis. Mr. Walsh's volume is a storehouse of facts which throw a strong and startling light on the inner meaning of the Oxford Movement—and serve to show from what sources it derived its inspiration, what were the motives which tended to increase its strength and promote its progress, what are the forces which are embodied in it, and what the issues for better or worse that are destined to be determined in the near future.

The author has reason to be thankful for the manner in which his volume has been received. The most powerful influences had been for many years enlisted on the side of High Anglicanism. The literary world had been won over by the glamour of Newman's genius even more than by the consummate skill of his *Apologia*. The name of Keble had been a tower of strength for the party of which he and Newman were the early leaders. The power of the great preacher Canon Liddon had taken strong hold of earnest Church people, and of not a few Nonconformists. On Pusey's death the two great political leaders, Gladstone and Salisbury, had joined hands to do honour to his memory as a great Church leader. Such a man as R. H. Hutton of the *Spectator* was a devoted admirer and even disciple of Newman both as a preacher and as a theologian and philosopher. Under these circumstances it seemed almost as if Evangelical Protestantism in England were a lost cause. And yet, was it to be believed by the people of England or by the adherents of reformed Christianity throughout the world that the cause of the Reformation in this country was lost, that English Nonconformity, Scotch Presbyterianism, and the vital Evangelical element in the Church of England were all doomed to final defeat, that the theology of Hooker and of Barrow, the gospel teaching of Leighton and Wesley, were destined to die out? The alternative was that either this must be the prospect of Christendom, or that a fatal flaw, a $\pi\rho\hat{\omega}\tau o\nu$ $\psi\epsilon\hat{\upsilon}\delta o\varsigma$, a fundamental fallacy, infected all along the line the teaching of the Oxford leaders. The subject was one which had occupied my mind for many years, and I felt constrained at length to undertake the task of showing that the whole line of Oxford High Anglicanism, from Keble and Newman onwards, was tainted by specific error, the same essential flaw and fault of conception and reasoning appearing and reappearing in different forms from point to point of its historic course. That there was something to admire in all the leaders of the movement I was prepared frankly to confess—I could myself see much to admire in some of them. But over all there seemed to lie the shadow of Anti-Evangelical superstition. Those who were most to be admired for genius or intellectual faculty, as it seemed to me, were most to be condemned for erroneous teaching in theology or philosophy, or both. Many writers had dealt with the subject partially, with the history and argument here and there; but the entire history was linked closely together in a continuous struggle and growth of half a century, and the needful work demanded that the whole linked line of misguidance should be tested, and the fundamental errors traced through every integral part of the long growth of theurgical superstition. I did my best, working slowly and brokenly, to grapple with the formidable task. My book has been received quite as favourably as my utmost expectation could have anticipated. I have now the opportunity of preparing a new and enlarged edition, which I trust may be more worthy of favour than the first.

It was not to be expected that such an attempt as I have described would escape hostile criticism from the organs of the Oxford High Anglican Movement. The wonder is, that so little has been accomplished by such criticism. Some trivial and technical inaccuracies have been pointed out, especially in a brief notice in the *Guardian*, for which service I owe the reviewer thanks. In the *Church Quarterly Review* a bitter and contemptuous article was published, in which the writer, it may be presumed, did his most and worst against me and my book. The temper of the article may perhaps be taken as a tribute to the effectiveness of the work criticised. The power of the reviewer is in an inverse ratio to his bitterness. He makes no attempt to meet any one position taken up in the volume, nor has he pointed out any error of importance in the history. He discovers a minute inaccuracy of statement here, and an unusual mode of expression there, such as no Oxonian could have perpetrated. But this hostile critic can find nothing to refute or expose in my book of more importance than a few such mistakes. By the press generally the volume was very favourably received. The *Times* did me the honour to publish a candid and generous notice on the day of publication. The crowd of journals which afterwards reviewed the volume, with few exceptions, dealt with it in the same fair and friendly spirit. If the High Church organs were unfriendly, the Nonconformist organs and those of the Evangelical Church were, as might have been expected, warm in their approval. Leading provincial journals, both in England and in Scotland, gave the book cordial commendation.

I have carefully revised this edition. I have also added many illustrative notes, chiefly from the controversial records of the last two or three years, and have made additions here and there to the text. I have not yielded, however, to the temptation to make many additions which have suggested themselves, lest I should make a "big book." I have to thank many friends for valuable information, though I have not always been able to use it. Some friendly critics have thought me too gentle in my tone. I know that I might justly sometimes have taken a severer tone, and that there are damaging facts which I have not used in exposing the errors of the Oxford leaders and their followers; and also, that there are able books, such as Dr. Abbott's volume on Newman, from which I might have borrowed weapons of attack against that leader. But my plan was fixed, to avoid acrimonious criticism and judgments *in malam partem* where main points of principle or of history were not in question. I desired to use as my chief authorities the writings of Anglo-Catholic leaders themselves, and not of their opponents.

Some have thought my chapter on Ward's life in the Roman Church irrelevant, or at least superfluous. I do not so regard it. In my view it is a chapter of chief importance, without which the lessons of the history would be incomplete, and the effectiveness of the volume impaired. The reason of this judgment is intimated in a note to the Preface to the first edition. In the present edition the close relation of that chapter to the whole book—its central relation—is indicated in a brief new chapter (chap. vii. in this volume) on "The End of the Oxford Tractarian Movement: Some Lessons of the History."

I have thought it well to add a supplementary chapter, giving a slight sketch of the course of that mighty reaction against Romanising ritual which during the last two years has occupied so much space in the public mind, and made its protests with such energy and such alarming effectiveness alike in the press, in public meetings, and in Parliament, compelling at length the serious and earnest attention of the bishops, and awakening the indignation not only of Nonconformists but of all true Protestant Churchmen.

I have also added two Appendices, one on what the Primate has said in his Charge on the subject of Consubstantiation as a doctrine not prohibited within the Church of England, the other containing some interesting correspondence relating to Newman, Pusey, and Manning, now for the first time published.

As now revised and enlarged I have good hope that this second edition will be found more complete and valuable than the first, and will bear its own share in the present combination of Protestant forces against the Romanising Neo-Anglicanism which has wrought so much evil in England and her colonies, and which, unless it had been challenged and checked as it has been, would have sorely changed for the worse the morality and manly virtue of our nation.[1]

BRIXTON, *November* 6, 1899.   JAMES H. RIGG.

[1] I owe my best thanks to the Rev. J. E. Harlow for the valuable service he has rendered in preparing the Index to this volume.

CONTENTS.

CHAPTER I.

THE FIRST LEAVEN OF THE OXFORD MOVEMENT:—

                                                     PAGE

THE EVANGELICAL REVIVAL—THE DIVINE RIGHT NONJURORS—KEBLE, HURRELL FROUDE, AND NEWMAN: THEIR MUTUAL RELATIONS—KEBLE'S LIFE AND CHARACTER—THE THEOLOGY OF THE *CHRISTIAN YEAR*—KEBLE AS A POET 1

CHAPTER II.

THE CRISIS OF DISTRESS FOR THE CHURCH OF ENGLAND—THE HELP NEEDED—THE QUESTION OF THE CHURCH'S UNITY AND CATHOLICITY—THE TWO UNIVERSITIES—HUGH JAMES ROSE AND NEWMAN—THE QUESTION OF A LEADER FOR THE CRISIS—NEWMAN WRITES AND PUBLISHES THE FIRST *TRACT FOR THE TIMES*—THE TRUE UNITY OF THE CHURCH . . 34

CHAPTER III.

THE *TRACTS FOR THE TIMES*—ANGLICANISM AND APOSTOLICAL SUCCESSION—NEWMAN AND WARD—THE ADVANCE ROMEWARD—WARD'S POINT OF VIEW—HIS UNIQUE IDENTITY—CONTRAST BETWEEN NEWMAN AND WARD—WARD'S PERSONAL HISTORY—HIS *IDEAL OF A CHRISTIAN CHURCH*—HIS DEGRADATION AND SECESSION 51

CHAPTER IV.

THE TRACTARIAN MOVEMENT AS DESCRIBED FROM THE INTERIOR :—

DEAN CHURCH'S *HISTORY OF THE OXFORD MOVEMENT*—CHURCH'S POSITION—HIS RELATION TO NEWMAN—HOW FAR HE WENT—FIRST PRINCIPLE OF THE MOVEMENT—KEBLE'S RELATION TO THE MOVEMENT—HURRELL FROUDE, HIS *REMAINS*—THE COTERIE AT OXFORD—OXFORD SIXTY YEARS AGO—NEWMAN'S LIFE AND INFLUENCE—HIS RESERVE AND AUSTERITY—WARD'S INFLUENCE OVER NEWMAN—WARD'S WITNESS AGAINST NEWMAN—*NOTE*, CHURCH'S LECTURE ON BISHOP ANDREWES 93

CHAPTER V.

THE MASTER SPIRIT OF THE MOVEMENT—EXTRAVAGANT EULOGIES OF NEWMAN—MR. HUTTON OF THE *SPECTATOR*—WAS NEWMAN A GREAT MAN?—HIS PHILOSOPHICAL SCEPTICISM—HIS *GRAMMAR OF ASSENT*—PURSUIT OF INFALLIBILITY—HIS VIEW OF FAITH AS APPLIED RESPECTIVELY TO CATHOLIC AND PROTESTANT POPULATIONS—TURNING WHITE BLACK AND BLACK WHITE—ROMAN CATHOLIC AND PROTESTANT MORALITY—*THE POPES NOT PERSECUTORS*—NEWMAN AND DÖLLINGER—ESTIMATE OF NEWMAN'S CHARACTER—HIS LAST YEARS . . 131

CHAPTER VI.

WARD'S LIFE AS A ROMAN CATHOLIC THEOLOGIAN AND PHILOSOPHER—THE LAST FORTY YEARS OF WARD'S LIFE—ENGLISH ROMANISM FIFTY YEARS AGO—AN ULTRAMONTANE IDEALIST—HIS FAITH AND ITS GROUNDS—DAILY ROUTINE—MANIA FOR THE SENSATIONAL DRAMA—CONTRASTED PHASES OF CHARACTER—WARD AND FABER—WARD'S EARNESTNESS AS A PROFESSOR OF THEOLOGY—HIS DISLIKE OF LIBERAL CATHOLICISM—ECCENTRICITIES—HIS MERITS—WARD AND TENNYSON . . . 168

CHAPTER VII.

END OF THE OXFORD TRACTARIAN MOVEMENT: SOME LESSONS FROM ITS HISTORY 196

CHAPTER VIII.

THE TRANSITION FROM TRACTARIANISM TO PUSEYISM—THE GOAL OF PUSEYISM 199

CHAPTER IX.

TWO GREAT CONTRADICTORY PARTIES IN THE ANGLICAN COMMUNION—FOR THE PRESENT CONDITION OF SCHISM PUSEY MORE RESPONSIBLE THAN ANY OTHER MAN—PUSEY'S FAMILY AND EARLY LIFE—SCHOOL AND COLLEGE—BYRON AND SCOTT—FOREIGN TOUR—FELLOW OF ORIEL—VISITS GERMANY AS THEOLOGICAL STUDENT—DEFENDS GERMAN THEOLOGY AGAINST ROSE—CHANGE IN HIS VIEWS—JOINS NEWMAN AND THE TRACT PARTY—WRITES TRACT ON BAPTISM—BECOMES A POWER IN OXFORD—HIS WEALTH AND GENEROSITY 205

CHAPTER X.

HOOKER AND ALEXANDER KNOX—PUSEY'S MIDDLE PERIOD—HIS TRACT ON BAPTISM—HIS DOCTRINE OF BAPTISM—EXPOSITION AND INTERPRETATION OF ST. PAUL—INFANT BAPTISM AND CONFIRMATION—THE REMEDY FOR SIN AFTER BAPTISM—SACRAMENTAL CONFESSION AND ABSOLUTION—THE CLAIMS OF ANGLICAN PRIEST-CONFESSORS . 233

CHAPTER XI.

FULLER DEVELOPMENT OF PUSEY'S DOCTRINE—CONFESSION AND THE EUCHARIST—HIS OWN PENITENTIAL HISTORY AND DISCIPLINE—KEBLE HIS CONFESSOR—BOYS IN THE CONFESSIONAL—COLERIDGE ON THE CONFESSIONAL SYSTEM—THE PRIEST-CONFESSOR—SISTERHOODS AND CELIBACY—PUSEY AND HUMAN NATURE—THE HOUSE OF MERCY AT CLEWER

—Bishop Wilberforce and Pusey—The Truth laid bare—Mr. Dodsworth and Mr. Maskell—Puseyism in Leeds—Pusey and Dr. Hook 257

CHAPTER XII.

Pusey's Doctrine of the Real Presence—Consubstantiation and Transubstantiation—Newman and Pusey—Pusey, Bossuet, and Newman—Pusey and Manning—Reunion with Rome—Pusey and Archbishop Wake—How Pusey outwent Newman—Gladstone, Lord Halifax, and the Pope—The One Hope of the Christian World . 305

CHAPTER XIII.

Pusey's Personal Characteristics—Belief in Contradictions—His Immobility—His Relations with Evangelicals and Nonconformists—Pusey and Manning on Churchmen and Dissenters—The Cardinal as Umpire—Pusey on Ritualism—Ritualism and Doctrine—Archbishop Benson's Judgment in the Case of the Bishop of Lincoln—The Attack on Protestantism—Romanising Advance—Small Popes—Sacramental Life . . . 328

CHAPTER XIV.

The Outlook—Sources of Pusey's Personal Influence—Signs of Reaction—Forecast 359

SUPPLEMENTARY CHAPTER—1895-1899.

The Course of Events since 1895—National Agitation and the Church Crisis—Pending Questions—Disestablishment—Reform in Discipline and Organisation—Perplexities and Possibilities 371

Appendix A. The Primate's Charge on Consubstantiation . 405
Appendix B. Correspondence relating chiefly to Newman, Pusey, and Manning 410

OXFORD HIGH ANGLICANISM AND ITS CHIEF LEADERS.

CHAPTER I.

THE FIRST LEAVEN OF THE OXFORD MOVEMENT:—

THE EVANGELICAL REVIVAL — THE DIVINE RIGHT NONJURORS — KEBLE, HURRELL FROUDE, AND NEWMAN: THEIR MUTUAL RELATIONS — KEBLE'S LIFE AND CHARACTER — THE THEOLOGY OF THE *CHRISTIAN YEAR* — KEBLE AS A POET.

IN an article on "The Evangelical Movement," which Mr. Gladstone republished[1] in the *Evangelical Magazine* for January 1895, it is ingeniously suggested that the Oxford Movement owes its parentage—indirectly, if not immediately—to the same religious revival which produced the recognised Evangelical Movement in and beyond the Church of England. In connexion with this suggestion, Mr. Gladstone refers to the fact that Newman's " conversion," which he ever afterwards regarded as the beginning of his spiritual life, took place under evangelical influences. This, no doubt, is true. Newman then gained,

[1] It was published originally in the *British Quarterly Review*.

for the first time, a vivid consciousness of his personal relation to God,—to the "living God,"—the sense and strength of which remained with him always thereafter, safeguarding him from atheism and materialism amid all his metaphysical questionings. This was the vital principle, giving a sort of unity and continuity to the history of his soul through all its movements, and with all its oscillations. But in the de-Calvinised transformation of his doctrinal belief, which was consummated at Oxford, no characteristic doctrine of the evangelical theology was left. As to the doctrines of faith, justification, and sanctification, he had ceased to be "evangelical" some time before the first idea of the Tractarian revival took shape in his mind. In fact, his principles as the active leader of the Oxford Movement were imbibed from his intercourse with Keble and Hurrell Froude.[1] Newman himself says expressly and emphatically that Keble was the real father of the Oxford Movement; and it was the influence of Froude which brought together Keble and Newman. It was Froude who effected

[1] The authority on whom I have mainly relied in this chapter is Mr. Keble's almost lifelong friend, the late Sir J. T. Coleridge, who wrote Keble's Life,—published in 1869,—who also wrote for the *Guardian* newspaper several communications of considerable length during the month (April 1866) following his death. The letters to the *Guardian* are full and very valuable, but the Life is somewhat disappointing. It contains no correspondence with either Newman or Pusey. The aged author, moreover, was very feeble, and lived not many days after the publication of the biography. Of course, I have also used Newman's *Apologia*, Church's *Oxford Movement*, and *Pusey's Life*, which makes large use of Keble's letters. It was not, however, till after the chapter was in print that I became acquainted with Mr. Lock's *Biography of Keble*. Having now read it, I find no reason to modify what I had written, though I recognise the merits of the biography as written from the point of view of the Sub-Warden of Keble College, who might be expected to be a loyal adherent of the Neo-Anglican School.

that blending and focusing of the sympathies and aims of Keble, Newman, and himself which furnished the first inspiration and impulse of the Oxford Neo-Anglican Movement. Newman, that is to say, though afterwards the leader, was first the disciple of Keble, and even of Froude; and Keble and Froude derived their Anglican indoctrination and inspiration, not assuredly from the evangelical revival, which they were brought up to hate,—and did both sincerely hate through life,—but from the High Church school of the early years of the eighteenth century, of which Dr. Routh was a living representative at Oxford for many years after Keble obtained his fellowship at Oriel. Bishop Ken, Robert Nelson, and William Law in his earlier period, before he had become Behmenised and ultra-mystical, were their ideals as Churchmen; their sympathies were with the Nonjurors, and their politics were of the Divine Right complexion. Clayton, the Jacobite Methodist of Oxford,—who, after he had become chaplain of the Manchester Collegiate Church, and when his intimate friends, the Wesleys, had entered upon their evangelistic career, disowned his friendship with them, and utterly refused to recognise them, either personally or ecclesiastically,—was a true representative of the school of Churchmanship in which the Kebles were brought up by their father, a clergyman of the old, old school; and with which Froude, Keble's much-loved pupil, as well as Keble's other pupils, Robert Wilberforce and Isaac Williams, were to be presently identified. The author of the *Christian Year*, indeed, has not been generally regarded as belonging to so extreme and exclusive a Church school as this, because the history of his secluded life was not known, and he never appeared before the public eye. But yet it is true that no Churchman of the century has been less tolerant of Dissent than John Keble—none more narrow and exclusive in his ecclesiastical principles and sympathies. In 1847 he published a volume of *Sermons, Academical and Occasional,* which Newman redeemed from obscurity by a well-known reference to one of them in his *Apologia* as an epochal utterance, as sounding the first clear note of the new spirit which was arising to awaken and uplift the Church and the age. In the Preface to this volume Keble distinguishes mankind, as respects their religion, into three classes—" Christians, *properly so called,*[1] *i.e.* Catholics; Jews, Mohammedans, and heretics; and heathens and unbelievers." Thus deliberately, in the fulness of his strength and the zenith of his life, he placed on record his judgment that Dissenters, not being Catholics, can only be classed as heretics, between whom and true Christians, Jews and Mohammedans have an intermediate place. With this position his course was in harmony to the end of his life.

And yet when, less than twenty years after the publication of this volume of sermons, and of that Preface as explaining the ecclesiastical tone and the main line of thought pervading the whole, Keble finished his earthly course, no remembrance—no sense whatever, as it would seem—of the fact that he had throughout been identified with Newman's course as an Anglican, standing by him to the last,—and that he had, in the passage I have quoted, gone very far beyond Newman in his antagonism to Dissenters,—marred the complete harmony of reverent and loving lamentation with which all denominations of Christians mourned his death. Very remarkable and very

[1] The italics are mine.

beautiful was the unanimity of affectionate admiration and regret with which the intelligence of his decease was responded to by Christian men of every shade of denominational colour. In that first week of April 1866, the *Nonconformist* vied with the *Guardian* in its tribute to his merits as a sacred poet and his goodness as a man. Even the literary critic seemed in this case to forget his craft. The chief, if not the only, exception to this last remark was in the case of the *Spectator*. That journal alone, so far as I could find, was so sternly true to its vocation as to criticise with strict fidelity the poetry of the *Christian Year*, and to attempt to enforce discrimination in the praise bestowed on that volume.

The reason for this immunity from harsh criticism, and this agreement in tender reverence, accorded to a man of extreme and unbending opinions like Keble, is worth particular attention. Indeed, unless we understand the reason, we shall hardly understand the man all round. In these studies my object is not merely to criticise the opinions of those who pass under review, but to see them in their living reality as men and Christians. If this be done justly and truly, needful dissent from opinions or condemnation of conduct will have its due weight; and will be recognised, even if severe, as an integral part of a fair and honest presentation of the men as they actually were in life among their fellows. Keble was the tutor and the loving and sympathetic friend of the bitter and contemptuous Froude, who "hated the Reformation," and reserved his utmost scorn and antipathy for "irreverent Dissenters." He was not only at other points the friend and counsellor of Newman, but he regarded himself as jointly responsible for Tract 90, of which he published a formal defence. Yet those who, not unjustly, were indignant against Froude, and those who utterly distrusted and deeply condemned Newman and his methods, cherished nothing like anger against the friend and teacher of Froude, and seemed even to condone Keble's complicity with Newman. Newman's *Apologia*, indeed, published not long before Keble's death, may have done something to prepare the way for gentle judgments of Keble. But this of itself will go no way towards explaining the generosity of affection with which lamentation was made by the Christian world for Keble. In fact, the sorrow at his death did but express the love which had been gathering about him during his life. For nearly forty years, with the exception of a brief interval in the very height of the Tractarian controversy, Keble, the Tractarian poet, had been growing in the esteem of his countrymen. He seemed to bear a charmed life. Those who spared none besides spared him. Several reasons concurred to produce this result. But perhaps the deepest and most really operative causes were not the obvious ones. Not a little was due, no doubt, to his character as a poet—as a sacred poet. A *vates* of pure and lofty spirit, even in these modern times, is looked upon with reverence as well as admiration. But there was much more than this.

Keble had led a secluded, saintly life, worthy of a Christian pastor and poet, far from the world's strife, far even from the Church's rivalries, declining all preferment, eschewing all ambition, holding to the friends of his youth, abiding in the parish to which his way was guided in early manhood, living for thirty years among the same scenes and the same people, dying as he had lived, and carried to his long rest among his own parishioners in his own churchyard from the beautiful church which he had built and adorned out of the profits of his own churchly poems. During all this long life he had entered actively into no controversy, whatever may have been his personal sentiments, or his religious habits and practices. In such a life there was a unity, a purity, a beauty, which could not fail to touch refined and Christian hearts. For the sake of all this, the nation forgave Keble's antique prejudices and extreme ecclesiastical principles. His personal opinions were extreme, so extreme as to lead him to admire the character of Froude, in spite of his immodesty, his intolerance, and his puerile asceticism; because there was in the young man such heartiness, such good fellowship, such zeal, such talent, and all consecrated to the cause of "Catholic" restoration and Christian progress, as he understood it; so extreme, again, were his opinions as to carry him along with Newman in all that he did, including the publication of Tract 90, until he seceded to Rome. But Keble's personal disposition was tender and loving, and his own administration was mild and peaceful. His Church principles were "sentiments"—to use the convenient French word in its proper sense—rather than energies. He dreamt, and mused, and meditated; but he did not seek actively to revolutionise. It is remarkable that in his beautiful church, with all its rare and costly adornments, ritualistic symbols and uses were not carried to a puerile extreme. He was the oldest and most intimate friend of Sir J. T. Coleridge, himself the dearest friend of Arnold. And widely as Arnold and he, who had been early friends, came to be sundered, each bore towards the other throughout a deep and affectionate regard. Such a man, and the friend of such men, could not but be loved in spite of Romanising sympathies and opinions.

It is not an insignificant circumstance, as affecting the character of Keble, that he was never at a public school. His father was vicar of Coln St. Aldwyn's, near Fairford, in Gloucestershire, and resided at Fairford, in his own patrimonial house. The father conducted the education of his two sons himself, and prepared them for the university. He was, we are informed, a man of no ordinary ability and character, and "he lived to his ninetieth year, in the occasional discharge of his duty up to within a few months of his death." The manner in which his son acquitted himself on his entrance within the university is decisive proof of the ability and scholarship of the father; while the reverence and love with which his son always spoke of him, may be taken as evidence of his moral worth. Young Keble was not quite fifteen when, in December 1806, he competed successfully for a scholarship at Corpus Christi College, of which college his father had been a Fellow. In Easter Term 1810, being but a little more than eighteen years of age, he obtained his B.A. degree—a double-first. A double-first at such an age was an extraordinary instance of precocious scholarship; and we have the testimony of Sir J. T. Coleridge that the first classes in that examination were very distinguished. Such high scholarship at so early an age was not likely to have been attained by one educated at any of the public schools of England more than fifty years ago. In the coarse and Spartan age when our grandfathers went to school, our public schools were much less efficient than they have been of later years. Neither, we may add, is it likely that if he had gone to Winchester or Harrow, to

Westminster or Eton, young Keble would have retained untarnished that bloom of youthful goodness which seems to have been eminently characteristic of him from the first. From his father's house at Fairford to Oxford was an easy ride; and the loving and home-nurtured youth seems never to have departed from the godly ways in which he had been trained under his father's eye. No doubt this fact has some relation to the exquisite simplicity and purity which distinguished Keble's character in after life.

The consequence of his success as a scholar of Corpus Christi was, that Keble was speedily elected to what, at that time, was counted the most distinguished honour his university could bestow—a fellowship at Oriel. Among the Fellows of Oriel were such men as Copleston, Davison, and Whately. Intellectually, Keble was not at any time of his life the equal of these men, although as a mere scholar he may have been superior to more than one of them. It cannot be imagined that at nineteen this "junior Fellow" could have been equal to sustaining his part with such intellectual athletes in what Sir J. T. Coleridge, writing in the *Guardian* soon after Keble's death, describes as the "learned and able, not rarely the subtle and disputatious, conversations round the fire in the Oriel common room." It is no wonder that his friend fancied that Keble "sometimes yearned for the more easy, yet not unintellectual, society of his old friends at Corpus." We may be permitted, perhaps, to imagine that such disputations as those in which Whately and his friends took part, may have tended to produce in the mind of their immature and unequal colleague some distaste for subtle and daring speculations, may have led a youth of his reverent spirit to fly for refuge to the traditions and authority of the Church, which in his poems he so often apostrophises as "his Mother"; and here, again, it is not out of place to remark, that if his home-breeding had preserved uninjured the bloom of his mind's virgin purity, the bold play and competition of tempers and wits at a public school might have tended to develop a manliness and self-reliance of character which might have preserved him from the errors of a superstitious externalism, and given to his intellect and to his poetry a distinctness and force, the want of which was one of his admitted defects.

The conscientious industry of Keble had enabled him to take the highest honours in the mathematical studies prescribed for the Honours course at Oxford. These studies, however, were not at Oxford at that time so advanced as Cambridge mathematics, and there can be no doubt that his chief success as a scholar, if he had devoted his life to scholarship, would have been in the classics and elegant literature.

In 1812 he won the Chancellor's Essay prizes both in Latin and English. At this time he might have been regarded as the most rising man at Oxford. But ambition was not one of his passions, although he could hardly have been altogether insensible to its solicitations. He seems to have been one of those happily constituted men in whom human affections are paramount. A devoted son, an affectionate brother, and a devout Churchman, duty and affection appear to have ruled him from his youth up. "If he had ambition in his nature," says Sir J. T. Coleridge, "he had very early and effectually suppressed it. The Church he had deliberately chosen as his profession, and he desired to follow that in a country cure." These were his principles; in such channels flowed the even current of his affections.

Keble began to take pupils in his college about the year 1814. Soon afterwards he was appointed one of the Examining Masters for the university, an office which he filled more than once in the course of his connexion with Oxford. He was Public Examiner in the Final Schools 1814–1816. He was ordained deacon in 1815, being twenty-three years of age, and priest in the year following. He served the curacies of two small parishes near Fairford, but at a considerable distance from Oxford. How Keble contrived to serve these parishes as curate, and at the same time to discharge his duties at Oxford, seems difficult to understand. He was, of course, in the frequent habit of riding to and fro between Oxford and Fairford. It has been suggested that his parishes were extremely small, and were contiguous to each other; and also that, as they were near to Fairford, he might count on the assistance of his father. It might also be suggested that curates eighty years ago did not work in their parishes as they do now. Keble, however, delighted in his parish work. At that period he was already beginning to write the poems which were afterwards published in the *Christian Year*. At the end of 1817 Keble was compelled to fix his ordinary residence during term time at the university, having been appointed college tutor.

It was in the year 1822 that Newman was elected a Fellow of Oriel. At that time Keble was one of the most eminent and honoured men at the university.

"The first time," says Newman in his *Apologia*, "that I was in a room with him was on the occasion of my election to a fellowship at Oriel, when I was sent for into the Tower to shake hands with the Provost and Fellows. How is that hour fixed in my memory after the changes of forty-two years—forty-two this very day on which I write! I have lately had a letter in my hands which I sent at the time to my friend John Bowden, with whom I passed almost exclusively my undergraduate years. I had to hasten to the Tower, I say to him, to receive the congratulations of all the Fellows. I bore it till Keble took my hand, and then felt so abashed and unworthy of the honour done me that I seemed desirous of quite sinking into the ground. His had been the first name which I had heard spoken of, with reverence rather than admiration, when I came up to Oxford. When one day I was walking in High Street with my dear earliest friend just mentioned, with what eagerness did he cry out, 'There's Keble!' and with what awe did I look at him! Then, at another time, I heard a Master of Arts of my college giving an account how he had just then had occasion to introduce himself on some business to Keble, and how gentle, courteous, and unaffected Keble had been, so as almost to have put him out of countenance. Then, too, it was reported, truly or falsely, how a rising man of brilliant reputation, the present Dean of St. Paul's, Dr. Milman, admired and loved him, adding that somehow he was unlike anyone else. However, at the time when I was elected Fellow of Oriel he was not in residence, and he was shy of me for years in consequence of the marks which I bore upon me of the evangelical and liberal schools; at least so I have ever thought. Hurrell Froude brought us together about 1828; it is one of the sayings preserved in his *Remains*— 'Do you know the story of the murderer who had done one good thing in his life? Well, if I was ever asked what good deed I had ever done, I should say that I had brought Keble and Newman to understand each other.' "[1]

Personal reminiscences are, perhaps, as little to be trusted about one's self as about one's friends. There must be some mistakes in the passage just quoted. Newman was elected Fellow of Oriel, Keble's own college, in 1822. Keble, Sir J. T. Coleridge tells us, was Examining Master for the university from Michaelmas 1821 to Easter 1823. Keble, therefore, must have frequently been in Oxford in 1822 and 1823. It was not, indeed, till his mother's death in May 1823, that he decided to leave Oxford and settle near his father. Moreover, it is hardly likely that the main reason of Keble's holding aloof from Newman at this time was the connexion which, some time before, Newman had had with the "evangelical and liberal school." Keble was for years the friend of Arnold— liberal of liberals ; he was also friendly with Whately and Milman. It can hardly be imagined that the slight tincture of liberalism which had passed upon Newman would alone have been sufficient to keep Keble aloof from one who, as it is plain, earnestly desired his acquaintance. This would scarcely have comported with the character of one so "gentle" and "courteous." Still less is it to be supposed that the mild and inoperative remains of Newman's evangelical opinions or tendencies would have made him distasteful to such a man as Keble. The reason of Keble's distaste for Newman is not, I think, difficult to divine ; although it could hardly be expected that Newman would have the gift to divine it.

This is a point of some importance as well as of much interest. Their characters were not likely to blend, except

[1] Newman's *Apologia*, pp. 75-77 (1st edition).

under the influence of some common solvent—some medium of overpoweringly strong affinity with both, through which characters so sharply contrasted might be combined in sympathy and united in counsel. Both had much that was feminine in their nature;[1] but Keble's nature resembled that of a quiet, meditative woman, devoted to home duties, to parish work, to pious musings, to country walks and garden pleasures, to poetry and music, and especially to sacred minstrelsy; whereas Newman reminds us of a woman of genius and force, at once dreamy and busy, benevolent and ambitious, devotional and speculative, refined and controversial, restlessly active, zealously propagandist—such a one as would found sisterhoods, write clever but extreme books, and revolutionise a religious community. Any who have studied human nature will at once understand, if two such women were brought together, with what mild but settled aversion the shy and quiet sister would regard her restless, unsafe, and ambitious compeer. Such a neighbour would disturb her tranquillity, spoil her meditations, interfere with her plans, and, like the baleful comet of which Milton speaks, "perplex with fear of change." Very much of this sort, I cannot but think, were the feelings with which, at first, Keble regarded Newman, whose mind was essentially speculative and sceptical, and whose temper was eminently ambitious; who, indeed, as Bishop Copleston once declared to a friend, was neither understood nor trusted by any of his colleagues at Oriel. It was the Anglo-Catholic enterprise which finally brought the two into harmony and mutual understanding. Nor could a fitter instrument have

---

[1] See the Note at the end of this chapter on "The Feminine Vein in Newman's Character."

been found for bringing about the union on this basis than Hurrell Froude. He was himself in several respects as great a contrast to Keble in character as even Newman. But then he had been Keble's pupil, and he remained his devoted and admiring friend. Whatever his pride and bitterness against those whom he regarded as heretics, he was dutiful and reverent to his former tutor. Moreover, although Newman in his *Apologia* speaks of Froude as "speculative," he was not metaphysically sceptical, and his speculations appear to have been confined within theologically safe regions. Froude, in fact, stood in fear of Newman's speculative tendency; and in one place, whilst expressing his delight in his companionship, expresses his doubt at the same time whether he is not more or less of a "heretic."

In no sense was Hurrell Froude doctrinally or metaphysically speculative. He had, seemingly from the first, bound himself to tradition. His affections went after antiquity; but, in particular, he doted upon the mediæval Church. His speculations never led him towards the verge of unbelief. Whilst his zeal was hot and his mind active, his intellect seemed to make good its safety by servility to traditional dogma. If he mocked at the Reformers, he held fast by the "saints." Furthermore, although such a zealot for traditional Church authority, and so bold and hot against all Protestants and Puritans, he was to his friends gentle, tender, playful, pleasant, and most open-hearted. It is easy to see by what ties such a man would be attached to Keble and to Newman. The former regarded him somewhat as a mother regards a high-spirited, spoilt, but frank, true-spoken, and affectionate son. She is proud of him, while she disapproves of some of his proceedings.

She reproves him, but gently, lovingly—too gently by far. She views all his conduct with a partial eye. His very faults seem to her but the exuberances of a noble spirit. It must be remembered also that Froude's animosities corresponded to Keble's dislikes, and that his enthusiastic and passionate admiration was bestowed in accordance with Keble's preferences. The tempers of the teacher and pupil were very different, but their tastes and opinions were well agreed; and, in fact, those of Froude had been formed by Keble. What Keble instilled by gentle influence became in Froude a potent and heady spirit. Keble, accordingly, forgave the violence of his pupil, in part for the sake of his orthodoxy, and in part because of his dutifulness and affection to him personally. His excesses were but the excesses of a fine young nature on behalf of what was good and right. "E'en his failings leaned to virtue's side." While such were the ties which attached Keble to Froude, Newman was drawn to him both by agreement in theological and ecclesiastical opinions and tendencies, and also by a strong natural affinity of disposition. No one can read Newman's description of Froude and of himself in the *Apologia* without feeling that he and such a man as Froude must have been most congenial companions. Both were intellectually what he describes Froude as being, "critical and logical," "speculative and bold." Newman, no less than Froude, "delighted in the notion of an hierarchical system, of sacerdotal power, and of full ecclesiastical liberty." "Hatred of the Reformers," "scorn" of Protestantism, are noted by Newman as characteristics of Froude.[1] And, as to himself: "I became fierce," "I was indignant," "I despised every rival system," "I had a thorough contempt

[1] *Apologia*, p. 85.

for the evangelicals "—such expressions as these abound in his delineation of his own character at this period of his life.[1]

It is no wonder, therefore, that Froude and Newman clave to each other; and it is easy to understand how, through the influence of such a common friend as Froude, and of their common ecclesiastical and theological sympathies, Newman and Keble came to be intimately associated and warmly attached.[2] Keble was Newman's senior as a university man, and was also much his superior in university influence. To make such a man his friend must have been a great object with Newman, especially as the feeling of a vocation to reform the Church and the spirit of a propagandist began to take hold of him. Newman, there can be no doubt, used every effort to win Keble. And when once Keble had overcome his aversion and distrust in regard to Newman, he, like nearly all who came into intimate relation with that magnetic man, fell under the spell of his personal fascination, and became strongly attached to him; so that Newman's secession to Rome was, as Sir J. T. Coleridge tells us, "the greatest sorrow of his life."

The *Christian Year* was published in 1827, when Keble was thirty-five years of age, and still unmarried. The work had been in silent progress during many years. Sir J. T. Coleridge tells us that he had himself "the hymns for Septuagesima Sunday, St Mark's Day, the

[1] *Apologia*, pp. 97, 113, 114, etc.
[2] It must not be forgotten that Keble and Newman were the joint editors of Froude's *Remains*—a book which was published contrary to the judicious advice of Sir J. T. Coleridge, but which did not a little to reveal the true and the extreme character of the views which were common to the three friends.

Purification, and some others in MS. as early as 1819." Keble's original plan had been to "complete the series of poems," to "go on improving it all his life," and "to leave it to come out, if judged useful, after he should be out of the way." Such was his statement to his friend Coleridge in a letter dated 1825; but, acting on the advice of his friends, he published the book, by which for nearly seventy years past he has been known throughout all the Churches of English-speaking Christians, in the year I have mentioned, 1827. It was in the year following the publication of the *Christian Year*, as we have seen, that Hurrell Froude was the means of introducing Newman to the friendship of Keble. From the union of these three the Tractarian Movement may be said to have received its first inspiration. Newman has spoken of Keble as the "true and primary author" of "that Movement afterwards called Tractarian."[1] He traces to the *Christian Year* influences which he imagines to have given such shape and impulse to men's thoughts and feelings as tended directly towards his own Tractarianism. He mentions, in particular, as pervading the volume, "the doctrine that material phenomena are both the types and the instruments of real things unseen,"—a doctrine which, he says, "embraces not only what Anglicans as well as Catholics believe about sacraments properly so called, but also the article of the 'communion of saints' in its fulness, and likewise the 'mysteries of the faith.'"[2] Newman also professes to have learnt his doctrine of faith in part from Keble, but supposes himself to have improved upon Keble's doctrine, with which, although "beautiful and religious," he was "dissatisfied," as not sufficiently thorough—as logically

[1] *Apologia*, p. 75.   [2] *Ibid.* pp. 77, 78.

altogether inadequate. If we were to accept Newman's account of Keble's views, probably few would think Newman's any improvement upon them; his doctrine of faith, indeed, being one of the weakest and worst parts of his system, as intellectually faulty and contradictory as it is unevangelical. I confess, however, that Newman's discoveries of his own system in Keble's *Christian Year* seem to me not a little fanciful. It is, indeed, very satisfactory that there is so little evidence to prove that Keble was in any sense a master spirit in the Tractarian theological development; or that his theological teaching in the *Christian Year* was imbued to any serious extent with such superstitions as make up the substance of that system of theurgic mysticism which our modern High Anglicans have substituted for the glorious gospel of the blessed God. The theological views of Keble during the ten years antecedent to 1827—the period during which the hymns of the *Christian Year* were composed—were as yet more or less eclectic, and fell far short of the exalted sacramental doctrine which appears in some of his later poems published in *Lyra Apostolica* and *Lyra Innocentium*. It was during 1828 and some following years that Keble settled definitely on the basis of confessional and sacramental Anglo-Catholicism, which was afterwards common to the whole Tractarian school; and which Newman, partly through Froude's influence, embraced in its full extent some while later than Keble. Newman, in his reference to Keble's theology, quotes no single passage from the *Christian Year*, and adduces no single fact to show that Keble took a leading part in moulding the doctrine or in dictating the policy of the Tractarian organisation, though there can be no doubt that after 1833 he was an intimate associate and fellow-worker with Newman, so far as one not resident in Oxford could be. The one fact which seems directly to connect Keble with the origination of the Tractarian Movement as a distinct force, is that Newman ever kept the anniversary of the day on which Keble preached the Assize Sermon at Oxford, which he published under the title of *National Apostasy*, as "the start of the religious movement of 1833." But that sermon, as the context in the passage in the *Apologia* [1] referring to it clearly shows, derived its emphasis and importance, in the view of Newman, much more from the crisis in the ecclesiastical and religious history of the Anglican Church, in conjunction with which it was preached, than from any quality or force in the sermon itself. The sermon must have been the mere occasion—in no sense the cause—of the combination from which the Movement arose; it was the taper by which a train was ignited. There is nothing wonderful or electrical about the sermon; it is a solemn but feeble threnody on the deepening politico-ecclesiastical liberalism of the nation, mingled with exhortations to the pious not to cease to pray for the country. But the "times were ripe" when it was preached. The hour and the man had come: that man was Newman, shielded and recommended by the support of Keble's churchly, decorous, and prudent-seeming goodness. The sermon itself contains no outline, suggests no idea, of the Tractarianism which was so soon thereafter to be organised by Newman.

Nor will even a keen-eyed critic find more in the *Christian Year*, as originally published, than the reverent High Church utterances of a tender and poetic spirit. The

[1] Pp. 96-100.

hymn on Holy Communion contains no high sacramental doctrine. No one, out of any hint in that poem, could develop Pusey's doctrine of the Eucharist. The hymn on Holy Baptism teaches the doctrine of baptismal regeneration broadly and strongly; but that doctrine does not imply all that is taught by Anglo-Catholics. What is said by Archbishop Trench in his poems as to baptism is much the same, in effect, as what Keble says in his hymn. The hymns on Confirmation and Ordination contain no doctrine in excess of what every reverent and tenderly devout High Churchman would feel to be appropriate to those solemnities. Nor will distinct traces of those pronounced opinions, which belong to the modern Anglican imitations of Roman doctrine and ritual, be anywhere found in this favourite manual of devotional poetry. In the hymn on the Annunciation, high honour is done to her who was hailed by the angel as blessed among women; but it would be difficult to prove that anything in this hymn involves really Romish doctrine. It is a high poetical rhapsody—a poetical apostrophe. But it would certainly be wrong to regard it as an invocation. As a precedent the hymn may have done harm. It may have sounded a false keynote. The transition is easy from poetical apostrophes to personal invocation. Still, remembering that poetical apostrophes to the memories of great men—heroes, patriots, poets, founders of ecclesiastical communities—have not been uncommon in any age, ancient or modern,[1] it would not be just or candid, on the ground of this hymn alone, to

---

[1] See the peroration to Robert Hall's grand sermon on the "Sentiments proper to the present crisis," and also the Preface to the same sermon.

condemn Keble as intending to lend countenance to Mariolatry. The most suspicious lines in the hymn are:

> Ave Maria! Thou whose name
> All but adoring love may claim.

Protestant admirers of Keble could wish that these lines had been blotted from the poem; but it must be remembered in reading it that Keble was obliged, in the prosecution of the plan of his book, to write upon the Annunciation; that the words of the Annunciation are: "Hail, thou that art highly favoured, the Lord is with thee: blessed art thou among women"; and that the stanzas of the hymn which have been objected to are little else than a highly coloured and overstrained paraphrase of the words of the angel. The one passage in the *Christian Year*, as now published, which teaches the Tractarian doctrine as to the Eucharist is, in fact, a change from the original made by Keble's executors in conformity with his explicit direction given under the influence of advanced Tractarian friends, in order to bring the teaching of the *Christian Year* up to the Tractarian level. In one of the stanzas on the Gunpowder Treason, there occurred the line: "Present in the heart, *not* in the hand," as applied to the Lord Jesus in the Eucharist,— words distinctly anti-Tractarian. These words were changed by Keble's executors into "Present in the heart *as* in the hand," and in that form the line appears in the present editions of the *Christian Year*. That change, made after Keble's death in accordance with his own express requirement, may serve in part to measure the difference between the theology of the *Christian Year* as Keble sent it forth in 1827 and the system of theology which a few years later he adopted, and which was identical with that of the Tractarian school, especially as set forth by Dr. Pusey.

I have referred to Keble's *Lyra Innocentium* as much more advanced in its theology than the *Christian Year*. The wide difference between Keble's earlier and later theological views would have been still more strikingly shown if he had not at the urgent request of some of his friends, Coleridge among the number, suppressed several hymns intended for this volume, which, if published, would have alarmed and incensed public feeling. One of these hymns Sir J. T. Coleridge felt it to be his duty to print in his biography of Keble. In this hymn Mary is addressed as "Mother of God"; and these lines appear—

>Whom thousand worlds adore,
>He calls thee Mother evermore.

Keble resolutely defended this language, and expressed his surprise that his friends should object to it. His theology in middle and later life was, in fact, very different from that of the *Christian Year*. In a letter to Coleridge, dated 18th of June 1845, there occurs the following sentence: "No doubt there would be the difference in tone which you take notice of between this and the former book; for when I wrote that I did not understand (to mention no more points) either the doctrine of repentance or that of the holy Eucharist as held, *e.g.*, by Bishop Ken, nor that of justification."

I have spoken in the earlier part of this chapter of Keble's deliberate intolerance of spirit. An illustration of this is given in his biography. Sir J. T. Coleridge says: "He writes playfully to me at an earlier time—'Hurrell Froude and I took into our consideration your opinion, that "there are good men of all parties," and agreed that it is a bad doctrine for these days; the time being come in which, according to John Miller, "scoundrels must be called scoundrels"; and, moreover, we have stigmatised the said opinion by the name of Coleridge's heresy.'" In another letter Keble says to his correspondent, "I speak the more feelingly because I know that I was myself inclined to eclecticism at one time; and if it had not been for my father and my brother, where I should have been now, who can say?"

The one thing to be said on behalf of Keble, Newman, and the whole of the ultra-High Church party is, that the premisses from which the whole system of so-called Catholic —*i.e.* of Anglo-Catholic or Neo-Anglican—doctrine may, with some plausibility, be inferred by one-sided and prejudiced interpreters, seem to be, in part distinctly and in part indistinctly, presupposed or implied in various formularies of the Church of England; and that this system in its essential rudiments has, in fact, been held and taught by a succession of Church of England divines, some of them bishops, others at least doctors or dignitaries, from the time of James I. to the present time, including especially some of those divines who were most intimately connected with the revision of the Prayer-Book and the passing of the Act of Uniformity in 1662. It appears certain that Keble honestly believed that Puritanism, as he called it, by which he meant the evangelical system of doctrine, was alien from the Church of England, was an intrusion and a heresy. His reading, it may well be believed, had been one-sided. He perhaps hardly knew how grand a succession of profound and scholarly divines in the Church of England had maintained views strongly opposed to those of his party. But he must surely have known that he and his fellows had gone a long way beyond his own special saint and hero Bishop Wilson, and that the theology of Hooker, whose works he edited, and of Barrow, was distinctly opposed to the system of sacramental and confessional theology which he upheld. The teaching of Hooker and of Barrow on the subject of justification by faith is fundamentally and completely irreconcilable with the views which Keble learnt from his father and brother, and which he and Froude and Newman embraced as the basis of Tractarian teaching. Nor is it possible for all the subtle casuistry of Newman's Tract 90 to transform the Thirty-nine Articles into a system of theology conformable to Tractarian teaching or unfavourable to the essential principles of what Keble stigmatised as Puritanism.

All Keble's sympathies went along with the Tractarian Movement as it proceeded. He did not write much, but Newman availed himself of his counsel in the publication of the *Tracts for the Times*. In particular, he was a direct party to the publication of Tract 90, and he wrote in its defence. He was also associated with Pusey and Newman in editing the *Library of the Fathers* and the *Anglo-Catholic Library*. He mourned most deeply over the secession of Newman, not, however, because he disapproved of Newman's doctrinal opinions either before or after his secession, but because, for himself, separation from the Church of England seemed to be at once an impiety and an impossibility. In his letter in explanation and defence of Tract 90, after quoting what some had formerly said about going to another Church if any did not like the Church of England, he says: "As if there were any other to which he could go." It has been said, not perhaps unjustly, that Keble had not the nerve to leave his own Church, and that, accordingly, like Pusey and all the clergymen in whom the domestic religious affections overpowered their doctrinal attractions to Rome, he remained in the English communion.[1]

Though he remained in the English Church, however, the ten years following the publication of Tract 90, that is, the period between 1841 and 1851, were for him years of very painful perplexity. He was determined he could not go to Rome; but for a considerable time he was in doubt whether he must not give up his position as a clergyman in the Church of England, or at least subside into the position of a communicant without a cure of souls. He did not see how to justify his Church's ecclesiastical position; while her doctrine, he felt, was painfully deficient, and her condition divided and distracted. On the other hand, the canonical position of the Church of Rome seemed to him perfect, but her doctrine to be corrupted with unwarrantable superfluities and with falsities. In the Preface to his one volume of sermons, Keble's defence of the Church of England is throughout faint, feeble, extenuatory; his objections to the Church of Rome timid and deferential. In fact, his one strong reason for remaining in the Church of England was, that he was actually there, and knew not whither else to betake himself. Such twine as this would not hold Newman and Manning; but of these, the one was unmarried, the other a widower. Keble was domestic, unenterprising,

[1] On hearing the news of Newman's secession, Keble wrote to his friend Dyson: "Every day things are happening, especially in our two sickrooms, which make it more and more impossible for me to do as he has done; it would seem like impiety," etc. (Coleridge's *Life of Keble*, p. 297, 1st ed.).

happily fixed in an honoured privacy, his hymns sung in thousands of English churches. He could not tear himself from the Church of his fathers, his friends, and his country. During the last fifteen years of his life, however, Keble seems to have found more to object to in Rome and Romanism, and to have become steadily settled in his own Church. The defection, in 1854, of Robert Wilberforce, who had been one of his pupils, was a severe trial to him. It touched him more than that of anyone except Newman. When he left the Church, Keble wrote as follows to his friend Coleridge: "I thought he was too good-tempered really to go there, besides his learning and truthfulness. But he had got into a Utopian dream, and rather than give it up, he shut his eyes and made a jump, and now he must, and I suppose will, keep his eyes shut all his life long." No sharper or more vivid description was ever given of the process by which such men as Wilberforce and Manning were first brought to embrace Romanism, and then hardened and sharpened into Ultramontanism.

I have not, thus far, noted that Keble was elected Professor of Poetry in Oxford in 1831, and that, according to the ancient usage, he read and published his lectures in Latin. On the death of his father, in 1835, at the age of 90, he removed from Fairford, accepted the vicarage of Hursley from his intimate friend Sir William Heathcote, and settled in its parsonage as a married man. From that period to the end of his days he continued to dwell at Hursley, leading a most enviable life, as it seems to human sight, of saintly seclusion, united with pastoral cares and duties. He religiously kept the wise man's injunction— "Thine own friend, and thy father's friend forsake not," and his friends in return clave lovingly to him. He was born on St. Mark's Day [1] 1792, and died on the 29th of March 1866. His old friend and biographer, whom I have so often quoted, says of him: " Looking back through an intimacy unbroken and unchilled for more than fifty-five years, he seems to me now to have been at once the simplest, humblest, and most loving-hearted man, and withal the holiest and most zealous Christian I have ever known."

As a Christian poet, Keble must be judged by his *Christian Year*. His *Lyra Innocentium* has not added to his reputation, although some of the choicest pieces in that volume, and some other poems contributed by him to the *Lyra Apostolica*, are thought to be higher in strain than almost anything in the *Christian Year*. What will be posterity's precise judgment of the *Christian Year*, it would be hazardous to anticipate. The volume has had great advantages. Besides its intrinsic beauty, its character as a companion to the Prayer-Book, and, in particular, to the successive special services of the Church Calendar throughout the year, could not but recommend it to the attention of a very wide circle of persons possessed of refined culture, of poetic taste, and of leisure for indulging their taste. The world could not furnish such a *clientela* for a denominational poet to appeal to as was open to an Anglican poet, who should provide week by week pleasant and pious portions of graceful verse and appropriate sentiment for the votaries of his Church—the Church of the gentle, the dainty, the leisurely, the cultured. In this respect Keble had an advantage far beyond even that enjoyed by the Wesleys in their Hymn-Book for " the

[1] April 25th. To give his birthday in this form, as his biographers do, is surely a pedantic ecclesiastical affectation.

people called Methodists." The Anglican Services, it must be remembered, are more or less observed, and the Prayer-Book is most extensively used, in all countries where the English language is spoken. The *Christian Year*, however, has won a popularity far wider than the area represented by the English Church Service. It was a denominational critic of the sterner Dissenting school who, in the *Nonconformist*, a few days after the death of Keble, paid a graceful tribute to the memory of the Tractarian poet, whom he described as "a good and great man, whose memory will last as long as Christian devotion expresses itself in the English tongue. We know what he was. He was a Tractarian; he was a sacerdotalist; he was a very rigid cleric; in almost everything that relates to Church life and outward Christian worship on earth he was opposed to us and to that which we most cherish. Yet, if we were to single out one man in the Established Church who was almost a personification of the Christian graces, we should single out John Keble. He was as gentle as the gentlest woman, and as spiritual as a saint. He was a saint—a good and holy man, with some human weakness; he perhaps knew as little of sin as any man who has lived in these times. Keble is to the Christian Church what Tennyson is to all of our own age, whether of Christ or not—the poet of lofty spirituality. We wish that he had not so often sung in sectarian dress, but we have always forgotten the dress when we have heard the song." Such was the judgment of this Nonconformist critic. It is possible, however, that just because he was a Nonconformist he may have been partial in the poet's favour. Nonconformists, it could easily be shown, have not seldom overpraised such Churchmen as they have praised at all, whether in regard to their talents or to their disposition. At all events, let us hear what the *Spectator* said about the poet of the *Christian Year*. The judgment of the *Spectator* is cool, without its spirit being caustic; besides which, being familar with Church of England circles of thought, what was said in this journal may represent the opinion of some who are not amiable and impressible outsiders, but to whom familiarity with Anglican habits of thought and feeling has given superior steadiness and clearness of vision. This authority, then, ventures to say that Keble's " one great faculty was for verse, of which he wrote a great deal that is very sweet, very thin, and very feminine." This judgment of the *Spectator* having been questioned, the journalist justified it in a subsequent article. He says : " The idea of the *Christian Year*, the idea of so mapping out the various little hints and allusions made in the Gospels, as to find a well-defined and appropriate mood of spirtual poetry for as many days as possible in the calendar, seems to us to have been popular rather for its faultiness than for its merit. Religious men and women in general, especially the latter, want something more to lean upon than God has actually given. There is something so oppressive to them in the infinite, untravelled night, lighted here and there by suns or planets, but stretching, for the most part, beyond our utmost reach of knowledge, that they catch with relief at the proposal of the Puseyite poet to trace out with mimic stars—really lamps lighted by human ingenuity, at the verbal suggestions of revelation—the yearly round of human exercises, by finding or forcing a mood of occasional piety out of the smallest items of historic incident or moral epithet in the great history of revelation. . . . The characteristic attempt of the Puseyite poet is not to throw the light of God's character and revelation on the new world in which we live, but to find some definite chain of pious and antique associations in connexion with the lessons or Gospels appointed for each of the days in the Church's Calendar."

These words I believe to be true, whether they sum up all the truth relating to the matter or not. It cannot, indeed, be disputed that in the *Christian Year*, to use Newman's words, Keble "struck an original note and woke up in the hearts of thousands a new music." But if Keble had been a greater poet he could never have clung so tenaciously throughout his *Year* to the calendared events and services of the Prayer-Book. He would have soared into the empyrean with angel-song, or he would have gazed with trembling reverence into the mysterious abyss. But his feminine genius clung like the ivy to the forms of the Church which he so often apostrophises as his "Mother"; and it is the one praise and merit of his poetry that it has draped and festooned the prescribed order of service with tender and graceful verse. Nothing can be more exquisite than many of his verses, and not a few entire poems are of rare beauty. At the same time, many of the poems are vague and formless, and connected by the very loosest allusion with the days for which they were written, while many separate stanzas are exceedingly, some hopelessly, obscure.[1]

Some writers have compared or contrasted Wesley and Keble. Not much is to be learnt by such com-

---

[1] Archbishop Alexander of Armagh, in his Preface to Mrs. Alexander's Poems, speaks of Keble's style of expression in the *Christian Year* as "too often puzzling and contorted."

parisons or contrasts. Keble occupies his own niche. It would be eminently unwise to attempt to cast down any other poets of great and true renown in order to exalt him. Refined and pure and pre-eminently reverent, all tenderness and gentle devotion, Keble's poetry, even when it lacks strength or loftiness, breathes, almost throughout, a "mystical faint fragrance" of sweet and delicate quality. We love him as all love him, and day by day his morning hymn seems to us to gather depth and beauty. Ken and Keble, two High Church poets, will teach daily duty and consecration to Christians from generation to generation.

In his relation to Newman and the Oxford Movement, I have felt it needful to speak the truth with impartial fidelity as respects the poet of the *Christian Year*. As a man I have tried to do justice to the unblemished purity and godliness of his character. As a poet his merits and his charm are the lasting possession of a Christendom vastly wider than was embraced within his recognition and sympathy.

NOTE TO PAGE 14.

The Feminine Vein in Newman's Character.

It was no less true of Newman than of Keble, that he had a marked feminine vein in his character,—a character much more complex than Keble's,—although the close seclusion of his life, not only after, but for several years before, he left Oxford for Rome, has not, perhaps, allowed it to be so generally recognised. He was not, indeed, effeminate; but he seems to have been without any specially masculine tastes, pursuits, or passions—at least outside the region of ecclesiastical study. He was addicted to no specially manly exercises. He was not an athlete, he had no tastes in that direction; he was an ascetic. He embraced celibacy with sympathetic facility. Mr. J. A. Froude, indeed, in his *Short Studies*, Fourth Series, compares him, curiously enough, to Julius Cæsar. But his comparison does not go to contradict what I have now said. " A disdain for conventionalities, a temper imperious and wilful, but along with it a most attaching gentleness, sweetness, and singleness of purpose," are a combination quite as likely to be found in a woman as in a man. If Newman gained a commanding influence over many minds, it was not by force of a masculine capacity for command. It was by virtue, in part, of a penetrating subtlety of sympathy and influence which carried his ideas into the consciousness of his closeted intimates, and, in part, of his captivating and persuasive sermons ; it was chiefly by means of qualities not less appropriate to the feminine than to the masculine temperament. As the history of the Oxford Movement is unfolded in this volume, the truth of this general description will appear with increasing distinctness.

CHAPTER II.

THE CRISIS OF DISTRESS FOR THE CHURCH OF ENGLAND—THE HELP NEEDED—THE QUESTION OF THE CHURCH'S UNITY AND CATHOLICITY—THE TWO UNIVERSITIES—HUGH JAMES ROSE AND NEWMAN—THE QUESTION OF A LEADER FOR THE CRISIS—NEWMAN WRITES AND PUBLISHES THE FIRST *TRACT FOR THE TIMES*—THE TRUE UNITY OF THE CHURCH.

NEVER since the days of the Commonwealth had the position of Anglican Episcopacy been so assailed and threatened as during the Reform Bill period, of which 1832 may be taken as the central date. In the *Apologia*, Newman has described in his vivid way the distress, the despondency and alarm of devout and earnest Churchmen. "The Whigs had come into power; Lord Grey had told the Bishops to set their house in order, and some of the prelates had been insulted and threatened." The Revolution had been consummated in France. Revolutionary principles seemed to be in the ascendant, both in England and almost throughout Europe. Against the Church, in particular, there was arrayed an unprecedented combination of parties, political and ecclesiastical, secular and sectarian, Christian and anti-Christian, while the Church itself was divided and disorganised, and seemed for long almost helpless. For all sacred and constitutional principles it appeared to Churchmen to be a life or death crisis. If the Church and the country were to be saved, the hierarchy must now rally the aristocracy to its aid; and, in return, the Church must throw its ægis round the aristocracy. A new Church movement—a movement of defence—was already beginning to take shape in the country before Newman began the Tractarian Movement, and throughout England Churchmen of high and resolute principles were looking for leaders and a defensive organisation adequate to the crisis. Now or never was the opportunity. Toryism throughout the country was rallying to its strongholds, and it was for the churchly friends of the Church to unite with its political allies, to take the tide of reaction at the flood, and so to float themselves onward to "fortune" and to victory. Some, indeed, who were earnest and resolute Churchmen, were hardly prepared to cast in their lot with a politico-ecclesiastical alliance. Newman himself was of this number. But all those who had any insight into the actual condition of affairs were agreed that, within the Church itself, there was need of a common ground for the defence of Church principles, and of union on that ground for defensive action. Above all, there was needed a spring of new life, and the uprising of a Church leader with a band of able and devoted followers.

The first man of high mark who made an effort to rally the tribes of the Anglican Israel against the foes who were arrayed in opposition to it, was the learned and able Hugh James Rose, of whom Newman has given a beautiful sketch in the *Apologia*, and to whom he dedicated, in 1838, the fourth volume of his sermons, as the man "who, when hearts were failing, bade us stir up the gift that was in us, and betake ourselves to our true

Mother." It was he who established and, till his death in 1838, edited the *British Magazine*, in the pages of which, chiefly from the pen of Newman, began to appear as early as 1832 the series of poems entitled *Lyra Apostolica*, which were afterwards collected and published separately. This magazine was intended to be the organ of the new Church movement, though it was afterwards superseded by the *British Critic*, which was Newman's special organ.[1]

It was at Rose's rectory at Hadleigh in July 1833 that a meeting was held of a few clergymen, of whom Hurrell Froude was one, but where Newman was not present, at which meeting it was resolved to fight for the doctrine of apostolical succession and for the integrity of the Prayer-Book. This seems to have been the first combined and definite undertaking on behalf of the Church of England entered into in those troublous times. Two months later Newman, who never joined this Movement, believing, as he explains in his *Apologia*, not in committees or organised associations, but in personal effort and influence, began the *Tracts for the Times*, as he states, "out of his own head," thus, by the first tract, taking the practical initiative of

[1] Mr. (afterwards Sir William) Palmer, of Worcester College, an Irishman who had migrated from Trinity College, Dublin, to Oxford, —the author of *Origines Liturgicæ* and other learned works,— published in 1843, and republished in 1883 with additions, a *Narrative of Events connected with the " Tracts for the Times,"* which is very valuable for its accuracy and for its completeness, though it deals rather with the surface of the history than the deeper causes and feelings involved in the Tractarian Movement. Mr. Palmer evidently regarded himself as qualified to give critical guidance in the difficulties of the time. Newman, while acknowledging his superior learning,— probably in ecclesiastical learning he had no equal among High Churchmen,—explains that he was quite incompetent to take the position he aspired to, partly for want of "depth," and partly because he was not an Oxford, but a Dublin man.

systematic defence and reconstruction out of Rose's hands.

Rose, however, is the leader whom, as a divine and a Churchman, Dean Burgon, in his *Lives of Twelve Good Men*, desired most of all to honour, and whom he thought of all the Churchmen of his age most worthy of the Church's confidence. His early death (at the age of forty-three) he regarded as, humanly speaking, the greatest calamity the Church had known in his generation. He gives his hero the title of "The Restorer of the Old Paths." According to his account it was Rose, rather than Newman, who really originated the Anglican Revival. Rose disapproved of Newman's errors and excesses, acted powerfully as a moderator upon him and his Oxford band, and, if he had lived, would, in Dean Burgon's view, have been such a counter-power as might have saved the Church of England from the calamitous collapse and the leakage from perversions which marked the period following 1844. He and not Newman would have been the true "restorer" and leader for the Church, and he was strong enough, Dean Burgon believed, to have held the position of arbiter or leader even in the face of Newman and his mighty influence.

Rose died in 1838, worn out with disease and overwork. Newman, to use his own words in his *Apologia*, was "from the end of 1841 on his deathbed as regarded his membership with the Anglican Church"; and in October 1845, to use Dean Burgon's words, " actually transferred his allegiance to that Church which a few years before he had publicly denounced with unsparing bitterness as under the actual domination of Satan." For some time before his death Rose had been growingly uneasy, not to say suspicious, as

to the tone and tendency of Newman's writings, and as to
the effect upon the rising generation of University men of
the spirit and influence emanating from Newman and his
congenial friend—perhaps we might say prompter—Hurrell
Froude. Dean Burgon publishes a number of Rose's letters
to Newman of this period, with small portions of Newman's
own share of the correspondence. From these it is evident
that Rose, as he was senior to Newman, and altogether
independent of him, and was also doubtless at the time
a man of wider theological reading and greater influence,
besides being of a firm character and settled purpose, felt
himself able and entitled to speak to Newman with a
plainness of speech such as no other person could use, and
that Newman deferred to him more than to anyone else.

It may well be doubted, however, whether, if Rose had
lived, he would have continued to preserve anything like
the same relation to Newman. The intellects of the two
men were incommensurable. Newman's influence arose
from sources altogether different from any faculty of
influence and authority possessed by Rose, and touched
accordingly a different order of minds. Newman's
"Catholic" intensity of bias and feeling derived much of
its quality from a transformed evangelical ecstasy and
experimental assurance which was altogether foreign to
the character of Hugh James Rose's Anglican orthodoxy.
Rose was content to walk in the old ways of traditional
Anglicanism. Newman had a vein of enthusiasm, a power
of imagination, and a gift of genius, which made it impossible that he should be confined within the same
limits.

Besides all which, Rose was a Cambridge man, and
Newman was magnetising the young men of Oxford, and

always gathering and radiating influence at that focus. The metaphysical and theological genius of the two universities has always been different. Cambridge had already received its revival through Simeon and his school. The revival of Oxford was now to come, with Newman to kindle it instead of Simeon. Between the Simeonite Evangelicals and the rising Broad Church, Cambridge was preoccupied. It had no faculty, no receptivity, no fuel to spare for the establishment of a new school of Anglican zeal and devotion. In 1832 the rising school of religious thought, for the moment, was that of Hare, which was presently stimulated and distorted into the Neo-Platonising mysticism of Maurice. It was the turn now of Oxford to have its Church revival. Oxford, according to its traditions, could hardly be widely swept by any but a High Church influence. But that influence was not likely to emanate from a stiff Cambridge High Churchman walking in the fetters of Caroline theology and Church theories.

Nor was this all. The general studies and tendencies of the age had brought earnest and systematic students of ecclesiastical principles face to face with the question of the historical unity and continuity of the Church. The works of Neander, in regard to this subject and to other ecclesiastical questions, represented a movement of the mind which was awakening inquiry, not only in Germany, but also in England. The writings of Archdeacon Hare are full of the evidences of this fact. The politico-ecclesiastical speculations of Coleridge directed attention to it. There were two wrong solutions of the question of the Church's historical continuity and unity which presented themselves to many minds; one, the Broad Church solution, which was expounded most fully and with great ability a few years later by Maurice in his *Kingdom of Christ*, and which, in a vaguer and less objectionable form, was adopted not only by Arnold, but, in the first instance, by Pusey, when, as his earliest writing, he published his defence of German Protestantism against the strictures of Hugh James Rose, and when his writing savoured rather of Rationalism than of Romanism. The other solution was that of the mediæval Catholic Church and the Anglican High Church—or, as we now speak, it was the Anglo-Catholic view. Both these solutions erred in placing the identity and continuity of the Church in Christianity *as visibly organised*. The first, or Broad Church view found the Christian Church in the national or other public communities, which, however loosely or generally, professed the Christian name and faith. Collectively, from generation to generation, these constituted the Christian Church. Of this view Maurice was, as I have intimated, the ablest and most complete expositor. The other, or "Catholic," view found the identity and continuity of the Christian Church in a direct succession of Churches, or of the same Church, in several Branches, holding the orthodox faith, and having a ministry or priesthood lineally derived from the primitive and apostolic Church. Both these views assume that Christianity is founded and rooted in external conditions. The true view, the Pauline view, regards the true and living Church of Christ as consisting of the whole multitude, from age to age, of living Christians spiritually united to Christ Jesus, their Divine-Human Head, and constituting His one ever-living mystical body, invisible in regard to its spiritual glory and beauty, inasmuch as the "life" of its members "is hid with Christ in God," although Christians individually are visibly connected with various Christian Churches and communions. This, however, is a view which appears rarely to have entered into the thought of High Churchmen as at all possible, or as even conceivable; although, besides its being the New Testament doctrine, it is the view which has always been held by the most spiritually united and devoted Christian brotherhoods from age to age. The succession of mystics of the better side, whether Catholic or Protestant; the German pietists, who, in the worst days of dead Lutheran faith and formalism, kept alive the light and tradition of living Christian experience in Germany; Protestant continental divines of the most profound spiritual intelligence and insight—such, for example, as Vinet in recent times; all evangelical Nonconformists, and nearly all thoroughly evangelical Churchmen—have agreed in holding this view. It was, with a sort of necessary and unconscious acceptance, assimilated as a part of Christian doctrine by that succession of earnest and experimental Christians at Cambridge, of whom for half a century Simeon was the recognised leader, and who were often honoured with the epithet of "Methodist"; it has always been a central part of the Christian faith of the followers of John Wesley, who learnt it from their Founder, who had freed himself from Oxford High Church externalism by embracing the true doctrine of faith and salvation. But it was a view of the Christian Church entirely opposed to the genius and all the traditions of Oxford, which, in this respect—unlike Cambridge, but always consistent with itself—has, since the light of Wiclif died out of its cloisters, held with unchanging tenacity to the externalist High Church view of ecclesiastical and religious questions. It is true that, even in Oxford, Whately led and Arnold supported an opposite view. But how uncongenial their teaching was to the atmosphere of the place was strikingly shown by the total failure of their influence to counteract in any degree the Tractarian Movement. It is true, also, no doubt, that the revolutionary changes of recent years have produced effects more or less disturbing in the tone of thought on this subject. But I am speaking of Oxford as it was forty years ago and more.

In the Oxford University of which we are speaking—the Oxford of more than half a century ago—the character and opinions of Hugh James Rose, if he had been a resident, might well have had great conservative influence. They would have been congenial to the place. But then he was not a resident; and that which Newman was to initiate was not a conservative restoration, but an ecclesiastical and religious revival, in which there should be an altogether new inspiration and influence. Newman himself, in his *Apologia*, indicates both these reasons as having been fatal to Rose's ascendency, or moderating power, in the destined Movement.

"There was another reason," he says, "which severed Mr. Rose from the Oxford Movement. Living movements do not come of committees, nor are great ideas worked out through the post. . . . Universities are the natural centres of intellectual movements. How could men act together, unless they were united in a sort of individuality? . . . But another condition, besides that of place, was required. A far more essential unity was that of antecedents—a common history, common memories, an intercourse of mind with mind in the past, and a progress and increase of that intercourse in the present."

In such words, and others to a similar effect, which go

fully into detail, the *Apologia* explains why Rose could not lead or inspire an Oxford Movement. But that autobiography of the Tractarian leader also indicates that no mere conservative restoration such as Rose would have desired to organise, would have been likely to succeed at that crisis of feeling in Oxford. Froude was the energetic and wilful partner of Newman in the new enterprise—Froude, who, with less genius, far less personal tact and persuasiveness, and no gift of public or pulpit suasion, such as Newman possessed in a wonderful degree, was a man of intense and resolute character, of great logical daring, of unsparing pugnacity, of far-reaching ideas, whom Newman, and, as we have seen, Keble also, greatly admired and even loved, though he was loved by few besides. These two men, Newman and Froude, were mutually complementary; together they planned the first lines of the Tractarian Movement, as the private enterprise of Newman and his coterie is vaguely but conveniently called. Dean Church in his history of the Movement, with which I shall have presently to deal, protests against its being spoken of as a "conspiracy." Let us, as far as possible, avoid the inconvenient and ill-omened word, though, in fact, Froude himself was the first, as we learn from his *Remains*, to describe himself and his comrades in the new movement by that very word—*conspirators*. Still we must note that the Movement was an enterprise privately planned, a scheme deeply laid and worked with great subtlety, the fell influence and effects of which at this hour are tainting with deadly poison the great, and in some respects admirable, Anglican revival; and, indeed, are threatening the very existence of the Church of England, not merely as an Establishment, but as a united organisation. With Newman and Froude it was impossible for Rose really to coalesce. " Mr. Rose," says the *Apologia*, " had a position in the Church, a name, and serious responsibilities. . . . Rose could not go ahead across country, as Froude had no scruples in doing." Froude applied to Rose in a " reproachful " sense, as Newman says, the epithet " conservative." " Froude "—we are told, and Froude was Newman's friend and fellow—" was comparatively indifferent to the revolutionary action which would attend on the application of the principles " which Newman and himself made it their business to teach, " whereas, in the thoughts of Rose, as a practical man, existing facts had the precedence of every other idea."

These considerations are sufficient to show that with Newman and Froude at Oxford together, in the first instance, and afterwards with Newman there supreme, when he became the sole guide and leader of the Neo-Anglican coterie, Rose would have had no chance whatever of influencing the University. The leaders of the new Movement intended something with a new soul in it, and with unlimited capacity of development and extension. The motto of Rose—as of William Palmer, of Worcester College, who, however, had not for a moment his finger on the real centre and spring of action, and who, before long, was left away in the background—was *Stare super antiquas vias*—to go back to the Anglicanism of the seventeenth century. This was not at all Newman's idea, nor would it have met the wants of the Church at that time. What Newman, with a truer apprehension of the problems involved, felt to be necessary, was to furnish a clear and adequate statement of the distinctive principles and claims of the Church of England ; and a restatement, adapted to modern conditions, of the Anglican relations to the Roman Church and its doctrines.

Newman had not been brought up a High Churchman, but an Evangelical. His father was a banker of Dutch descent—the family name in England had been *Newmann*; his mother belonged to a well-known French Huguenot family.[1] His extraction was more foreign than English, and he had been trained in no Anglican Church principles. He was, in reality, at this time rather ignorant of Caroline Churchmanship, and never seems greatly to have cared for it. In abandoning his early evangelical principles, or, as he would call them, prejudices, he retained a vivid conviction of the reality of his evangelical conversion. This conviction abode with him through all his changing phases and subsequent developments of opinion. He was, and he remained through life, "more certain of his inward conversion than that he had hands and feet." The writer who made a deeper impression on his mind than any other, and to whom, he tells us, "humanly speaking," he "almost owed his soul," was the evangelical commentator, "Thomas Scott, of Aston Sandford." With these experiences and memories graven on his consciousness, the writer of the *Apologia* tells us that he came to Oxford. Here, in contact with the influences of the place, he gradually exchanged Low Church for High Church views. But, not being at the time a man of either much learning or trained habits of logical investigation, he leaped impulsively to extremes, as shallow evangelical Christians, who exchange any of

---

[1] See Mr. Lilly's careful and exact article in the *Dictionary of National Biography*, the article of a friend and co-religionist, but a trustworthy outline of facts and personal history.

their original distinctive principles or prejudices for any one High Church principle or view, are very apt to do. That able and guarded High Churchman, Dr. Hawkins, the provost of his College, seems to have given him the first impulse which, not by any means necessarily, but because of the unfurnished and untrained condition of his own mind, and because of his natural susceptibility of temperament, set him distinctly on the road to the theology of mere tradition and development. Dr. Hawkins taught him what many Low Churchmen overlook—the office and worth of tradition, especially, as in the first instance, the one primitive and oral teacher of Christian doctrine. Not perceiving that the truth in this view left intact the authority of Scripture as the surest and only unerring test of primitive doctrine, Newman lost his interest in the Bible Society, and soon after withdrew his name from the list of subscribers. Thus he started on the way to Rome—not really on the way to Caroline Anglicanism. Bramhall and Laud and Cosin were not his masters; he had not been brought up in their school, and he never really took to them. Thomas Scott had been more to him than they ever were. High and dry Anglicanism was not congenial to him; he had been introduced to the life of conscious salvation; he continued to believe in high and rapt religious experience, though now what he admired and longed for was of the mediæval or monastic type. He had no admiration for a ponderous machinery of religious externalism, and no personal taste for mere brilliance of ritual display. His loving contemplation and desire went back, not to the *origines* of the Church of England as purged and reformed, though he might fall back on them as an intermediate study and a proximate guide and authority, but to the earliest ages of the Church—the ages of primitive (or quasi-primitive) zeal, of the grand historical victories and development of Christianity, of the great Church councils, when Catholic doctrine was defined and determined. He was bent upon identifying himself and his Christianity with the grand course of Christian history and development. Having taken the postulates of externalism with him from the beginning of his inquiries and speculations,—having missed the only true solution of the question of the Church's continuity and unity,—it was, indeed, a foregone conclusion that such a mind as his could not eventually find any resting-place till he was constrained to seek refuge in Rome. But as yet this was hidden from his view. From the first, however, it was impossible for him to be a mere High Churchman of the past. It was impossible that he should remain shut up within the barriers of Anglicanism, as if that were the "happy valley" from which he might in tranquillity survey the whole schismatic universe of Christianity around him—on the one hand, schismatic Nonconformity; on the other, schismatic and corrupt Roman Catholicism, with the incommensurable Eastern Churches far away in the dreamy distance. Newman was, at heart, a mystic; he was, both in religion and philosophy, a transcendentalist; he was a poet and a dreamer; and, above all, in virtue of his devotion, his enthusiasm, his industry, his combination of unworldliness with knowledge of character and with subtilty of adaptation to worldly conditions, and his unique charm as a preacher,—a charm which had in it the elements of intellectual distinction and force, of persuasiveness, suggestiveness, and even at times of spiritual ecstasy,—he was the absolute and unquestioned master, the admired and almost adored disposer, of a multitude of earnest and enthusiastic spirits. Such a man, with such followers, could never have coalesced with Hugh James Rose; nor, able as Rose was, and much more widely read as a theologian and as a European scholar than Newman, was it possible that he could ever have prevented the supremacy of Newman, least of all in Oxford. Dean Burgon's idolatry of Rose, and his attempt to show that he, and not Newman, might best and most fitly have been the leader of the High Church revival, is merely evidence of the limited *calibre* of the dean himself. The worship of Caroline Anglicanism could never reanimate the Church of England. With all his errors, Newman was far too large and gifted a man to be reduced to contemplate such an aim. We may justly lament with bitter grief for England and the Church of England the effects of his influence, and still more of the deadlier influence exercised within the Church of England by his friend and early co-worker, Pusey. The joint result is that a fatal leaven of essentially Romish doctrine, of Romanising superstition, has taken deep hold of England. England will yet be sorely shaken by the controversies that must result. Agnosticism and unbelief have been very greatly strengthened. The Church of England may not improbably be disestablished, not because of outward assaults, but of internal errors and schisms, and, if thus disestablished, will be divided into two, or possibly even three, distinct Churches; all this seems not unlikely to happen.[1] All

[1] In the *Guardian* for February 27, 1889, the Rev. Mr. Enraght published a letter criticising the Bishop of Liverpool's address on the subject of the Sacrament and Sacramental Superstitions—which address has been a bitter pill for the Romanising section of the clergy to which Mr. Enraght belongs. In this letter Mr. Enraght, with characteristic modesty and decency, speaks of the dislike felt towards

this perhaps must happen, if ever the implicated superstitions and corruptions which now deform and consume the life of the Church are to be purged out. But one thing at least is certain—Revived Laudianism could never have reanimated the Church of England or won the allegiance of the English nation.

My business, however, is not to prophesy, but to note the points and progress of an historical development. For the reasons which I have now suggested, the work of rallying and reviving the forces, of organising and developing the resources of the Church of England, was one which, while it could only be accomplished from a university centre, could not be accomplished from Cambridge. Newman had the gifts and the qualities of character fitting him to become the master-spirit in a movement of seminal Church reform and reorganisation, of which Oxford was the congenial centre. There he established a sort of school of the prophets. There he trained instruments and prepared the materials of propagandism. He restated the principles of the Church of England; and he began the work of re-defining the Anglican position in regard to Rome, but broke down before the work was really finished, and ended by capitulating altogether to Rome. For his characteristic work at Oxford, Newman had been prepared by the influence of Keble and Froude. To quote Dean Church, " Keble had given the inspiration, Froude had given the impetus, then Newman took up the work." If Froude had

" the Eucharistic sacrifice " by " the Bishop of Liverpool in common with *his co-religionists.*" It seems accordingly that Mr. Enraght had already decreed an ecclesiastical separation between Evangelical Churchmen, the " Bishop and his co-religionists," and himself and *his* " co-religionists." Dissenters could not have been more distinctly cut away from Church communion. That phrase speaks volumes.

lived a few years longer, it cannot be doubted that he would have gone over the imaginary line of division, and would have found himself consciously and professedly at Rome. Keble had neither logic nor courage to take him across the line, and therefore remained a beneficed clergyman of the Church of England, while his esoteric principles were those of a Gallican Romanist. In the secret place of his doctrinal sympathies he was one at heart with Bossuet or Dupin. Newman, alone of the three, slowly and reluctantly, but by force of sincere and overmastering convictions, followed his principles out to the complete end, and so finished his career a cardinal of the Church of Rome.

CHAPTER III.

THE *TRACTS FOR THE TIMES*—ANGLICANISM AND APOSTOLICAL SUCCESSION—NEWMAN AND WARD—THE ADVANCE ROMEWARD—WARD'S POINT OF VIEW—HIS UNIQUE IDENTITY—CONTRAST BETWEEN NEWMAN AND WARD—WARD'S PERSONAL HISTORY—HIS *IDEAL OF A CHRISTIAN CHURCH*—HIS DEGRADATION AND SECESSION.

IN 1832 and 1833 Newman and Froude took a continental tour together, spending much time in Italy.[1] They separated before the tour ended, Froude returning to England first. Newman returned on July 9, 1833. On July 14, Keble preached the Assize Sermon at Oxford in the University Church, the sermon which he published with the startling title, "National Apostasy," and the date of the delivery of which Newman thereafter solemnly kept as "the start of the Oxford Movement." In the following September, Newman published the first tract

[1] From Froude's *Remains* we learn that Newman and he at Rome "got introduced to Dr. Wiseman to find out whether they"—the Romish Church—"would take us in on any terms to which we could twist our consciences," and found to their dismay that it would be absolutely necessary for them "to swallow the Council of Trent as a whole." Newman, as co-editor with Keble of the *Remains*, explains that this was Froude's "jesting way" of telling a friend that they wanted "to ascertain the ultimate points of issue between the Churches." The statement of Froude and the explanation of Newman are equally characteristic of the writers respectively.

of the famous series of *Tracts for the Times*, a tract in which he laid down what he assumed to be the foundation principles of the Church of England, apostolical succession being the main "plank" of the "platform." Eight years later, in 1841, he published Tract 90, which brought down the hand of Church authority to put an end to the series. First the Heads of Houses—the Hebdomadal Board—severely censured the tract. Then the Bishop of Oxford, Newman's kind friend, Dr. Bagot, officially requested that the series of tracts might be discontinued. Presently the bishops, one after another, in due succession, condemned the tract in their charges; condemned, also, the series generally, of which this was to be the last. The object of the tracts throughout was to educate Churchmen, especially the clergy, in the principles, the practices, and the policy which befitted the claims and character of the Apostolic and Catholic Church of England. The great authorities recognised were "the Fathers" of the first four centuries, especially of the third and fourth centuries. Their teachings, and the Church practices which their writings disclosed, were assumed to be the teachings and the practices of the primitive Church, although, in fact, the actual development of the Church during the first four centuries of its existence had so modified, had indeed so corrupted and transformed the teachings of Christ and the apostles into conformity with the spirit of "the world,"[1] and the seductive precedents and practices of surrounding paganism, as to make up a whole of Church organisation and influence strangely and sadly in contrast, at many points, with the purity, simplicity, and unworldly majesty of true primitive Christianity. The

[1] 1 John ii. 15–17.

general effect of the teaching of the tracts was to lessen continually, and at point after point, the differences between the Anglo-Catholic and the Roman Catholic Church, as regarded by the disciples of the Tractarian school. To effect this result discreetly and without weakening too much the position of the Church of England, was the most difficult problem for Newman to solve. The purpose of Tract 90 was to show how much of Romish doctrine might be held by an Anglican priest without legally or indisputably violating the Articles of the Church. The attempt, however, though exceedingly subtle and skilful, was too daring, and brought, *as such*, the whole Tractarian Movement to the ground.[1]

Of the ninety tracts, indeed,—of the greater part of which Newman was himself the writer,—there are three which stand out from the rest as of pre-eminent importance, and as affording together a sufficient indication of the tendency and purpose of the whole series. These are the first and the last, to which I have already referred, and Pusey's unfinished but voluminous and epoch-making tract, or treatise, on Baptism. The first— on Apostolical Succession—marked out the line Romeward; the last—No. 90—defined the fatal extent of concession and approach to Rome to which Newman had already, in 1841, advanced in his conduct of his disciples, bringing the party close up to the gates of the Papal City.

[1] Newman himself says that the immediate cause which led to his Tractarian career was his being deprived of his college tutorship, and his public career at Oxford being brought to an end by his quarrel with his provost (Hawkins) as to the scope of his tutorial powers and responsibilities. He considered his office of a religious nature, which Hawkins did not. Deprived of his tutorship, he went with Froude to the Continent. It was Newman's own influence which had turned the scale in favour of Hawkins' election as provost, as against Keble, who, though "an angel," was not fit to be provost.

Thus the law of the Movement was fixed on the strictly ecclesiastical side. Pusey's tract was complementary in its character. It did not deal with questions of Church order, but with the theology of sin and salvation; and it laid the foundation of that degrading and demoralising doctrine of Confession and Absolution, and of sacramental efficacy *ex opere operato*, which lies at the heart of the special system of papal superstition and hierarchical domination from which it had been hoped that the Reformation had delivered the people of England. The Tractarian Movement was thus inspired by the teaching and influence of Newman and Pusey.[1] Other points there were connected with those I have now noted, such as the *disciplina arcani*, the doctrine of reserve, the ascetic and the celibate life, and the mystical interpretation of Scripture. But those I have marked out from the rest were the points fundamental and essential to the whole scheme of the Movement. Round these, moreover, the conflict still has to be carried on in that larger Movement of which Oxford has all along been the chief centre, and into which the original Tractarian Movement has developed.

I have spoken in the last page of Newman as having, by his tract on Apostolical Succession, marked out the line to Rome. It does not enter into my purpose to argue at length against the doctrine of Apostolical Succession. If logic and sound argument could have killed it, it would not have survived the unanswerable demonstrations of its

---

[1] Pusey, indeed, did not really identify himself with the Movement till two years after its commencement. But his accession, when he did join, added to it not a little of moral weight, and still more of University credit and social prestige, though he never really took an active lead in its direction. But of Pusey there will be much to say in my later chapters.

absurdity given by Macaulay and Whately, not to speak of the cogent and conclusive arguments of Henry Rogers. But this doctrine is necessary to the ecclesiastical existence of the High Anglican, and takes rank as an article of faith which must be accepted like any other mysterious dogma. It is, however, a point to be noted in its bearing on the character and history of our modern Anglo-Catholicism that this doctrine did not come to Anglicanism from any *corpus theologicum* or ecclesiastical decree of the Mother Church of Rome. It was a mere invention of the hard-pressed High Churchmen of the last period of Elizabeth's reign, seeking for a handy weapon of defence against the Divine-Right claims of the Presbyterian leaders of English Puritanism. For fifty years after the separation of the English Church from Rome no such argument was heard of. The late Dr. Nicholas Pocock was a distinguished High Anglican authority on the history of his Church in the period of Elizabeth and the Stuart kings. Writing in the *Guardian* in 1892 (November 23) he says roundly that "the belief in the Apostolical Succession in the Episcopate is not to be found in any of the writings of the Elizabethan Bishops." He affirms that "probably not a single Bishop was to be found who believed in his own Divine Commission or in the efficacy of the Sacraments." It was not, indeed, till the year 1588, the year of the Armada, that Dr. (afterwards Archbishop) Bancroft, preaching at Paul's Cross, first of all, so far as history knows, suggested —rather than asserted—the Divine Right of Episcopacy in the English Church, thus seeking to make good its position on the one hand against Rome, and on the other against the Puritan party with its New Testament model of Presbyterian discipline. This claim involved the desertion of the ground hitherto held on behalf of the English Reformers by Jewell, Whitgift, and Hooker. Shortly afterwards, this novel contention was set forth and maintained by Dr. (afterwards Bishop) Bilson in an elaborate argument. It was, however, opposed not only to the views of Whitgift and Hooker before him, but of Andrewes after him.[1] No authorities have been more loftily cited by Anglo-Catholics as on their side than Hooker and Andrewes, but they might more justly be cited on behalf of the Puritans, so far as regards this fundamental point.

As the power, the pertinacity, the Divine-Right assumptions, of the Puritan party, however, grew more and more formidable during the reigns of the first two Stuart kings of England, High Church controversialists made more and more of this newly invented argument. It became a shibboleth of the Laudian school, and with this pretension in their mouth, High Churchmen, after the Restoration, started their new lease of power. It was less heard of, however, as Puritanism decayed, and it all but died out with the Nonjurors. It was forgotten when Latitudinarianism, to use an unfriendly name for the liberal ecclesiastical school founded by Tillotson and Stillingfleet, rose to the ascendant. Its revival by Newman was the manifesto of a new attack upon the evangelical principles of the Reformation—though those principles, as embodied in the Church's teaching of the Evangelical Revival, whether as represented by Wesley or by Simeon, were by no means identical with the Presbyterian principles of such Puritan divines as Cartwright and Travers. For all evangelical Churchmen— the common ground of antagonism to the sacerdotalism— the "Apostolical Succession" exclusivism—alike of Ban-

[1] *Church and State under the Tudors*, by Gilbert W. Child, p. 238.

croft and Laud in the Stuart period and of Newman's tract, is clearly indicated by the Duke of Argyll in a letter to the *Times*, occasioned by some strong anti-State-Church letters written by Dr. Parker of the City Temple:[1] "I know very well what has driven Dr. Parker into this reckless theory. It is dread and dislike of the sacerdotal theory, as represented by Roman and High Anglican theology. No one is a more thorough disbeliever in that theory than I am. I have no sympathy with the gushing gratitude with which a few Anglicans have thanked God that the Bishop of Rome has condescended to inquire into what they and he are pleased to call the 'validity' of Anglican Orders. The very word implies an assumption which I believe to be irrational. In all such matters my own opinions are in accordance with the views of Nonconformists and of the most learned writers of the English Church down to and including the late Bishop Lightfoot of Durham." Elsewhere in a pamphlet (*Words of Warning to Presbyterians*) the same able and accomplished Christian nobleman speaks of "that extraordinary doctrine which makes the whole apparatus of Christianity (sacraments and all) hang on the local preservation of one order in the ministry for which in the New Testament there is not even a distinctive name."

To return, however, to the Movement in its early history whilst Newman was shaping the course for himself and his associates. Whilst feeling his way along the perilous line I have described, Newman, in 1837, published a volume on *Romanism and Popular Protestantism*, in which, though conceding much to Rome, he insisted strongly on some of the errors and corruptions of the Romish Church. It was written after the death of Froude, and was an attempt

[1] *Times*, 12th June 1896.

to discover a line of safety—a *via media*—lying between popular Protestantism on the one hand and Romanism on the other. This *via media* charmed many ultra-High Churchmen, and after Newman had abandoned it, some still clung to it. In after years he poured contempt upon it. Perhaps, if that strong Romaniser, Froude, had still been by the side of Newman, his criticism of Rome would have been gentler than it was, and his concessions still larger. At all events, the *Apologia* furnishes evidence that not long after its publication Newman doubted whether he had been just to the Romish Church in his book. In 1838, Ward, a yet stronger and much more trenchant Romanising critic of the Church of England than even Froude had been, had become a close friend of Newman, and his influence was daringly, and even recklessly, pro-Romish, as will be shown in this chapter. With him as his friend and prompter, Newman carried on his series of tracts, and finally published Tract 90; a tract, however, which, it should never be forgotten, had been beforehand read and approved by Keble, and was afterwards defended in detail not only by Keble but by Pusey. In February 1843, in his subtle and secret way, Newman anonymously, yet with significant intimations which to the well-informed revealed his identity, published in an obscure journal, never heard of, as it has been said, before or since,—the *Conservative Journal*,—a retractation of all the hard things he had said against the Church of Rome.[1]

[1] In the recantation to which I refer, sent to the *Conservative Journal* in 1843, Dr. Newman gives the following explanation of his severe censures of certain features of Roman teaching and policy, published in a magazine in 1834:—

"If you ask me how an individual could venture to publish such views, I answer that I said to myself—'I am not speaking my own

The view maintained by Ward with increasing pressure of logic and of will was, that the ecclesiastical position of Rome gave it an indisputable superiority over the Church of England, and that this position carried with it the whole question as between the two Churches. From the premisses which he learned and adopted from Newman this was a legitimate conclusion. The only thing, therefore, for Newman to do, who knew not how to resist this contention, and who was in reality inferior to Ward in keenness and force of logic, was to Romanise as far as possible the Church of England, and to bring about, if that should be possible, a reconciliation between the two Churches. Ward had joined him as a disciple implicitly trusting and obeying a master; but the disciple presently began to dominate his teacher. The faults and disabilities of Rome, as Newman was now brought to think, were, however serious, less serious and formidable than the schismatic attitude and course, and the grievous deficiencies in doctrine and ritual, and, above all, in ecclesiastical

words, I am but following almost a consensus of the divines of my own Church. I wish to throw myself into their system. While I say what they say I am safe. Such views, too, are necessary for our position.' Yet I have reason to fear that such language is to be ascribed, in no small measure, to an impetuous temper, a hope of approving myself to persons' respect, and a wish to repel the charge of Romanism." Among the words which he thus recants are these: "The Roman Church I will not blame, but pity—she is, as I have said, spellbound, as if by an evil spirit; she is in thraldom." "Old Rome is still alive. In the corrupt Papal system we have the very cruelty, the craft, and the ambition of the republic"—and more to the same effect. This article, thus recanted, was written shortly after his return from a long visit to Rome and Italy. I have not seen the article myself,—the journal in which it appeared is hard to find,—but I quote from a volume, by Major-General H. Aylmer, entitled *Transformers* (Nisbet & Co.), which contains much authentic and valuable information.

authority and position, of the Church of England. Hence the publication of Tract 90, the arguments and the assumptions in which excited the almost universal indignation and alarm of the bishops and the older clergy, and still more of the laity of the Church of England, rousing especially to righteous rage the powerful Evangelical section of the Church.

It was thus towards the close of the interval covered by the publication of the tracts, and at a time when Froude had lately been removed by death from the side of Newman, that W. G. Ward became his intimate counsellor and friend. Ward, as Newman's counsellor and prompter, was to carry forward the process which Froude had begun until Newman had worked out the logical results of his premisses, and by his definitive secession to Rome had followed to its end the highroad which he had chosen for himself, and into which he had allured so many others, of whom it is sorrowful to think how many—and painful, at the same time, to think that perhaps too few— followed him to the same goal. Ward became Newman's chief, and by far most urgent, counsellor in 1838 or 1839, two or three years before Tract 90 was published. He remained in intimate association with him till 1845, the year in which first Ward and afterwards Newman actually joined the Romish communion. Mr. Wilfrid Ward, the son of Newman's friend, has published his father's life, of which the first volume is entitled, *W. G. Ward and the Oxford Movement*.[1] That volume takes us into the heart of our subject. Of its singular accuracy as a history of facts, and of its not less remarkable fairness of spirit,— though it is written by the Roman Catholic son of such a

[1] Macmillan & Co.

convert to Rome as W. G. Ward,—there can be no doubt whatever. As to the second stage of the Tractarian Movement, properly so called, after the death of Froude, and when the spirit and tendency of the tracts came to be understood with increasing distinctness, a stage of which Newman's account in the *Apologia* is by no means complete, never even referring to Ward,—this volume furnishes us with invaluable information. It supplies a critical deficiency in our available materials. Ward and Newman, as we shall see, though they had strong points of mutual sympathy, had also antipathetic points of character; and after they had gone over to Rome represented contradictory tendencies as to Church policy,—a fact which comes out strongly in the second volume of Mr. Wilfrid Ward's life of his father, with which we are not concerned in this chapter. This fact may perhaps account for Newman's silence as to Ward in the *Apologia*.

The special period of the Movement which Mr. Wilfrid Ward's volume covers is that between 1841 and 1845, during which, the *Tracts for the Times* having with Newman's No. 90 found their climax and come to a collapse, Newman himself was in retirement, chiefly at Littlemore. It was the period during the earlier years of which the *British Critic*, with Mr. Thomas Mozley as its editor, and Ward as one of its chief writers, was the organ of the now increasingly advanced and Romeward movement. When, in 1843, after passing all bounds of possible toleration in its ever-increasing Romanising and its incessant attacks on the Anglican position and claims, the *British Critic* came to an end, Ward, no longer able to use it as his organ, wrote his *Ideal of a Christian Church*, which he published in June 1844, and that publication was followed, in February 1845, by the formal censure of the University. Convocation not only condemned the *Ideal*, but degraded the writer of the condemned work, so that, though still a Fellow, he was reduced to the status of an undergraduate. The natural result very shortly followed. Ward, having in the meantime married, joined the Romish communion, and became a professor at St. Edmund's College. Newman also, whose hand Ward's active influence had forced as early as 1841, went over to his destined haven and home in the same communion very soon afterwards. It was, indeed, only by the official veto of the proctors that Tract 90 escaped formal condemnation in 1845 by the same Convocation of the University which degraded Ward. The Oxford Tractarian Movement was thus brought to an end, although the influences which emanated from it have since continued to spread through the churches and parishes of England, in some respects in a more intense degree and form than were ever known in Oxford during the rise and development of the Movement as such.

Since 1841, Ward had well-nigh outgrown the position of a disciple. In the last phase of the Tractarian evolution he may be said to have exchanged places with his former master, and he became the leader in the final clash and conflict. Oakeley, of Margaret Street,—the common friend of Newman and Ward, friend also of Hope-Scott and Gladstone,—who, like Ward, had long been really a Romanist, took his place by the side of Ward, being received into the Church of Rome within a few days of his friend. Of the earlier part of his father's history, up to the crisis I have now spoken of, Mr. Wilfrid Ward writes in the volume before us. In a volume published three years later he has dealt with the remaining forty years of his father's life, which he passed as a member of the Church of Rome. With Ward in this his second phase of character, however, I have not to do in the present chapter.

Reserving for a later place in this chapter a consecutive sketch, in outline, of Ward's earlier life while still professedly an Anglican, let me first endeavour to present the man himself in his unique identity as revealed in his son's narrative, and described by his Oxford friends or acquaintances, especially in his relations to Newman—relations of likeness and unlikeness, of sympathy and contrariety, but always interesting and important, because no man had such an electrical influence on Newman as Ward.

Ward was from the beginning of his student life—was even at school—a bold and ardent abstract thinker, with no taste for the concrete in any form. He loved abstract, but hated applied or mixed, mathematics. He was a good linguist and grammarian, but could never be induced to get up the collateral history or illustrations which related to any author he was reading. History he detested, and throughout life remained phenomenally ignorant of it. He had no taste for poetry. And if for music he had a real passion, yet as to art in general, and architecture, he was a mere barbarian. His tastes for abstract study were balanced and counteracted only by a passion for fiction, burlesque, and, as I have said, music. To the opera and the burlesque stage he remained a devotee even after he had become a devoted and ascetic Romanist; but of high dramatic art he seems to have shown little appreciation. He became a well-read Roman

Catholic theologian, and especially delighted in the systematic and logical theology of the Jesuit masters. But a really learned theologian he never did become, because he cared almost as little for ecclesiastical as for other history, and because he had never studied the historical development of theology. In pure metaphysics he revelled in his mature and later life, as in his earlier life he had revelled in pure mathematics. But he knew no more of physiology or physiological psychology than he did of mechanical theories or applied mathematics. Student as he was of systematic theology and ascetic books, he seems to have known nothing whatever of Biblical exegesis or New Testament criticism. The illustration, from any external source of light or knowledge, of the Scripture text, regarded as history or narrative, seems never to have been recognised by him as a matter of importance. Very little in this way, as Dean Stanley has remarked, in a well-known article in the *Edinburgh Review*,[1] was done by his master, Newman. Ward seems to have been altogether insensible to the attraction of any such work. His ascetic exercises were a discipline he felt the need of, but which he set as far as possible to music. His religion outside the practice of moral duties and of prescribed rules and services was an abstract science—mere theology and metaphysics. So far did he carry his abstractions that he denied that there was any special or necessary duty of love to parents as such, or attachment to one's country; he refused to recognise patriotism as in any sense a virtue.

In his early life Ward was strongly attracted towards Bentham and, especially, Mill—their abstract argumenta-

[1] For April 1881.

tion and their hard matter-of-factness were very much to his taste. Mill's strict, though utilitarian, regard for ethics and practical morality also impressed him favourably. But, notwithstanding his logical hardness, Ward had a profound religiousness of nature. Conscience within him bore strong and peremptory witness to the being and government of God. With this the intrinsic agnosticism of Mill's philosophy was irreconcilable. For some time Ward wavered in painful and agitating suspense—for a long time he was tormented with doubts. The immorality of which he had been witness at Winchester School, the low standard of morality which he saw in the nominally Christian world around him, had strengthened the attraction for him of Mill's equitable character and enlightened ethical teachings, and had conspired with his merely intellectual difficulties to tempt him to scepticism. But in good time the character and influence of Dr. Arnold, and especially the high practical tone of his Christian teaching, helped the young student in his struggles against the philosophy of Mill. When he received deacon's orders, Ward signed the Thirty-nine Articles as a disciple of Arnold, although when he received priest's orders he signed them as follower of Newman—or, as his son uses the word, as a Newmanite. Newman drew him from Arnold. All through, indeed, Ward had missed in Arnold's teaching the abstract basis, the ground of authority, the completeness of grip and scope, which his mathematical genius desiderated. What he wanted was not a mere practical system of Christianity, with a working doctrinal compromise at its base, such as Arnold's teaching offered him; he craved a complete and logical system of faith and religious practice founded on abstract principles. Even when drawn towards Mill he had, feeling his want of such a resting-place, turned a longing and half-fascinated look towards Roman Catholicism, as affording the sort of system in which he might, if only he could accept it, find the repose he craved. Newman seemed to furnish Ward with at least the promise and earnest of what was necessary in this kind. At the same time, the great preacher's ethical tone, and his severely chaste and restrained, but persuasive, eloquence charmed and fascinated the young inquirer, while his sidelong hints and questionings subtly searched again and again the flaws and faults of Mill's material utilitarianism.

Ward thus, within a few years after gaining his Balliol fellowship, became a follower of Newman—an enthusiastic, devoted, and, for some time, an implicitly trustful disciple.[1] What he seemed to himself always to need was an infallible guide, and Newman was, in effect, his Pope. This is very evident from many passages in the volume before us. Nevertheless, there was such a difference—such a contrast —in temper and intellectual tone between the master and the disciple, that it was inevitable, sooner or later, that they should cease to keep even step and close company. For long, indeed, before their mutual relations were sensibly changed, the questions and continual urgency of the disciple, however respectful, however deferential, had been felt by the master to be unwelcome and embarrassing— they were as goads to one who disliked to be urged by anyone to quicken his speed, or hastily to adventure new

---

[1] He was fond of quoting Carlyle's dictum—"True guidance in return for loving obedience, did he but know it, is man's prime need." For several years he thought he had found all he needed in Newman.

departures, one who was supremely anxious to do everything with all caution, and according to the requirements of the most skilfully calculated policy. Ward was a much bolder and more direct man than Newman. The disciple, after a time, began to point in advance of his master, and to ask if the way were not onward in the direction of Rome. Ward embodied the logic of principle, and, in his foresight of inevitable consequence, he also represented the logic of coming fact, which, as he foresaw, was destined to overtake Newman's cautious and tentative policy, a policy which was obliquely suggested by means of hints contained in his tracts and sermons, or was intimated in his private whisperings,—hints and intimations which went to make up the substance of a new, though undeclared and undeveloped, system,—a system nominally Anglican, but virtually Romanist. Newman threw out these suggestions as an evolutionist feeling his way out of the perplexities of Anglo-Catholicism into the solid—or solid seeming—and symmetrical system of Roman Catholic theory,—a system which, however unreasonable it may appear to the impartial intellect, however unnatural and really impracticable it may be, yet within its own sphere of artificial abstractions, of imaginary qualities and quantities, appears to be closely compacted, logical, and complete. Ward was impatient of his master's timid and dilatory process, and desired to be led boldly onward to the destined goal. Thus it came to pass that while Newman was first Ward's guide and oracle, who had delivered his disciple from scepticism, Ward became afterwards almost as a prophet and leader to Newman, interpreting him to himself in distinct utterance, and showing him in the Romish Church the only possible fulfilment of his ideas and the necessary goal of his wavering, but gradually advancing, footsteps. All this had been more or less known before; but never before has it been set in the full light of complete evidence before the eye of the inquirer into this strangely, and in many respects sadly, interesting chapter of English Church history, as it is now shown in Mr. Ward's volume.

Newman's real deficiencies as a thinker combined with his fine special gifts to heighten the contrast between himself and Ward. While Newman was an adept at using the analytic scalpel in the investigations of microscopic introspection, he was greatly wanting in synthetic power, a fact of which his *Grammar of Assent* affords striking evidence and illustration. He felt his way from point to point, almost with the preternaturally quick and subtle sensibility of the sightless traveller; but his was not the bright, keen, far-reaching vision which reveals to the wayfarer at one view the country that lies before and around him, the goal towards which he is journeying, and the roads among which he must choose his path. With this natural want of far-sighted perspicacity another quality combined to make him slow and cautious in his movements. Alike from his personal experience and his long and intimate fellowship with earnest Anglicans of different shades of opinion, and also from a natural fineness and delicacy of sympathetic sensibility, he was keenly alive to all the prepossessions and scruples of English Churchmen. Corresponding to this, also, he possessed a wonderful faculty of persuasiveness in answering, or, still more effectually for his purpose, in anticipating and seeming to clear away beforehand, without formal statement or argument, difficulties or objections which appeared to stand in the way of his present counsels or conclusions. Hence, for all these reasons, it was eminently characteristic of Newman to be slow, patient, tentative, circuitous in his movements and the guidance of his party. In all the particulars I have noted, Ward was a complete contrast to his leader. Ward had no tenderness for Anglican traditions, or sympathy with Anglican scruples and sensitiveness. He was, indeed, a man destitute of fine susceptibilities, except, perhaps, upon the point of honour. Large, strong, almost elephantine in physical frame, he was governed intellectually by unmitigated logic, save only that he had a strong sense of religious responsibility. Regardless of prepossession, or prejudice, or sentimental scruple, he would have marched boldly and swiftly, from step to step, along the line of his argument, driving remorselessly home his conclusions, however harsh or even revolting they might appear to others.

The contrast between the character and methods of Newman and Ward, during the time that they stood to each other nominally in the mutual relation of leader and follower, and almost up to the time when Ward set his teacher the example of leaving the English Church for the Roman communion, is very well set forth by his son in the following paragraphs :—

" To undo the work of the Reformation, and to restore to the English Church her original Catholic character, with the ultimate, if distant, prospect of restoration to the papal obedience, was his " (Ward's) " declared aim, and the programme which he advocated for the Oxford school. . . . If this programme differed from that of the earlier phases of the Movement, much more did the method in which it was advocated differ from that of the early tracts. And it was the peculiarity of this method which brought things to a crisis and ultimately broke up the party. If Ward's theory was unwelcome to Anglicans, his mode of advocating it could not but make it more so, as the unwelcome elements were those he most insisted on. The early tracts had appealed to English ecclesiastical patriotism. There was a Church with a noble history, immemorial traditions, a beautiful liturgy, a roll of saints in her calendar—all this rich inheritance of English Churchmen was being set aside by the accidental views and ignorant bigotry of the moment. They protested against an invasion of Protestantism as against the inroads of Popery. They refused to take their theology from Geneva as they refused to take it from Rome. They said that the English Church should be true to herself and her own past. Augustine had brought to England the faith of the early Fathers. These were the spiritual ancestors of English Christians. Rome had deflected from the original traditions, though she had likewise preserved, as was natural, tokens of their common parentage. Both Churches had been in different ways untrue to themselves. The concern of Englishmen was with their own Church. Let them study the past records of her history and its existing witness in her liturgy, and restore to nineteenth-century Anglicanism the spirit which the lives of Bede, Cuthbert, Anselm, on the one hand, and the Church of England Prayer-Book on the other, breathe in every page. Whatever the precise view taken of the Reformation by the different writers of the tracts, and the precise period at which the English Church was supposed first to have been untrue to herself, it is evident throughout that the appeal is of the kind here indicated—an appeal to *esprit de corps* among English Churchmen, to their pride in the Church's liturgy, in its institutions, in its history, in its monuments throughout the land. . . . Mr. Ward's tone was the very reverse of this. Whilst in theory he was bent on restoring the Anglican Church to what she had been before the Reformation, he preached practically a doctrine of humiliation before a foreign power. He dwelt throughout—partly perhaps from his love of looking at the furthest consequences of his principles, and viewing his theory as a whole, partly from an almost unconscious taste for what seemed startling and paradoxical —on all those results and aspects of his view which were most irritating to English Churchmen. He defended his tone on the ground that perfect frankness and straightforwardness were imperative in a party which had been accused of preaching Popery in secret, and of being generally disingenuous. Moreover, he did, no doubt, think that all Anglican explanations of the Movement *did* veil or make little of what was, in his view, essential. The spirit of loyal submission to papal authority, and of readiness to accept the doctrines taught by the Roman See—these were not minor points, but integral parts of the Catholic position as he viewed it. To win converts by concealing this seemed to him unfair" (pp. 222, 223).

Ward's strength was that of the intrepid logical reasoner, who shrinks from no clear or sure consequences which flow from his reasoning. His weakness was that of the man who endeavours to apply abstract reasoning where it cannot be applied; to define out of his own head where concrete facts of history alone can help us to a true analysis of phenomena or a true definition of principles. His assumptions as to fact and as to doctrine were often erroneous; the premisses of his arguments were thus fatally flawed. One defect which invalidated all his reasonings and judgments in regard to Church systems, was his amazing ignorance of history. He may be said to have known nothing of history; he cared nothing for it; he loudly confessed, he almost boasted of, his ignorance. He was as ignorant of ecclesiastical as of general history. Whilst professing, in some sort and in certain respects, to be a Catholic theologian, he had not even begun to study the times and lifework of Athanasius; he knew almost as little of patristic lore as if he had been a Baptist City Missionary. And yet history is, alike in Christian theology and Christian apologetics, the necessary complement of abstract thought and argument. In the facts of history, justly interpreted,—in a true induction applied to the facts of history as taken in connexion with the facts of consciousness,—are to be found for religion, as in the facts of nature inductively interpreted are to be found for science, the principles of truth and the theory of life. For religion as well as for science, for faith as well as for reason, it is in the verified records of fact— in the one case the facts of history and consciousness, in the other the facts of natural existence—that we must find respectively the demonstrations, on the one hand, which stand in relation to our spiritual intuitions, and those, on the other hand, which establish the physical laws of the universe and stand in relation to our faculty of inductive or scientific reason.

When, in his later life, and as a Roman Catholic professor, Ward had to deal within the comparatively narrow, but profound, sphere of the highest metaphysics, with the relations of the human spirit to God and to moral law, with questions which touched only the sphere of consciousness, and with which neither history nor physical science stands in any relation, then his wonderful keenness of logical understanding enabled him to expose, as very few besides could have done, the fallacies of the materialistic school of sceptical thought to which he was so strongly drawn in his youth. He had gained from Newman some pregnant hints which, aided by his deep religious feeling, pointed him at the time to the way of escape from that danger. These hints, after he had become a teacher in a Roman Catholic university, he developed in a series of powerful arguments, which were immeasurably superior in piercingness and in linked strength and closeness of thought to anything in the way of metaphysical writing which has been done by Newman. But that subject more properly belongs to the latter period of Ward's life, and to a later chapter in this volume.

Ward's phenomenal ignorance of history should have prevented him from attempting to write such a treatise as his *Ideal of a Christian Church*. If he had had any competent knowledge of the history of Christendom he would not have attempted to exhibit the Church of Rome as fulfilling his ideal; he would have understood that his "ideal," confronted with the reality of the history of the Roman communion, could only have the effect, at many points, of a withering satire. Nor, if he had made himself really master of the history of Luther and Lutheranism, instead of using for his purpose detached second-hand passages borrowed from Sir William Hamilton and Moehler, would he have laid himself open to Archdeacon Hare's scathing criticism in his *Vindication of Luther*, much less would he have made his own travesty of Lutheranism stand as the common description of evangelical Protestantism everywhere. Neither would he have subjected himself, by his monstrous misrepresentation of all that relates to the Reformation in England, to such a castigation as that inflicted upon him by Mr. Gladstone in the *Quarterly Review*.[1] For a man so totally devoid of any knowledge of history, before or after the time of Christ, to undertake the writing of such a work as the *Ideal of a Christian Church*, was nothing less than farcical. It is scarcely a matter of surprise that the judgments contained in the book are as arrogant and the tone often as bitter as the treatise, in its historical references, is ignorant throughout. Had Ward really known both the history of Christendom and the vital elements of spiritual religion, according to the apostolic doctrine and the primitive experience of the Christian life, he would have learned that the divine unity of the Church is not to be sought in any organised communion or communions, but can only be fulfilled in the mystical and invisible body of Christ; that in that spiritual Church alone is the New Testament ideal to be realised. But he would also have known that, notwithstanding all errors and all divisions, Christians throughout the world, and the different Churches of Christendom, are helping towards the fulfilment in a continually growing measure of the grand principles of the Lord Jesus Christ's life and teaching. One cannot but wonder what Ward might have become if, as a student of Church history, he had sat at the feet of Neander and, in his longing after Church unity, had entered into fellowship of spirit with Julius Hare, and, above all, if he had also been made in early life a partaker, in full and clear consciousness, of personal salvation through faith in Christ his Saviour. This would have been the best cure for his

[1] October 1844. See also Gladstone's *Gleanings*, vol. v.

scepticism. This would have relieved that continually threatening melancholy, to remedy which he sought diversion in society and discussion, or excitement at the theatre, or consolation and inspiration in music. Had he been a partaker of the peace and joy of evangelical faith, he would have been better fitted to be a profound theologian, and might have refreshed and relieved his mind and heart by assiduous attendance, not at special offices of the Roman Catholic Church, but at Christian meetings for devotion and fellowship of the true primitive type.

"In Mr. Ward's view," we are told by his son, "the ceremonial of the Church was a grand antidote against the constant sceptical imaginings to which he was a prey. At times, when the spiritual world seemed totally unreal, when the difficulties against faith, with which, as we have seen, the material creation abounded in his eyes, tried him most, it helped his imagination to look at the outward symbols of great religious mysteries. The doubts were, to a great extent, imaginative rather than intellectual, and a remedy was required appealing primarily to the imagination" (p. 147).

After all, we find here an unexpected link of alliance between the high Roman Catholic idealist and the fervent Cornish Methodist, or the earnest and spiritually awakened captain of the Salvation Army. All alike make physical influences and sensuous symbolism contributory to the purposes of devotional realism and spiritual ecstasy.

I must not pass away from the subject of the *Ideal of a Christian Church* without referring to the doctrine of conscience as there set forth. It forms part and parcel of Ward's theory on the subject; but, though founded on one side on a great and deep truth of human consciousness, it is yet, as he sets it forth, scarcely less misleading or liable to abuse than any fanatical errors as to the conscience ever broached by the most unenlightened sectaries of the Commonwealth period. The authority of conscience, according to his teaching, stands in no relation to the understanding. It must not even seek for information or enlightenment. Its "feeling" is at once and absolutely to be obeyed. The conscience of the "holy" man is sure to be a true guide. To seek light from the understanding would be for the conscience to abdicate its rights. A doctrine this which seems to us to be very near akin to the error of Ward's master, Newman, in regard to faith, as taught both in his university sermons and in his *Grammar of Assent*, according to which faith and reason are so far in opposition to each other, as that the man who believes the most upon the least evidence or ground of mere reason, is the man of the greatest and truest faith; and so to believe absolutely all that the Church teaches, apart from all reason or evidence, is the perfection of faith.[1] It is in strict accordance with this view that his son represents Ward as teaching that "Church authority is the external embodiment of a perfect conscience" (p. 74). Viewed from another side, Ward's confused and incoherent doctrines as to conscience cannot but remind us of the error of the extreme "Plymouth" sectary which makes him his own pope, and his conscience, or what he supposes to be such, to be the absolute rule of truth both for himself and others.

Such was the man himself, while still a member of the Church of England and the University of Oxford. A

[1] *London Quarterly Review*, January 1871, Art. v. Newman's *Grammar of Assent*. See also Froude's *Short Studies*, Fourth Series.

sketch of his earlier life will enable us more fully and exactly to appreciate his unique personality.

The family of William George Ward has been settled for more than a century in the Isle of Wight, where the Ward property is contiguous to that of Lord Tennyson, who was a friend of Ward's in his later life, and who wrote some memorial lines on "the most generous of all Ultramontanes." At the same time, the Ward family were eminent in the circles of City finance, and Ward's father was Tory member for the City of London,—where Ward was born in 1812,—and was also one of the most famous of cricketers. Ward himself seems not to have taken after his father; at anyrate, he had no taste or capacity either for commerce or cricketing.[1]

Ward's mother was Miss Combe, of the well-known brewery firm, her brother, the head of the firm, being also a popular master of hounds in Surrey. The son seems to have in no respect resembled in taste or character any of his relatives. "Even as a child," we are told, "his likes and dislikes were very intense. He had a passion for music and the drama, and for mathematics. He detested general society." He seems to have grown up under undesirable influences, and altogether without proper, if

[1] Among the collateral relatives of his father was Robert Plumer Ward, who was a member of several Tory ministries, and author of *Tremaine*, a novel of considerable ability, and which contained the outline of a thoughtful argument in favour of Christianity, a book which the writer of this volume remembers with pleasure and gratitude after the lapse of more than half a century. It is certain, however, that nothing of the tone or spirit of *Tremaine* was reproduced in the writings of William George Ward. Another distinguished member of the Ward family was the son of the author of *Tremaine*, Sir Henry Ward, G.C.M.G., who was at one time Lord Commissioner of the Ionian Isles, and died Governor of Madras in 1860.

any, discipline. He hated the commonplace of life—even of boy-life—from the first. He could not live without intense excitement, either of thought or of dramatic representations. When very young, the reaction after the play sometimes made him cry from depression of spirits. He could not endure even a few minutes' interval of rest and quiet. Between the acts of the play he would be busy with his mathematics. He knew the names of all the actors and supernumeraries, of subordinates as well as principals. At the same time, he was deep in logarithms at an early age.

He was, withal, a clumsy, shy, unsociable boy, given to biting his nails, sitting or standing apart, and looking generally bored. Taken to a children's dancing party, he left abruptly and walked home through the country roads in his dancing shoes, notwithstanding the pelting rain. He was not asked to go to another party. When eleven years old he went to Winchester School as a commoner. Here he was shocked and disgusted with the wickedness of the school, and seems to have found no compensations. He had no aptitude for games. This fact, added to his natural shyness and his moral austerity, made him generally unpopular. Lord Selborne, a schoolfellow, says of him: "Physically he was strong. In appearance ponderous, in manners brusque and eccentric, he was no cultivator of the Graces, and was not at his ease in strange society." "He despised, or affected to despise, poetry and romance." At the same time, with his friends he was "good company. He had a pleasure in paradox and a keen sense of the ludicrous, and far from being offended at the amusement others found in his peculiarities, he was quite capable of entering into a joke at his own expense." His memory was remarkable, and stood him in good stead both in his classical and mathematical studies. But he quite refused to work seriously at the versemaking of which classical Winchester made so much. He gained the gold medal, however, for Latin prose composition in his eighteenth year, against such competitors as Roundell Palmer [1] and Robert Lowe.

He loved, even in his schoolboy days, abstract discussion and reasoning. The contrast between his quick perceptions in mathematics or ethical speculation, or in the details of the ideal world of the dramatic stage, and his inadvertence in matters of common life, was from the first remarkable. A story is told of his asking, at twelve years of age, when eating a sole, what it was; and when the name of the dish was told him, saying, "It is very nice; where do they grow?"

At the same time, this strange, uncouth boy was strictly moral, with a deep sense of religion, of which he sometimes spoke to his eldest sister, and to a governess of his younger sisters, whom other people seem to have regarded as dull, but who was an earnest evangelical Christian, and whose society he so much sought as to give rise to family pleasantries on the subject. This same sense of religion seems to have led, his son tells us, "to a horror at the immorality prevalent at Winchester, startling in its degree to most of those who conversed with him on the subject." Probably this deep sense of morality was connected with the insurrection against his authority as prefect which broke out in the school, and which was immediately occasioned by his determination to punish an offending boy. He was mobbed and dragged off by a large

[1] The late Lord Selborne.

number of the boys. Six boys were expelled in consequence. The matter got into the newspapers, and Ward was condemned rather than applauded by the guardians of society in the press. The offender was a young man of good family and position. The method of discipline at Winchester which gives to the prefects the right and duty of "tunding" offenders against discipline has often been brought unhappily under public attention, and certainly affords no good model for other schools. But what public school is much better in this respect? It is hardly even a question of degree; there seems to be very little to prefer among them all, though all, no doubt, are improved since the period when Ward was at Winchester, and Trollope at Winchester and Harrow.

It is no wonder if so strange a boy as Ward was not understood even by his relatives. His parents do not seem to have made much of him, and in after years he did not pretend to feel any special, or, as others would have expressed it, "natural" affection for them. His holidays were generally spent either with his grandfather, Mr. George Ward, in the Isle of Wight, or with his uncle, the brewer and sportsman, at Cobham. It was at his uncle's that his qualities were first, in part, discovered; not, it need hardly be said, by his uncle, but by "an eminent and cultured dignitary of the Anglican Church," whose name one would be glad to know. After this discovery of his powers of reasoning and of conversation, he was looked upon by his relations in a more respectful light. Already the intense melancholy which preyed upon him through life had become a part of his character. Had he been differently brought up, it may be fairly supposed that it would not have established itself as it did. A gentle, kindly, religious nurture, a true Christian training instead of a regimen of playgoing from his babyhood, with no system of discipline whatever, would have produced a different character from that which I have described. He left Winchester in 1829 and entered Oxford in 1830, having in the interval devoted himself to the study of mathematics and of political economy and philosophy as taught by Bentham and Mill.

At Oxford, Ward became almost at once a distinguished debater at the Union. He was called the "Tory Chief" of the Society, and was elected its President in 1832. Though called a Tory, however, he soon showed that he had been sitting at the feet of Radical teachers. In 1833 he brought forward a motion—which, of course, was lost—for the admission of Jews to the Legislature. His great passion, however, in his undergraduate days, as Archdeacon Browne in particular testifies, "was for music, in every kind of which he took the greatest delight, from the operas of Mozart and Rossini to the burlesques at the Olympic." His reading was miscellaneous, and he was in no sense a student. "He had no idea," his son tells us, "of taking honours until his father's embarrassed circumstances made it a matter of importance that he should obtain a fellowship." With this view he stood for a scholarship at Lincoln, and was unanimously elected in 1833. But nothing could induce him to work at subjects not to his taste; and when given by his tutor, on the eve of a critical examination, a set of specially important formulæ in mechanics to learn, he sat up reading one of Miss Austen's novels instead. "The rapidity and accuracy of his work in pure mathematics were said to be wonderful; but he could not bear applied mathematics." Experimental methods and approximate results were especially distasteful to him. "The study of fractions," he used to say, "makes me feel literally sick." So again, in classical scholarship, in Latin especially, he greatly excelled. "But in the matter of collateral knowledge," says his son, "as to the history of the works he was reading, the circumstances of their composition, the lives of their authors; and, again, as to the history of the times with which they dealt,—except so far as it was conveyed in the actual works themselves,—he professed total ignorance. He said that such things did not interest him, and that he did not understand them, so he simply left them alone." It is hard to understand such stupid indolence as this in the case of a man of undoubted capacity, and of liberal education, brought up in contact with general intelligence. It was evidently a form of selfishness and self-will, as well as of intellectual indolence, and indicated a narrow range of sympathies, a cramped "humanity," an undisciplined mind and character. Here was at least one professedly Christian student and destined clergyman who could not appreciate the force and beauty of the famous heathen apothegm—"Homo sum: nihil humani a me alienum puto." This fatal defect in his character and intellectual equipment, however, remained with him to the end. It had much to do with the one-sided development of his mind.

Even when under examination for his degree Ward amazed his examiners by the singular and wilful negligence, not to say contempt, which he displayed of all relating to the subjects of examination that was not, as he chose to think, "in his line."

"One of Cicero's letters to his brother Quintus is chosen, and the examiner tells Ward to turn to a particular part. Ward reads it admirably. Attention is aroused. The audience, consisting of a large number of undergraduates and a good sprinkling of dons, is on the *qui vive*. The construing comes next, which, if not so good as the reading, still bears out the expectation of first-rate ability. At the end, the examiner says: ' Well, Mr. Ward, now let me ask you, what are the principal extant letters of Cicero ? ' Ward (without the slightest hesitation) : ' I really don't know.' The examiner (surprised, and after a short pause): ' The letter from which you have just construed was written on the eve of a very eventful time ; can you tell me something of the events which immediately followed ? ' Ward : ' I know nothing whatever about them.' Examiner : ' Take your time, Mr. Ward, you are nervous.' ' No, sir,' replies Ward, ' it is not nervousness ; pure ignorance.' Examiner (making another attempt): ' In what year was it written ? ' Ward (with energy): ' I haven't the slightest idea '; his last replies being given almost in a tone of resentment " (p. 27).

Though far from being as ignorant as Ward, Newman also, as we know, was weak on the side of history, having no taste for its original and impartial investigation, resorting to its stores and sources only when he had a special conclusion to establish, a brief to support, for which it was necessary that he should gather some evidence. " History is not my line," said Newman to Ward in 1841 (p. 180). In the case of both Newman and Ward, this special defect in the point of historical knowledge was closely connected with their theological errors. A curious illustration, in the case of Ward, will presently be added to what has already been said on this subject.

Ward's passion for music and the drama was still

greater at Oxford than in his school-days. This is said to have been owing to the insupportable attacks of melancholy to which he was subject. "He fled from the perplexities and religious doubts to which he was subject, and threw himself into any form of congenial recreation with the utmost unreserve. Music and the drama were his great means of transporting himself into this ideal world, and he availed himself of them continually."

Such statements sound somewhat strange in regard to one to whose "deep seriousness" and consequent "dignity" of character we also receive emphatic testimony. But his seems to have been a character in which startling contrasts were combined. His shyness was not incompatible with real *abandon*, when the ice was broken and he found himself in congenial and stimulating society, as when he went, as the Archbishop of Canterbury describes, to a party at Balliol, where there was to be a large and lively gathering, with music and dancing. He made up his mind to go after mastering some serious scruples of conscience as to the lawfulness of the recreation, and the different claims of duty. But as he walked home with his friend he said: "My dear Temple, what a delightful evening—one of the pleasantest I ever spent — and what delightful ladies. I could have proposed to any one of them on the spot."

Ward took his degree in 1833, attaining a second-class, notwithstanding his wilful negligence and wayward faults as a student. In 1834 he was elected Fellow of Balliol. Some time after this he came under the influence of Newman. For a long time he had refused even to go near him. "Why," he asked, "should he listen to such myths?" But having been cleverly seduced into St. Mary's Church by a friend one Sunday evening when Newman was to preach, he came immediately under the preacher's spell, and, before long, submitted wholly to his ascendency. "That sermon," the late Professor Bonamy Price wrote, "changed his whole life." Newman's sermons and lectures were more than a match for Ward's mere uninformed dialectics. They seemed also, as I have already observed, to furnish him with a way of escape from the teachings of Mill. He yielded to the fascination which enthralled almost the whole generation of earnest and religiously disposed young men at the university. Before, however, he finally surrendered himself to the influence of Newman, he determined to visit his friend Bonamy Price, then a master at Rugby, and talk the matter over with him. The result, curiously illustrative of Ward's one-sidedness of intellect and judgment, and of his impatience of historical inquiry, will best be told in Professor Price's own words:—

"I received a letter from Ward which stated that he was on the point of changing his religious views, but that before carrying out the change he wished to discuss with me the religious elements involved in this grave matter. He hoped, therefore, that I would be willing to receive him at Rugby as my guest for a week, which would allow time for a thorough examination of the principles at issue. I replied that it would give me great pleasure to welcome him at my house, and to do my best to carry on the discussion, . . . so accordingly he came. The first day passed very pleasantly, and the discussion proceeded smoothly. On the second day, to my infinite surprise, Ward broke out suddenly with the remark: 'Had I known beforehand the treatment I was to receive here I should never have come.' I was thoroughly taken aback. I exclaimed: 'Have I been rude or discourteous, my dear

Ward? I had not the slightest intention of being so; but if I have, I will ask for your forgiveness most sincerely.' 'Oh, dear, no,' he rejoined, 'but you have been eminently disagreeable.' ... Undoubtedly his remark was true; I had been very disagreeable, and I could not help it. But why, and how? I had discovered that he had come down, if I may say so, to play a trick literally, not on me, but on his conscience. He had resolved, under the inspiring influence of Newman's preaching, to adopt his view of religion, but he had neither time nor inclination to analyse the problem to the very bottom, so it occurred to him to go down and have a talk with 'that Protestant Price.' He would say to himself that his arguments were all rubbish, and so he would be able to effect the conversion with greater ease and confidence to himself. On making this discovery I saw clearly what had to be done. I resolved to personate that conscience which he was trying to silence. I put myself in its place, and asked those very questions which he wanted to shirk. I said to him: 'You assert that a certain fact occurred and a certain doctrine existed at the very beginning of the Church different from the opinion held in the Protestant Church of England; have you examined the evidence on which you make that objection?' 'Oh, dear, no,' he replied. 'Then why do you adopt it?' 'John Newman says it is so.' After a while he again brought forward a doctrine built on alleged fact, which differed from the view taken in the English Church. Again I asked: 'Have you searched out, and can you state the evidence on which you contradict the view you have hitherto held?' Again the answer, 'No,' rolled from his lips, and again he took his stand on what Newman said. Some more questions followed, all ending in the same answer. Therefore I remarked: 'Then Newman is your sole authority. His word is the only thing you stand upon. Has he worked a miracle on which to claim your assent?' It was then that he spoke the angry words which put an end to the whole discussion."

It was in 1838 that Ward became a "Newmanite." To the Rev. James Lonsdale he said soon afterwards: "My creed is very short: 'Credo in Newmannum,'" although I may observe, in passing, that this characteristic saying does not square with what Mr. Lonsdale tells us of his "apparent desire of fairly sifting all questions to the bottom." Ward's sifting took no account of any historical evidence; it was the sifting of a dialectical gladiator— it was mere logical sword-play. This sort of work is valuable in its place, but will not avail to sift questions to the bottom.

Ward had many and distinguished friends at Oxford. He was a brilliant conversational debater, and was perfectly good-tempered; he was in his personal relations a frank and generous man. Among his closest friends were Arthur Stanley and Clough the poet. Their friendship began at the time when he was a brilliant and dangerous—sometimes also an irreverent—rationalist, at least in his ordinary course of conversation and discussion. It is said that his clever talk did no harm to Stanley. It is admitted, however, and it was a matter of painful and remorseful confession on his part in his later life, that he was largely instrumental in destroying the hopeful and happy early faith of Clough. On the whole, he must have been somewhat of an *enfant terrible*. Dean Church says of him in his contribution to Mr. Wilfrid Ward's volume:—

"The most amusing, the most tolerant man in Oxford, he had round him perpetually some of the cleverest and highest scholars and thinkers who were to be the future Oxford; and where he was, there was debate, cross-questioning, pushing inferences, starting alarming problems, beating out ideas, trying the stuff and mettle of mental capacity—always rapid and impetuous, he gave no quarter. . . .[1] But he was not generally persuasive in proportion to his powers of argument. Abstract reasoning, in matters with which human action is concerned, may be too absolute to be convincing. . . . Ward, in perfect confidence in his conclusions, rather liked to leave them in a startling form, which he innocently declared to be manifest and inevitable. And so stories of Ward's audacities and paradoxes flew all over Oxford, shocking and perplexing grave heads with fear of they knew not what. Dr. Jenkyns, the Master of Balliol,—one of those curious mixtures of pompous absurdity with genuine shrewdness which used to pass over the university stage,—liking Ward, and proud of him for his cleverness, was aghast at his monstrous language, and driven half wild with it."

Excessive and burlesque jocoseness was a striking feature of Ward's character. Although deep seriousness is spoken of repeatedly as the foundation of his character, this opposite characteristic would appear to have been much more "in evidence" when he was with his companions. Nor was any occasion serious enough to restrain him. "Dulce est desipere in loco" may be a

---

[1] The effect of a visit of a few days, which he paid to Dr. Arnold at Rugby, in school-term time, was, that after his departure Arnold had to take to his bed for a day. His evenings with Ward, following his work in school, had completely knocked him up.

good motto for a companionable life. But to play the fool out of place and out of time is not an estimable or pleasing feature of character. This is what Ward did on the day and on the morrow of his degradation in connection with the condemnation of his *Ideal*, as may be read on pp. 343, 344 of his son's record. On one of these occasions Cardinal (then Archdeacon) Manning administered a not ungentle, but dignified, rebuke. An instance of his extraordinary faculty for mixing up things sacred and profane, or at least devotional and altogether worldly, is also furnished in the following anecdote. The narrator is Professor Jowett.

" He once took me, on a Sunday evening in the middle of summer, about the year 1839, to Mr. Newman's church at Littlemore, where he was to preach. We drove out after dinner, and walked home. Two things I remember on that occasion which were highly characteristic of him. The sermon which he preached was a printed one of Dr. Arnold's, but with additions and alterations, which, as he said, it would have driven the author mad to hear. We walked back to Oxford in the twilight, along the Iffley Road. He was in high spirits, and sang to me songs out of ' Don Giovanni' and other operas, with which his memory was well stored. He was not the less serious because he could pass an hour or two in this way."

On the Lord's day evening, after the holy service,—such it should have been to a serious " Catholic " preacher, —he could, it seems, without impairing his seriousness, sing songs out of the Don Juan opera for an hour or two ! Is this after the Catholic and Apostolic model and spirit ?

Ward, as we have noted, became a " Newmanite " in

1838. Between 1841 and 1845 he led the advanced Romeward Movement, Newman having retired from the front after the condemnation of Tract 90. In 1844, Ward published his *Ideal*. In 1845 his book was condemned by the Convocation of the university, and he was degraded. In the same year he married, his engagement having been made public during the Convocation which condemned his book, and soon afterwards he and his wife were "received" by Father Brownhill in the Jesuit Chapel, Bolton Street.[1] When they made confession to the Jesuit Father, "he showed," we are told, "such knowledge of human nature. He told Mrs. Ward to make a retreat and to practise certain austerities; but he told" Ward himself "to unbend as much as possible, and to go to the play as often as he could." They went soon afterwards to reside at Old Hall, near the College of St. Edmund, Ware. Here Ward built a house, of which Pugin was the architect. Ward, however, knew nothing of architecture, and had no reverence for Gothic, having, indeed, never

---

[1] A writer in the *Guardian* for March 25th, 1891, reviewing Dean Church's book on *The Oxford Movement*, refers to Ward as "that curious creature and lovable man," who so loved the ludicrous that he could bear with perfect good humour and almost rollicking fun to see himself the object of the laugh, and as one who, "with wonderful simplicity and extraordinary impudence, would obtrude what most men would reserve." " Perhaps," he adds, "this culminated in his apology for his marriage, which he defended on the plea that, if the Church of England were what it claimed to be, she could never have admitted him into the priesthood." His engagement was announced at the crisis of the fight in Convocation, and was received in the theatre at Oxford "with universal, immense laughter." A sedate colonial bishop, at the end of a dinner-table, was heard to say in the quietest of voices: "I presume that, in the next edition of the *Ideal*, there will be this epilogue: 'On such a day Mr. Ward was married, and the lady and gentleman are now a happy couple.'"

heard of "mullions" till he met Pugin. He tried the patience of Pugin by insisting on having windows "of large number and goodly size." Here his son leaves him at the end of this volume, poor as yet, but steadfastly anchored in the haven of the "Roman obedience." Here also I leave him for the present, reserving to a later chapter a review of his uniquely interesting and instructive history after he had become a Roman Catholic theologian and an Ultramontane philosopher of the high spiritual school.

As a son's biography of a father's life before he had found his spiritual settlement and home, or taken up the final work of his life,—as an account of that period of his life which was full of controversy and conflict, and which was more or less out of harmony with the last forty years of his history—as a record sent forth by the son for the information, in the first place and chiefly, of readers professing a creed and holding principles of the highest and most sacred import in opposition to the creed and principles both of the subject and of the author of the biography,—it is a singularly impartial production. The views are here most fairly presented of all the survivors from among Ward's most distinguished university friends—including such men as Dean Stanley and Jowett, as Dean Church and Dean Goulburn;—of men who were best fitted to speak of his character and position,—of whom several have now followed their early friend into the unseen world; —and of all these none are Roman Catholics. Still, nowhere throughout the volume is any representation given, is even a glimpse afforded, of the true spiritual and evangelical Church theory, which is neither Broad Church nor High Church, nor, in any distinctive and definite sense, nationalist.

In some of the books whose titles are given below, truths are set forth of which not only William George Ward, but all his university friends seem to have been totally unaware, and by which the eyes of young students may perhaps be preserved from the dazzle and confusion apt to be produced by the study of such a book as the one with which we have been chiefly concerned in this chapter.[1]

[1] *The Holy Catholic Church, the Communion of Saints.* By the Rev. B. Gregory, D.D. *Methodism in the Light of the Early Church.* By the Rev. W. F. Slater, M.A. I may here also refer to Dr. Jacob's valuable volume on *The Ecclesiastical Polity of the New Testament* as a modern volume by an English Churchman which expounds the true spiritual view of the Church. I will venture also in this connexion to refer to a volume of my own, entitled, *A Comparative View of Church Organisations—Primitive and Protestant* (3rd edition).

CHAPTER IV.

THE TRACTARIAN MOVEMENT AS DESCRIBED FROM THE
INTERIOR :—

DEAN CHURCH'S *HISTORY OF THE OXFORD MOVEMENT*—
CHURCH'S POSITION—RELATION TO NEWMAN—HOW
FAR HE WENT—FIRST PRINCIPLE OF THE MOVEMENT
—KEBLE'S. RELATION TO THE MOVEMENT—HURRELL
FROUDE, HIS *REMAINS*—THE COTERIE AT OXFORD—
OXFORD SIXTY YEARS AGO—NEWMAN'S LIFE AND
INFLUENCE—HIS RESERVE AND AUSTERITY—WARD'S
INFLUENCE OVER NEWMAN—WARD'S WITNESS AGAINST
NEWMAN — *Note* CHURCH'S LECTURE ON BISHOP
ANDREWES.[1]

THE materials for the late Dean Church's volume on *The Oxford Movement* must have been in preparation for many years. It relates strictly and properly to the Tractarian Movement—it closes with the secession of Newman in 1845. Its author belonged to the Inner Tractarian circle, and was an intimate and cherished friend of Newman. Fulness of knowledge, mastery of details, ripeness of judg-

[1] *The Oxford Movement* (1833–1845). By R. W. Church, M.A., D.C.L., etc. Macmillan & Co. *Letters and Correspondence of J. H. Newman during his Life in the English Church.* Edited by Anne Mozley. Longmans.

ment—from the author's own point of view—distinguish the history from first to last. The book accordingly, though posthumous, may be regarded as the mature and finished product of the writer's mind.

It had been for some time known among the intimate friends of the late Dean that he was writing the history of the Oxford Movement, and that the work was nearly ready for publication. It was, of course, looked for with great interest. Church had not only himself been one of Newman's friends and disciples at Oxford, but he had retained his close friendship with him through the whole of his life. As one of the university proctors—the junior of the two— he had, on occasion of the condemnation in 1845 of W. G. Ward's *Ideal of a Christian Church*, borne his part in the responsibility of the veto pronounced by his colleague on the proposal brought before Convocation by the Hebdomadal Board of the university (after having condemned and degraded Ward) to pronounce a formal censure on the principles taught in Newman's Tract 90, published nearly four years before. Soon afterwards he left Oxford, and during many years of retirement from public life, years spent for the most part in the seclusion of an obscure country parish, he was understood to have devoted himself very largely to those wide and various studies of literature and ecclesiastical history, chiefly continental, of which the results are found in his well-known and justly valued works. It was therefore expected that, notwithstanding his well-understood High Church principles, his Oxford training and history, and his friendship with Newman, his account of the Oxford Movement would be written with a detachment of mind and a freedom from prejudice—especially after the lapse of nearly fifty years—such as could not be expected in the case of anyone who had taken part in the intermediate history and controversies as a recognised public leader of the party which had followed, first Newman and afterwards Pusey, along the line of doctrinal development and ecclesiastical controversy. As regards this point, the volume before us is somewhat disappointing. Rarely indeed is Dean Church at all unkindly in his tone; his temper in speaking of the adversaries of his party is sometimes generous, and nearly always respectful; only, indeed, in the case of Dr. Hampden do his censures seem to savour of unfairness, or any other narrowness than such as was necessarily imposed upon him by the principles which belong to his Church party. But to those principles in this book he holds tenaciously. It is only from 1840 that his views begin to diverge in any important sense from those of Newman. As to what are really main principles, it would seem as if he had never differed from the views which Newman taught at Oxford; he held fast also, at least in general, to Pusey's views, which, it is virtually acknowledged by Pusey himself in his *Eirenicon*, and now made still more evident in his *Life*, were in essential agreement with all the necessary *agenda et credenda* of the Roman communion, except only the vulgar Mariolatry and the Papal Infallibility. The position of Dean Church, indeed, as disclosed in this volume, does not appear materially to differ from that of Pusey. He does not regard any as "Roman" so long as they do not approve or accept the Curial Policy of the Papacy—the special Papal Development—Mariolatry, Infallibility. The list he gives of men "not Roman," who were in full sympathy with Newman and his teachings up to 1840, is sufficient evidence on this point. Chief among these Tractarians who were "not Roman" he sets down Pusey, joining with him such men as Isaac Williams and Charles Marriott.¹ The true Protestant view is very different. It is that Puseyism is essentially Popery; not, like the Laudian Movement, Popery revived from its embers in a nation of which the great mass of the people had never really embraced the Reformation, but Popery revived after ages intervening in which England, through all its ranks and classes, had ceased to be Popish, and, with whatever shortcomings, had yet been an enlightened and Protestant nation, delivered alike from the gross superstitions and the spiritual despotism of Rome. The two plague-spots of Puseyism—of High Church Catholicism—are its sacramental perversions, whereby the holy seals of the Christian faith and profession are turned into superstitions; and its dehumanising doctrine of the confessional. And these two roots of error being once accepted, there is no tenet, either of Tridentine or of modern Popery, which may not be received. Those who, following Pusey, have learned to regard the priest-confessor as a searcher of hearts and the healer and absolver of the soul, gifted for his office with corresponding attributes and authority from God, need find no difficulty in addressing prayers to the Virgin Mary, or to perfected saints, and can find nothing too hard for them in the doctrine of the Pope's Infallibility, when speaking *ex cathedrâ*, as the "Vicar of Christ."

Dean Church would, no doubt, have accepted for him-

[1] Both these men were High Tractarians, and went far along the Romeward road, though neither of them wholly followed, or always fully trusted, Newman. Isaac Williams was a true poet, but a man of little or no active influence. Marriott was the self-effacing, absent-minded scholar of the party.

self the ecclesiastical character or description of an "Anglo-Catholic." He was a Catholic; he followed Newman in accepting that designation; but he would not have dropped the qualifying *Anglo*. He held to the character of an English Churchman. But he would not have allowed himself to be regarded as a simple English Churchman, apart from all that is implied in the special designation *Catholic*. The position represented by Dean Burgon in his *Twelve Good Men* would have been regarded by Church as too narrowly national, too strictly Anglican. He was a High Anglo-Catholic.

His history of the Movement is, of course, strung upon a succession of names of leaders. It will be found, however, that in this history, as given · by Church, the number of actors—of actual leaders—is very small. As the whole Movement, so far as it is dealt with in Dean Church's volume, only embraced thirteen years, this is what might be expected. Pusey is little more than a name— to the Movement in its earlier stages he contributed comparatively little, and the full meaning and scope of what he contributed was not at first apparent. Church has less to say of him than even of Charles Marriott, who was little more than a literary drudge, an editorial hack, working to the order of others, chiefly Newman. Both Pusey and Marriott were absolutely blind to the intellectual and ecclesiastical laws and influences which governed the Movement and drove its leaders to their destiny. The vital links in the succession of personal forces which ruled the original Tractarian Movement were Keble and Newman. With Newman must be bracketed Froude and Ward. Isaac Williams was an echo of Keble, who had been his tutor, and the strain of his influence soon died away. What in this volume is most valuable relates to the four men whom I have specially named. Of the four, Ward is the marplot —or the over-zealous partisan—through whose unrestrainable impetuosity and honest, though always more or less ill-informed, perversity the grand "catastrophe," as Dean Church calls it, took place, which broke up the Tractarian alliance, and brought the Movement to an end, by the secession of Newman, following Ward, to the Roman communion. The drama which ended with this "catastrophe" is the subject of this volume, and Newman is its hero, with whom, more and more, as we advance from stage to stage of the history, all the interest and fortunes of the narrative are identified, and with whose passing off the Oxford stage the volume terminates. With a force of language and in a style altogether unusual in the tranquil writing of Dean Church, he refers (p. 276) to "the strange and pathetic events of 1845" as having "for a time hushed even anger in feelings of amazement, sorrow, and fear," and as having "imposed stillness on all who had taken part in the strife, like the blowing up of the *Orient* at the battle of the Nile."

How it was that Church did not accompany his admired teacher and friend in his parting from the Church of England—at what precise point in his course he found himself unable further to follow him—how, whilst agreeing with so large a part of his premises, he escaped his ultimate and decisive conclusion—it is by no means easy to discover. The question is not distinctly dealt with by Dean Church, and it is only by a careful observance of the places where he fails directly or indirectly to indicate his agreement with Newman, and a few places besides where the turn of expression or the form of reflection shows that the author is speaking distinctively for himself, and at the same time is gently criticising or intimating his difference from his master, that we are able to learn in what respects Dean Church fell short of his master in sympathy with Roman doctrine. The upshot of the whole is, that, knowing much more history than Newman, and being at the same time less practically logical as a speculative reasoner and less under the sway of ecclesiastical considerations and motives, he could not, although conscious of the false position of the Church of England,[1] leave it for a Church which had such a history as that of Rome in respect of its hierarchy, especially its Popes, and in respect of its corruptions, such as those which stirred up the indignation of Luther, including indulgences and relic worship, and the excesses of Mariolatry and other forms of hagiolatry. He held that the objections on such grounds against the Church of Rome were as grave and as undeniable as any objections which Rome could urge against the Church of England, and therefore that it was his duty to remain in the Church of his nation, and of his early choice. Possibly the fact that he was of Quaker descent, of Irish parentage on one side and German on the other, and that, born in Spain, and spending his early youth in Italy, he had no Anglican antecedents or connexions, may have contributed to Church's comparative detachment of mind and feeling.

If Dean Church, however, had been a less biassed thinker, he would have seen that this argument of his in apology for the defective notes and titles of the Church of England, as co-heir with the Church of Rome of the Catholic character and inheritance of the true Church of Christ, is an irresistible weapon of defence,

[1] See Note at the end of this chapter.

which he places in the hands of continental Protestant and of Nonconformist Churches, for their own use and service against Anglo-Catholic as well as Roman Catholic pretensions. For, first, it cuts away the ground from under the assumption which Dean Church accepted from Newman —as set forth in the first of the tracts—that the Catholic Church character descends of necessity and exclusively by the line of apostolico-episcopal succession. That principle, as Newman in the end came to see and feel, must, for all that hold it fast, invest the Romish communion, notwithstanding all its faults and corruptions, and especially as against the claims of an excommunicated Church like the Church of England, with an indefeasible supremacy, reducing the Church of England, as Cardinal Manning, criticising Pusey's *Eirenicon*, long ago insisted with unanswerable force and pungent emphasis, to a relative position towards the Church of Rome, corresponding very closely to that which Churchmen assign to Nonconformist communions in England. Then, in the next place, if, notwithstanding the superior ecclesiastical claims of the Church of Rome, Dean Church, for such reasons as he assigns, felt himself bound to maintain his allegiance to the Church of England, by parity of reason the Nonconformist Churches, such, for example, as Wesleyan Methodism, might well, in view of the frequent blemishes and stains of that Church's history, of the abuses, the irregularities, the worldliness, the barrenness and impotence which have too often marked its annals, sometimes for several generations in succession, and especially which, by confession of its own best and greatest sons, gave to its history during the eighteenth century a peculiar flagrancy of discredit,—hold fast their allegiance to their own Church principles and ecclesiastical organisations, even if they were prepared to admit, as they are not, the superior ecclesiastical claims and titles of the Church of England.

The following passage expresses, in part, the feeling of which I have been speaking, as enabling Church to resist the influence of his leader's example in going over to Rome:—

"The English Church was after all as well worth living in and fighting for as any other; it was not only in England that light and dark, in teaching and in life, were largely intermingled, and the mixture had to be largely allowed for. We had our Sparta, a noble, if a rough and an incomplete one; patiently to do our best for it was better than leaving it to its fate, in obedience to signs and reasonings which the heat of strife might well make delusive. It was one hopeful token, that boasting had to be put away from us for a long time to come. In these days of stress and sorrow were laid the beginnings of a school whose main purpose was to see things as they are, which had learned by experience to distrust unqualified admiration and unqualified disparagement; determined not to be blinded even by genius to plain certainties; not afraid to honour all that is great and beneficent in Rome, not afraid with English frankness to criticise freely at home; but not to be won over, in one case, by the good things, to condone and accept the bad things; and not deterred, in the other, from service, from love, from self-sacrifice, by the presence of much to regret and to resist" (p. 347).

With this passage may fitly be compared the Dean's description of the Tractarian Movement in the stage of its best early promise and hopeful vigour:—

"It might well seem that it was on its way to win over the coming generations of the English clergy. It had on its side all that gives interest and power to a cause. . . . It had the promise of a nobler religion, as energetic and as spiritual as Puritanism and Wesleyanism, while it drew its inspiration, its canons of doctrine, its moral standards, from purer and more venerable sources—from communion, not with individual teachers and partial traditions, but with the consenting teaching and authoritative documents of the continuous Catholic Church" (pp. 193, 194).

The "continuous Catholic Church" is a large and impressive phrase, but is scarcely more than a phrase. And notwithstanding its supposed derivation and descent from this hypothetically defined but scarcely verifiable organisation,—scarcely verifiable at least by an English Churchman,—the Church of England, according to the showing of Dean Church, had fallen into such a state of lethargy and confusion, of neglected duties and traditions or of divided counsels, that the violent remedy of the Movement had become necessary to correct its errors and to reorganise and revive it, and the highest point of success which that Movement had in this its vigorous youth attained, was that "it had the promise of a nobler religion, as energetic and as spiritual as Puritanism and Wesleyanism." Surely, in the light of such testimony, "Puritanism and Wesleyanism" may quite as fitly, and to the full as boldly, maintain their ecclesiastical position against the unlimited claims to superiority and allegiance of the Church of England, as that Church assert its legitimacy and authority against the claims of the Church of Rome.

In another passage, with which, of course, one cannot but sympathise, and which, it is evident, is part of a contemporary record of Church's own reflections and mental struggles in the later agonies of the Movement, a Tractarian is described who shrinks with all his heart from the thought of giving up his "best friends and the most saint-like men in England," in order to "escape the very natural suspicion of Romanising," and yet "has no feeling towards Rome, does not feel, as others do, the strength of her exclusive claims to allegiance, the perfection of her system, its right so to overbalance all the good found in ours as to make ours absolutely untrustworthy for a Christian to rest in, notwithstanding all circumstances of habit, position, and national character; has such doubts on the Roman theory of the Church, the Ultramontane, and such instincts not only against many of their popular religious customs and practical ways of going on, but against their principles of belief (*e.g.* divine faith = relics), as to repel him from any wish to sacrifice his own communion for theirs" (p. 345).

Such was Church's own position in the interval between 1840 and 1845, while Newman, urged continually by Ward, was coming nearer and nearer to Rome. During the latter part of this interval, indeed, Newman was engaged in building that bridge of argument in his *Essay on the Development of Christian Doctrine*, by which, as he imagined, he made for himself a sure and solid roadway from the position of advanced Tractarianism which he had reached in 1840, into the territory of the Roman communion which, simultaneously with the publication of the work to which I refer, he at length entered in 1845.

Up to 1840, or, at anyrate, 1839, Church went entirely with Newman, as will be seen from the following comprehensive and unqualified eulogy which he pronounces on the Movement and its leaders during the earlier period of their history :—

"Anglicanism was agreed, up to this time—the summer of 1839—as to its general principles. Charges of an inclination to Roman views had been promptly and stoutly met; nor was there really anything but the ignorance or ill-feeling of the accusers to throw doubt on the sincerity of these disavowals. The deepest and strongest mind in the Movement was satisfied; and his steadiness of conviction could be appealed to if his followers talked wildly and rashly. He had kept one unwavering path; he had not shrunk from facing with fearless honesty the real living array of reasons which the most serious Roman advocates could put forward. With a frankness new in controversy, he had not been afraid to state them with a force which few of his opponents could have put forth. With an eye ever open to that supreme Judge of all our controversies, who listens to them on His throne on high, he had with conscientious fairness admitted what he saw to be good and just on the side of his adversaries, conceded what in the confused wrangle of conflicting claims he judged ought to be conceded. But after all admissions and all concessions, the comparative strength of his own case appeared all the more undeniable. He had stripped it of its weaknesses, its incumbrances, its falsehoods; and it did not seem the weaker for being presented in its real aspect and on its real grounds. People felt that he had gone to the bottom of the question as no one had yet dared to do. He was yet staunch in his convictions; and they could feel secure.

"But a change was at hand. In the course of 1839 the little cloud showed itself in the outlook of the future;

the little rift opened, small and hardly perceptible, which was to widen into an impassable gulf" (pp. 194, 195).

Of what nature the "little rift" was, and into what a "gulf" it opened during the four or five following years, has been indicated in the previous quotations. The last quotation shows how absolutely Church was able to identify himself, not only at the time, but permanently, with Newman's course up to 1839 or 1840, and with his original principles as the founder of the Tractarian party. Let us then turn to the very first of those tracts, those "early tracts," which, as Dean Church writes, "were intended to startle the world, and succeeded in doing so," and learn from it on what foundation, first and most of all, Newman built up his ecclesiastical system of principles and aims. "I fear," he says, "we have neglected the real ground on which our authority is built—OUR APOSTOLICAL DESCENT. We have been born, not of blood, nor of the will of the flesh, nor of the will of man, but of God. The Lord Jesus Christ gave His Spirit to the apostles: they in turn laid their hands on those who should succeed them; and those again on others; and so the sacred gift has been handed down to our present bishops, who have appointed us as their assistants, and in some sense representatives" (p. 101). This postulate of Tractarianism Church accepted and held fast. He embraced all that followed in the long series of tracts up to No. 90, as to some points in which he appears to have had doubts and scruples. Among the preceding eighty-nine, besides those tracts which contained Newman's own development of his opinions, some of which (especially No. 71) had anticipated the methods and processes of No. 90, although they had not disclosed the whole scope of its purpose and meaning, there were Pusey's portentous misinterpretations of baptismal texts and references, and the monstrous errors of doctrine he built upon these false interpretations, in his tract or tracts on Baptism, and there was Isaac Williams' tract on "Reserve in Communicating Religious Knowledge," to say nothing of Keble's on "The Mysticism of the Fathers in the Use and Interpretation of Scripture." The whole of this series Church had accepted as true and timely teaching, or, if there were some points as to which he might have doubts, they involved nothing serious or material.

He was therefore, in this respect as well as in others, eminently fitted to write a history of the Movement as seen and known from the interior. Although his was not naturally the temper and spirit of the partisan, although his temper was serene, and his disposition habitually liberal and kindly, he was steeped to the lips in the spirit of the Oxford Movement, and he appears, with all his breadth of culture, never to have outgrown his Tractarian habit of thought and feeling, although, like Pusey, he never became an extreme ritualist of the now prevailing type. The volume he has left may therefore be regarded as a most authentic relation of the main history of the Movement from beginning to end as regarded in the most favourable light, written by one of its most reasonable and least extreme adherents. It is accordingly unique in its authority and importance. The *Apologia* was the personal defence of the head and chief of the Movement after he had led his followers to destruction from the Anglican point of view, and had himself taken refuge in the enemy's citadel, and become the censor and satirist of his former disciples. Mr. Wilfrid Ward, in the Life of his father, W. G. Ward, has described the Movement from the point of view of a Roman Catholic bred and trained as such, although he has shown himself a man of remarkable candour, insight, and fairness in dealing with all parties concerned, and by no means a mere partisan or eulogist of his father, the logical driver and the *enfant terrible* of the Movement. From such narrators Dean Church stands sharply distinguished. He was a loyal disciple of Newman, until it could no longer be hidden from any but recluse and one-sided men like Pusey and Marriott, that, with whatever hesitation and windings, Newman was leading the way down a steep declivity towards the Roman territory, which he had already approached within measurable distance. When he could no longer follow his leader, Church retained his personal relations of friendship with him, and to the end, even when he had himself reached one of the most eminent positions in the English Church, he kept up his intimacy with him. No wonder the Cardinal always treated the Dean of St. Paul's with distinguished regard. At Oxford he had owed not a little to the junior proctor who bore half the responsibility of shielding the author of Tract 90 from the express condemnation of the University. His memory was to owe still more to the writer of *The Oxford Movement*. The Dean's book was written as the history of the lifework, as an Anglican, of his still surviving ancient friend. It is evident, as has been already intimated, that he was carrying out a long-cherished idea. His intimate familiarity with every detail of the history, as wrought out on the side of Newman and his immediate co-workers, is manifest on every page. The volume must have been largely composed from contemporary documents, journals, or letters. Some of his references, by way of illustration, in the text, and especially in the notes, tell of a leisurely study and revision of the narrative in its details and in its points of analogy with the records and remains of ancient as well as later literature.

Dean Church follows Newman in recognising Keble as the "true and primary author" of the Tractarian Movement. In a qualified sense, this is no doubt true. His influence contributed much to the Movement; it was one of the chief sources from which emanated the ideas that prepared the Anglican mind, not only at Oxford, but still more outside of Oxford, for the reception of Newman's teaching. It was natural, also, that Newman should be disposed to place the name of so distinguished and revered a man as Keble in the forefront of his own group of intimate associates, and not less natural that Church, himself, in some marked respects, a man of Keble's sort and of Keble's spirit, should follow Newman in this. But Church's own description of the two men sufficiently settles the question as to which of them was the real leader and the informing spirit of the Movement. To the Movement, as a Movement, Keble seems to have actively contributed no momentum whatever, although his reputation, like Pusey's later on, lent it a powerful sanction. To Newman belongs all the merit or demerit of the Tractarian line of policy and action. Without him the Movement would never have taken form or gathered way. Froude was, very early, a powerful and energetic colleague—indeed, without him Newman would not have been what he was, or done what he did. And Froude's principles were taught him by Keble. But as to Keble, let the words of Dean Church be noted:—

"Mr. Keble had not many friends, and was no party chief. He was a brilliant university scholar, overlaying the plain, unworldly country parson; an old-fashioned English Churchman, with great veneration for the Church and its bishops, and a great dislike of Rome, Dissent, and Methodism, but with a quick heart; with a frank, gay humility of soul; with great contempt of appearances, great enjoyment of nature, great unselfishness, strict and severe principles of morals and duty" (p. 23).

On the preceding page we read that "he had no popular aptitudes, and was very suspicious of them"; that "he had no care for the possession of influence—he had deliberately chosen the *fallentis semita vitæ*, and to be what his father had been, a faithful and contented country parson, was all that he desired." Of Keble's character, genius, and life I have written at some length in my first chapter. There is nothing in Dean Church's volume but what is in agreement with the view I have ventured to set forth. All we know goes to establish the conclusion that Keble was of too absolutely old-world a character, was too inflexible in his views, too narrow and limited in his personal sympathies, to have inspired and shaped the policy of a new party in the Church, or to have led a great movement. What he was as a poet we know, but he was in no sense a leader of men. He did, however, as we have seen, impregnate with his intense and intolerant High Church spirit one who became, with Newman, the joint originator of the Tractarian Movement. Froude had been the pupil of Keble, and, Dean Church tells us, "Keble attracted and moulded Froude—he impressed Froude with his strong Churchmanship, his severity and reality of life, his poetry and high standard of scholarly excellence. Froude learned from him to be anti-Erastian, anti-Methodistical, anti-sentimental, and as strong in his hatred of the world, as contemptuous of popular approval, as any Methodist. . . . In accepting Keble's ideas, Froude resolved to make them active, public, aggressive; and he found in Newman a colleague whose bold originality responded to his own. . . . Keble had given the inspiration; Froude had given the impulse; then Newman took up the work, and the impulse henceforward, and the direction, were his" (pp. 27, 28).

Of Froude, also, I have written at some length in my first chapter. But something more should be said here as to his direct relation to the Tractarian Movement as a co-worker with Newman. The chief interest attaching to Froude is that, being what he was, he so powerfully influenced Newman, who said of him, in his *Lectures on Anglicanism*, that he, "if any, is the author of the Movement altogether"; a saying hardly, however, consistent with the statement already quoted from the *Apologia* as to Keble's relation to the Movement. Froude was a man of much force of will and superior natural gifts; he was handsome and attractive, a bright and lively companion, a warm and affectionate friend, a "good fellow," but very free indeed of his tongue; he was ignorant, self-confident and audacious, as intense a hater as he was a warm friend, a bitter bigot, a reckless revolutionist, one who delighted to speak evil of dignities and of departed worthies and heroes reverenced by Protestant Christians at home and abroad. Church, who did not know him, but took his estimate of him mainly from Newman, makes a conspicuous figure of him, giving much more space to him than to Pusey, more even than to Keble. That this should be so shows how deeply Church had drunk into the spirit that prompted and inspired the tracts. Even his friendly hand, however, cannot omit from his picture certain features which, to an outsider who is not fascinated by the *camaraderie* of the Tractarian clique as it was in the early days of the Movement, will be almost sufficient, without further evidence, to warrant the phrase, "a flippant railer," in which Julius Hare—himself assuredly no evangelical bigot or narrow sectary—describes the man whose *Remains* were edited and published by his two great friends, that Anglican Churchmen might be led to admire the zeal and devotion, and to drink into the spirit, of this young hero of the new party. According to their view, his early death, in the odour of sanctity, although of true Christian saintliness in temper or spirit he seems to have had as little tincture as any persecuting Spanish saint, left an aureole of glory upon his memory.

Such was Froude's hatred of Puritanism that, as may be learnt from Dean Church, he was "blind to the grandeur of Milton's poetry." Church speaks himself of his "fiery impetuosity, and the frank daring of his disrespectful vocabulary." He quotes James Mozley as saying: "I would not set down anything that Froude says for his deliberate opinion, for he really hates the present state of things so excessively that any change would be a relief to him." He says that "Froude was made for conflict, not to win disciples." He admits his ignorance. "He was," he tells us, "a man strong in abstract thought and imagination, who wanted adequate knowledge." He quotes from the *Apologia* Newman's admission of two noticeable deficiencies in Froude: "he had no turn for theology"; "his power of entering into the minds of others was not equal to his other gifts." Such a power, we may note, is very unlikely to belong to men of fierce and hasty arrogance and self-confidence. It finds its natural home in company with the "wisdom from above," which is not only "pure," but "gentle and easy to be entreated," the characteristics of a saintliness of another sort than that of Froude. Dean Church admits that the *Remains* " contain phrases and sentiments and epithets surprisingly at variance with conventional and popular estimates"; as, for example, we may explain, when Froude speaks of the illustrious Bishop Jewel, whom Hooker calls "the worthiest divine that Christendom hath bred for the space of some hundreds of years," as "an irreverent Dissenter." Church adds that "friends were pained and disturbed," while "foes exulted, at such a disclosure of the spirit of the Movement." The apology he offers is that, "if the off-hand sayings of any man of force and wit and strong convictions were made known to the world, they would by themselves have much the same look of flippancy, injustice, impertinence to those who disagreed with the speaker or writer. . . . The friends who published Froude's *Remains* knew what he was; they knew the place and proportion of the fierce and scornful passages; they knew that they did not go beyond the liberty and the frank speaking which most people give themselves in the *abandon* and understood exaggeration of intimate correspondence and talk." To which the reply is obvious—If the editors (who were no other than Newman and Keble) had disapproved of the tone and style of these *Remains*, as it is evident that Dean Church himself, notwithstanding his strong friendly bias, could not help disapproving of them, they would either not have published them, or would at least have suggested some such apology as that suggested by Dean Church. But, in fact, they published them without any such apology, and it cannot be seriously doubted that they rather rejoiced in than condemned such gross improprieties. Further, if this sort of writing is common in the intimate correspondence of responsible clergymen, how is it that it is so hard, if it is at all possible, to match the flippancy and insolence of these *Remains* in any other correspondence or remains of men of Christian culture and character known to modern literature? Dean Church, indeed, cannot but admit that "Froude was often intemperate and unjust," and that "his strong language gave needless exasperation." He endeavours, however, to make one point in favour of the Movement from the publication of the *Remains*. Whether it was wise or not, he argues that "it was not the act of cunning conspirators; it was the act of men who were ready to show their hands and take the consequences—it was the mistake of men confident in their own straightforwardness." I have no wish to revive against the first leaders of the Movement, as represented by Froude and the admiring editors of his *Remains*, the charge of being conspirators, though, as I have already stated, Froude himself was the first to describe the Tractarian Movement as a "conspiracy." Certainly Froude, in the earlier stage of the Movement, like Ward in its later stages, had little in him of the conspirator's subtlety or craft, whatever may be said as to Newman. But an unbiassed historian would hardly describe the act of publication as Dean Church does; he would rather say that it was the act of men whose honesty may be admitted, but who were sanguine partisans—men strongly biassed by their sectarian temper, by their overweening self-confidence.

But it was a strange little world—the world of Oxford—in which Froude was regarded as a bright and leading character sixty years ago. It seems as we look back upon it to be very much farther away than half a century, and to belong almost to a different planetary sphere. Here is a scene as described by an early friend of Newman and Froude, the late Lord Blachford, better known by his earlier style and title as Sir Frederick Rogers, long Under-Secretary of State for the Colonies, and who was ennobled by his school and college contemporary and lifelong friend, Mr. Gladstone :—

"I remember one day his (Froude) grievously shocking Palmer, of Worcester, when a council in J. H. N.'s rooms had been called to consider some memorial to which Palmer wanted to collect the signatures of many, and particularly of dignified persons, but in which Froude wished to express the determined opinions of a few. Froude, stretched out his long length on Newman's sofa, broke in upon one of Palmer's harangues about bishops and archdeacons and the like, with the ejaculation: 'I don't see why we should disguise from ourselves that our object is to dictate to the clergy of this country, and I, for one, do not want anyone else to get on the box'" (p. 54). "He would," we are told by the same relator on another page "(as we see in the *Remains*) have wished Ken to have the 'courage of his convictions,'" by setting up a little Catholic Church, like the Jansenists in Holland.

It was, in fact, a young and ignorant, as well as bigoted, circle in which the idea of the Oxford Movement first germinated. Newman, doubtless, was far superior in knowledge, in ability, and in depth and gravity of feeling, as well as in insight and caution, to those who were in the closest fellowship with him. It was a schoolboyish sort of clique, and in wildness, enthusiasm, ignorance of the actual forces and the gathering movements of the world outside, their projects and dreams remind us of schoolboy plans and projects for moving the world and achieving fame and greatness. The Tractarians lived in an unreal world all through their party history. Newman, it cannot be doubted, crossed over in his dreams from Oxford to Rome. Even the last "catastrophe" was but as an interval of sharp disturbance and partial awakening to a dreamer, and having crossed the border he dreamed again. Oxford was a semi-monastic, secluded, academic world. That most quaint antique, Routh, like a survival from the seventeenth century, was its great ancient. The principles of Jacobite times and parties had descended through successive generations, who had inherited from old-fashioned and hereditary clerical families or fossilised gentry the traditions of the Stuart Church and State. Hence the possibility of such sentiments as those cherished by Froude,—as expressed in the last quotation,—and which, no doubt, had been strengthened by his association with Keble. These things must be borne in mind in trying to understand the character of the Oxford Movement. The special *camaraderie* of the place must also be remembered. Schoolboys' friendships are often intense and romantic. Those of Newman and his circle were passionately deep and warm, —more like those of boys in some respects than of men, perhaps still more like those of women who live aloof from the world in the seclusion of mutual intimacy,— intimacy suffused with the fascinating but hectic brightness of a sort of celibate consecration to each other, apart from any thought of stronger or more authoritative human ties that might some time interfere with their sacrament of friendship. This *morbidezza* of moral complexion and temperament, this more or less unnatural and unhealthy intensity of friendship, was a marked feature in Newman's relations with those around him. There is no doubt a touching side to this feature in the Tractarian society of Oxford. Dean Church speaks of "the affection which was characteristic of those days," and adds that for both Isaac Williams and William John Copeland, "Mr. Newman had the love which passes that of common relation" (p. 57). Of the mutually feminine attachment which bound Newman and Froude together, there is no need to say more than has been said in a preceding page. The *Apologia* sets it forth all the more fully because Froude was no longer living. It was indeed one of Newman's greatest powers for the work that he had taken in hand, that he fascinated, not only into admiration, but into entire and enduring friendship, so many of his companions, although at the same time he inspired most of them, as Isaac Williams, for example, with more or less of distrust. They admired him, were fascinated by him, obeyed him, but he was yet a mystery to them, and they stood in awe, and sometimes in doubt, as to what his deepest purposes might turn out to be.

The following description of Oxford as it was at the beginning of the Tractarian Movement is interesting and instructive in relation to the points which have been suggested:—

"The scene of this new Movement was as like as it could be in our modern world to a Greek πόλις, or an Italian self-centred city of the Middle Ages. Oxford stood by itself in its meadows by the rivers, having its relations with all England, but, like its sister at Cambridge, living a life of its own, unlike that of any other spot in England, with its privileged powers and exemptions from the general law, with its special mode of government and police, its usages and tastes and traditions, and even costume, which the rest of England looked at from the outside, much interested but much puzzled, or knew only by transient visits. And Oxford was as proud and jealous of its own ways as Athens or Florence, and like them it had its quaint fashions of polity; its democratic Convocation and its oligarchy; its social ranks; its discipline, severe in theory, and usually lax in fact; its self-governed bodies and corporations within itself; its faculties and colleges, like the guilds and 'arts' of Florence; its internal rivalries and discords; its 'sets' and factions. Like these, too, it professed a special recognition of the supremacy of religion; it claimed to be a home of worship and religious training,— *Dominus illuminatio mea,*—a claim too often falsified in the habits and tempers of life. It was a small sphere, but it was a conspicuous one; for there was much strong and energetic character, brought out by the aims and conditions of university life; and though moving in a separate orbit, the influence of the famous place over the outside England, though imperfectly understood, was recognised and great. These conditions affected the character of the Movement and of the conflicts which it caused. Oxford claimed to be eminently the guardian of 'true religion and sound learning'; and therefore it was eminently the place where religion should be recalled to its purity and strength, and also the place where there ought to be the most vigilant jealousy against the perversions and corruptions of religion. Oxford was a place where everyone knew his neighbour, and measured him, and was more or less friendly or repellent; where the customs of life brought men together every day and all day, in converse or discussion;

and where every fresh statement or every new step taken furnished endless material for speculation or debate, in common rooms or in the afternoon walk. And for this reason, too, feelings were apt to be more keen and intense and personal than in the larger scenes of life; the man who was disliked or distrusted was so close to his neighbours that he was more irritating than if he had been obscured by a crowd; the man who attracted confidence and kindled enthusiasm, whose voice was continually in men's ears, and whose private conversation and life was something ever new in its sympathy and charm, created in those about him not mere admiration, but passionate friendship, or unreserved discipleship. And these feelings passed from individuals into parties, the small factions of a limited area. Men struck blows and loved and hated in those days in Oxford as they hardly did on the wider stage of London politics or general religious controversy" (pp. 139-141). This was the world in which Newman exercised an unrivalled —a unique—ascendency over the minds of many earnest young High Churchmen, men of intense religious character.

A picture of Newman, drawn from the life by his admiring friend, explains in some degree his power:—

"Mr. Newman, who lived in college in the ordinary way of a resident Fellow, met other university men, older or younger, on equal terms. As time went on a certain wonder and awe gathered round him. People were a little afraid of him; but the fear was in themselves, not created by any intentional stiffness or coldness on his part. He did not try to draw men to him, he was no proselytiser; he shrank with fear and repugnance from the character— it was an invasion of the privileges of the heart. But if men came to him, he was accessible; he allowed his friends to bring their friends to him, and met them more than half-way. He was impatient of mere idle worldliness, of conceit and impertinence, of men who gave themselves airs; he was very impatient of pompous and solemn emptiness. But he was very patient with those whom he believed to sympathise with what was nearest his heart; no one, probably, of his power and penetration and sense of the absurd, was ever so ready to comply with the two demands which a witty prelate proposed to put into the examination in the Consecration Service of Bishops: 'Wilt thou answer thy letters?' 'Wilt thou suffer fools gladly?' But courteous, affable, easy as he was, he was a keen trier of character; he gauged, and men felt that he gauged, their motives, their reality and soundness of purpose; he let them see, if they at all came into his intimacy, that if *they* were not, *he*, at anyrate, was in the deepest earnest. And at an early period, in a memorable sermon, the vivid expression of which at the time still haunts the recollection of some who heard it, he gave warning to his friends and to those whom his influence touched, that no child's play lay before them; that they were making, it might be without knowing it, the 'Ventures of Faith.' But feeling that he had much to say, and that a university was a place for the circulation and discussion of ideas, he let himself be seen and known and felt, both publicly and in private. He had his breakfast parties and his evening gatherings. His conversation ranged widely, marked by its peculiar stamp—entire ease, unstudied perfection of apt and clean-cut words, unexpected glimpses of a sure and piercing judgment. At times, at more private meetings, the violin, which he knew how to touch, came into play" (pp. 161, 162).

At the same time, the artist who paints this description has to add that Newman's influence was limited, and more or less marred by what seemed like "over-subtlety," and that "his doctrine of the Church had the disadvantage of an apparently intermediate and ambiguous position." Newman was accessible and conversible, was an adept in the arts of conversational persuasion and casuistry,—especially evasive casuistry,—but appears to have been very rarely frank and outright, even when most confidential. Froude was more extreme in his language, but then he was always outspoken—leaving no suspicion of an undisclosed meaning or an *arrière pensée*. Hence, quiet men like Isaac Williams, though disapproving of his violence, felt they understood and could trust him; while much as they admired the abler and more cautious Newman, they were, in regard to him, haunted by a sense of distrust. Their relation to Newman, accordingly, was "a curious mixture of the most affectionate attachment and intimacy, with growing distrust and sense of divergence" (pp. 64, 67, 68). Froude in the earliest, Ward during the later stages of the Movement, were powerful motive forces by the side of their leader. Both of them alike were easy to read; they used plain speech, and spoke aloud so that all might hear. Their leader's object was to win over adherents one by one, by every lawful art of persuasion, to detach them gradually from their old principles, to transform the very aspect and colour of the traditional Church of England to their medicated vision, to bring them unawares to points of view from which the past should appear to them altogether different from what they had heretofore understood it to be. Hence, his methods were in contrast with those of his outspoken friends.

Hence, too, even those who admired Newman much, and could not resist his spell, in following him felt that they did not share his deepest counsels, and could not foresee whither he might lead them, or into what perplexing or even alarming position he might bring them in the end. This being so, we are not surprised to learn from Dean Church that a certain "austerity" was felt as tingeing the relations of Newman with his disciples, or that these regarded him with more or less of "awe."

This volume does not add much to our previous knowledge of the main points in Newman's history as an Anglo-Catholic, or the most marked features in his character and influence. He was a very gifted man within a limited range of personal and intellectual influence; he was a man of sympathy and insight in regard to character, and the relation of character and conduct to circumstances and environments; he was an exquisite writer of English; he was a man of true poetic genius. He was a preacher of extraordinary power of persuasion and penetration when dealing with conduct, motives, the realities of character; not a popular preacher, not a preacher for any but cultivated people, people of disciplined habits of mind, but a soul-searching preacher. His preaching, in fact, was a yet greater power than his private influence; and his personal influence would not have prevailed as it did in private intercourse apart from the power of his pulpit ministry at St. Mary's, though his audiences were very rarely numerous—were generally, indeed, small.

His main logical instrument as an ecclesiastical leader and innovator was always the same,—he used continually the same leverage. By degrees he drove home the master principle of external Church unity, as defined by the postulate of apostolical succession laid down in his first tract. In dealing with shortsighted people it was, perhaps, one cause of his success that he himself was almost as shortsighted as they were. His principles could not but lead to Rome; but it took him many years to find this out. When at length this truth began to take definite and solid shape to his vision he was terribly alarmed—hesitated, shuddered, would, if possible, have drawn back. But the slow compulsion of his first principles gradually, through years of agony and latterly of seclusion, wrought out its necessary results upon one who was at bottom sincere, and whose logical faculty, though only quick when playing a short-distance game of verbal fence or subtlety, was yet, in its power of slow and gradual evolution of results from accepted principles, a living force that could not but in the end obtain the mastery. It led him, by a singular combination of unwarranted assumptions, erroneous views of history, and ingenious, though unconscious, sophistry, to the results embodied in his final argument, or, I might say, apology, for completing his passage to Rome;—his Development theory, by which he was enabled to accept the mediæval corruptions of the Roman Church as part of the whole authorised teaching of the One True and Apostolic Church—a theory which served his turn, but has been utterly neglected since.

The Movement began, Dean Church expressly tells us, in Mr. Newman's determination "to force on the public mind in a way that could not be evaded the great article of the Creed, 'I believe one Catholic and Apostolic Church.'" Into what form and attitude the Movement had shaped itself long before the "catastrophe" came—five years before—is vividly described by Dean Church:—

"Thus a great and momentous change had come over the Movement, over its action and prospects. It had started in a heroic effort to save the English Church. The claims, the blessings, the divinity of the English Church, as a true branch of Catholic Christendom, had been assumed as the foundation of all that was felt and said and attempted. The English Church was the one object to which English Christians were called upon to turn their thoughts. Its spirit animated the *Christian Year*, and the teaching of those whom the *Christian Year* represented. Its interests were what called forth the zeal and the indignation recorded in Froude's *Remains*. No one seriously thought of Rome, except as a hopelessly corrupt system, though it had some good and catholic things, which it was Christian and honest to recognise. The Movement of 1833 started out of the anti-Roman feelings of the Emancipation time. It was anti-Roman as much as it was anti-Sectarian and anti-Erastian. It was to avert the danger of people becoming Romanists from ignorance of Church principles. This was all changed in one important section of the party. The fundamental conceptions and assumptions were reversed. It was not the Roman Church, but the English Church, which was put on its trial; it was not the Roman Church, but the English, which was to be, if possible, apologised for, perhaps borne with for a time, but which was to be regarded as deeply fallen, holding an untenable position, and incomparably, unpardonably, below the standard and the practical system of the Roman Church. From this point of view the object of the Movement was no longer to elevate and improve an independent English Church, but to approximate it as far as possible to what was assumed to be undeniable—the perfect Catholicity of Rome. More almost than ideas and assumptions, the tone of feeling changed. It had been, towards the English Church, affectionate, enthusiastic, reverential, hopeful. It became contemptuous, critical, intolerant, hostile, with the hostility not merely of alienation, but disgust. This was not, of course, the work of a moment, but it was of very rapid growth. 'How I hate these Anglicans!' was the expression of one of the younger men of this section, an intemperate and insolent specimen of it. It did not represent the tone or the language of the leader to whom the advanced section deferred, vexed as he often was with the course of his own thoughts, and irritated and impatient at the course of things without. But it expressed but too truly the difference between 1833 and 1840" (pp. 210, 211).

How narrow with all its keenesss and subtlety, was the intellect of Newman, cannot but be evident to any unfascinated person who will exercise serious thought, from the fact that it was Dr. (afterwards Cardinal) Wiseman's quotation of St. Augustine's words in reference to the Donatist controversy, *Securus judicat orbis terrarum*,[1] "ringing continually in his ears, like words out of the sky," which really vanquished Newman. That saying "opened a vista which was closed before, and of which he could not see the end." Nor is it less indicative of intellectual weakness on the part of Newman, notwithstanding his gifts and accomplishments, that "one of the blows which broke" him, as he himself says in the *Apologia*, was the business of the Anglo-Prussian bishopric of Jerusalem. Only a man already under the spell and bondage of an intrinsically Romish superstition could so have felt. Such weakness as

[1] "The judgment of the whole world must stand good."

is thus disclosed was a main part of Newman's character. Not less marked was that perhaps amiable, but extreme and almost ultra-feminine, self-consciousness which is disclosed in his correspondence, especially that with his sister, in regard to the ecclesiastical questions which wrung his soul. The letters are touching; they reveal a character which had its aspect of true sincerity as well as acute sensibility; but they do not well harmonise with the idea either of mental or moral greatness.

That Newman, the fashioner of the Tractarian school of thought and character, was himself a man of large and enlightened intellectual and moral character; that he was accustomed to live consciously in an atmosphere of straight and truthful thinking,—is more than any impartial critic can be expected to admit. He did not believe in logical truth as an instrument of spiritual influence or instruction. He did not believe in objective truth at all, as scientifically or intellectually regarded. All truth for him was merely relative, except what was directly disclosed to him in consciousness or made known by divine revelation. His doctrine of faith and obedience stood in no relation whatever to history or argument; the only faith he acknowledged was immediate and implicit, recognising the direct authority of God, or of the Church, and the priests of the Church, as representing God, and ignoring besides this, the whole world of thought and fact, of feeling and consciousness. Reason for him, as such, had no authority. A man habitually dwelling in such an atmosphere of unreal thinking must, however sincere, be devoid of the intellectual sensibility which compels the trained Christian reasoner, no less than the critical philosopher, to recognise the laws of thought, alike in history and in abstract science, by which truth is discriminated from falsehood. Hence, although it led to some harsh judgments, which strict and impartial investigation has compelled later generations to modify, there was a natural and by no means unreasonable ground for the views which prevailed fifty years ago as to the subtlety and deceitfulness of the whole Tractarian system of thought and teaching, and which were held by men of such high character and ability, and so well-informed, as Dr. Arnold, Dr. Whately, and Henry Rogers.[1]

Perhaps the ablest and the most spirited part of Dean Church's volume is that in which he deals specially with W. G. Ward and his relations to Newman and the Movement. He gives many pages to Ward's *Ideal of a Christian Church*, and his account and criticism of that famous, but very little read, book may fitly be described as masterly. It hardly lies, however, within the scope of this volume to say more as to that eccentric production than has been said in the preceding chapter. It is a huge and tedious, though clever and curious, book; and it has had no appreciable effect on the course of events, or even on the course of controversy, "because," to use Dean Church's words, "on the face of" this even more than "his" other "writings,"—and he wrote much in the *British Critic* and elsewhere,—Ward "was so extravagantly one-sided, so incapable of an equitable view, so much a slave to the unreality of extremes." He was totally ignorant of history; he wove his argument in the main on the basis of mere

[1] What Mr. J. A. Froude says, from personal knowledge, on the points touched on in this paragraph, is decisive testimony. (See his account of Newman in *Short Studies*, Fourth Series.) But this evidence is only a small part of the whole to the same effect. I shall return to this subject in the next chapter.

assumptions; he adapted his assumptions to his preconceptions; his preconceptions were those of a mere idealist who dwelt in the region of abstractions; and thus he composed his *Ideal of a Christian Church*, in which he was keen to show the inconsistencies and logical dilemmas of the Church of England, while he attributed to the Romish Church all the perfections which his *Ideal* required. It is, however, important to note the influence which Ward exercised on Newman, and how this contributed to what Dean Church speaks of as the "catastrophe" of Newman's leaving the Church of England. Church's description well agrees with the view which Mr. Wilfrid Ward gives, and which has been quoted in the last chapter, as to the mutual relations of Newman and Ward.

"Mr. Ward," says Dean Church, "was continually forcing on Mr. Newman so called irresistible inferences: 'If you say so and so, surely you must also say something more.' Avowedly ignorant of facts, and depending for them on others, he was only concerned with logical consistency. Accordingly, Mr. Newman had continually to accept conclusions which he would rather have kept in abeyance, to make admissions which were used without their qualifications, to push on and sanction extreme ideas which he himself shrank from because they were extreme. . . . He had to go at Mr. Ward's pace and not his own. He had to take Mr. Ward's questions, not when he wanted to have them and at his own time, but at Mr. Ward's. . . . Engineers tell us that, in the case of a ship rolling in a seaway, when the periodic times of the ship's roll coincide with those of the undulations of the waves, a condition of things arises highly dangerous to the ship's stability. So the agitations of Mr. Newman's mind were reinforced by the impulses of Mr. Ward's."

Newman, in fact, found in Ward the Nemesis of his own errors. The inferences which Newman disliked were based by Ward on the "facts" which he had taken for granted on the authority of Newman. Newman knew far too little of history, and depended too much on misapplied logical processes. Historical induction as applied to theological and ecclesiastical questions he was unable to use to any serviceable extent. In theological science also, as derived from apostolic teaching, he was strangely weak— weak and ill-informed. Ward was a keener and stronger logician than Newman, but was absurdly ignorant of history. His intellectual character was a striking but grotesque caricature of Newman's. Hence he, in effect, brought his master's claims and contentions, as an Anglican, to a *reductio ad absurdum*. With a light heart, and almost as if the whole Movement were a huge and ridiculous absurdity, he exploded the Tractarian mine. He went over laughingly to Rome, and dragged Newman after him. On the 14th February 1845 the Oxford Convocation condemned Ward's *Ideal*, and degraded the writer, reducing him to the position of an undergraduate. On the same day Tract No. 90 was rescued from the formal university censure, which the Convocation were prepared to pronounce upon it, by the interposition of the proctors,—Church being one of the two,—who had power so to interpose in suspension of any proposed decree of Convocation. The proposed decree of censure might conceivably have been renewed and adopted in the following year, when new proctors would have come into office. But before that period Newman had left the Church of England. After a seclusion of many months he was, on the 8th October 1845, received into the Roman Catholic Church by Father Dominic the Passionist.

I ought not to pass away from the view of Ward's relations to Newman, as presented by Dean Church, without referring to the fact that, as to the controversy on the subject of Tract 90, Ward in his *Ideal* goes over, so far as the case between Newman and his Anglican censors is concerned, to the side of those who, as Anglicans, condemned Tract 90. He contended that the articles of the Church, though "*patient* of a Catholic meaning, were *ambitious* of a Protestant meaning; whatever their logic was, their rhetoric was Protestant." "With characteristic boldness, inventing a phrase which has become famous, he wrote, 'Our twelfth Article is, as plain as words can make it, on the Evangelical side; of course, I think its natural meaning may be explained away, for I subscribe it myself in a non-natural sense.'" After such a confession from the lips of his closest counsellor and confederate, it was hardly possible that Newman should continue to maintain the position of an English Churchman. That position had become on every side untenable. Nor was it either unnatural or unreasonable that Convocation, besides condemning Ward and his *Ideal*, should have been prepared explicitly to censure Tract 90. In fact, Ward may be justly cited as a witness to prove the charge of disingenuous subtlety which the great majority of competent judges had brought against the casuistry and the non-natural explanations of Tract 90.

NOTE TO PAGE 99.

The account of Dean Church's views in regard to the Church of England given in the foregoing chapter is strictly and fully warranted by the language he uses in the volume with which the chapter deals, as my quotations show. Nor is there any qualifying passage which I have left unnoticed. It is impossible to escape the conclusion that he himself writes in that volume as one "conscious of the false position," ecclesiastically regarded, "of the Church of England." To find that for Dean Church no other conclusion seemed possible was to myself a disappointment. I searched most carefully for indications to the contrary. Since the death of Dean Church, however, in a volume entitled *Pascal and Other Sermons*, a lecture has been published on Bishop Andrewes, delivered by the Dean at King's College, in 1877, which does justice to the character and position of the English Church, as a Reformed Church, and, in general, to the "English Reformation." Of narrow sacerdotalism there is no trace in this lecture. If the spirit and arguments of that lecture had ruled in the Oxford Movement of 1833, Newman would never have seceded to Rome. The position of the English Church of Edward and Elizabeth, with all its difficulties, is justified. The transfer of supreme authority from the Pope to the Crown is frankly defended as, for that season of our national history, an absolute necessity. To reconcile the views taught in that lecture with the Dean's volume on *The Oxford Movement* is no part of my responsibility. It is satisfactory, however, to find an unexpected support to the principles of the English Reformation in this posthumous publication of so learned and well-considered a summing up of the whole question. It would seem as if a recurrence to early memoranda and correspondence, as if the steeping of himself afresh in the memories of the Oxford of his youth, had had power to obscure the conclusions which, in the mature vigour of his powers, a direct study of the times and of the personal histories of the English Reformation period for the purpose of giving a lesson to young English Churchmen had led him to form and to set forth in his King's College Lecture. Andrewes, it is certain, though a High Churchman, was no Romaniser, but a true son of the English Reformation, on its Episcopalian side.

CHAPTER V.

THE MASTER SPIRIT OF THE MOVEMENT—EXTRAVAGANT EULOGIES OF NEWMAN—MR. HUTTON OF THE *SPECTATOR*—WAS NEWMAN A GREAT MAN?—HIS SCEPTICISM—HIS *GRAMMAR OF ASSENT*—PURSUIT OF INFALLIBILITY—VIEW OF FAITH AS APPLIED RESPECTIVELY TO CATHOLIC AND PROTESTANT POPULATIONS—TURNING WHITE BLACK AND BLACK WHITE—ROMAN CATHOLIC AND PROTESTANT MORALITY—THE POPES NOT PERSECUTORS—NEWMAN AND DÖLLINGER—ESTIMATE OF NEWMAN'S CHARACTER—HIS LAST YEARS.

TO be gentle and generous to the memory of the dead is a maxim which pre-Christian civilisation has handed down to modern times; and never was it so generally or generously acted upon as at the present day, especially in the case of men of genius. In commemorating the deceased, genius is made to cover a multitude of sins. When, besides, genius is united with eminent rank and with distinguished achievements, and when its renown lends lustre to a protracted old age, admiration on the part of the English public is apt to grow into something like idolatry. The faults, however grave, of a famous life, much of which seems already to have become ancient, are forgotten. A sort of mythical haze and splendour gathers around the memory of a renowned and venerable man, as the gathering glories of the sunset attend the parting day.

Most of all is this so when the deceased, whether with or without genius, has been a famous leader,—military, political, or ecclesiastical,—who having in his time borne hard blows and sometimes unjust or excessive censure, has left at length the scene of his life's conflicts and vicissitudes. The general interest and enthusiasm in such cases knows no bounds. Illustrations of what I have been saying will recur to the memory of all my readers. The names of Wellington, Palmerston, Pusey, Beaconsfield, Gladstone, will come at once to mind. Nor is it a grateful task to undertake to say anything by way of chastening the exuberance of such feelings, even though they may be altogether excessive. Nevertheless, there are instances in which it may be necessary so to do.

Protestants generally, however liberal and well-informed, still believe that Popery as such—by which I mean the organised ecclesiastical system of which the Pope and Papal Court at Rome are the head and centre, with its unchanged policy, its aggregate of Bulls and Decretals, of General Councils, and conciliar Acts—constitutes a vast and pernicious perversion of Christianity, and that in regard to no perversion of truth in the world's history is the proverb more justly applicable, *corruptio optimi pessima*. I say this whilst retaining all charity towards individual Roman Catholics, and whilst recognising that not a little that is good has always been found within the limits of the Roman Catholic Church, that some of its Popes, especially in the early Middle Ages, acted the part, among rulers and nations, from time to time, of beneficent powers in a barbarous and distracted period, and that the roll of its hagiology includes many true saints as well as many false.

Of late years, however, over a considerable area of cultivated society in England, there has been a marked bias Romeward. Capital is made by Romish and Romanising writers out of the extravagant eulogies on Cardinal Newman, with which, after his death, the public press was inundated: eulogies written, I cannot but believe, either by personal friends and admirers, by Romish or Romanising partisans, or by writers very little informed as to the true history of Newman's life, or his real character and merits as a teacher and writer.

How far this tendency will yet develop, or how long it will last, it would be rash to conjecture. We can but hope that the tide may turn before very long. But, in the meantime, the influence of Mr. Hutton's monograph [1] on Cardinal Newman is all in the wrong direction. For some years there had been rumours from time to time to the effect that the editor of the *Spectator* was about to join—indeed, there were rumours that he had already joined—the Roman Catholic communion. It was scarcely possible for those who had long known and, on the whole, greatly admired the writings of this distinguished man, and the devout and religious spirit in which he had conducted his journal, to lend any credit to these rumours, notwithstanding the increasingly and surprisingly High Church tone and tendency of his newspaper for many years past. After reading his book on Newman, however, many will feel that it would scarcely surprise them if they were to learn before very long that he had joined the communion which it is evident that, on the whole, he admires more, if he does not more fully agree

[1] *Cardinal Newman.* By R. H. Hutton. Methuen & Co.

with it, than any other Church.¹ Considering the point from which he started, some forty years ago or more, on his doctrinal ascent as a thinker and writer; considering the avenue of thought through which, under the guidance of Mr. Maurice, he found his way on to the platform, and within the precincts, of the Church of England,—the last thing that would have been expected, in the case of Mr. Hutton, would have been that he should end his course on the margin of the Romish Church. In 1850, however, it appears that he heard Father Newman deliver his lectures on the *Difficulties of Anglicanism*. He was fascinated by the lectures, and especially by the gifts of the lecturer. Subsequently he became a personal friend of Father Newman. Few Englishmen, outside of Newman's own circle as a Roman Catholic, who have ever come into close contact with him, have been able altogether to escape his "spell." The result in the case of Mr. Hutton appears in the partial and one-sided account which he has published of Newman and his life-work.

There is another sort of view of Newman given by a namesake of Mr. Hutton's in three numbers of the

---

¹ "Is there truer worship anywhere, in spite of its greedy traditionalism," asks Mr. Hutton, "than in the Church of Rome?" Referring to Newman's final "birth" into the communion of the Church of Rome, he speaks of that Church as "the one Christian Church which has a historical continuity and an external organisation as impressive and conspicuous as even his heart could desire for the depository of revealed truth." The Church of Rome "the depository of Revealed Truth"! *

---

* It need hardly be said that this was written before Mr. Hutton's death. I find no reason from anything which has since appeared to alter what I have written as to Mr. Hutton, in his relations to Dr. Newman.

Expositor.[1] Mr. Arthur Hutton writes as one who lived with Cardinal Newman for years at the Birmingham Oratory. His account bears every mark of being a genuine and truthful transcript of the writer's personal knowledge and experience, not discoloured by prejudice or temper, but written with the calm impartiality of a friendly though disenchanted witness, who had been long accustomed to see Newman in his own cloistral home, in his everyday life, both in its strictly religious and in its more or less secular aspects, in full dress and undress, and in all his varying moods.

It would seem that the editor of the *Spectator* has, in common with journalists generally, been fascinated by the gifts, the genius, and the personal ascendency of Cardinal Newman, and on the strength of these has been prepared to regard him as what he styles him in the title of his first chapter, a "great man."

I demur, however, *in limine*, to such a description of Cardinal Newman, and ask what are the qualities which entitle him to be called a great man? He was, doubtless, a gifted man, and a man of great personal influence; he was even a man of genius. But to say this is not to say that he was a great man. Was Newman a man of truly great character? Was he even a man of great and fruitful intellect? Was he a great theologian, or a great administrator, or a great philosopher? Was he even a great scholar? Was he a man of great and sterling attainments in any leading branch of humane or liberal knowledge—as, for example, in history? He led far

[1] *Reminiscences of Cardinal Newman.* By Arthur Hutton, M.A. *Expositor*, September to November 1890. Mr. Arthur Hutton represented Cardinal Newman at the funeral of Dr. Pusey.

astray many followers; but is he on this account to be regarded as great? For a few years at Oxford he was a great preacher to a special class. When he had gone over to Rome, however, he preached no more great sermons, though he delivered, not very long after that passage in his history, some clever and daring lectures in disparagement of the Church and people of England. On what ground then is he to be exalted as meriting the magnificent title of a great man,—as belonging to the enthroned circle of earth's peerless immortals? The world has seen very many men of rare gifts, many men of genius; but of these comparatively few have been admitted within the ranks of the great men of the earth.

Mr. Hutton professes to base his judgment as to the greatness of Cardinal Newman "chiefly on the ardour and energy which he devoted to adequate objects." But surely this is a very inadequate definition of human greatness, and one which, if adopted, would admit into the category of great men a vast multitude of persons who have, indeed, devoted ardour and energy to worthy objects, but whom the world has never begun to look upon as great. In the sentence following the words I have quoted (page 6), Mr. Hutton speaks of the "vividness of his faith in divine guidance," and his "exultation in the wisdom and spiritual instinct of his Church," as having "furnished him with his confidence and guaranteed his success." What Mr. Hutton means by "his success" it is hard to understand. To me his life appears to have been anything but a success in any such good sense of that word as should entitle a Christian thinker and leader to the character of greatness. Mr. Hutton, however, proceeds to speak of his intellect as having "taken exact measure of the depths of the various channels by which he might safely travel to the 'haven where he would be'; the care with which he has buoyed the quicksands and the sunken rocks, and the anxious vigilance with which he has traced out the winding and often perilous passages in the way." Where and how Newman did anything of the sort here described I think Mr. Hutton would be unable to point out. The description appears to be perfectly inapplicable to the mode of procedure by which Newman found his own way into the "haven" of the Romish communion, and still less applicable as a description of any method of instruction and guidance which at any time he made known to others. Indeed, Mr. Wilfrid Ward's Life of his father furnishes sufficient evidence that Mr. Hutton's description of his hero is purely imaginary. There is no book except the *Apologia*, so far as I know, to which the words could even be imagined to have any possible application; and that volume, though it explains in part the process by which he himself "went sounding on a dim and perilous way," does not really answer at all to the description I have quoted.

Mr. Hutton's words suggest a reminiscence of a well-known passage in Newman's *Difficulties of Anglicanism*, in which, in an insolent and ungenerous strain, he satirises his own Anglican followers, the Tractarian residue whom he first misled and then forsook for the Roman communion.

"Their idea," he says, "was simply and absolutely submission to an external authority; to it they appealed, to it they betook themselves; there they found a haven of rest; and hence they looked out upon the troubled surge of human opinion, and upon the crazy vessels which were labouring without chart or compass upon it. Judge, then, of their dismay when, according to the Arabian tale, on their striking their anchors into the supposed soil, lighting their fires on it, and fixing in it the poles of their tents, suddenly their island began to move, to heave, to splash, to frisk to and fro, to dive, and at last to swim away, spouting out inhospitable jets of water upon the credulous mariners who had made it their home" (*Lectures*, etc., p. 124).

It was Newman himself who had professed to "measure the depths of the channels" by which his comrades and followers might make their way to *this* deceitful "haven," and to "buoy the quicksands and the unseen rocks." Mr. Hutton's language would go to imply that, after Newman had escaped from their company and found refuge in Rome, he had really done such a service as Mr. Hutton describes for such of the forlorn and deceived mariners as might be "credulous" enough to trust him as their leader on a second venture, in "sounding on" still farther their "dim and perilous way" till they should find, with him, the true "haven of rest" in the Roman obedience. But unless Mr. Hutton means to say that Newman has done this in his *Essay on Development*, of which Mr. Hutton has himself sufficiently exposed the fallacies to show at least its utter untrustworthiness, or in the two series of clever and occasionally brilliant, but paradoxical and utterly unauthentic and unhistorical, lectures which he delivered at Birmingham, from one of which I have taken my last quotation, and to which I shall presently have occasion to refer at some length, I cannot hazard a guess as to when or how he can be imagined to have done it.

Mr. Hutton further speaks of the "profound and passionate conviction which lay beneath all this delicate intellectual appreciation of difficulties." Doubtless within narrow limits a profound conviction of spiritual realities—

that is, as Newman himself explains, of "himself and God," derived from the experience, in early life, of his own "conversion," whilst still a Calvinistic "evangelical"— did underlie his intellectual movements, however vacillating and uncertain.[1] This fact, however, carries us noway towards the conclusion that, in any adequate sense of the phrase, Cardinal Newman was a great man. He was an idealist; he was a poet of fine genius; he was an exquisite writer of English; he had in perfection the gifts of a special pleader; his power of personal fascination and influence over university men of devout and churchly minds was extraordinary; and, understanding perfectly the character of university society, and of the average Anglo-Episcopal mind, he adapted his written addresses with consummate skill to the special audience for which they were intended. But all this taken together is far from warranting such an exaltation of Cardinal Newman to a place amongst the great men and heroes of the world as that which Mr. Hutton claims for him. As has been shown in preceding chapters, Newman's was a characteristically feminine nature; it was feminine in the quickness and subtlety of his instincts, in affection and the caprices of affection, in diplomatic tact and adroitness, and in a gift of statement and grace of phrase which find their analogies in the conversation, in the public addresses, and not

[1] He uses the word "conversion" in the *Apologia*. He speaks of himself as "resting in the thought of two, and two only, supreme and luminously self-evident beings—myself and my Creator." "I believed," he says, "that the inward conversion of which I was conscious—and of which I am still more certain than that I have hands and feet—would last into the next life, and that I was elected to eternal glory." He adds that, though he regarded himself as predestined to salvation, he did not think of others as predestined to eternal death, but thought only of the mercy to himself.

seldom in the written style of gifted women. He was wanting in manly strength, and we cannot easily accept as a great man anyone who is not a truly manly man. Hurrell Froude, his chosen and most congenial friend, was more feminine still than Newman—feminine in his faults as well as in his gifts and his defects. For sympathy and mutual intelligence the two were wonderfully well assorted, Newman delighting in the very faults of Froude, though at the same time it was his work to chasten and restrain his friend. Ward, on the other hand, as has been shown in his biography, was, in the frank and masculine traits of his undiplomatic character, was in his blunt manliness, a striking contrast to Newman. But, apart from this special weakness of character, where can we find in Newman, regarded in any capacity in which he might have been supposed to claim the character of a thinker or leader, the characteristics of a great man?

Mr. Hutton seems not to have fathomed the true character of his hero. Nothing can be more amazing than his denial of Newman's natural intellectual scepticism. The argument he gives to the contrary,—his only argument, it would seem,—that amidst all his perilous soundings and questionings Newman never lost hold of the conviction he derived from his early religious experience as to the existence of a personal God and his own personal relations to Him, is, I venture to think, nothing whatever to the purpose. His habit of mind, on the purely intellectual side of his nature, was pre-eminently sceptical. Mr. Froude's statements in his *Short Studies*, already referred to, are strong evidence on this point. But, indeed, the testimony of those who knew him most closely, and the evidence of his writings, agree absolutely to the same effect. Mr. Hutton appears not to have mastered the general principles and scope of Newman's *Grammar of Assent*. That book, which furnishes the key to Newman's intellectual character in its aspect towards metaphysics and philosophy, Mr. Hutton dismisses with a slight and inadequate description towards the end of his volume; a description so slight and inadequate as to suggest that the writer did not comprehend the significance of the book, the intricate obscurities of which, indeed, it is exceedingly difficult to follow, by reason especially of its continual fallacies and self-contradictions. The very dilemma propounded in that book is, that "assent" and "certitude" are in no sense possible on any ground of logic or philosophy or induction, and are only attainable through religious faith and obedience, leading up to Church infallibility as the one sole guarantee for mankind of divine truth and reality.

Mr. Hutton's admiring sympathy with Newman has enabled him to do such justice to the best side of Newman's character and gifts as has hardly been done before. Putting himself in Newman's place during the years in Oxford when he was slowly moving Romewards, Mr. Hutton has shown the pathos, and set forth the power, of his searching, subtle, persuasive, and sometimes pathetic, sermons, preached at St. Mary's, as no other critic has done. Those sermons, doubtless, are many of them masterpieces of their kind. They show a spiritual power, as Mr. Hutton seems in effect to admit, such as no later writings of Newman's show. They suggest a style of life and consecration, and an earnestness of character, much superior to that which is revealed to us as having belonged to Cardinal Newman in the later years of his life at Birmingham, so far as we may judge from the plain and direct evidence furnished by Mr. Arthur Hutton.

It is not wonderful that an admiring friend of Cardinal Newman should have dwelt at length on his ministry at St. Mary's, and should have given a more thorough and complete account of that than of any other part of his life and life's work. It is surprising, however, that Mr. Hutton has not exposed the monstrous perversions of history of which Newman was guilty in the lectures which he delivered after he had joined the Roman Catholic Church. Some very slight intimations, indeed, of the glaring paradoxes and perversions which Father Newman set forth as facts of history Mr. Hutton has given, but his dealing with these productions of Newman's Roman Catholic life, the genius and brilliancy of which he highly praises, is strangely inadequate, and this side of Newman's professional work is treated with a gentleness which is scarcely faithful to the requirements of truth. Newman's lectures were full of libels upon his nation and travesties of history. Mr. Hutton should not have gently passed over such faults as these.

No trained metaphysician who studies Newman's *Grammar of Assent* could admit any claim on behalf of the writer to be a metaphysician or even a logician. The blunders in logic in that book are as signal as the faults in metaphysical definition and statement, and are yet more frequent, so that a well-known writer, who signed himself " Cantabrigiensis," in commenting, in the *Times*, on the excessive eulogies of Newman which were flooding the press, was justified in speaking of him as the writer of " the best English and of the worst logic " in his generation.

The late Mr. James Macdonell, the brilliant leader-writer of the *Daily Telegraph*, and finally of the *Times*, took in hand to read the *Grammar of Assent*, with a strong predisposition to admire the intellect and logic of the writer, being, like most other journalists of his time, smitten with admiration generally of the author of the *Apologia*, who, if he had been a writer for the daily press, would no doubt have easily excelled most competitors, even of the rank of Mr. Macdonell. In one of his letters Mr. Macdonell expresses, somewhat naïvely, the puzzled feelings with which he read, or tried to read, the treatise. Writing to a friend, to whom in advance, and with great expectations as to the value of the volume, he had sent the *Grammar of Assent* as a present, he finds himself constrained to say, "I confess that I never saw more painfully inconclusive reasoning come from a logical pen than that which I note on some pages." "Logic is good, and so is mysticism; but as I find myself cast alternately from one to the other as Newman finds convenient, I confess that my sense of logical precision and my faculty of faith, such as it is, are both irritated."[1] The effect of this volume is completely to sever faith from reason, and philosophy from religion. Among other things, Newman teaches (p. 4) not only—as he might truly maintain—that a man may be a believer of "unhesitating faith," though he knows nothing of Christian evidence,—of the argumentative reasons of his faith,—and never regards his religious faith as sustained by any "conclusions of reason"; but, that *such* a "man of unhesitating faith" is the very ideal of a "believer," is the purest and truest type of a Christian;—as if true philosophy and true religion were not in harmony with each other; as if

[1] *James Macdonell, Journalist.* By W. Robertson Nicoll (p. 180).

philosophy incapacitated for faith; as if grounds of reason did not form part of the true and only stable support for the believer's " unhesitating faith "; as if, in a word, reason had never lighted the way to faith, and reason and faith could never coalesce in the heart of the enlightened but humble Christian into an absolute unity of solemn conviction and reverent trust. This is Newman's deliberate science on the subject of faith and reason. It is the full and, so far as we know, final development of the doctrine taught in his Oxford sermons, to the effect that faith and reason were so far in opposition to each other as that the man who believed the most upon the least evidence or basis of mere reason was the man of the greatest faith, so that to believe all that the Church teaches, absolutely apart from all sense of fitness or ground of evidence, is the perfection of faith.[1]

Many of Newman's difficulties in this book are due to the fact that *faith* throughout the volume stands merely in relation to *creed*, and is used to mean the unshaken and immovable acceptance by the mind as infallibly true of a certain modicum of belief. Hence he teaches (p. 181) that " we cannot, without absurdity, call ourselves at once believers and inquirers also." And yet it is certain that for many men the way to an immovable faith, in the true comprehensive sense of the word faith, leads by the avenues of many doubts,—doubts not indeed welcomed as such, but yet considered in the clear light of reason until distinctly understood, and kept in view till, by the help of the Spirit of Truth, the answer has been learnt and can be given. Nor is it possible to read this very book, the *Grammar of Assent*,

[1] See as to this point also, Froude's testimony in his *Short Studies*, Fourth Series.

without feeling that he who writes in it of doubt and belief, of investigation and implicit faith, of inference and assent, is one to whose own restless intellect doubt has been as familiar as faith and religion are to his susceptible, shrinking, clinging heart.

For a somewhat detailed review of the *Grammar of Assent*, I may refer to an article in the *London Quarterly Review* for January 1871, from which some sentences in the last page have been borrowed. That article, notwithstanding much criticism in the sense just indicated, did not fail to recognise the beauty, felicity, and instructiveness of a good deal of what the book contains on the subject of the unconscious illative processes of our mind. At the same time, it speaks of what is described as Newman's "sceptical heresy," and the result of an analysis is given in these words :—

"He does not believe in any absolute certainty, except such as may be established by mathematical or syllogistic proof. He does not believe in the 'intuitions of the mind,' or in objective truth. Inductive certainty with him is the mere accumulated probability of the world's experience. Dr. Newman holds with Hume and Mill that experience alone has generated our faith in the constancy of nature,—that it is in no sense primary and intuitive, and that all our assurances are but the feelings or opinions which grow up within us from the impressions produced by experience. He teaches throughout that certainty is altogether relative and subjective. He gives up all hope of finding a 'common measure' of truth in any province of thought, or any 'criterion' by which to test principles and conclusions. In a word, he is a sceptic in philosophy."

Newman does not believe in "assent" and what he calls

"certitude," except only as resting on authority and determined by the will. His, in short, is the fit philosophy of a man of keen and sceptical intellect, who has settled his doubts and difficulties by betaking himself to the infallible direction and authority of the Roman communion. Faith with him is merely and absolutely the response of the conscience to authority. Faith, as understood in the sense, and as resting on the grounds indicated in a well-known volume by the late Dr. Dale,[1] is a thing totally unknown to the theology or experience of Cardinal Newman. Such a teacher is not entitled to rank as a master, either in philosophy or theology.

The truth is, that to this dominantly sceptical habit of Newman's mind was due the whole course of his ecclesiastical and theological development; for his development was first ecclesiastical, and only secondarily theological. He himself says, in his lectures on the *Difficulties of Anglicanism* (p. 120), when describing the progress of Tractarianism, and referring to the Tract writers, that "the principle of these writers was this,—an infallible authority is necesssary. We have it not, for the Prayer-Book is all we have got; but since we have nothing better, we must use it as if infallible."[2] It was this pursuit after infallibility which continually led forward Newman as he "went sounding on his dim and perilous way," coming ever nearer and nearer to Rome. Intellectual scepticism, accordingly, is the one and only key by which to explain Newman's course. In philosophy he was an empiric; but, holding

[1] *The Living Christ and the Four Gospels.*

[2] So also, in a passage already quoted, he says, "Their idea was, simply and absolutely, submission to an external authority. To it they appealed, to it they betook themselves: there they found a haven of rest."

as he did to his spiritual conviction of the existence of God, and of himself in relation to God, he was bound to look always for some living representative of God whose voice was to give assurance to the believer, and whose authority could command obedience. Prophets represented God under the Old Testament; Jesus and His apostles under the New; the Church, and, as representing the Church in its unity and authority, the Pope, for all after ages,—all these being personal and divine authorities. From these sources alone could come assurance, moral certitude, rest and peace to the searching spirit. Such, in brief, is a summary of Newman's faith and philosophy.

That Mr. Hutton should have missed the real key to Newman's whole character and course,—his despair of human reason as affording any light or help in regard to objective truth, natural or spiritual,—and should have taken upon himself to deny the fundamental and overmastering scepticism of his mind, is matter of astonishment. In this he differs from all those of Newman's contemporaries who had most closely studied his writings and his character, and who were most competent to judge. I might quote, for instance, Henry Rogers, a writer and a critic not easily to be surpassed in dealing with the borderland of thought which belongs to theology and to philosophy, and who criticised Newman's writings and ecclesiastical course with singular ability in his Essays, of which the main substance was originally published in the *Edinburgh Review*. I might cite the language of Bishop Wilberforce, who surely had the means, as few besides could have, of understanding intimately the character and tendencies of Newman's mind and teachings, and who, to quote a pregnant expression in one of his *Addresses to Candidates for Ordination*, speaks, with a manifest reference to Newman, of those who have taken their flight " on the wings of an unbounded scepticism into the bosom of an unfathomed superstition." But, above all, I may adduce the authority of Archdeacon Hare, the most learned, the most acute and searching, the most competent, in regard to all the largest questions of controversy with Newman, and at the same time the most polished and courteous of Newman's contemporary critics, who seems, moreover, to have carefully read all that Newman had published. This master alike of philosophy and theology—as also, I may parenthetically note, of history —thus describes Newman's course of intellectual development :—

"Probably it will have seemed to many, when they terminated their wanderings through the mazes of his *Lectures on Justification*, that the text prefixed to the first lecture ('*Who is this that darkeneth counsel by words without knowledge?*') has been selected under a judicial blindness as the aptest motto for the whole work. Moreover, when we look back upon the author's subsequent career, when we reflect how he has gone on year after year sharpening the edge of his already over-keen understanding, casting one truth after another into his logical crucible, and persuading himself that he had dissolved it to atoms, and then exhibiting a like ingenuity in compounding the semblance of truths out of fictions,—when we call to mind how in this way he appeared to be gradually losing the faculty of distinguishing between truth and falsehood, and the very belief in the existence of any power for discerning truth, nay, as it seems at times, in the existence of any positive truth to be discerned, and how, taking refuge from the encroachments of a universal scepticism, he has at length bowed his neck under a yoke which a man, gifted with such fine qualities of mind and character, would hardly assume until he had put out the eyes of his heart and of his conscience as well as of his understanding,—it is not in scorn and triumph, but in deep sadness and awe, that we repeat, ' *Who is this that darkeneth counsel by words without knowledge ?* ' " [1]

These words were written by Archdeacon Hare long before the *Grammar of Assent* was published. They do but anticipate the judgment as to the character and tendencies of Newman's mind which that volume so completely establishes.

In the preceding observations I have been led to speak of Newman's teaching as to faith. Mr. Hutton has given no clear or adequate idea of Newman's doctrine on this subject, and leaves his own views altogether in a haze. I must dwell briefly on Newman's view of faith as regarded from another side, because it gives character to his whole system of theological teaching. I have indicated the relations of faith to reason as taught by Newman. I wish now to give a view of his teaching as to the relations of faith to spiritual life. Spiritual and truly Christian faith then, according to Newman, signifies implicit belief inwrought in the soul through the grace of baptism, and standing in no relation to love or good works, or the "fruits of the spirit." It differs absolutely and completely from faith as understood by all evangelical teachers; it stands entirely apart from any such conception of faith as that expressed in Wesley's well-worn words, " faith which works by love and purifies the heart." In his

[1] *Vindication of Luther,* pp. 99, 100.

Difficulties of Anglicanism (p. 223), Newman says explicitly: " Catholics hold that faith and love, faith and obedience, faith and works, are simply separable, and ordinarily separated in fact; that faith does not imply love, obedience, or works." "It is," he says, "a certainty of things not seen, but revealed, preceded ordinarily by the instrumental Sacrament of Baptism, but caused directly by supernatural influence." Of this faith, indeed, he speaks as a "spiritual sight," applying to it, because he must find Scripture for his view, the really inappropriate and inapplicable words of Heb. xi. 1. In no respect, however, is faith, according to his teaching, a high moral or a true spiritual grace, open-eyed to the revelation of God's character and the Saviour's mission and work: it is mere implicit belief. Archdeacon Hare says of such faith as Newman describes, that it is not spiritual but magical. "A spiritual power," he says, "acts upon the will and the conscience, and through them: a magical power produces its changes arbitrarily, independent of the will and the conscience. Such is the belief which Newman calls faith, and which he supposes to manifest itself by outward acts, by the repetition of prayers by rote, without any renewal of the spirit; such is the baptismal change of nature as substituted for the new birth; such is the belief of a string of propositions on the authority of another, without any inward personal conviction of their truth; such is the infallibility ascribed to Popes, without any reference to their moral or spiritual condition."[1] In the foregoing words Hare has summed up the description of faith and its effects, as gathered from Newman's Lectures on the *Difficulties of Anglicanism*. That Newman should

[1] With what is said above may be compared Newman's *Theses de Fide*, as given in the *Expositor* for November 1890.

speak of such faith as this as a spiritual sight of the unseen, applying to it the words of the Epistle to the Hebrews, serves to show how bold and unhesitating a polemic he was. But this comes out much more fully in his *Grammar of Assent*, when he is contrasting religion among Catholic populations with religion in England, and among Protestant populations generally. " Religion among Catholic populations," we are instructed, " is real ; in England, speaking generally, it is but notional." The astonishing sentence I am about to quote points the contrast as Newman conceived it : " As to Catholic populations, such as those of mediæval Europe, or the Spain of this day, or quasi-Catholic as those of Russia, among them assent to religious objects is real, not notional. To them the Supreme Being, our Lord, the Blessed Virgin, angels and saints, heaven and hell, are as present as if they were objects of sight ; but such a faith does not suit the genius of modern England."[1] Here tawdry images are confounded with real spiritual vision. Newman selects the worst examples of corrupt and degraded " Catholic " Christianity,—the semi-paganism of mediæval Europe and of the Spain of this day, the superstitious and ignorant devotion of the Russian peasantry,— and parades this as " real religion " in comparison with which the average and staple modern English Protestantism, as professed and practised by persons of decidedly religious character, is but " notional," " an empty form and routine of Bible reading," as he describes it, and " stereotyped aspects of facts." This is a wantonness of daring and of insult of which it might have been thought that Newman would have been incapable. What was the " religious realism " of mediæval Europe ? What is the " religious

[1] *Grammar of Assent*, p. 53.

realism" of Spanish and of Russian villages and towns? The paintings in mediæval cathedrals and in Russian churches may help us to understand its character and quality; paintings of the Persons of the Trinity, pictures filled with "angels and saints, heaven and hell"; paintings of our Lord and the Blessed Virgin, who, we are told, are as "present as if they were objects of sight" to the "real" devotion of Catholics. This is the realism in religion of Catholic populations which Newman has dared to place as in favourable contrast with the "notional" religion of England. This is the vision of the unseen furnished by the faith of which he speaks.

Mr. Hutton all through his volume appears to be ignorant of the true character and quality of faith as taught by Newman. In closing his chapter on Newman at St. Mary's he writes the following sentence, which is the last in a fine paragraph: "I cannot help thinking that Newman, though he always insisted on the certainty of the communion between God and the individual soul as the very starting-point of revelation, has conceded too much to those who speak of God as only presenting Himself to us through sign and symbol and mediate adaptation, and has hardly dwelt enough on those aspects of revelation in which we see the very majesty and the very holiness of His character without a film to hide its splendour and its purity from our eyes." This sentence refers to Newman's sermons at St. Mary's when, as yet, he had not left the Church of England, though his theology was even then, essentially, much more Roman than Protestant. His doctrine of faith had even then almost altogether lost the touch and quality of evangelical reality which had been derived originally from his Calvinistically evangelical sense of converting experience. What remained to him of that experience was rather a metaphysical assurance as to the personal relations between God and his own soul, coupled with the keen and clinging sense of moral dependence and need, than any high vision of God in Christ, as Father and Saviour. Hence the omission, throughout even the series of sermons which he preached at St. Mary's, and to which in real elevation and moral power nothing that he wrote after he joined the Church of Rome can for a moment compare, of all such views of revelation in its high moral and spiritual aspects as those the want of which Mr. Hutton so justly and impressively points out. But it is evident that the real reason of this want is hidden from Mr. Hutton. He does not see that Newman's view of faith was one which did not lead him at all to a contemplation of the moral and spiritual effects of the gospel-revelation, in its grandeur and tenderness, upon the believing soul. Already at Oxford the tone of his urgent admonitions, the strain of his severe analysis and scrutiny of character and motives, is that of a teacher with whom faith is merely the force urging to religious observances, to moral austerity, to legal obedience, not the faith which derives joy and strength and evangelical motives to holiness from the vision of God in Christ reconciling the world unto Himself. If Mr. Hutton had penetrated to the real character of Newman's theology and religion, he would not have expressed in gentle words of surprise his sense of the deficiency of which he speaks. He would have understood and pointed out its reason and source. It is, however, still more remarkable that throughout the volume Mr. Hutton never seems to have become aware of the character or the reason of the defect he has thus indicated.

Even later, and when referring to Newman as a Roman Catholic, he intimates similar mild surprise. He heard, as he tells us, the Lectures on the *Difficulties of Anglicanism*, or some of them; but they do not seem to have disclosed to him their main theological lesson as to the character of Newman as a Christian believer and teacher.

The historical illustration just quoted from Newman of his views as to the quality and effects of Roman Catholic as contrasted with Protestant religion among the nations of the world, leads me naturally to notice one of the great features of Newman's teaching as a Roman Catholic lecturer, as to which Mr. Hutton has scarcely spoken at all. I have referred to the point some pages back. I desire now to give illustrations of my meaning. Archdeacon Hare speaks in one place of Newman's "Circean talent for metamorphosing historical facts," and, in another, of his "favourite feat of turning white black and black white." The language is not too strong. It was his business, in his Lectures on the *Difficulties of Anglicanism*,—lectures which made such a critical impression upon Mr. Hutton,—to show the superior moral and spiritual condition of Roman Catholic countries as compared with Protestant. The following passage is a sample of the style in which he accomplishes his work. He is describing, and in comparison vindicating, the moral and spiritual condition of Roman Catholic countries:—

"Vice," he says, "does not involve a neglect of the external duties of religion. The crusaders had faith sufficient to bind them to a perilous pilgrimage and warfare; they kept the Friday's abstinence, and planted the tents of their mistresses within the shadow of the pavilion of the glorious St. Lewis. There are other pilgrimages besides military ones, and other religious journeys besides the march upon Jerusalem.

. . . . . .

"It is a mixed multitude, some most holy, perhaps even saints; others penitent sinners, but others again a mixture of pilgrim and beggar, or pilgrim and robber, or half gipsy, or three-quarter boon companion, or at least with nothing saintly and little religious about them. . . . Yet one and all, saints and sinners, have faith in things invisible which each uses in his own way. Listen to their conversation, listen to the conversation of any multitude, or any private party; what strange oaths mingle with it: God's heart, and God's eyes, and God's wounds, and God's blood; you cry out how profane. Doubtless, but do you not see that the special profaneness above Protestant oaths lies not in the words, but simply in the speaker, and is the necessary result of that insight into the invisible world which you have not. . . . It is the consequence of mixed multitudes all having faith; for faith impresses the mind with supernatural truths, as if it were sight, and the faith of this man and the faith of that is one and the same, and creates one and the same impression. Sin does not obliterate the impression. Ordinarily speaking, once faith always faith. . . . It is just the reverse among Protestant people. . . . They have no certainty of the doctrines they profess. They do but feel that they ought to believe them, and they try to believe them, and they nurse the offspring of their reason as a sickly child, bringing it out of doors only on fine days. They feel very clear and quite satisfied while they are very still; but if they turn about their head, or change their posture ever so little, the vision of the unseen like a mirage is gone from them. So they keep the exhibition of their faith for high days and great occasions, when it comes forth with sufficient pomp and gravity of language and ceremonial of manner. Truths slowly totter out with Scripture texts at their elbow as unable to walk alone. Moreover, they know if such and such things *be* true, what *ought* to be the voice, the tone, the gesture, and carriage attendant upon them; thus reason, which is the substance of their faith, supplies the rubrics, as I may call them, of their behaviour. This some of you,[1] my brethren, call reverence; though I am obliged to say it is as much a mannerism, and an unpleasant mannerism, as that of the Evangelical party. . . . They condemn Catholics, because, however religious, they are only unaffected, easy, and cheerful in the mention of sacred things, and they think themselves never so real as when they are solemn."

In his Lectures on the *Present Position of Catholics in England,* delivered in 1851, he undertakes to vindicate in its results the doctrine of celibacy as inculcated by the Roman Catholic Church. He maintains, not only that matrimony does not prevent cases of immorality among Protestant ministers, but that celibacy does not cause them amongst Catholic priests. His argument on this subject is subtle and ingenious, but, I need hardly say, totally opposed to the great stream and volume of historical evidence. He is bold enough to say:—

"I have as much right to my opinion as another to his, when I state my deliberate conviction that there are, to say the least, as many offences against the marriage vow

[1] He is addressing High Anglicans, the companions he had left behind.

amongst Protestant ministers, as there are against the vow of celibacy amongst Roman Catholic priests" (p. 129).

The literature of Roman Catholic countries, especially of France, Spain, and Italy, is itself a sufficient argument upon this subject as a whole. It is notorious that of the gross and licentious tales of these countries a large proportion of the grossest and most licentious are told of priests and monks. If some Protestant countries to-day furnish discreditable records as to this subject, an examination of their history prior to the Reformation will show how immeasurably worse things were then than now, and that the Reformation itself marked the period of improvement in this as well as in other respects. But Newman had his brief; and the logic of his faith compelled him to maintain the historical paradox to which I refer, and not only to maintain this paradox, but greater and more outrageous paradoxes still.

As to the Church of Rome and her persecutions, Newman, in the Lectures from which I have last quoted, uses the following language:—

" In the course of 1800 years, though her children have been guilty of various excesses, though she herself is responsible for isolated acts of most solemn import, yet for one deed of severity with which she can be charged there have been a hundred of her acts repressive of the persecutor and protective of his victims; she has been a never-failing fount of humanity, equity, forbearance, and compassion."

Newman further proceeds to quote and adopt the words of Balmez:—

" We find in all parts of Europe scaffolds prepared to punish crimes against religion, scenes which sadden the soul were everywhere witnessed; Rome is the one exception to the rule. . . . The Popes, armed with a tribunal of intolerance, have scarce spilt a drop of blood; Protestants and philosophers have shed it in torrents" (p. 213).[1]

Referring to the reign in England of her whom he calls "Bloody Elizabeth," he speaks of the severities exercised in her reign without the slightest intimation of the political grounds, which, indeed, were the only grounds, of those punishments. On the other hand, he pleads that the "burnings in Queen Mary's reign" were the acts of an English party inflamed with revenge against their enemies, and were opposed by Cardinal Pole. He takes care not to state that the "English party" of which he speaks included the whole body of the English Romanists, with the bishops at their head; and he conceals the fact that Cardinal Pole, who, at the Council of Trent, had incurred suspicion as being too favourable to Protestants and Protestant views, and was obliged to quit the Council, was also superseded in England as legate by the Pope, his milder policy failing to meet the papal approval. "Protestantism," he says (p. 209), "has ever shown itself a persecuting power. It has persecuted in England, in Scotland, in Ireland, in Holland, in France, in Germany, in Geneva." "To be sure," exclaims Archdeacon Hare, in fine irony, "did not the Dutch burn Alva and his army in the Netherlands? Did not the Huguenots massacre Charles IX. and Catherine de Medici, and every Roman Catholic in Paris, on the famous night of St. Bartholomew?" Newman must have been well aware that for the Huguenots' massacre in which the numbers slain

[1] "Philosophers," who were *not* "Protestants," but were themselves brought up within the pale of Romanism.

amounted to 50,000, Pope Gregory XIII. went in procession to St. Mark's to return thanks to Almighty God; and yet he pretends that there is one spot upon earth, namely, Rome, where reverence for liberty of conscience is a native growth, and one heart from generation to generation in which it has always been inherent—the heart of the Pope. "To the Pope," as Archdeacon Hare says, "has the glorious privilege been granted of transmitting the sacred principle of toleration from age to age." If there be any appearance of truth in the statement that, in the immediate territory of Rome itself, there has been less persecution than elsewhere, the reason is obvious enough. All life and liberty had been absolutely trampled down and suppressed within that territory; nor could healthy independence of thought breathe in its mephitic air. Butler, the Roman controversialist, adjured Southey as a Christian and a gentleman to say on which side the balance of persecution lies: the Roman Catholic or the Protestant. "Put the Inquisition in the scale," was Southey's reply, "and nothing can be found to counterpoise it, unless hell itself be plucked up by the roots." Newman, however, undertook to maintain that Rome had been a "never-failing fount of humanity, equity, forbearance, and compassion." Such and so monstrous historical paradoxes as these, which form a large and leading part of Newman's Lectures, should have been duly characterised by Mr. Hutton, instead of which he passes them over in silence, praising the Lectures generally as "giving the fullest scope to his powers of orderly and beautiful exposition, and opening out a far greater range to his singular genius for gentle and delicate irony than anything which he had previously written." He speaks of one of the Lectures as delivering "one of the most powerful attacks ever opened on the Anglican theory of the Church as independent of the State," and of another as powerfully describing the "collapse of the Anglican theory of the Church when applied to practice." But of such portions of the Lectures as I have referred to he has nothing to say, except that Newman's observations "raise as many difficulties as they remove," and that the Lectures are "much more powerful in attack than in defence."

I have referred to these Lectures as illustrating the want of historical knowledge and of the historical sense in Newman, and as showing how he has travestied history in such daring and paradoxical misrepresentations as have been quoted. In further illustration of the same quality in his character, I may refer to a very searching analysis of some portions of his letter to the Duke of Norfolk, written in reply to Mr. Gladstone's "Expostulation" on the subject of the Papal Syllabus, which forms a note in Mr. Arthur's learned and able work on *The Pope, the Kings, and the People*, and is entitled, *Dr. Newman on the Syllabus* (vol. i. pp. 183-194).

As to the point which we have been considering, I may fitly quote some illustrative matter from Mr. Arthur Hutton's "Reminiscences" of Cardinal Newman in the *Expositor*. "It is natural," he says, "to compare or contrast Newman with Döllinger. . . . Döllinger had visited Newman a few years before, and the two men had found it hard to get on with each other. 'It was like a dog and a fish trying to make friends,' so the latter described it some time later. The ultimate basis of Newman's dogmatic theology was feeling; that of Döllinger's was history. . . . It is never easy to estimate what a man's historical knowledge may be unless he has written on that period which we have ourselves specially studied. My impression is that in this respect Newman was vastly inferior to Döllinger. Of course, there was a period which he had made his own, that of the Arian controversy. Doubtless, too, there were sundry episodes and sundry personages belonging to other epochs about which he had good information and clear and correct ideas; but of the earlier centuries he appeared to know but little, and not to care much for what could be known, while he scarcely entered upon the great field of Church history subsequent to the days of Arianism and extending to our own times." [1]

Newman, in fact, was not a really well-informed man in respect of the deep and exact knowledge proper to the character either of a student of history or a student of theology or biblical criticism. Of biblical criticism he knew less than he did of philosophy or of metaphysical science. Mr. Arthur Hutton may here again be quoted. "Behind the Vulgate, Newman, as I knew him, never cared to go. Of recent criticism of the Greek Testament, he knew nothing; and, as to the Old Testament, never having studied Hebrew or its cognate languages, he was not in a position to do more than follow the received Latin or English texts. So far as I can judge, he had never so much as heard of recent theories; and as he knew no German, and never had occasion to meet the English exponents of the German and Dutch criticism, I believe that this was really the case."

I have spoken more than once of the idealistic tone of Newman's mind, and of the feminine quality of his character.

[1] See Appendix (B) at the end of the volume.

In his *Apologia* he paints his own portrait, and sketches his own opinions as held in his earlier Oxford life (pp. 90–93). From the interesting account there given of himself, we may form an estimate of the basis of his character through life. The description he gives is not that of a calm philosopher, of a profound divine, of a wise and true expositor. There is fancy, susceptibility, genius, dreamy speculation; but what some might take for philosophy is at best but poetry. The exposition of his views does not even pretend to be founded upon any basis of reason or sober thought. From his boyhood he was at once fanciful, sceptical, and superstitious. Never brought into contact either with the various strife and life of the outer world, or with the practical claims and duties of home life, the youth grew up to be a cloistered enthusiast, a student, a scholar, though by no means in his scholarship exact or profound, a controversialist with many accomplishments, with such faculties as are the instruments of private discussion and personal persuasion most highly cultured, most fully developed, but without that steadfast, self-suppressing devotion to the study of history for its own sake as the record of humanity, to the study of nature and science for their own sake as the revelation of the God of the universe, and above all to the study of the word of God in its own simplicity as the revelation of the God of holiness and love, without which speculation cannot but degenerate into fancy, controversy into word-play, and theology into traditional error and priestly invention.

Later on, in the same record of his history (pp. 111–118), we have a picture of himself which is certainly not attractive, which exhibits a combination of intellectual and hierarchical pride and ambition from which it was not likely that the fruits of truth and peace would grow. He is depicted by his own hand as full of an overweening self-confidence, as a sort of hierarchical champion, proud of his Church and his Orders, and prouder still of his logic, and in this spirit conceiting himself to be the destined leader of a second and a better and greater Reformation. He speaks of his " fierceness " and of his " sport." He took Froude for his prompter, of whom he says that " he delighted in the notion of a hierarchical system of sacerdotal power and of full ecclesiastical liberty " (p. 85). I have referred to this before; but it is necessary to refer to it here again in attempting to give a general and comprehensive estimate of his character. It was through the force of sympathetic prepossession, not of reason or strict inquiry, that Newman became what he was from point to point, changing from Calvinism to High Anglicanism, and so onward till he joined the Roman Church. With Newman, as with people of a commoner sort, feelings, prepossessions, prejudices, determined the creed; his logic was ever an afterthought and a mere instrument of defence or persuasion. In this as in so many other respects Newman's was, I must be allowed again to repeat, a characteristically feminine mind, poetic, impressible, receptive, and reproductive, rather than original and commanding; and with the feminine mind was joined a feminine temperament.

Mr. Arthur Hutton, in his " Reminiscences," confirms and illustrates this view of Newman's character. He speaks of him in his old age as a venerable man, "singularly winning, courteous, and considerate, very feminine in his affection, yet withal very dignified and fitted to command respect"; adding that he was by his temperament unfitted to be a ruler, or, at all events, that he made no attempt to rule. With this statement may be combined the passage I am about to quote :—

"One of his short poems, 'The Married and the Single,' written in 1834, expresses very clearly the view of the relation between the two sexes to which he held consistently throughout his life. It is the view of the Catholic Church, which makes the celibate state essentially the higher one for all. The outcome of this view is to degrade the idea of all love between man and woman that is more than friendship: and it was remarked to me of Newman, by one who had known him long and well, that he never could distinguish between such love and lust. . . . On the whole, he held the sex in something like contempt. 'You know I think them great liars,' he once said to me, smiling; and seemed shocked at his own boldness."

What has now been brought forward justifies fully, as I think, the statement made in the early part of this chapter, to the effect that Newman was wanting in manliness; as indeed were most of the group of Anglican clergymen with whom he was closely identified.

In his later years Newman was a venerable and interesting figure, but Mr. Arthur Hutton's "Reminiscences," the genuine and authentic character of which impresses one more strongly the more they are studied, show that his moods were not all or always attractive. His Protestant visitors, such as Dean Church, Canon Liddon, or Lord Coleridge, were sure to be well and even affectionately received, and would carry away a delightful impression of his brightness and affability. It was otherwise when his visitors were Roman Catholics. It was often with difficulty that even distinguished ecclesiastics from other countries could obtain access to him; and to such visitors he had little to say, and was seldom otherwise than reserved. The visits, we are told, of his own bishop he hardly affected to treat otherwise than as a bore. Another very peculiar point relating to his Sunday social habits is mentioned by Mr. Hutton. The Oratory School at Birmingham stands in the midst of residential houses. In spite of remonstrances from Protestant neighbours he supported the boys of the Oratory School in playing cricket and other games on Sunday afternoons; while at the same time within the house the recreation room was made merry with the sounds of violins and other instruments, he himself never failing to be present when any concerted music that interested him was to be performed. With ascetic severity, indeed, he seems to have had, as an Oratorian, very little, if any, sympathy. A sort of "indolence" appears to have been one of his not infrequent characteristics. He was diligent, however, in reading his *Times* daily, following with keen curiosity public affairs.[1] He found congenial recreation and employment in editing Latin plays for the Oratory boys to act, and in taking the part of theatrical manager for all the details of the acting, and of the costumes and scenery. He studied with close attention the whole of the intricate ceremonial connected with his appearance as Cardinal at all functions whatever. In these things he found interesting occupation and hearty pleasure. He corresponded

[1] From the *Short Life* of the Cardinal, by his admiring friend and co-religionist, J. S. Fletcher, we learn that he was also a diligent novel reader, and that the library in his country retreat (Rednal), on the slope of the Lickey Hill, contained a choice collection of the best English modern novels.

also with some chosen friends. But to the weightier matters of biblical or theological study he seems to have given no attention. Nor do social or philanthropic subjects, even those closely touching the most pressing questions of humanity, seem to have in the least commanded his attention. In this respect, as in some others, he was a striking contrast to his brother Cardinal, Manning.

Newman, in his *Apologia*, vindicated his general good faith and personal honour; indeed, his secession to the Church of Rome, considering the potent motives which might have bound him to the Church of England, is itself an evidence of his conscientiousness, however ill-lighted or perverted his conscience might sometimes have been. Especially, when placed in contrast with the conduct of others as essentially Romanising as himself, who remained within the Anglican pale, Newman's conduct rises in our estimation. But yet his vindication of his good faith was effected at the expense of his intellectual reputation. The *Apologia*, perfectly written as it is, is nevertheless a humiliating tissue of disclosures. It reveals an acute, subtle, sceptical intellect, penned up within narrow limits, and exercising its faculties in a dim and darkling sphere, groping its way from premiss to consequence, often from fallacy to fallacy, and only discerning the error of the latest fallacy through which it has passed in order to plunge into a new, subtler, deeper, and more perilous error, until at last, utterly wearied out, it sinks down self-blinded, to find its rest henceforth within the arms of Popish despotism and superstition.

He has gone from his "haven of rest" in the Oratory to his eternal rest. Every heart will sympathise with the sentiment of his Church's benediction—*Requiescat in pace.*

Most gladly would I have been silent as to his errors, as I look back from his tomb over the course of his life. But when both by Catholics and, however inconsistently, by Anglo-Catholics—and by mere men of the world also—lessons are drawn from his life in favour of Romanism or of Romanising tendencies, and the whole effect of the current exaggerations and misstatements is to assist the great and terrible work of doctrinal corruption and ecclesiastical usurpation which is spreading over England, I have felt that it is the time not "to be silent," but "to speak."

CHAPTER VI

Ward's Life as a Roman Catholic Theologian and Philosopher [1]—The Last Forty Years of Ward's Life—English Romanism Fifty Years Ago—An Ultramontane Idealist—His Faith and its Grounds—Daily Routine—Mania for the Sensational Drama—Contrasted Phases of Character—Ward and Faber—Ward's Earnestness as a Professor of Theology—His Dislike of Liberal Catholicism—Eccentricities—His Merits—Ward and Tennyson.

MR. WILFRID WARD'S first volume on his father's remarkable history closed with the reception of W. G. Ward into the Roman Catholic communion. The volume which forms the subject of this chapter takes up the biographical story where the first volume left it, and thenceforward opens out to view phase after phase of the "Catholic Revival," not only as it has taken form in England, but as it has developed on the Continent, using the course of Ward's life, after his secession to Rome, as the line of movement from which successive views are given of the whole course and field of modern Romanist advance.

[1] *William George Ward and the Catholic Revival.* By Wilfrid Ward, author of *William George Ward and the Oxford Movement.* Macmillan & Co.

If Mr. Wilfrid Ward's first volume was exceedingly interesting and valuable, the second appears to us scarcely less so, though in a different way. The first greatly helped towards completing our knowledge of the Oxford Movement, and our understanding of the character and ascendency of its chief leader, who sat at the centre, and, when he ceased to guide by articulate counsel, did not cease to influence those who had been of his intimate companionship. But the second volume introduces us to spheres hitherto almost utterly unknown, even to cultivated Englishmen, although some have had a dim inkling of movements going on there, coupled with a profound and curious interest in what, to nearly all people, were regions of mystery. Led by Mr. Wilfrid Ward, with his perfect English information and insight, and at the same time his familiar knowledge both of English and continental Romanism, to the inner history of which he seems to have command of all the keys, we are introduced, in succession, to a range of views of extraordinary interest. The first scenes are in England. From the quiet, secluded, unambitious, unintellectual old-fashioned English Catholicism of St. Edmund's College, Ware,—where the inmates, and the families which frequented and sustained the college, and made up the Roman Catholic colony with which it was connected, are described as a *gens lucifuga*,—the steps are traced by which the *régime* of Bishop Challoner and Bishop Griffiths, under whose sway the comparatively mild Roman Catholic principles of Alban Butler formed the recognised standard of English orthodoxy, passed into the much loftier dispensation of Cardinal Wiseman, with which was associated the revival in England of the organised Roman Catholic hierarchy and the corresponding " Papal claims "; and afterwards into the yet more fully developed Catholicism, so speciously and seductively presented, so cleverly economised, so skilfully administered by Cardinal Manning. At a later point in the volume, the origin and progress of the great "Catholic Revival," which, during the larger part of the century now closing, has been developing on the Continent, are unfolded, from the first faint stirrings and timid movements during the period of the great Napoleon onward, from point to point, till now, when that revival has taken a wide and powerful hold of continental Catholicism, especially in the Rhine provinces of Germany, and still more in France, in which country Romanism was, perhaps, never so powerfully organised or so active and zealous as it is to-day. These are matters which, known more or less to careful and candid inquirers and students for twenty years past, have now in this authentic volume found, for the first time, in outline, an orderly and historical record in our own language. It is of the utmost importance that the truth as to such questions should be understood by evangelical Protestants, who should always remember that one part of the power of the "Catholic Revival" results from the fact that evangelical truths have, so to speak, filtered from the Reformed Churches into the old hierarchical communities, and especially that the attitude of Romanism in regard to the Bible has, however slowly and with whatever caution and reluctance, to a considerable extent been modified, so that Bible reading and preaching from the Scriptures prevail among Roman Catholic communities more widely than many Protestants suppose. In the social and civil commerce, direct and indirect, of the nations and of the various Churches, there is more of occult mutual sympathy, more of mutual influence, more participation in common tendencies and movements, for good as well as for evil, than is generally recognised. The Bible Society, also, it must never be forgotten, has been perpetually, and over the whole breadth of the Continent, for fifty years past, but especially in Germany and France, diffusing the knowledge of the Scriptures among Catholic as well as Protestant populations.

Another little-known region into which, following the line of his father's history, Mr. Wilfrid Ward introduces his readers, is the Metaphysical Society of London, a society founded in 1861 by Mr. James Knowles, afterwards and at present editor of the *Nineteenth Century*, and which Mr. Ward describes as "an attempt to form a microcosm of the English intellectual world," a society where the representatives of all forms and fashions of speculative thought met on the ground of frank and friendly discussion, including such opposites as Ward and Mill, Stirling and Huxley, a society of which Ward at one time was president. The chapter on the "Metaphysical Society" is one of the freshest and most interesting in the book, and is fitly followed by a chapter on "The Agnostic Controversy," in which the course of the important controversy between Ward and Mill is described.

On these wide and momentous subjects, however, it would be beside the purpose of this volume for me to enter at any length. The personality and experiences of Ward himself, as a refugee from scepticism and Protestantism to the coverts of Romanism, are of profound and unique interest, and, for evangelical Protestants, possess an instructiveness all their own. He was a man altogether apart from other men, and combined in himself seeming contradictions. I do not think that the critics, even the best informed critics, of the son's volume have succeeded in bringing distinctly into view the peculiarities of Ward as faithfully but modestly and gently indicated in his son's biography, or in exhibiting, as a living whole, a character which, in its special combination of strong qualities and of weaknesses, of virtues and faults, is without parallel. In an earlier chapter an attempt was made, from the materials afforded by the first volume of the biography, so far as these were available, to make a sketch of the man himself. The second volume, however, gives much fuller information, and enables us to gain a larger and more lifelike view of William George Ward as he fulfilled his course during the last forty years of his life, and to gather some, at least, of the striking lessons taught by his unique history.

It may seem strange to describe as a fanatic a man who could meet in frank social and intellectual intercourse men of all schools of thought, including agnostics and misbelievers,—one who, being a Roman Catholic, even corresponded on friendly terms with Mill and Bain, one who for a time was president of the Metaphysical Society. Yet a fanatic he was, albeit a personally tolerant fanatic; and without bearing this in mind it is almost impossible to understand his conduct or his course, his private habits or controversial life. He was a Papal fanatic, with all the one-sided zeal and enthusiasm of a pervert and neophyte who has looked only on one side of the field of a great controversy. I may venture to add, viewing the controversy in its whole breadth and complexity, that he was a fanatic, because in regard to a great part of what is regarded as general culture he was either altogether ignorant, or was at best a man of very shallow knowledge or information. This was shown in his attitude in the Infallibility controversy, in which he took the most extreme position possible, such as it would have been thought only an ignorant monkish devotee or a Spanish bigot could have taken. He was intoxicated with the doctrine of Papal Infallibility, and enamoured of Papal Bulls and decrees, so that he said, of course more or less jocosely, but yet as conveying an intimation of his serious views, that he should enjoy his breakfast the more if, morning by morning, he had a fresh Bull always laid on the table.[1] This spirit linked him with Veuillot in opposition to Dupanloup, and produced a long estrangement from Newman. No man with a scholarly tincture of historical knowledge, with anything of the spirit of historical criticism, could possibly have taken such an extreme position. Speaking of the difference between Newman and Ward, Mr. Wilfrid Ward says: "He (Newman) could not forget the human elements which affected policy, though they could not touch the essence of doctrine. Saints have been called on to rebuke Popes, though Popes can define doctrine infallibly and saints cannot. Ward's sanguine trust appeared to be based on an ideal of guidance from on high, which, however desirable, had not been in fact vouchsafed" (p. 282).[2] That is to say, Ward dwelt in the world of abstractions, uninstructed by the realities of history. We have in this a special illustration of the

[1] His words were: "I should like a new Papal Bull every morning with my *Times* at breakfast" (p. 14).

[2] In another place the biographer says: "Ward's attitude was far simpler (than Newman's). The narrow field in which his intellect moved so actively did not include many of the problems which perplexed Newman; and thus, while the latter had very much to consider before he could interpret the decrees to his satisfaction, the former applied them without difficulty in their simplest and most obvious sense, and rejoiced in them as fresh light without any shadow."

ill-balanced character of his mind. Of history, as was shown in a former chapter, he knew nothing, and did not care to know anything; for what was concrete he had no faculty. Of the limitation of his knowledge and faculties as to concrete facts, a curious illustration is given in this volume. Father Vaughan, now Cardinal Vaughan, was visiting Ward at Old Hall, where he lived, being at the time professor at St. Edmund's Catholic College. It was Father Vaughan's first visit to Ward. "What fine beech trees," Father Vaughan remarked, as they turned into an avenue. The reply to this not very pregnant observation startled him. "Wonderful man!" exclaimed Ward. His visitor waited for an explanation. "What a many-sided man you are," pursued Ward; "I knew that you were a dogmatic theologian and an ascetic theologian; and now I find that you are acquainted with all the *minutiæ of botany*." "The Vice-President" (Father Vaughan), adds the biographer, "was thoroughly puzzled; and it took him some little time to realise that to his new acquaintance the difference between a beech and an oak was one of those mysterious truths which, although undoubted, nevertheless brought home to him painfully and sadly the limitation of his faculties" (p. 48).

Ward certainly was not a "many-sided man"; his intellect seems to have been developed only on one side. He may almost be said to have been intellectually a monster; his faculties for abstract thought were abnormally developed, while nearly all his other powers were undeveloped. Except his musical faculty, and his taste for fiction and burlesque and spectacular plays—*not* for the Shakespearian, the historical, or in any sense the classical drama—all else on the intellectual side of his nature seems to have been strangely stunted. He was like some misshapen men, a combination of giant and dwarf, half Hercules, half cripple. That this arose in some measure from his own obstinate wilfulness from childhood upwards, rather than from any natural incapacity, leaves the actual result the same.

Hence his rapid and natural passage into Popery, so direct and decisive, and in such contrast with that of Newman, who, though weak, as he himself confessed, in his historical grasp and range, was vastly better informed than Ward, and possessed a faculty of historical imagination which, though not fully disciplined or informed, and consequently predisposed to illusion, was yet vivid and powerful. Ward's faith in Popery was founded on abstract argument, and had no respect whatever for any facts of history, either ancient or modern. Having, by metaphysical and logical reasoning, established the existence of God and Divine Providence, he deduced thence the principles of Divine Revelation, Divine Redemption, Divine Guidance for God's people, one Divine Saviour, one Holy Church, infallibly taught and led, and one human head of the Church, representing its Divine-Human Head, and infallibly guided into all spiritual truth as such guidance came to be needed. Given the Godhead, the Papal infallibility for Ward followed by logical and necessary sequence. His one fundamental, and his only grand, controversy was the theistic controversy. This, with its necessary metaphysical correlates, among which the law of causation and the question of the liberty of the will held a central place, was the great argument of his life. Here he felt that he could hold his ground against whatever adversaries. He had fought

and conquered his own doubts, and he found nothing really
and radically new in the doubts of others. He enjoyed
this conflict, because the more victories he won over others
the more he strengthened his personal position. What had
once been his own doubts were publicly slain when he
overthrew such antagonists as Bain and Mill, and a wide
audience "assisted" as witnesses at their overthrow. Such
opponents were "foemen worthy of his steel." He understood and respected their difficulties and objections; the
like difficulties had at one time or other arrested him. To
prove himself more than a match for the greatest champions
that represented the enemy's side in his own internal
conflicts, was to gain attestation to the reality of his
victories over the temptations which had darkened his own
spirit. He thus kept himself in heart, and fortified his own
faith and confidence in that which for him was the one
point in question; he secured his hold on the one premiss,
on which, in his view, the whole argument on behalf of the
Christian faith hinged. Nor did it distress him, or ruffle
his pleasant and almost cordial relations with his antagonists, that they were defending the citadel of infidelity
from which all moral evil and eternal misery naturally
flowed. He made great use, for the purpose of charitable
hope, of the allowance made by Roman Catholic theologians
for "invincible ignorance," especially in the case of men
whom he regarded as honourable and sincere, though
misguided; and, through his refutation of them, he trusted
that the writings of these leaders of unbelief would prove
greatly helpful to the final victory of divine truth.

An amusing instance is given of the manner in which
he would humorously fall back on the plea of "invincible
ignorance" on behalf of his friends—in the instance now

to be given, not of an unbelieving, but of an Anglican friend.

"I need not say," says Dean Goulburn, in a paper of reminiscences, "that all the walks I had with him became, if they did not start by being, argumentative. Argument was to him what whist is to many—one of his most favourite pastimes. . . . Once, when I had expressed surprise to him that seriously-minded Roman Catholics could, in view of the dogma *Extra Ecclesiam nulla salus*, have any comfort or happiness in thinking of their Protestant friends, he expounded to me the theory of 'invincible ignorance,' as excusing a large amount of heresy, and placing heretics who have erred under its influence within the pale of salvation. 'And I am quite sure, my dear Goulburn,' he added, with the greatest earnestness and emphasis, 'that your ignorance is *most* invincible'" (p. 77).

A direct consequence of the peculiarity in his intellectual character of which I have been speaking was, that his faith in Christianity seemed to derive little or no support or brightness, and his soul no conscious comfort, from the sense of life and reality, from the felt "grace and truth," which evangelical and experimental Christians, who are also close and loving students of Scripture, derive from their Bible readings, and especially from the study of our Lord's life in the Gospels. To not a few Christians the revelation of Jesus Christ contained in the Scriptures is itself the most living and convincing evidence of the truth and reality of the gospel revelation. There is not a trace, not a hint, throughout the two volumes of Ward's Life of any such use or comfort of the Scriptures in his case. His faith in Christ seems to have rested solely on high *à priori* grounds. He held it fast most firmly when he was full of the sense and force of abstract argument. But, if he ceased to feel the argumentative compulsion, his faith suffered, or was tending to suffer, occultation. Anything like the tranquil enjoyment of the sense of the divine reality of the gospel history, as history, as history of transcendent self-evidencing power, as history so full of divine light and power and consolation, that out of its fulness, as from the fulness of the Incarnate Word Himself, believing students feel themselves to be receiving into their souls both truth and grace,—any such enjoyment as this appears to have been a thing unknown to Ward. His religion was nothing if not strenuous; his faith faltered when it ceased to be argumentative and more or less combatant. The views which this volume affords of his peculiarities, and his daily course of life and working, illustrate and confirm the view of his character now given, as will be seen from the extracts which follow, a selection taken from one chapter—that on his " Closing Years."

Tennyson was Ward's next neighbour in the Isle of Wight, where his large landed property was situated, and where, at Weston Manor, he chiefly resided during the later years of his life. His biographer points some of the contrasts between the two men :—

"Tennyson's love of trees, and his love of all Nature, were a part of the intensely sensitive perceptions and concrete mind of the poet, in marked contrast to Ward's imperfect observation of the concrete and love of the abstract and mathematical. . . . Minute beauty did not appeal to him, because he could not perceive it at all. He could not distinguish one tree or flower from another. A bird was an object of vaguest knowledge to him. It was primarily a thing which made a noise and kept him awake. Trees shut out the fresh air, shut out the grand views which he loved, however little he marked their details" (pp. 396, 397).

"His daily routine was precise and methodical. Rising at half-past six, he went to chapel at seven for meditation or mass. The number of his meditation books, and the numerous pencil references in them, show how systematic a work this was with him. He breakfasted at eight in his study, reading at the same time the evening paper of the previous day. He went to chapel again at nine. Then he read and answered his letters—nearly always answering by return of post. Then came the serious work of the day—the philosophical essay on which he was engaged, or the address to the Metaphysical Society, or the theological controversy; or the reading necessary for any of these works. The other fixed items in his programme were a walk and a solitary luncheon in his study at one o'clock, a drive at two, and then another walk. He generally came to the drawing-room for five o'clock tea, and dined with his family at half-past seven. . . .

"After a year spent at the Gregorian University in Rome (in 1878), I arrive in the afternoon, and the message comes that I am to go into his study at 4.30. I appear, as I think, at the appointed time, and, after cordial greetings, he points to the clock and observes that I am whole two minutes late. The talk with me is to last a quarter of an hour. He is using his dumb-bells, which have taken the place of the riding of a former date. He does not pause in his gymnastic exercises, but begins at once a conversation about Rome. The professors at the Collegio Romano are discussed. The length of the course and the nature of the work are elicited with great rapidity. . . .

"The quarter of an hour is passed before the subject has been pursued far; the dumb-bells are put down, and he returns to his study table, on which lie in order five books, each with a marker in it. One of them is Father Kleutgen's work, *La Philosophie Scolastique*; another, a volume of Newman's *Parochial Sermons*; a third, Planché's *Reminiscences*; a fourth, *Barchester Towers*; the fifth, Sardou's comedy, *Les Vieux Garçons*. 'My working powers are getting so uncertain,' he explains, as he takes up Planché's *Reminiscences*, 'that I find I have five different states of head, and I keep a book for each. Kleutgen is for my best hours in the morning, Newman comes next, then Planché, and then Trollope; and, when my head is good for nothing, I read a French play.' . . .

"We meet at a punctual half-past seven dinner. 'When you left me,' he begins, 'I read a great deal of Planché. Some of the anecdotes are delightful.' . . .

"Dinner can scarcely pass without some reference to Oxford and Newman, a subject which ever arouses deep feeling. 'Was there ever anything in the world like Newman's influence on us?' he repeats for the hundredth time. And the scene at Littlemore during the farewell sermon on the 'Parting Friends,' often described before, is told with even fresh pathos. . . .

"After dinner he retires early to his study, and a message, half an hour later, summons me for further conversation. I find him in high good humour, buried in a French play, the third he has read in the course of the day. 'This is a delightful play,' he explains; 'truly French. The height of romance and self-devotion, as long as it can be combined with breaking a large proportion of the Ten Commandments.' . . .

"He points to a large cupboard full of French plays. 'I read these things so fast now,' he explains, 'that I sometimes get through six in an evening—being fit for nothing better;—that is, I read as much as I want to, and master the plot. I therefore wrote to Stewart to send me every French play that has ever been written. I am leaving them to you in my will.'

"The rest of the conversation is on things dramatic. The autumn opera season, and the prospect of Mr. and Mrs. Bancroft moving from the Prince of Wales' Theatre to the Haymarket especially interest him" (pp. 382–387).

The foregoing extracts, nearly all taken from an account which occupies several pages of the son's intercourse with the father, during one day, furnish a lively picture of some of Ward's peculiarities, and especially his mania for the sensational drama, and, in particular, for French plays, notwithstanding their impiety and nastiness. His son, however, informs us that he did not inherit the legacy of French plays which his father had led him to expect. The vast collection was kept till within a year of Ward's death, when he resolved to burn them. To complete the view of Ward's character, I must add some other extracts:—

"No picture of Mr. Ward at this time would give him 'in his habit as he lived' without reference to two phases of his thought and conversation which were at opposite poles—the one his deep sense of the melancholy aspect of life, the other the relief he found in talking elaborate and fantastic nonsense. His sense of the amount of unhappiness in the world was constant; and, although his faith and religious habits became, he said, more and more supporting as life went on, he never got rid of the habitual trial to which he was subject from the thought of the more terrible side of religion, and the difficulties which beset 'the probation of many of our fellow-creatures.' . . .

"The strain of an overwrought mind would bring a reaction, and he used sometimes to take refuge in talking utter nonsense for an hour at a time. It was often brought forth, however, with the deepest mock seriousness. Nonsense was talked with such intense gravity and such elaborate logical sequence, that a stranger would think he must have missed the drift of his words."

The biographer proceeds to give examples of his father's nonsense—the most laboured, cold-blooded, and extraordinary nonsense ever heard, I suppose, from the lips of a sane philosopher, or, indeed, a sober sensible man of any kind. One trick of wearisome absurdity centred round the name of a Mrs. Bright, of Trentham, and was, with minor variations, repeated again and again. He had been to Stoke to see his daughter at the Dominican Convent, and in reference to this journey he engaged in some interesting discussions with Father Dalgairns as to the monastic system. Diverging, in grave continuity of observation, from this subject, he went on to say that "the most remarkable thing about the village of Trentham is that it is *not* the birthplace of Jeremy Bentham." The company protested against such nonsense; but he proceeded: "You don't believe me. I assure you it is so. I made inquiries and there is no doubt whatever about it." Further protests were useless; and he went on with his unaccountable fooling, which was as devoid of humour or amusingness as of reasonableness or any sort of meaning. "I found out more than this," he continued, and went on to say that "a dear old landlady, a Mrs. Bright," with whom he was staying at a pretty old-fashioned inn, and who was some eighty years old, and knew all the local history, had told him that her inn had originally been a private house; and there seemed to him to be no doubt that that was the identical house in which Bentham was *not* born; adding that he believed his room was the very room, though that point was uncertain, as it rested only on a "vague tradition." And so for half an hour he held on his way. This particular joke frequently came up again, suddenly reappearing in a new form. After nearly a year's interval, however, during which his family had heard nothing of it, and had begun to hope they would never hear it again, he asked one day, "Where do you think I went last week?" His son looked up, expecting to hear of some new opera. But the answer came, "To see our old friend, Mrs. Bright." His son had forgotten the name, and what belonged to it. "Don't you remember?" said Ward. "At Trentham." Vainly his family tried to burke the story. Ward went on with his nonsense. "Yes, but you don't know what a curious visit it was. By a most singular coincidence I was there on the 26th of July. Now the 26th of July is the anniversary of the very day on which Jeremy Bentham was not born." After further vain remonstrance, he proceeded with a touch of sad seriousness: "The world does not forget as easily as one is apt to think. Jeremy Bentham was a great man. You have no idea of the number of people, and the *kind* of people, who didn't come in honour of the occasion. The Prince of Wales, the Archbishop of York, the Bishop of London, the Dean of Westminster, and a considerable number of minor clergy

—I daresay upwards of a hundred—didn't come. It was very remarkable."

It is hard to know what to make of this elaborate and empty nonsense-making, which cannot be construed into satire, and has in it no real touch of fun or humour, although its continuous solemnity of unaccountable absurdity did at length, in some cases, provoke laughter from strangers. To his family such exhibitions were a painful annoyance, and they would not laugh, that they might not encourage him in his eccentric habit. The habit, however, seems in later life to have become a characteristic of his free family intercourse; it is a feature which his filial biographer thought it necessary to describe at length, and it cannot properly be omitted in a picture of him as he lived. That he indulged in such fooling when he visited, as he not seldom did, his great neighbour and familiar friend Tennyson, would seem to be impossible.

Mr. Wilfrid Ward, as we have seen, explains this peculiarity as a reaction from the strain of an overwrought mind, and after giving nearly two pages to an account of it, he recurs very soon to the same subject of his pessimism and his melancholy, in connection with some reminiscences furnished by Father Haythornthwaite, Ward's chaplain. The chaplain relates, that after a dinner-party, at which Ward had been the life of the company, he would be found in his study in a state of brooding melancholy, or even in tears. "Pessimistic views and the remembrance of death coloured all his thought. 'I don't think,' he said, 'the thought of death is absent from my mind for five minutes in the day.' Truly," continues Father Haythornthwaite, "the saving uses of Christianity were never so apparent as they were in his case. The sense of God's presence in which he lived, and the graveness of his under-life, made all life a serious and a deeply interesting business."

Surely this life, so revealed to us, in all its phases and with contrasts so violent, is a unique mystery. Reading the last passages quoted, we feel them to jar strangely as we think of the French plays, and of other matters in this biography. For many years Ward was accustomed, during some portion of the year, to exchange his Isle of Wight home at Freshwater for Hampstead. Of all the advantages and delights of Hampstead—beyond its salubrity, beyond the society placed within his reach of such men as his friend, R. H. Hutton, beyond everything else—"above all," he rated this one advantage, that he "could go every night to the play or opera." This, however, he regarded as necessary to his health. To his sons he wrote, in 1879, "the Haymarket is the region whence salvation cometh. Hampstead is only the *sine quâ non*. Long live Captain Armit, of whom, however, you have probably never heard." In a footnote his son explains that Captain Armit was "one of the *dramatis personæ* of some play."

An amusing story told by his son in his account of the familiar intercourse between Ward and Father F. W. Faber, the poet (known also as Dr. Faber, as he received the diploma of Doctor in Philosophy from Pio Nono at the same time as Ward), illustrates rather vividly the peculiarities of Ward on the side to which I have been referring. The anecdote relates to the period when, having lately left St. Edmund's College, he was often at the Oratory in London, in the company of his spiritual director, Father Faber, and the other Fathers of the Oratory. It was in 1858 or thereabouts. A discussion was in full course between Ward and Faber on Grace and Predestination, Faber taking the Thomist view, Ward supporting the less rigorous opinion of Alfonso Liguori. " Definitions, citations from the great scholastics, are quoted with the exact memory and knowledge of men whose lives are absorbed in the study of such authorities." Ward, in particular, is in a white heat, swaying to and fro as he argues with intense earnestness. In the violence of his bodily movements, a pamphlet falls from his pocket. One of the Fathers present picks it up, and, mechanically opening it, instead of the title *De Actibus Humanis*, or some such title, is startled to read, " Benefit of Mr. Buckstone. The celebrated comedian will appear in his original character of Box, in ' Box and Cox,' " and so forth. The argument goes on, but the audience becomes distracted. The playbill, after having circulated, finds its way back to its owner. Ward drops the discussion and joins in the laughter. *Risu tabulæ solvuntur.*"

Faber, whose saintliness no one will dispute who is familiar with his life and writings, especially his hymns, was Ward's " Spiritual Director " for a good many years about this time. He was sympathetic and indulgent in his treatment of Ward. Nothing can be more unlike the " sobriety " of the Anglican Church as characterised by Keble, than the ecstasies and spiritual excitement of the Roman Catholic Church. Faber and Ward, we are told, " seldom meet without some electric shock occurring in the course of conversation." " Shall I go into retreat ? " Ward asked one day, when he felt that the absorbing interest of his intellectual work needed some counteracting spiritual influence. " A retreat ! " exclaimed Faber. " It would be enough to send you to hell. Go to the play as often as you can, but don't dream of a retreat." So it was. Ward was always at an intense strain, but could not endure any considerable interval of religious solitude and meditation. He gave two or three brief spaces in a day to a sort of ordered, half-mechanical, half-active meditative exercise on religion; but natural, unrestrained, peaceful, and happy spiritual converse with God and divine things was no part of his religious life. When strenuous religious work, by way of argument or of high and intense text-book meditation, of mass, or other ritual, or of prescribed activities of teaching or of charitable works, did not occupy him, he had no peace, and his escape from collapse or pessimistic misery was found in the theatre, or in fiction, especially French plays.

Of literary culture, of the enjoyment of general reading, Ward seems to have known very little. He "dearly loved a parson," we are told, and liked much to have a "rector" next to him at dinner. Perhaps, on that account, he seems to have appreciated Trollope's novels. But *Barchester Towers* and "Trollope" are the only words in the volume that remind us of general literature. Walter Scott is never referred to. For poetry, Ward professed as complete distaste as for history. Tennyson was his next neighbour in the Isle of Wight, and was his friend, but Ward seems never to have read the poet. *In Memoriam* he declared himself unable to understand. Throughout all his writings we catch not the most distant or general allusion to the "world of letters"—to general literature, or to any favourite authors belonging to that world. The region of abstractions—the world of abstract thought—was his home. If he left it, it was for the strangely contrasted world of comic, sensational, or musical dramatic entertainments. Such was the man; and his character and life afford a unique study; he was altogether *sui generis* —a specimen apart. Yet he was a profound reasoner; he has rendered signal service to his generation; he was the friend of R. H. Hutton; the friendly correspondent, as well as redoubtable antagonist, of Mill; the champion of Theism, free will, and the spiritual world; the intimate friend of the saintly Faber; and the valued co-worker of three great Catholic Signori—Wiseman, Manning, and Vaughan.

The way in which, notwithstanding his singularities and his disadvantages as "a convert and a married man," he surmounted prejudice and opposition at St. Edmund's College, where he was first Professor of Philosophy, and afterwards Teacher of Theology, is exceedingly remarkable. From his intense earnestness, and from his spirit and special aims as a teacher, evangelical professors and teachers may have something to learn. Father Lescher, of Notting Hill, who was one of his pupils, describes his lecturing in some striking paragraphs, part of which I must quote:—

"What chiefly gained our hearts was his wonderful earnestness. He carried us away with him, and often we came out of his lecture as if we had been to a retreat sermon. . . . His great love of the poor also, and his extreme desire that we should carry to them the real substantial food of the gospel, of doctrinal truth, won the love of all of us. He got quite moved to tears, whilst, with uplifted face to heaven, he dwelt on their unfair position; the beautiful truths of the Church often unknown to them, and nothing to gratify their propensions but sin.

"Coming from his lectures was like coming from the lectures of St. Thomas, whose heart burned with what he taught. I shall never forget the way in which he brought before us strongly the presence of God amongst us, and the ingratitude of forgetting One who, though our greatest benefactor, stood like a forgotten friend in a corner of the room. It was like an electric shock" . . . (pp. 36, 37).

I must add a few sentences taken from his final address to his students when he resigned his professorship and left St. Edmund's College, where, as a married layman and a convert from Protestantism, his position had never been quite easy and congenial, although he was throughout sustained by the warm support of Cardinal Wiseman and of Father (now Cardinal) Vaughan.

"For what purpose," he asked, "has God revealed those great truths which we contemplate in theological studies, whether those which concern Himself directly, or those which relate to His operations in the souls of men? For what purpose, except that we may spiritually grow on such truths—that we might be more and more conformed to the likeness of that God, of that crucified Saviour, whom theology places before us? . . . May God ever protect you from an increased zeal for intellectual activity, which shall not be accompanied, in at least a corresponding degree, by an increased love of the interior life, by an increased yearning for those only true joys which the Holy Ghost reserves for those who abandon to Him their whole hearts! May God ever protect you from seeking any part of your rest and peace in the empty, delusive, and most unspiritual pleasures of mere intellectual excitement. . . . Who am I, and of what kind is my daily life, that I should dare so to speak? . . . Willingly, willingly would I have been silent, but that I have been stung with the remembrance of those great principles which I have just been stating. Had I succeeded in obtaining your deep interest in a purely intellectual view of that great science committed to my charge, I should have been your worst enemy. I should have been preparing the way for the greatest calamity, which under ordinary circumstances can hereafter befall you—I mean the habit of *effusio ad externa*, of being carried away by the excitement of present work from the heart's deep and tranquil anchorage in God" (pp. 54, 55).

On Ward's retirement from St. Edmund's College (in 1858), he began to visit London more frequently than he had done, and he renewed a number of old friendships. He was, as we have noted, much at the Oratory, and in the company of Father Faber. It was at this period also that he resorted, for the sake of his health, to that form and method of riding exercise which Dean Goulburn has so amusingly described in an account from which paragraphs have appeared in journals of all sorts. Nothing can be more grotesque or ludicrous than the picture given of his six horses, each hired to trot under him ten minutes at a time, and each of which was well tired with the work, so heavy and so unwieldy was the passive body that bumped upon the saddle during the successive periods, till the full hour of exercise was accomplished in the riding school, to which place a theological work was latterly brought him to read "between the acts," while he rested and the horses were changed.

But his mental energies could not be satisfied merely by society and devotional duties, intermingled with doctrinal discussions. "Coming fresh upon the world from the absolute seclusion in which he had lived for fourteen years, Mr. Ward was at once struck with what Mr. Mill has called the 'mongrel morality' of the later nineteenth century, with its intellectual confusion," and with "the growth of the secularist spirit." Looking at the disturbed scene from the point of view of an Ultramontane Catholic, he naturally cast his eyes across the Channel to where France and Germany, but France especially, had for many years been passing through the earlier stages of what is spoken of as the "Catholic Revival," a revival which was, in fact, one of two contrary, but mutually connected, movements generated as a consequence of the French Revolution, the other being the democratic advance throughout Europe which dated from that terrible upheaval, while the "Revival" was the reactionary and complementary movement. In a long and instructive chapter Mr. Wilfrid Ward describes the views and influence, in succession, of Chateaubriand, de Maitre, de Bonald, "the founder of Traditionalism"; de Lamennais, who aimed at fusing and developing Ultramontanism and Traditionalism, but ended by bending his efforts to transform Ultramontanism into a democratic movement; of Montalembert and Lacordaire, who, following Lamennais, brought in the first stage of the "Liberal Catholic movement"; of Veuillot and the *Univers*, which became the organ of the Neo-Ultramontanes; of Abbé Gaume and his extravagances; of Dupanloup and Ozanam. He describes also the "Catholic Revival" in Germany, bringing into view Stolberg and Schlegel, Overbeck and the Romantic School, Möhler and his Symbolism, the Prussian Government and the Archbishops. He mentions as a feature common to the French and the German "Revivals," that they "both invoked Catholic tradition against a destructive philosophy." He thus prepares the way for explaining Ward's relations to Liberal Catholicism in

England; his opposition to the *Rambler*, a Roman Catholic journal (called afterwards the *Home and Foreign Review*), because of its "liberal" laxity of tone and doctrine; his private controversy and his strained relations, during not a few years, with Newman, who for a short time edited the *Rambler*; his connexion with the *Dublin Review*, of which he became eventually the editor, and in connexion with which he did the great work of his life by contributing to it a number of masterly articles in opposition to the materialism of Mill and in defence of theistic philosophy. A considerable part of the volume is occupied with the matters I have thus slightly indicated, and, as connected with them, is concerned with Ward's extreme Ultramontanism on the subject of the Syllabus of Pius IX. and the Infallibility decree of the Papal Council of 1870, in contradistinction from the somewhat less unreasonable Ultramontanism of Newman.

Ward was at the height of his Ultramontane zeal and partisanship, when, in 1869, or soon afterwards, he joined the Metaphysical Society. The two chapters on this society, and on the Agnostic Controversy, are, as I have intimated, of special interest; as also is the "Epilogue," in which, as between his father's extreme Ultramontanism and what may, perhaps, be described as Cardinal Newman's liberal Ultramontanism, Mr. Wilfrid Ward sums up, as it seems, rather in favour of Newman than his father, though he pronounces no judgment on the controversy as a whole. There are, besides, three valuable appendices, one of which contains a number of letters from Newman to Ward; while "two psychological studies" of Ward, one by Baron F. von Hügel, and the other, by Mr. Hutton of the *Spectator*, are very interesting contributions towards the comprehension of one of the most original characters which this century has produced.

Original, Ward certainly was; his eccentricities verged, at some points, on repulsiveness. We learnt from the first volume of his biography that he refused to recognise patriotism as in any sense a virtue. This, however, though a singular and undesirable opinion, is intelligible, and might be taken as a sign of cosmopolitanism, or even as a form— though Cardinal Manning would not have allowed this—of Papal Catholicism. But he also denied, as we are informed in the same volume, that there was any special or necessary duty of love to parents, as such.[1] From this second volume we learn that he manifested no natural affection to his children as infants, and all but ignored their existence till they were old enough to be intelligent companions. Nevertheless, as they grew up, he showed himself a good father, and treated them with frank confidence and steady generosity. In all our judgments of him it must be remembered that he knew nothing in his tender years of any tender nurture or wise training; that his strong religious sensibilities received no welcome or guidance from a well-instructed or devoutly-disposed parent; and that at Winchester School the barbarities and the immoralities which prevailed darkened and depressed his mind and heart. His noble powers at no time received any recognition, much less any guidance and culture, except a chance recognition from a dignitary of the English Church, whose name is unknown, who sometimes met Ward at his uncle's. Ward was brought up, from his very babyhood, on a diet of perpetual playgoing; while, at the same time, his shyness and awkwardness made him avoid society, no one about him having skill or sym-

[1] *Ward and the Oxford Movement*, p. 124.

pathy enough to draw forth his really bright faculties for society, or his companionable qualities, which, though latent, were strong. Thus he grew up the eccentric, angular being so vividly described in his biography; full of contradictoriness and wilfulness, though at heart also full of fun, frankness, and generosity. Thus he grew up the shy, seclusive, absent-minded, inadvertent man, with no eye for material phenomena, for anything visible on the surface of life, with a dislike of all details, strangely ignorant of common things, disliking all records of facts, even the facts of history, and only happy in the inner world of abstract thought, where his powers found a free and undisturbed sphere—revelling in mathematics, in metaphysics, in abstruse argumentative discussions, but otherwise finding no pleasure, no congenial occupation,—except in music, for which he had a passion, in fiction, burlesque, or spectacular plays,—*i.e.* always in an emotional world of excitement,—never in the actual play and commerce of life. Such a man came across Mill, and but for his deep and awful sense of God's reality, and the reality and life of the soul as related to God, would probably have yielded himself to that master of discussion; then he found his guide and oracle in Newman during a critical period of his life, and was at least weaned from Mill, and brought into deep and earnest religious relations with God and Christianity; then, following what seemed to be the laws of abstract logic, divorced from history and actual life, he threw himself passionately into the arms of the Roman Catholic Church, and became the most ultra of the Ultramontanes. Throughout life Ward was the same restless, strenuous spirit as when, in his boyhood, he equally refused all customary recreation and all quiet. Rest he could not;

he must be always vehemently engaged about something. When he had not some good and useful thing to do, he must needs be amused, or else be given over to misery. Thus the passion of his childhood for the theatre remained the passion of his mature life, even to his latest years. But, at anyrate, by his magnificent contributions to Christian philosophy of the highest quality, philosophy the most abstract and abstruse,—but also the most central, sublime, and far-reaching,—W. G. Ward did for the theistic controversy and for the doctrine of humanity, as involving the relations to the Creator of a free spirit, moral, responsible, and immortal, as great a service as any man of his generation.

Nor must we forget how highly Ward was esteemed by Tennyson, and in what terms the poet expressed, in the epitaph which may be read on Ward's monument at Weston Manor, his opinion of the qualities of his neighbour and friend, totally ignorant though that friend was of the poet's writings. The tribute to Ward's generosity contained in the poet's lines is true, albeit Ward was so extreme a Papist. I may not unfitly close this chapter, in which the grievous faults and errors and the singular intellectual deficiencies of Ward have been pointed out, with Tennyson's kindly lines on his friend—

> Farewell, whose living like I shall not find,
>   Whose Faith and Work were bells of full accord,
> My friend, the most unworldly of mankind,
>   Most generous of all Ultramontanes, Ward,
> How subtle at tierce and quart of mind with mind,
>   How loyal in the following of thy Lord!

CHAPTER VII.

END OF THE OXFORD TRACTARIAN MOVEMENT—SOME LESSONS FROM ITS HISTORY.

OUR study of the history of Tractarianism, properly so called, is now finished. The Movement may be said to have begun with Tract No. 1; it culminated in Tract 90. Then came the period of "thunder and eclipse" which ended in the passage over to Rome of Newman and his fiery comrade, Ward. After a season of seeming triumph, but also of painful controversy, the vivid current of Newman's life, which seemed to flow so deep and strong in his middle course at Oxford, subsided into the dead level of the "sleepy hollow" at the Birmingham Oratory. It had been "turned awry" in mid course, and now crept silently towards the final silence. Rome swallowed him up with all his brilliant faculties and ripened powers, and for years before his death he was as if no more, scarcely ever heard of, almost as seldom seen or felt. In this result his revival of the English Church by way of the apostolical succession principle had ended—so far, at least, as he was concerned. His fate remained as a warning to many. Ward, with a bolder, freer step, strode onward to the citadel and centre of Romanism, and there, unlike Newman, enrolled himself as one of the Pope's bodyguard. His logic applied to Newman's ecclesiastical principles and claims, in total disregard of history, or precedent, or experience, led him to the utmost heights of Ultramontanism. All had unfolded from Tract No. 1, and all was the direct result of Newman's teaching, unfalteringly and blindly followed. Ward was destined to furnish in his own career, as a lesson to all who have eyes to see, a *reductio ad absurdum* of Newman's first principle. How a man of such exceptional ability could go forward so blindly, exposing himself unawares to the world, and even to the satire of the most advanced Romanists of the older school, is a problem which it would have been impossible to solve but for the revelations contained in his son's biographical narrative. From that we learn that Newman's defects as to the knowledge of history and the principles of science were immeasurably exaggerated in the ignorance of his stalwart follower; that to all the lessons of knowledge, insight, mental discipline, relating to the successive generations of men, to the ways of Providence in the government of the world, to Nature and the divine teaching of Nature, he was utterly blind and insensible. It was thus that the brilliant metaphysician was able to maintain himself in an obstinate and immovable Ultramontanism. The lessons of Ward's life complete the lessons taught by the life of Newman, and from both the lives together we learn to what apathetic helplessness the embrace of Popish principles brings the sensitive, subtle, questioning intelligence, such as was Newman's, and to what blind and servile allegiance and obedience it brings the Polyphemus-like votary, such as Ward, who in the world of religious thought has no eye except for a set of abstract statements, accepted on merely traditional and often spuriously traditional authority. Following the *ignis fatuus* of "apostolical succession" Newman was forced reluctantly to Rome, and in the end was led into a swamp. Ward followed his one-eyed logic boldly to Rome, and found that for him Romanism meant Ultramontanism. The history of Oxford Tractarianism would not be complete without both lessons, both histories. We shall pass now from the region of abstract argument and ecclesiastical principles to that of theological teaching and practice as taught at another level of thought and feeling by Newman's friend Pusey. From Tractarianism we advance to Puseyism, and so enter on a new field of study. The same underlying ecclesiastical postulates are assumed, but now on the basis of blind theory is built up within the Church of England a system of legal bondage and morbid, ascetic superstition.

CHAPTER VIII.

THE TRANSITION FROM TRACTARIANISM TO PUSEYISM—
THE GOAL OF PUSEYISM.

IN the foregoing chapters we have seen the beginning and end of the *Tractarian* Movement, as such. The first tract, Newman's original manifesto and appeal, went on the ground of episcopal orders and an uninterrupted ministerial succession. This ground was spoken of, in brief, as the principle of apostolical succession. Evangelical Nonconformists hold, and, if the laity are counted, as they ought to be, a majority of well-educated Churchmen have always held, with John Wesley, that the "uninterrupted succession" is "a fable." With modern High Churchmen, on the contrary, it is an article of faith, to be received, on divine authority, like any other divine mystery, as unquestionably true. Being thus accepted, it leads earnest and resolute logicians, unyielding and intrepid doctrinaires of the High Catholic school, direct to Rome. This principle is the basis and bond of hierarchical externalism and exclusiveness. At first the ultra High Church neophyte welcomes the idea of a threefold Catholic Church, one in three branches, the Greek Catholic, the Roman Catholic, and the Anglo-Catholic, the third being the most enlightened, the purest, and the most truly primitive. But, unfortunately, the English Church has cut itself off from, and has been excommunicated by, the Romish Church, and is held to be schismatic by the Greek or Eastern Church, while Anglo-Catholic Churchmen dare not pretend to unchurch either the Roman Catholic or the Greek Catholic Church. Thorough doctrinaires, accordingly, like Newman, Ward, Robert Wilberforce, Faber, Oakeley, Hope-Scott, and many more, following out their principle to its thorough-going logical conclusion, went over to Rome. If others, who sympathised with Newman, did not follow him to Rome, the reason could only be that they practically abandoned the ground that Christian life and salvation absolutely depended upon the legitimate succession of bishops and of duly ordained priests.[1]

Some there were, indeed, apparently incapable of feeling the force of the logical arguments which appealed so strongly to the consistency and sincerity of men like Newman and Robert Wilberforce. Of this number were Keble and Pusey. Of Pusey as yet little has been said. His line of thought and feeling was different from Newman's; he worked on another level. Pusey proceeded, indeed, on the same postulate of "Catholic" ministerial character and authority, as descending exclusively through the line of "apostolical succession"; but he simply assumed that the English and the Romish Church in common possessed this apostolical succession and concomitant transmitted authority, and set himself to study the conditions under which the ministerial prerogative in the Anglo-Catholic Church must be exercised, so as to make that Church, to all who join its communion, the unfailing channel of grace and salvation, desiring and expecting that some day Canterbury might be reunited to Rome, the archbishops

[1] See Note at the end of the chapter on William Palmer.

be brought under the primacy of the Pope. What was necessary was to show a way of salvation which, while it did not provide for the conveyance of saving grace to any but "Catholic" communicants, should open forth to every such sincere communicant a sure and safe channel of salvation, alike in the English and in the Roman communion. He believed himself to have found what was necessary in the doctrine of sacramental grace, by means of baptism and the Eucharist, duly administered by duly ordained priests; and especially in the correlated doctrine of the efficacy of the "sacrament," as he described it, " of confession and absolution"; with which, as a part of the complete sacramental view, he combined a dogma of the Real Presence, scarcely to be distinguished, if at all, from the doctrine of transubstantiation, as taught by some of the most subtle and famous among Romish theologians. In this way Pusey, working ever in harmony with Newman's principles, though he did not follow Newman to Rome, provided a foundation within the pale of the Established Church of England, on which all the essential doctrines of Rome—all those against which the Reformers had protested—might be built up. Auricular confession, priestly prerogative and influence, not only in the pulpit, but in the most secret recesses of family life, and especially over the souls, individually and apart, of women and children, sacramental penance and absolution, the confessional priest in schools, sisterhoods under priestly direction and with life-vows, all these elements of Romanism Pusey made it his business to introduce into the Church and into society, and lived to see them take deep root, and spread far and wide. All this was hardly included in the idea of Tractarianism as first initiated by Newman. But Pusey, working ever silently and with much secrecy and subtlety, had begun his work, and sown much seed carefully and deeply, before Newman passed out of view, and the Tractarian Movement proper came to an end. After Newman's secession, he was recognised as the head of the resulting Movement, still largely an "Oxford Movement," which grew out of the Tractarian Movement, and which has gone so far during the last generation in Romanising the Church of England. He has thus prepared many Anglican priests and some lay devotees, including a few men of education, such as Lord Halifax, to welcome and work for such an identity of doctrine, ritual, and practice with the Church of Rome as may prepare the way for attaining what is now confessed to be the goal of their efforts, an extensive reunion of English clergy and Churchmen with the Roman See and the Latin Catholic Church. The remainder of this volume, accordingly, will be occupied chiefly with the life and lifework of Pusey.

NOTE TO PAGE 200.

The Case of William Palmer.

Of the difficulties and confusions involved in the principle of lineal priestly succession, taught as the test and credential of the true Church, a very remarkable illustration is found in the history of William Palmer, the elder brother of the late Earl of Selborne. This history is given in detail by Lord Selborne himself in his Memorials. Led astray by the delusions and chimeras of so-called Catholic externalism, William Palmer, a brilliant Oxford scholar, the eldest son and for some years the hope and pride of his father, an exemplary country clergyman, spent much of his life in fruitless, and indeed ridiculous, efforts to obtain the recognition in his own person, alike by the Greek and the Roman Churches, of his right as an Anglican Churchman to Catholic communion beyond the limits of his own

Church, without any separation from that Church. In the Church of England he took orders as a deacon, but he never got any further. He knocked at the door of the Greek Church for admission. Disappointed there, he turned to Rome, and after years had passed became a communicant of that Church. He was never ordained "priest." He had spent more than twenty years in seeking for the magnetic pole where his spirit might rest, before—reluctantly and with reservations —he at length yielded to the commanding authority of Rome. In a paper drawn up in 1855 for the benefit of his family and friends, he explained the process by which he was at length led to such a result. Seven years, from 1832 to 1840, he spent, to use his own words, in "cultivating or filling up and correcting his inherited Anglican traditions," with the result that he found himself in agreement with the Greek Church at all points except as to the Procession of the Holy Ghost. After seven more years he came to agree with the Eastern Church in this point also, and to confess that his own Anglican Church had fallen into grave errors. For eight years more, down to 1855, the date of his explanatory document, he remained in the same position, and yet all the time his heart was being drawn more and more towards the Roman communion, and all the more because the Greek Church did not admit the validity of his Anglican baptism. Under these circumstances, at last, in 1855, after twenty-three years of research and vacillation, he finally concluded to join the Church of Rome. He has need, he says, of the sacrament, of a valid absolution and communion; of these he is deprived so long as he halts between the East and the great Western Church. He finds himself, to use his own words, "passing judgment on all visible Churches, and having no certain ground on which to stand himself. Meantime," he adds, "death is approaching, and to die without the sacraments is dangerous." In 1855, therefore, he determined "immediately to submit himself to the Roman Pontiff, as to the chief doctor and ruler of the Apostolic Church," even though the form of submission might "contain some things inconsistent with his own private judgment, not only in certain particular doctrines, *but even respecting the definition of the Church*, on which they depend." Thus he submits, as it were, to the *force majeure* of the Roman Church. He never sought orders in that Church, but lived a student's life, between Rome and England, being recognised by the learned world as an exceptionally erudite scholar and antiquarian, whose books of research are valued highly by scholars, and being the intimate friend of Newman as long as he lived. This great "failure" was, for his learning, sought out at Rome by scholars of all Christian Churches, especially of the Greek Church, in which he had many friends. Two of his special subjects were *Egyptology* and *Early Christian Symbolism*. His whole career may well be regarded as a *reductio ad absurdum* of the select principle of successional externalism on which, as their unique foundation, High Anglicans build everything for time and eternity, with a frankness of rash confidence such as outdoes the precedents of Romish defensive logic and argument.

CHAPTER IX.

Two Great Contradictory Parties in the Anglican Communion—For the Present Condition of Schism Pusey more responsible than any other Man—Pusey's Family and Early Life—School and College — Byron and Scott — Foreign Tour — Fellow of Oriel — Visits Germany as Theological Student — Defends German Theology against Rose — Change in his Views — Joins Newman—The Tract Party—Writes Tract on Baptism—Becomes a Power in Oxford—Wealth and Generosity.

ARCHDEACON SINCLAIR, in an address delivered at the Church Congress of 1893, on the subject of the English Church Union, drew attention to an authoritative publication put forth by that Union, which, to quote the Archdeacon's words, " pointed out with great frankness the mistakes of the Reformers in our present Prayer-Book, proposed the omission of the Ten Commandments, advocated mediæval additions to the Church office to bring it into line with Sarum, pronounced fasting reception to be necessary, urged the practice of reservation, proposed the introduction of the Romish service of Benediction, wished to alter our cathedral services so that there should be Mass every morning, longed that everybody should recognise that our chief religious duty was the oblation of the Lamb of God, insisted on the restoration of the word *Mass*, and deplored the disastrous effects of the Reformation." If to this authentic enumeration we add, as among the objects aimed at, the establishment of sisterhoods and monasteries, and the restoration of the confessional, with all that it implies, we have a fairly representative but by no means complete account of the retrograde movement towards the mediæval practices of the Church of Rome, which has seemed lately to be in the ascendant, within the limits of the Reformed Church of England. Words fail to describe the fatal meaning and tendency of this movement. A passage, however, from the *Guardian* for October 1893 may fitly be placed by the side of what has been quoted. The *Guardian* knows its market and weighs its words; it represents the highest faculty and best informed judgment of the High Anglican party. The following is the passage. It occurs in an article on the subject of "Reunion," as brought before the Church Congress of that year:—

"No doubt, according to a pregnant sentence of the Archbishop of Dublin, there is more difference between High Churchmen and Low Churchmen within the Church of England than there is between High Churchmen and Roman Catholics on the one side and Low Churchmen and Dissenters on the other. But then this is the result of an ecclesiastical accident. The combination in one and the same Church of opinions so widely divergent can be explained historically, but not logically. It is hardly conceivable that it could have existed, if the Church had not been established, or that it should continue to exist if the Church ceased to be established. Any religious and intelligent Dissenter, who was invited to come into the Church, would naturally, we think, ask into which Church of England am I to come? Is it the Church of Lord Halifax, or the Church of Sir Robert Leighton?"

This passage teaches, in terms of unmistakable plainness, that the difference is altogether less between High Anglicanism and the Church of Rome than between High Anglicanism and the Evangelical and Protestant portion of the Established Church; and that, but for the coercion of the State bond, there would, of necessity, be a complete organic separation of the one party from the other—the High Anglican section being the true Church of England, and Evangelical Episcopalians no part whatever of that Church. It teaches that the true Church of England is as narrow, as exclusive, as ritualistic as "the Church of Lord Halifax," which is no other than the Church of the "Church Union," Lord Halifax being the official head and the presiding spirit of the Union. This Romanising sect, according to the *Guardian*, is the true national Church of England. The claim is a grotesque absurdity. But the deliberate utterance of such a judgment by the *Guardian* is a very dark sign of the times. It shows that in the opinion of that journal there is no need any longer to keep on terms with the evangelical section of the Established Church. In anticipation of the day of disestablishment, that journal distinctly and deliberately looks forward to the division of the existing Established Church into at least two sections, of which that alone is to be accounted as representing, and indeed as being, the true Church of England, which is in close affinity and sympathy with the Church of Rome, and which severs itself completely from the Evangelical and Protestant portion of what has hitherto been deemed the Church of England, and from the convictions and sympathies of the great majority of Englishmen.

It seems not improbable, indeed, as has been intimated on an earlier page, that there will be, in the event of disestablishment, not two, but three distinct sections—a Romanising, an "evangelical," and a Broad Church section. Such is the prospect which faces us. How far the Romanising Neo-Anglican section, the Church of the Church Union, would be likely to go when freed from the State bond and organised into a separate sect, must remain a question. But, judging from what we know of the zeal and extravagance of the high sacramental sections of our Colonial Churches in South Africa and Australia, even in the midst of what in England would be regarded as middle-class social conditions and democratic institutions; judging also from the recent developments of ritualistic superstition and bigotry in the United States, and from the increased and strengthened tendency of even the Anglo-Irish Episcopal Church towards Ritualism and High Sacramentarianism, since Disestablishment took place, it might fairly be doubted whether in the England of Laud and of Pusey the adherents of the "Church of Lord Halifax" would shrink from any ritualistic and Romanising extreme short of acknowledging the Papal politico-ecclesiastical claims, if even they would refuse to acknowledge those claims.

The greatest force in bringing about the present lamentable condition of things was unquestionably the teaching and influence of Pusey. He more widely, more diligently, and with more of personal influence than any other man, sowed the seeds of the harvest which our country is now reaping. Keble, Newman, and Pusey, these are the three men whose names must always be associated as the founders of the Romanising Movement in the Church of England of the last two generations. Keble, however, alone would only have handed down to a few the tradition which had come down to him from the Divine Right Nonjurors of the last century. There was no motive energy, no propagandist force in him. Newman was the man of magnetic influence, the man of intellectual superiority and force. It was he who laid the ferment and supplied the ideas which were to start, to inform, and for ten years to inspire and guide the whole Movement. But, after his secession to Rome, the Movement must have died a natural death before many years had passed, if it had not been taken up and fostered for nearly forty years by Pusey, who, though not a man of any originality, combined in himself many of the qualities which go to foster ideas, and to build up a school of religious devotion. In some respects, indeed, he had points of special superiority as the leader of a party. Newman and his shortlived but powerful comrade Froude were able, astute, and daring—daring almost to recklessness. But these bachelor fellows, being at first men of no school or set, were also men of no social position, and at the beginning of their work had little personal influence. For a while at least they unsettled and alarmed more powerfully than they attracted or persuaded. What Pusey did for the new Movement is told by Newman himself in his *Apologia*. Newman says: " Without him we should have had no chance of making any serious resistance to the Liberal aggression. He had a vast influence in consequence of his deep religious seriousness, the munificence of his charities, his professorship, his family connexions, and his easy relations with the university authorities." He was able to give " a name, a form, and a personality to what without him was a sort of mob." He lent dignity and prestige to the Tractarian Movement, though he never led in its counsels. To the end he gave his moral support to Newman, though he did not follow him to Rome. After Newman's death he became the prophet and teacher of the Tractarian residue, and extended his influence more and more widely and deeply through the ranks and circles of the ultra High Anglican devotees.

At length, after many years of expectation, we have the advantage of studying Dr. Pusey's biography. Dr. Liddon, Pusey's disciple and intimate friend for many years, had done much in the way of preparation, but he had not altogether finished even the collection of matter for the work, nor had he throughout perfectly moulded his own material into form. The published volumes, however, are sent forth as substantially the work of Dr. Liddon.[1] Notwithstanding its voluminous character, the biography fails to give a complete exposition of Pusey's views, or a complete account of his work and influence. Even Dr. Liddon, it would seem, had not ventured to go thoroughly into the meaning of all Pusey's work, or exactly and fully to expound his doctrine. His life was the life of a saint, but a saint of a morbid and misguided school. His history is capable of being written in its main personal outlines, which are generally interesting and sometimes touching; without undertaking to exhibit fully the inner meaning of his line of development in doctrine and in

[1] When the first edition of this book was published, the last of the four volumes of the biography had not been published. That volume, however, adds nothing to modify the history or the criticism contained in this book.

spiritual counsels. There are also facts connected with his history which may be gathered elsewhere, but which are not necessary for the continuity of the narrative, and the insertion of which might not appear to be advantageous to his memory as a divine of the Reformed Church of England. Yet some of the information omitted may be necessary in order to a just estimate of his work, and to the needful counteraction of the grievous mischief which he wrought, not only within the Church of England, but, more or less, throughout all English-speaking countries.

The name of Pusey did not belong to the ancestors of the future ecclesiastical leader, but to the estate which came to his father as a gift from two sisters bearing the name of Pusey, who were co-heiresses of the Pusey property, and sisters-in-law of the first Lady Folkestone, Pusey's grandmother. His father was the Honourable Philip Bouverie, son of the Earl of Radnor; he took the name of Pusey with the Pusey estates. The Bouverie family were Walloons, who became naturalised English subjects in the latter part of the seventeenth century, and were ennobled in the eighteenth; the family, before it migrated to London, having been for more than one generation settled as part of the Walloon colony at Canterbury. Pusey was therefore descended from Low Country Protestants of the French Reformed Confession, who had been driven from their country on account of their religious faith. He recognised in himself the strain of Walloon breed and temperament. He would sometimes say, with a smile, "You know I am phlegmatic, and indeed Dutch." Canon Liddon intimates that his business instincts and habits might have been in some sort inherited from his commercial line of ancestry. His mother traced her descent to an Anglo-Saxon family which was already ancient in the time of the Plantagenets. She was the daughter of the Earl of Harborough, was married when very young to Sir Thomas Cave, and was left a widow at twenty-one. At the age of twenty-six she married the Honourable Philip Bouverie Pusey. Her father, though an Earl, was also a clergyman, and she undertook the religious education, after a plain, old-fashioned Anglican fashion, of her children. "She used to talk to her son as if she represented a religious temper which had belonged to her race in earlier days. 'All that I know of religious truth,' Pusey used to say, 'I learnt, at least in principle, from my mother.'" She taught her children their Catechism, and read the Scriptures largely with them.

So much, in brief, we gather as to the ancestors of Pusey from a very long genealogical appendix, of which the greater part refers to the Puseys, with whom, whether in respect of blood or of training, the inheritor of their name had nothing more than a legal and incidental connexion. His wealth came mainly from them, but that was all. What strikes one on looking over his pedigree is that diligence, common sense, and business training seem to have been hereditary; but that along the whole line, at least since the days of the De Bouveries of the Burgundian Court in the Middle Ages, there is no glimmer of real distinction either in Church or State, in arms or learning. Pusey House did not contain a library of any value. Pusey belonged, however, to the *noblesse* of England; he called such a nobleman as the Earl of Shaftesbury his cousin; he inherited a large estate.

Edward Bouverie Pusey, the second son of his parents, was born in 1800 at Pusey House, a mansion situated in Berkshire, twelve miles from Oxford, near a hamlet consisting of some dozen cottages, and in the midst of a sandy region timbered mostly with fir trees. Here, through the greater part of his life, was his study and home; his fellowship first, and afterwards his professorship and his canonry, being at Oxford, where the pulpit of Christ Church, sometimes exchanged for St. Mary's, was his place of power. After his elder brother's death, the paternal home seems to have become Dr. Pusey's property. He died, however, at a Cottage Retreat, near Ascot, to which he was accustomed to retire when he sought perfect privacy.[1]

Pusey's first schoolmaster, the Rev. Richard Roberts, of Mitcham, to whose care he was sent at the early age of seven, taught and disciplined him as a classical scholar of 1807 might have been expected to do. He flogged him once for cutting a pencil at both ends; he flogged him out of false quantities; he made him an adept for his age, both in Latin and Greek verse; he prepared him thoroughly for Eton. Pusey used to say in after life that he could have passed the University Little-Go before he went to Eton. He worked more than ten hours a day, though he was only eleven when he left Mitcham. Dr. Keate was his master at Eton. There he continued the same course of application into which he had been introduced at Mitcham. The late Rev. Edward Coleridge, who sat on the same bench with him, wrote of him in 1882 that he "did not engage in sports, did long exercises, and was very obscure in his style." "The child was father of the man"—of the "portentous student" of after days, who knew the rules of Latin and Greek syntax and prosody

[1] *Annual Register*, 1883.

but not the niceties of style and composition in his mother tongue, which he never learned to write elegantly or idiomatically. With English literature he seems never to have gained any considerable acquaintance, and his residence in Germany in early manhood probably did not tend to supply the defects of his earlier education, but rather to aggravate the imperfections of his English scholarship.

There was one respect, however, in which he acquired the accomplishments of an English gentleman whilst still young. He learnt to shoot well, and was a good rider across country. It was a saying of Charles Kingsley—to which I have before had occasion to refer—that all the Tractarian leaders were wanting in virility, *i.e.* not so much effeminate, as naturally more woman-like than masculine. Few who have closely studied the characters of Newman, Keble, Froude, and some others of the foremost Tractarians, will, I think, deny the general truth of the observation. In some respects also it seems to have applied to Pusey; but in the point now noted, at anyrate, perhaps also in some other points, Pusey was more masculine than his chief Tractarian associates. At Eton his religious character, as might be expected, was not developed. His period there, however, coincided in great part with that of Napoleon's greatest victories, with the amazing growth and the culmination of his power and ascendency, and with his overthrow. These critical years of the world's history "contributed to develop that sense of the presence of God in human affairs, as attested by swift and awful judgments, which coloured so largely his religious convictions." Altogether his Eton course appears to have been studious and creditable, but not distinguished. He was no doubt moral, but of special religious character or experience there is little trace. He gained no school honours. On leaving he went to read, at Buckden, near Huntingdon, with a private tutor, Dr. Maltby, afterwards Bishop of Durham. Here, during his stay of fifteen months, he seems to have made good progress in classical studies in preparation for university honours at Oxford. He said in after life that he was "very happy with Maltby; there were no black sheep at Buckden"—an evident reference to the "black sheep" of Eton, with whose character and conduct it is clear that he had no sympathy.

In January 1819, Pusey went to Oxford, and, as an Eton boy, naturally entered Christ Church. Among his friends at Oxford was his cousin, the future Earl of Shaftesbury. Their friendship, however, was checked by Pusey's declining to read for lectures with Lord Ashley. Had this check not occurred, and had the future heads—one as a clergyman, the other as a layman—of the two antagonistic bodies of the modern Church of England grown into public life as intimate friends, the Anglican history of the century might, perhaps, have been materially different from what it has been. Another friend was John Parker of Sweeney Hall, Shrewsbury, afterwards a clergyman. I refer to him because he tried, in vain, to bring his friend to study and master a good and true style of English writing. "It is easy," he warned him, "to write moderate English, but far from easy to write it finely. I am sorry to say that almost the only man who writes English with purity, though he is frequently vulgar, is that infamous William Cobbett." When, in 1828, Pusey sent him a copy of his *Theology in Germany*, Parker replied: "I will carefully read it, and criticise the style, as that is the only part where my opinion would be of use to you." Certainly in that publication there was ample scope for criticism of style. Another intimate friend of Pusey's undergraduate life—a friend also in after years—was R. W. Jelf, afterwards Canon of Christ Church.

Just before going up to the university, Pusey had become deeply attached to the lady to whom he was eventually married, and who must have been as interesting and attractive a woman as she proved herself to be a sympathising and devoted wife. Of her history and family connexions, however, little or nothing is to be learned from the biography, except that she had been baptized by a Dissenter. For some reason, not disclosed, Pusey's father refused his consent to his son's engagement to this lady, to which her own family also seem to have been opposed. Nor was it till after her father's death, in 1827, that the way was cleared for the engagement to be contracted with all proper consents. During the years that elapsed before the obstacles to his engagement were removed a settled cloud rested upon his mind. No other object seems even for a day to have distracted his desire or affection. His disappointment overcast his college life, and at one time threatened to interfere with his university work for the schools. However, after prodigious work during his last year at college,—to the extent sometimes of sixteen or seventeen hours a day, so that he himself described his later undergraduate life at Christ Church as "that of a reading automaton who might by patience be made a human being,"—he finally gained a first class. His strength, however, as we are told,—but should scarcely have needed to be told,—"lay in accurate verbal scholarship rather than in philosophy."

His degree won, he went with a college friend to

Switzerland, spending three months on the tour. Under the influence, at least in part, of his disappointed affections, he indulged, as his Diary shows, in not a little morbid sentiment—in what his biographer describes as " Byronism," as he himself, indeed, called it. This Byronic mooning is not what would have been expected in the case of such a young man as Pusey; it is deliberate and elaborate, as the passages quoted from his Diary show. At the same time these passages evince more than a little susceptibility to the grand and beautiful features of natural scenery, and show also that he took a lively interest in the history, topography, and geology of the regions through which he passed, especially the glorious Savoy scenery between Geneva and Chamounix. Pusey's Byronism did not affect his religious faith or his morals, but it made him indulge, with a sort of self-satisfaction, in gloomy and morbid ideas and feelings. His own account in after years was as follows:—

" The extreme force and beauty of Byron's poetry, combined with a habit of deep, and in some degree, morbid feeling, which had always more or less a shade of gloom, induced us to give our assent to, and even in some measure exult in, feelings of whose full extent we were either at the time not aware, or at least against which we half, and but half, shut our eyes."

This description is not perspicuous, but it is sufficiently intelligible, and it harmonises, in some sort, with his characteristics through life. He seems almost always to have been surrounded, more or less, by an atmosphere of depression, and to have been full of sorrowful foreboding as to the course and aspect of the times, though he was free from religious doubts and intellectually full of self-confidence. He was always, on the other hand, very hopeful and indeed sanguine in regard to the health and well-being of those with whom his heart's affections were bound up.

So self-confident was he, at the early age of which I am writing, when he was but twenty-three years old, that, although philosophy and speculative thought were all through his life uncongenial and foreign regions of thought to him, and therefore he must have been peculiarly incompetent to play the part of "Christian advocate," as a representative champion against speculative unbelief, he nevertheless undertook an argumentative correspondence, which seems to have continued during many months, with a well-read sceptic and atheist of the French school, who had been a friend of his at Eton. The correspondence ended as might have been expected. Pusey was not in the least, so far as appears, disturbed in the solidity of his own Christian faith, nor his correspondent at all influenced by Pusey's arguments. One effect this correspondence had on Pusey which gave a colour to his life, it produced the conviction " that the faith of Christ had, in the very heart of Christendom, implacable enemies just as ready to crush it out of existence, if they could, as any who confronted the apostles of the Church of the first three centuries."

It is amusing to read that—

"As Byron to a certain extent spoiled Pusey's view of the Swiss mountains, so Pusey at first read Walter Scott with Byron's eyes. His brother Philip induced him to read *Rokeby* by telling him that he had a great deal of Wilfrid in his character. 'I read the book,' he said long afterwards, 'most carefully, and found it so: it became from that time my greatest favourite. Maria, of course [the lady he loved], occupied the place of Matilda. My destiny was, I know not how far, identified with Wilfrid's. You may, or rather cannot, conceive the effect of the beautiful "cypress wreath," or the few last words which Wilfrid addresses to Matilda.' The love of study, the love of nature, the pensive melancholy mood, were to a certain extent common to Edward Pusey and Wilfrid."

Dr. Liddon goes on to quote, as more or less applicable to Pusey, some of Scott's lines, including these four—

> No touch of childhood's frolic mood
> Showed the elastic spring of blood:
> Hour after hour he loved to pore
> On Shakespeare's rich and varied lore.

The first three lines seem to apply remarkably well, but as to the fourth there does not appear to be a glimmer of evidence that Pusey was a loving student of Shakespeare.

Pusey returned from his tour in time to be present at the marriage of his elder brother to Lady Emily Herbert, daughter of the Earl of Carnarvon. This happy marriage gave him an accomplished and charming sister-in-law, of a strongly religious character, and, in after life, was one of those family or social connexions which contributed not a little to his influence and authority as a Churchman.

"For more than thirty years, to her husband's delight and satisfaction, Lady Emily corresponded constantly with her brother-in-law. . . . This friendship lasted undimmed to Lady Emily's last hours. He admitted her [after his wife's death] to share his thoughts and hopes and fears in those years when his heart and mind were taxed to the uttermost by the demands of the great Movement in which his share was so great and so responsible; and he found in her a sympathy more intelligent and responsive than that of any other member of his family. In her last hours he was at her bedside, and in his ministrations and words she found her greatest comfort and support."

Lady Emily wrote at least one novel, of which the title is not given, but in which, we are informed, she introduced Edward Pusey into her pages under the name of Edgar Belmore, setting forth his high and strict religious character, as she conceived it, and reproducing a part of his early history.

Returning to Oxford, Pusey applied himself to the work of gaining a settlement there, and took his line for life as a scholar and a divine. His ambition, though sedate, was high and steadfast, an Oriel Fellowship was his mark—Oriel, at that time, being the selectest garden of intellectual and religious culture in the university. The Fellows of Oriel were men of high accomplishments, and especially of disciplined intellect. Without doubt Pusey was intellectually below the Oriel standard. Copleston was Provost. Whately, Keble, Hawkins, Jelf, were Fellows. Davison and Arnold had but lately ceased to be Fellows. Newman was in his year of probation. The college was famous for its pre-eminence in logic. It was coarsely said to "stink of logic." To the end of his days Pusey was singularly defective in logic and logical methods of thought and teaching. He himself confessed that he was quite wanting in the speculative faculty which was the distinction of several of the Oriel Fellows. Most of the Oriel men also were distinguished for the simplicity and purity of their English style, whereas Pusey's style was often rugged and sometimes almost barbarous. Nevertheless he gained his Fellowship.

It is evident enough that his was a favoured suit

for preferment from the very outset. In those times intellectual merit and scholarly attainments counted for less in the competition for Fellowships than they do at present. Character, connexions, and position counted for much more. Even as a classic, whilst his reading, no doubt, had been large, and his grammatical knowledge must have been exact, it is more than doubtful whether he ever attained to the elegancies of style and composition which have distinguished high university scholars both in earlier and later times. He was, however, elected. A description of him is quoted from one of Newman's letters when Pusey was an undergraduate of twenty-two years of age, but already aspiring to an Oriel Fellowship, and when he was a guest of his friend Jelf at Oriel high table—

"His light curly head of hair was damp with the cold water which his headache made necessary for his comfort; he walked fast with a young manner of carrying himself, and stood bowed, looking up from under his eyebrows; his shoulders rounded, and his bachelor's gown not buttoned at the elbow, but hanging loose over his wrists. His countenance was very sweet, and he spoke little."

During the examination for the Fellowship, Pusey had one of his bad headaches, and broke down. He tore up his essay, saying that there was no good in going on with it. Jenkyns, one of the examiners, picked up the bits, put them together, and showed the essay to the Fellows. Newman says that it was a capital essay. Later in the examination, after an hour's unsuccessful effort, he wrote a letter begging to retire from the competition, and left the hall. The Fellows, however, requested the Rev. C. J. Plummer to go over to his lodgings and persuade him to revoke his decision. The result was that Pusey persevered and gained his Fellowship. The porter at the college gate was asked on the last day who would be elected, from which it may be inferred that quick and acute porters sometimes hear a good deal, and know more than many. " What do you think, sir," was the reply, " of that gentleman in the chapel ? " Pusey was alone in the chapel or ante-chapel on that day.

" It must be owned," Dr. Liddon remarks, " that the Society of Oriel did not endow Pusey with its characteristic excellence of clear writing." Pusey quotes and adopts a description of himself at that time from the letter of a friend as " shy," and expressing himself with hesitation and obscurity. " To the end of his life," according to Dr. Liddon (vol. i. p. 144), " Pusey's sermons were marked by a complete indifference to method and rhetorical effect." It is evident that this fault in his writing was the result of simple incapacity. A mind insensible to logical relations in thought is a mind incapable of method in discourse or argument, and destitute of the faculty which must lie at the basis of effective rhetoric. It is easy to understand a judgment upon Pusey which was passed by two young men at the time of his preaching his first sermon in 1828. A relative of Mrs. Pusey's writing about Edward Pusey, as she calls him, says : " He is entirely engrossed with the subject of divinity, and unless upon that point is a silent man ; he listens and makes great observation on character, and always leans to the most amiable side in his judgment ; but he is not by the generality thought agreeable ; Thomas and Reginald think him very stupid."

His Fellowship being gained, and his position in his university assured, Pusey undertook—in 1825—the critical enterprise of visiting Germany, that he might study in its most distinguished universities, and make acquaintance with its greatest scholars. It was a bold step to take, and affords a measure of the scholarly zeal and the thirst for learning which were characteristic of Pusey. The strongest motive, however, which determined his decision was the advice of Dr. Lloyd, at that time Professor of Theology at Oxford, and afterwards Bishop of the Diocese. People were saying—such was Pusey's own account to Liddon in later life—that the new German theology was full of interest. Only two persons in Oxford were understood to know German. One day Dr. Lloyd said to Pusey : " I wish you would learn something about those German critics." In the obedient spirit of those times, Pusey set himself to learn German, and afterwards went to Germany himself. There he made acquaintance with Eichhorn, Tholuck, Schleiermacher, Neander, Freytag, Lücke, Sack, and others ; attended lectures at Göttingen, Berlin, Bonn, and elsewhere ; paid particular attention throughout to Hebrew and Arabic studies ; and finally returned in 1827, after spending the greater part of two years in that country. This visit largely determined the after-course of his life. " My life," he said to Liddon, " turned on that hint of Lloyd's."

Whilst he was studying in Germany the Rev. H. J. Rose published his four discourses, delivered at Cambridge in May 1825, on *The State of Protestantism in Germany*. These sermons created a deep impression in England, and were soon the subject of severe criticism in Germany. Pusey, full of friendly feeling for his German friends and teachers, was displeased at the tone, here and there, of Rose's strictures, and regarded the sermons on the whole as giving an incorrect and injurious impression of the state and prospects of the Protestant religion in Germany. He therefore, with characteristic self-confidence, formed the purpose, whilst still in Germany, of replying to Rose. Mr. Rose at that time was a clergyman of high distinction and great influence, though he was scarcely more than thirty years of age. Pusey was only twenty-six, and not yet a Deacon. He was a young layman who knew little of theology, and who, as to German studies and history, must be regarded as still only a neophyte. But he had no hesitation as to measuring swords with Mr. Rose. At that time " the history, the results, the temper, and the tendencies of German Protestant theology were as little understood in England as though they had belonged to another and a distant continent, far beyond the pale of Christendom and civilisation."

Pusey returned from Germany in 1827, but did not publish his reply to Rose until the following year. In the meantime his friend and patron at Oxford, Dr. Lloyd, had succeeded to the Episcopate. He himself, about the same time, became engaged to the lady to whom for eight years he had been attached, her father having died, and all opposition to the marriage having passed away on the side of his father. This lady having been baptized by a Dissenter, it may be presumed that her family had at one time been members of a Dissenting congregation. She had latterly with her family attended the ministry, at Cheltenham, of Mr. Close, the well-known evangelical clergyman, afterwards Dean Close, of Carlisle. She was full of religious knowledge and religious scruples and questionings. The correspondence between Pusey and herself was most voluminous, and dealt with many bristling points of controversy, religious and ecclesiastical, including also moral and social questions. Eventually she became as High a Churchwoman as any High Churchman could have desired, and became also her husband's helper—largely his amanuensis. She was a devoted wife, and possibly her health was undermined by the strenuous sympathy and co-operation she continually gave to her husband. Her death, in 1839, marks an epoch in the history of her husband's religious development.

In 1828, the year following Pusey's engagement, his father died at the age of eighty-one. Pusey was ordained Deacon, and shortly afterwards married; and what Pusey would probably have thought still more important even than his marriage—John Keble was rejected, Dr. Hawkins was elected, in succession to Copleston, as Provost of Oriel. The Puseyite school, with one consent, appear to have been of opinion that if Keble, who was at one with Newman and Pusey in regard to the whole teaching of the Oxford Tracts, had been chosen, the High Church party would have escaped all the troubles which followed, and which they regard as so disastrous, especially the condemnation of Tract 90, and the consequent secession of Newman. There is, however, another way of reading history which would regard the election of Hawkins instead of Keble as peculiarly providential, and the condemnation of Tract 90 as a beneficial event in the history of the English Church, one altogether necessary to its consistency of character and to its well-being. There can be no doubt that it was Newman's influence which cast the die in favour of Hawkins, and that he so prepared the way for his own official censure. It also cannot be doubted that, for all the ordinary official responsibilities of a Provost, Hawkins was a much fitter man than Keble.

In 1828, Pusey published his reply to Mr. Rose, under the title, *A Historical Enquiry into the Probable Causes of the Rationalist Character lately predominant in the Theology of Germany*; and two years later, under the same general title, he published the second part of the *Enquiry*, containing an explanation of some points misconceived by Mr. Rose, and further illustrations. This second pamphlet was a reply to strictures which Mr. Rose had published in the interval on his former pamphlet. The first of these pamphlets issued from Messrs. Rivington's house before its author had received his appointments as Professor of Hebrew and Canon of Christ Church, and before he had been ordained Priest. The second, which is much the larger of the two, was published when he had been ordained Priest, and had been appointed Professor and Canon, but had ceased to be a Fellow. Throughout these remarkable first-fruits of his theological studies, Pusey wrote as an English divine of the moderate High Church school, whose views had been enlarged and liberalised by intercourse with the best and ablest continental divines, might have been expected to write sixty years ago.[1]

He was, however, in 1830, far from being a Low Churchman, although, as yet, he had not entered within the coils of extreme High Church principles, in which he was so soon afterwards entangled. He refers, without disapproval, to the Lutheran form and practice of confession, as in use in the earlier and better times of Lutheranism. He mentions, in particular, the fact that the saintly Spener was the confessor of the Elector of

---

[1] For a view of the scope and contents of Pusey's *Enquiry*, I may refer, not only to what is said upon the subject in the biography, but to my *Character and Life Work of Dr. Pusey* (pp. 26–35).

Saxony, observing, however, that because of the growing hollowness and formalism of the times, Spener was thankful to retire from his confessorial office. But, at the same time, throughout this *Enquiry* he speaks habitually of "Churches" generally, besides those calling themselves "Catholic"; and of the "German" Church, as well as of the "Roman" and the "English" Church; no exclusive epithet, no employment of the word "Catholic," as is now customary among High Churchmen to distinguish "Apostolic" and "Episcopal" communions from other sects, being found in the *Enquiry* from first to last. He speaks enthusiastically of "the immortal heroes, the mighty agents of the Reformation." Mr. Rose had attributed German heterodoxy largely to three causes—the want of diocesan episcopacy, the absence of binding Articles, and the want of such a liturgy as that of the English Church. Pusey objects that Mr. Rose's view "involved the abandonment of the fundamental principles in Protestantism and derogated from the independence and the inherent power of the word of God." In after years Pusey came to agree very closely with the views of Mr. Rose. Undoubtedly his own view as to the state of religious belief in Germany was much too sanguine. It is almost amusing to think that in 1828, with Baur and Strauss and their followers yet to come, Pusey in the title to his pamphlet speaks of the rationalism "lately predominant in Germany." But Mr. Rose was, of course, utterly at fault in supposing that bishops and Articles and a liturgy could have saved Germany from the devastations of rationalism. The rigid suppression of anything like ecclesiastical autonomy or liberty, under the iron hand of the State, together with the entire absence of any freedom of evangelical life and fellowship within the German Churches, were the chief causes of German rationalism.[1]

At the point where Pusey stood when he wrote these pamphlets, he was not far removed from the position occupied by Archbishop Tait throughout his course,—a position completely opposed, as the Church and the world were to learn during many years of controversy, to that maintained by Pusey during his long history as leader of the Oxford Movement. It is an interesting question how it happened that, holding such a position in 1830, he came within five short years to the position marked out by his Oxford *Tract on Baptism*. Of the chasm between his position in 1830 and that occupied by him in 1835, Pusey himself, indeed, would seem to have been unconscious. It was one of his peculiarities that he fancied himself, and the Movement of which he came to be the centre, to be all along fixed and stationary as to points of Church-principle.[2] There can be little doubt, however, that it was the question of the historic unity of the Church of Christ which determined his position in after-life. To use striking words, originally applied to Sibthorp by Bishop Wilberforce, who, High Churchman as he was, never lost hold of the root-principle of evangelical life and unity, Pusey "held the $\pi\rho\hat{\omega}\tau o\nu$ $\psi\epsilon\hat{v}\delta os$, that unity is to be gained by the members of the Church Catholic through union with one visible centre."[3] He knew little or nothing of evangelical teaching and experience on the point, and he was dazzled by the picture of

---

[1] See "Religion in Germany," vol. ix. of the *London Quarterly Review*.

[2] "Stationary" was his own word.

[3] Wilberforce's *Life*, vol. i. p. 203.

visible external unity, as presented in the writings of the hierarchical "fathers" of the patristic age, who had themselves departed from the spiritual simplicity and majesty of St. Paul's teaching as to the Church. Just here is the watershed which divides two systems of ecclesiastical and theological thought and obedience. For an English ultra-Churchman, the way just here goes off direct to Rome. Here is brought into view the difference between the citizenship of the "Jerusalem above," "which is free," and of the Jerusalem of the Roman unity, which "is in bondage with her children."

Considering his antecedents, and especially his experience in Germany, Pusey might well, one would think, have shrunk from embracing the High Church sacramentarian system of doctrine; but, missing the true principle of apostolic doctrine as to the Church of Christ, it may have been that to him the alternative seemed to lie between accepting the whole scheme of hierarchical and theurgical transcendentalism or going the entire length of the German rationalism within which it is hardly too much to say that he had felt the danger of being entangled. It is certain that, having put his hand to the ritualistic plough in the Oxford furrow, he never looked back. Of his adhesion to the hard and extreme externalist school, he gave the pledge and first-fruits, not so much by his tract on *Fasting* in 1833—one of the earliest of the Oxford Tracts—as by that on *Baptism* in 1835.

Perhaps I should note, in this connexion, that it was not until after Pusey's marriage and his settlement at Oxford in 1830 that he came closely and fully under the spell of Newman. At an earlier period Newman had taken a liking to him, and had drawn him out, encouraged him, and more or less patronised him. The shy young man had responded feelingly to Newman's attentions. But now Pusey was not only a college don, but a university professor and a canon; he was, to use Newman's own words, in "easy relations" with all the university authorities, and also with many people of rank and influence. Mrs. Pusey's Diary shows that, however secluded was Pusey's life after his wife's death, ten years later, they kept good company, and saw a good deal of it, for some years after he went into residence at Oxford. Newman henceforth cultivated Pusey assiduously, and Pusey felt sympathetically the power of that superior mind and the fascination of Newman's influence. Pusey rapidly graduated, accordingly, in the new Oxford school, and, before long, fairly kept step with him whom, in common with the rest of the Tractarian company, he recognised as leader. Still, we find that, as late as 1835, in delivering the "Inaugural Address" to the "Theological Society" which he founded, and of which he was the first Moderator, he laid stress on the advantages of the Reformation, and spoke of the Lutheran and Reformed "Churches." In starting the Society, moreover, he tells his wife in a letter that he sees elements of disunion, in that John [Newman] will scare people (vol. i. p. 336). As yet, therefore, he must have been sometimes a little restive. In the account which his biography gives of the rise of the Oxford Movement, there is, as the critics have said with one consent, little that is new. There was, indeed, little left to tell, although, in a biography intended to be historical and monumental, and relating to the second, and, in later years, the sole leader and chief of the school, an adequate chronicle of the whole growth and progress of the Movement was a matter of necessity. Some things, if it had been Dr. Liddon's intention completely to exhibit the life and conduct of his hero in all its aspects and influences, should have found a place in the record which are actually wanting, and those things would have been less known and more interesting than much of what is told. But the biographer has been prudent as well as authentic, and has discreetly left in the shade certain points which it will be necessary to bring into the light.

From 1830 to 1838, in which year the state of Mrs. Pusey's health obliged her husband to live much away from Oxford, and to give up his generous hospitalities, Pusey used his wealth in such a way as to make not a few his grateful debtors. For some years he had received students into his house, James B. Mozley being the chief of these, as the readers of his letters will remember. When his wife's condition of health obliged him to give up this practice, Pusey took another house for the same purpose, of which James Mozley seems to have been the head, and where, for a time, Mark Pattison resided. The effect on Pattison, as we know from his autobiography, was by no means happy; and, on the whole, this second arrangement proved a failure. The house was closed in 1840. Pusey's reputation, however, was already established in 1837 as "the great benefactor of Oxford," the Cambridge visitor who so describes him adding, that "he supports five divinity students in his own house, and his benefactions to the poor are very great." This unnamed visitor further states, after referring to the immense excitement produced by Pusey's 5th of November Divine Right sermon in that year, that he was said to "possess an indirect but great influence over the whole clergy of Oxford," including even those who were not favourable to his views (i. 406). At this time (1837) Pusey had already published his famous tract on *Baptism*; but as to auricular confession, we learn that he feared it was " a grace which had been lost to the Church, and could not be restored " (p. 407).

Here, then, we see Pusey established as a great and growing power in Oxford just as Newman's influence was approaching its climax, which was so soon to be followed by his fall. As yet Pusey's designs are not unfolded—he does not himself at present see how far they are to take him. The beginnings of his confessional theory perplex him. But his work differs altogether from that of Newman. He does not live in a world of ideas and abstractions, but of penitential feeling, of theological contemplation, and patristic studies. Newman's secession will not move him, for logic does not govern his thoughts or his aims.

CHAPTER X.

HOOKER AND ALEXANDER KNOX—PUSEY'S MIDDLE PERIOD
—HIS TRACT ON BAPTISM—HIS DOCTRINE OF BAP-
TISM—EXPOSITION AND INTERPRETATION OF ST. PAUL—
INFANT BAPTISM AND CONFIRMATION—THE REMEDY
FOR SIN AFTER BAPTISM—SACRAMENTAL CONFESSION
AND ABSOLUTION—THE CLAIMS OF ANGLICAN PRIEST-
CONFESSORS.

IT will be convenient, at the beginning of this chapter, to note that Dr. Liddon quietly throws over two errors which at different times have found a good deal of support from Anglican writers, and even in the columns of the *Guardian*. One of these has been that Hooker sanctions the high sacramental doctrine of Pusey and his followers. The author of the great sermon on Justification ought never to have been supposed to hold such doctrine; the idea is strangely astray. The allusions to the subject of the Lord's Supper in the *Ecclesiastical Polity* do not lend the slightest colour of support to such an idea; they plainly imply the contrary. Dr. Liddon, in effect, concedes this, and, as accounting for Hooker's failing to agree with the standard of high sacramental orthodoxy taught by the Laudian school, and revived by the Oxford Tractarian writers, refers to the "Calvinistic tinge" which remained in Hooker's teaching. This phrase seems to indicate the source of the error on this subject which has prevailed.

Because Hooker was the defender of Anglican Episcopacy against Calvinistic Presbyterianism, it appears to have been imagined that he must have been High Anglican all round. This erroneous assumption is born of far-reaching ignorance. In fact, the great champion of English episcopal government was as little of an apostolical successionist, in the sense of modern ultra-High Churchmen, as of a High Oxford sacramentarian. On all points he held the scales fair and even between the opposing schools; he was neither Lutheran nor Calvinist; he was neither patristic nor Zwinglian; he was Pauline and scriptural; he was an evangelical English Churchman, a true son of the English Reformation in its best, its ripest, its most justly balanced form. Not less unfounded is the other error to which I refer, viz. that Alexander Knox was in some sense a forerunner of the Oxford Tractarian school. He was the intimate friend of Wesley for many years, and after his revered friend's death continued to delight in the preaching of Wesley's most eminent "assistants," especially Adam Clarke. His doctrine of faith is identical with that taught by Wesley in his *Appeals to Men of Reason and Religion*, and nearly resembles that of Luther, and also that taught by Archdeacon Hare; it is contradictory to that taught by Newman and Pusey. His doctrine as to the Eucharist, also, is very far removed from Pusey's doctrine of Consubstantiation or Transubstantiation and the Real Presence.[1]

It is my aim in this chapter especially to note the points of progress and development in Pusey's growth out of the "liberal" High Churchmanship of his early manhood, into the extreme Romanising position which he maintained

[1] As to the sacrament of the Lord's Supper, in particular, I may refer to his letter to Hannah More (*Remains*, iv. pp. 308-311).

for nearly half a century. It has been noted that of his adhesion to the Tractarian school he gave the pledge, by his tract on *Baptism* in 1835, five years after he had published the second part of his *Enquiry* in answer to Mr. Rose on the subject of German rationalism. His earlier tract on *Fasting* was distinguished from the other tracts of the series by the signature of Pusey's initials, and it contains nothing characteristic of the special sacramentarian teaching of the Tractarian school. The unsigned tract on *Baptism* took its place strictly and fully as one of the anonymous series of *Tracts for the Times*.

By it he laid the foundation of that definite doctrine on grace, and all that relates to the innermost and essential Christian life, which has since been the peculiar characteristic of the modern Sacramentarian school of Oxford. Here also he began to mark out sharply for the Oxford school that line of evident divergence from the spiritual doctrine of the Reformation which before long alienated Samuel Wilberforce from the new High Anglican party. He was, indeed, but a clumsy exponent of the new views, which were afterwards presented in a more plausible form by Robert Wilberforce, who was able to give a delusive aspect of philosophical system and method to what was really not so much transcendental as contradictory and impossible—as contradictory as that two and two make five, as impossible as a fourth dimension in solid geometry. But, however clumsily, Pusey, a pious and earnest Christian, so taught his doctrine as to make it appear, to those who received it, a vital part of spiritual theology, as exhibiting in its first beginnings the work of the Holy Spirit in renewing and sanctifying the soul. This he did with a gravity, a solemnity, one might almost say an unction, which impressed many of his readers, however much they might be puzzled by some parts and startled by other parts of his teaching. Dr. Liddon has hardly done justice to his subject at this point. He seems himself to hesitate as to endorsing or professing to understand all that his master has written. He leaves the reader to infer from what he quotes, as said by eminent High Churchmen, as to the difficulties raised by Pusey's teaching, and from his own silence, that the tract raised serious questions in the minds of the ablest High Church divines, recognised authorities in their own school, difficulties such as he himself cannot undertake to remove. He quotes also admissions from Pusey himself that he had not clearly or satisfactorily explained his own views; and he gives us to understand that, though the tract was afterwards enlarged, though several editions of it were published, it was never so enlarged as to supply what was needed, and was at last left by its author unsatisfactory and incomplete. But the biography contains no real explanation of the special teaching of the tract, although some pages are occupied in vague statements, partly quotations, intended to indicate its general purpose and drift. This deficiency I must endeavour to supply.

What I am about to write is founded on a first-hand study of the tract and of Pusey's sermons. The promised sequel to the tract was never published; the necessary explanations Pusey never gave in any connexion with the tract. We may reasonably conclude that he had not fully worked them out when the tract was written, and so far as he saw them coming into view, shrank at that period from making them known to an unprepared English public. But the sequel and the needed explanations were in effect involved in that full-blown confessional system which it was to be the business of his after-life covertly to introduce, and which, to the bitter grief of his archbishop, and the bishops of the southern dioceses especially, harassed and disturbed Pusey's episcopal superiors during all the later years of his life,—that confessional system which, as we have seen, when he set about writing his tract, he regarded as a "grace and blessing lost to the English Church."

The first occasion on which Pusey aroused public attention on the subject of baptism was when he preached at Christ Church his remarkable sermon—Thomas Mozley, in his *Reminiscences*, calls it his "great sermon"—on "Sin after Baptism." Unless the order of the *Reminiscences* is hopelessly confused, this sermon was preached at an earlier period than the publication of the tract. The text was Heb. vi. 4–6. Mr. Mozley says: "Every corner of the church was filled; one might have heard a pin drop. Every word told. The keynote was the word 'irreparable,' pronounced every now and then with the force of a judgment." The sermon does not appear to have been published. But Mozley's account of it shows what was the leading idea of the exposition and of the commination fulminated by the preacher. He made the language of the terrible passage refer directly and properly to baptism. In *baptism* the Hebrew reprobates had *once for all*, ἅπαξ, been "enlightened," and through confirmation had been "made partakers of the Holy Ghost." Such baptized persons having "fallen away" from grace by wilful sin, it was impossible to "renew again unto repentance." Their loss was "irreparable." It is no marvel if the sermon was never published, for deliberately to justify its exposition to the satisfaction either of divines or of New Testament scholars would have been impossible.

The exegetical ignorance which could so misinterpret a text—the reference of which to publicly apostate Jews, who in returning to the camp of blaspheming antichristian Jews, " crucified to themselves the Son of God afresh and put Him to an open shame," should have been very plain to a biblical student—is beyond what could well have been thought possible in an Oxford Professor of Hebrew even in the era of Lord Grey's or Lord Melbourne's Ministry. Nor is it wonderful that the alarming question as to Sin after Baptism first raised by a sermon not to be forgotten, then raised again vaguely, but with emphasis, in his tract on *Baptism*, a question left quite unanswered, should have been cast up against Pusey by one after another even of his High Church friends, and should be implicitly recognised by his biographer as a problem unsolved. How Pusey came to solve it afterwards will be presently explained.

Meantime I proceed to show that other parts of his teaching on the subject of baptism, as these are set forth in his tract, if not so dark and repulsive as this, are scarcely less difficult or incredible. He gathered up the substance of the first part of his tract, as several times revised and as very greatly enlarged, in a volume entitled, *The Doctrine of Holy Baptism*. In this volume he makes baptism the one means and channel of the whole Christian life at its initiation, whether for adults or infants. Herein, and only herein, is conveyed forgiveness, and the new birth, and the gift of the Holy Ghost. The meaning and operation of faith in the case of penitents are restricted to the preliminary work of accepting the authority of the Church and the teaching of the priest as to the way of salvation. According to Pusey, St. Paul knew nothing whatever of Christian grace until after his baptism by

Ananias. "As yet," he says, "neither were his sins forgiven, nor had he received the Holy Ghost; much less was he born again of the Spirit, until it was conveyed to him through the Saviour's sacrament." "Before his baptism, he appears neither to have been pardoned, regenerated, justified, nor enlightened." During the three days and nights of his blindness and agony he was unvisited by any illumination of the Spirit, or any influence of the special grace of Christ. All that transformed him from the state of bondage, darkness, and terror was accomplished in and by his baptism at the hands of Ananias. In that his pardon was declared, his soul regenerated, and the Holy Ghost imparted to him in sudden power and fulness.

The case of Cornelius, indeed, is admitted to be a sort of exception to the law of divine influence, as laid down by Pusey, the solitary exception, except the primary and palmary case of the disciples who, on the Day of Pentecost, were baptized with the Holy Ghost in order to qualify them for baptizing others "with water and with the Holy Ghost." The case of Cornelius and his household, Pusey virtually identifies with that of the first disciples in the upper room on the Day of Pentecost. Unfortunately for any such identification, the first disciples on the Day of Pentecost had not been baptized unless with John's baptism; while, on the other hand, Cornelius was baptized immediately *after* receiving the Holy Ghost. That is to say, when he had already received the Holy Ghost, he afterwards received that baptism of which the characteristic virtue is, according to Dr. Pusey, that in and by it the gifts of pardon and of the indwelling Holy Spirit are conveyed to the baptized.

Pusey's name is great, and the object of his biography

is to make it greater than ever, not only as a man of saintly devotion and life, but as, of this age, the greatest "Master in Israel." For this reason my readers must bear with me while I exhibit still more fully the actual teaching of the Oxford High Church rabbi—the great theologian of his school. St. Paul declares (1 Cor. i.) that to the Corinthian believers Christ had been made "wisdom from God," "and righteousness and sanctification and redemption." The reference of the apostle here, Pusey teaches, was strictly and directly to the baptism of the Corinthian Christians as the immediate source of all these high and heavenly blessings. He teaches this without appearing to note the contradiction he thus gives to the apostle's own words almost immediately preceding, in which he says that Christ sent him "not to baptize, but to preach the gospel," and even thanks God that he had himself baptized only two persons at Corinth, "lest any man," as he explains, "should say that ye were baptized into my name." So, again, Pusey's interpretation makes St. Paul teach that it was in and by baptism, as the direct and only means and instrument, that the Corinthians "were washed, were sanctified, were justified, in the name of the Lord Jesus and by the Spirit of our God" (1 Cor. vi. 11); although this would imply, that with this great work, inasmuch as, with a few specified exceptions, St. Paul did not himself baptize the Christian believers in Corinth, the apostle had nothing to do. The words of John the Baptist, "I indeed baptize with water, but there cometh One after me, who shall baptize with the Holy Ghost and with fire," are interpreted as finding their direct and proper fulfilment in the effects of Christian water-baptism as administered by the disciples and their converts on and after the Day of Pentecost.

The Ephesians, we read, were "sealed by the Spirit of God unto the day of redemption," "were sealed with that Holy Spirit of promise which is the earnest of our inheritance." This sealing, Pusey teaches, is only another name for baptism. Similarly, when the apostle says in his Second Epistle to the Corinthians that God had "anointed" and "sealed" the Corinthian believers, and given them the earnest of the Spirit in their hearts, the full and proper meaning of the passage is said to be satisfied by referring it to the direct and necessary results of the water-baptism of these Corinthians. Nay, even when St. John, in his First Epistle, speaks of the "unction from the Holy One," the reference, according to the Puseyite theology and exegesis, is to the gift and blessing bestowed in and by the act of baptism as means and instrument. With characteristic intrepidity, with the sanguine thoroughness of purpose which, as Newman has taught us, in the case of Pusey, was unconscious of any "intellectual perplexities," the plough of Tractarian superstition is thus driven straight through the plainest teaching of apostolic doctrine—and this in the name of apostolicity!

The following passage will serve to present in his own words a summary view of Pusey's doctrine as to baptism:—

"No change of heart, then, or of the affections; no repentance, however radical; no faith, no life, no love, comes up to the idea of this 'birth from above'; it takes them all in and comprehends them all, but itself is more than all: it is not only the creation of a new heart, new affections, new desires, and, *as it were*, a new birth, but it is an *actual* birth from above or from God, a gift coming down from God, and given to faith, through baptism; yet not the work *of* faith, but the operation *of* 'water and the

Holy Spirit.' . . . Faith and repentance are the conditions on which God gives it; water, sanctified by our Lord's baptism, is the womb of our new birth."

Here, in passing, let us note that the faith of which Pusey here speaks is not at all that "faith of the Son of God," that "faith of the operation of God," of which St. Paul speaks, and whereby he tells us that he lived (Col. ii. 12; Gal. ii. 20); it is faith *before* grace, faith apart from any special influence of the Holy Spirit. What it may be understood to mean in the case of the baptized *infant*, Pusey makes no attempt to explain.

Thus much, however, we learn as to infant baptism—that infant baptism and confirmation are part and parcel of the same sacrament. According to this view, in baptism "original sin is washed away and divine grace imparted" through the Spirit of Christ; in confirmation, regarded as part of baptism, the fuller and richer gifts and influence of the Holy Ghost are, under the laying on of the bishop's hands, imparted to the catechumens. Pusey approves and adopts the expressions which speak of confirmation as "part of baptism," as "the complement of baptism"; and he quotes with approval from Bingham the language of Haime—a High Church writer—which affirms "in so many words—'The gift of the Holy Spirit is given in *baptism* by the imposition of the bishop's hands.'"

I add another quotation, the reference of which is to infant baptism. After referring to the earliest memories of happy homes, and to "bright visions of the past" in childhood's happiest days, Pusey proceeds as follows:—

"It is not then in vain, surely, that throughout His whole Church He has blended with that early past one brighter spot which sheds its lustre over all, and from which the light of their sun shines sevenfold, our baptismal morn. . . . Our baptism is of inexpressible value and comfort, even because it is the act of God; it has nothing earthly mixed with it; it was simply His who chose us 'to the sprinkling of the blood of Jesus Christ,' and 'predestinated us unto the adoption of children by Jesus Christ unto Himself.' . . . Our comfort, our joy, our peace, our consolation, our glory, is to have what we have purely from Him, and conveyed by a formal act of His, whereby, 'not according to works of righteousness which we did, but according to His mercy HE SAVED US, through the washing of regeneration and the renewing of the Holy Ghost.'"

Such was Pusey's teaching as to the new birth and the gift of the Holy Ghost in baptism, equally for adults and infants. The Christian life so begun in the soul was, of course, as he taught, to be nourished and maintained by the "Holy Eucharist," in which our Lord in His perfect fulness, as God and man, as Son of God and Christ, is consubstantiated with every particle of the consecrated bread and wine. But on that subject I shall not enter in the present chapter. I will try to show, hereafter, what that doctrine involves.

The question as to sin after baptism now, however, comes back to us. The sources and channels of the divine life, the Christian life, in man, according to the Puseyite teaching, have been shown. But what is the case of those who, by wilful sin after baptism, have lost the life imparted, have fallen from grace and from Christ, and incurred an "irreparable" forfeiture? This is what Pusey did not explain in his tract, but what on all sides, after his awful sermon at Christ Church, he was expected to explain. The explanation was never given as a part of his *Doctrine of*

Holy Baptism. The demands of his friends were never explicitly dealt with. Expectations were held out that he would explain; he intimated that in a larger treatise, dealing with the whole Christian life, what was needed might be supplied. But the direct explanation never came. Indirectly, however, Pusey's views were at length made known in print, and then it was not difficult to understand why they were not earlier and more plainly and fully set forth. When he had fully defined and developed his views on the subject, he thought it prudent to keep back the publication of his remedy for post-baptismal voluntary sin until he had privately prepared the mind of his disciples for receiving and applying it. Like all his school, he believed in the doctrine of reserve, taught in more than one of the tracts. In brief, his remedy was *The Confessional*, with priestly absolution, effectuated and completed by the reception of the Holy Eucharist.

Among his published sermons—sermons published many years after the tract on *Baptism*—are some on this subject. I am about to quote from the preface to his first sermon on *Entire Absolution to the Penitent.*

Referring to penitents, he says: "They wish to be, and to know that they are, in a state of grace. God has provided a means, however deeply they have fallen, to replace them in it." And then he explains what is the means so provided of God. "By His absolving sentence," he says, "God does efface the past." But, inasmuch as they "cannot estimate their own repentance and faith, God has provided physicians of the soul to relieve and judge for those who 'open their griefs' to them." Such was Pusey's doctrine. It is not the Spirit of God, the "Spirit of adoption," imparted from above to the penitent and believing suppliant, that delivers from the "spirit of bondage unto fear." It is the voice of the priest-physician, declaring "the absolving sentence" of God, whereby He "effaces the past." It is the priest-physician judicially "estimating the repentance and faith" of the penitent, who "judges for" and, when he is satisfied, "relieves those who open their griefs" to him. As the priest, under the Mosaic law, examined the leper, and either pronounced him clean, or sent him back to his seclusion as unclean, so the Anglican priest, the Anglican "physician," according to Pusey's doctrine of faith and salvation, examines and judges as to the state of the penitent, and either "estimates" his repentance and faith to be sufficient, and accordingly restores him to the congregation of the faithful, declaring, as God's voice, that the "past is effaced," or else judges them to be insufficient, and sends him back to prolonged penance, with directions to return and submit himself for judgment on a future day.

Thus the penitent may earlier or later get comfort from the priest, and from him alone can receive any sure or lawful comfort. Here, in this "sacrament of confession and absolution," and here alone, is the rightful source of consolation for the troubled conscience. For venial sin, indeed, for hasty and unconscious transgression, the daily confession in the public prayers at church, and the public absolution from the priest following thereupon,—the whole service being read and interpreted under High Anglo-Catholic light,—might be sufficient. But for all wilful sin that troubled the conscience, the one true and legitimate remedy was the confessional.

This was Pusey's consistent docrine, although the fear

of episcopal censure often led him to use language which rather implied than straightforwardly expressed it,—language which laid down the principle, but did not in full distinctness draw out the conclusion,—and his practice for forty years was in strict agreement with his doctrine. Most earnestly and repeatedly did Bishop Wilberforce endeavour to gain from Dr. Pusey some substantial concession as to this point of his teaching; but he completely failed. Pusey neither frankly told the whole truth as to his own teaching and example, nor gave any pledge as to his future course.

Pusey's preaching, when not addressed to believers, was of the most stern, searching, and awakening character, —sometimes, indeed, startling and scathing in its bold and almost fierce outspokenness,—but rarely if ever coupled with any direction of sinners immediately to Christ as their Saviour; its characteristic effect was to drive his hearers to the priest and the confessional. There indeed, according to Pusey's special system of doctrine, lay the only way of help for the awakened soul. One sentence in the preface to the first volume of his *Parochial Sermons* puts in very strong light the antagonism between his views and those of John Wesley as to the point which is now before us. "Wesleyanism," he says, "substituted its doctrine of 'present salvation' for the comfort through the ordinance of confession and absolution." If we turn this sentence round, the truth comes out in the following form: Puseyism substitutes for the blessed doctrine of a present and conscious salvation, through "repentance towards God, and faith toward our Lord Jesus Christ," such comfort as may be obtained from confession to a human priest, and absolution pronounced by his lips. If this prime and deadly element of Popery, together with the essentially Romish doctrine of the Mass, are now widely spread through England, and if they are in course of increasingly active propagation, Pusey, more than any other man, contributed to the lamentable result.

What shall we say to such teaching as this? With what prerogative of heart-searching does it invest the priest! "I the Lord . . . try the reins," so we read in Scripture. But here it is the parish priest who "searches the hearts and tries the reins of the children of men." This is the provision whereby we common, unordained sinners, coming to the young curate of our parish, who was ordained priest last week, may be assured, "however deeply we have fallen," that we are restored, and may be made to "know that we are in a state of grace." This is "the means which God has provided." One shrinks from using the only words which can truly describe such teaching. To a serious thinker, who comes fresh from the contemplation of the divine majesty and grace to the view of this dogma, it is a hard thing to refrain from whispering to himself the question: "But is this less than blasphemy,—to invest poor, frail, and fallible young mortals, fresh from college, with such attributes as these?" While to the man who comes direct from personal intercourse, in flesh and blood and broadcloth, with the priests and "physicians" of whom this great Churchman speaks, the pretensions set up on their behalf cannot but appear ludicrous in their absurdity. Indeed, but for the intrinsic impiety of these claims, they might be expected to dissolve amid "inextinguishable laughter."[1]

What I have now stated will enable the readers of

[1] See Note at the end of this chapter (*Archdeacon Garbett's Charge*).

Pusey's biography to understand the feeling excited by his tract, as otherwise they hardly could understand it. To the "terrible" sermon the biography makes no reference. And yet that sermon explains some references in the biography. Mr. Rose, for example, we are informed, thought that Pusey "ought to have answered the serious and pressing question—'What is that grievous sin after baptism which involves a falling from grace?'" The reference here, no doubt, is in part to certain obscure phrases or allusions in the tract; but, still more, it can hardly be doubted, the reference is to the sermon. Rose, we are told, understood Pusey to teach "no remission of sin after baptism." Pusey himself said in later years, and the quotations I have made from his later sermons throw on his words a full light such as the biography does not afford: "From the moment of my completing the tract on *Baptism*, I felt that I should have written on Christian repentance, on confession and absolution." The tract was originally published in three parts. The first part, which consisted of forty-nine pages, was republished in a volume of 400 pages, intended to form the first part of a treatise, this volume being the book from which I have quoted. Parts II. and III. were never republished. "Part II.," Pusey wrote to Keble in 1841, "will be suspended till I can read about absolution." "The remainder," he wrote about the same time to Archdeacon Harrison, "must wait a while, until I can read more on absolution and the absolving influence of the Holy Eucharist." He waited forty years, but never completed his tract or, rather, treatise. Meantime, through the organisation, far and wide, of the confessional movement, he continued to develop his teaching and influence, working especially by means of sisterhoods and of schools. Even boys of tender years were trained to practise confession. But this practical development of his doctrine belongs to his later life, and is beyond the scope of this chapter.

From the period of his publishing this famous tract, Pusey took his position as the great spiritual teacher and preacher of the patristic revival. The solemnity of his tone continually deepened, his consecration of life was more and more recognised, his earnestness was profound and contagious; sin and holiness, the solemnities of life and death, were the themes of his awakening sermons. The great sorrow of his life—the loss of his wife—came upon him before the excitement occasioned by his baptismal utterances had passed away. Even in connexion with her death there is a touching, but surely also a painful, example of the manner in which his legal and, to speak plain truth, his Pharisaic teaching had taken hold of the wife he so passionately loved, and who seems to have been so worthy of his love. As I have already noted, Mrs. Pusey had been baptized by a Dissenter. In her last lingering illness this matter disturbed her peace. She could not find "rest to her soul" simply in her Saviour; she could find no peace till "conditional baptism" had been administered to her. Newman accordingly rebaptized her, and her gratitude to him for this act was painfully abject. It is all but certain that, if she had been under the spiritual guidance of Cardinal Manning, no such scruple would have been allowed by him to vex her soul. Her death (in 1839) left Pusey disconsolate. Not only so, he regarded this sorrow and bereavement as a chastisement laid on him for his sins, and himself as only fit to be treated as a lifelong penitent, who was to take his place alongside guilty sinners at the feet of Jesus—his duty through life being *facere pœnitentiam*. This feeling deepened the sombre tone of his saintliness—for we may not deny that he was, notwithstanding his errors, a devoted and saintly man—and increased the severity of his discipline both towards himself and others. From this time he lived an absolutely secluded life. He shut up the drawing-room door at his Christ Church house, never to open it again; he did not go into public; he shunned society.

This must be borne in mind when we come across such traces of his character and influence as are to be met with in the biography of Mr. J. R. Hope, afterwards Mr. Hope-Scott, whom Pusey, in effect, trained into a Romanist, though he himself never thought of entering the Romish communion, and though he seemed to be no less amazed than grieved, in Hope's case as in that of Newman, Manning, and many more, when he saw one whom he had encouraged in his approaches Romewards pass forward to the obvious goal which had long fascinated his vision, but which Pusey himself was so blind as never to have seen standing full in view at the end of the road he was taking.[1]

[1] "None are so blind as those who will not see," so says the proverb. Nearly seven months before Newman seceded to Rome, he wrote—it was in March 1845—a long letter to Pusey, explaining frankly and fully his position. In this letter he says: "I cannot hold precisely what the Church of England holds, and nothing more. I must go forward or backward, else I sink into a dead scepticism, into which too many in Oxford are now sinking. You cannot take them a certain way in a line, and then, without assignable reason, stop them." If there had been anything in Pusey of logic or speculative power of thought, this might have awakened or in some way intel-

In the year 1844, Pusey wrote a letter to Mr. Hope—not as yet Hope-Scott—which Dr. Liddon has not thought necessary to quote or to refer to in this biography, exhaustive as it is supposed to be, but which I quote here because it is important as an illustration of the real character of Pusey's influence —of the frightful lengths to which he went himself, and encouraged others to go, in the Romeward direction. Mr. Hope was travelling on the Continent, and Pusey in his letter gives his friend a number of commissions. One of these commissions is reserved for the postscript, and is given as follows :—

" There is yet a subject on which I should like to know more, if you fall in with persons who have the guidance of consciences—what penances they employ for persons whose temptations are almost entirely spiritual, of delicate frames often, and who wish to be led on to

lectually moved him. Its only effect seems to have been to restrain him from in any way opposing the claims of Rome ;—all its essential and necessary doctrines, as at that time authoritatively set forth, all that was "of faith," he already held as fully as Newman. Incredible as it may appear, four months later, in July, he actually "wrote to Newman for advice with regard to some people under his own charge who were tempted to join the Church of Rome." Within a few days after Newman's secession, Pusey wrote a long letter to the *English Churchman*, in which he suggested that Newman had, in answer to the long-continued and earnest prayers of a multitude of persons in the Church of Rome for his conversion, been given to that Church, and taken from the Church of England, where there was no scope for his great faculties ; he had, by Providence, to quote Pusey's words, been "transplanted into another part of the vineyard, where the full energies of his powerful mind can be employed, which here they were not." Such were the views, such the spirit, of the man whose memory is worshipped by the "Church of Lord Halifax" as the leader who has moulded the theology and disciplinary character of modern High Anglicanism. (Vol. ii. pp. 449–463.)

perfection? I see in a spiritual writer that even for such, corporeal severities are not to be neglected; but so many of them are unsafe. I suspect the 'discipline' to be one of the safest, and with internal humiliation the best . . . could you procure and send me one by B.[1] What was described to me was of a very sacred character; five cords, each with five knots, in memory of the five wounds of our Lord. . . I should be glad to know also whether there were any cases in which it is unsafe—*e.g.* in a nervous person."[2]

It was almost immediately after the death of his wife, and in order to carry out his plans of penitent self-sacrifice, that Pusey conceived the thought of building a church in Leeds. The melancholy and instructive history of that plan and of its accomplishment is partially given in the last chapter of the second volume of the biography, and is resumed and finally disposed of in the third volume. I shall return to the subject in my next chapter, having in this given a fuller and more precise account of his teaching as to baptism than has before been published. Here, however, I desire to close the chapter with a few explanatory words. I have felt it my duty plainly to expose Pusey's errors, fraught, as they were, with incalculable mischief to the cause of evangelical truth and life in England; but at the same time I have acknowledged, and desire once more to acknowledge fully and frankly, Pusey's sincere and earnest piety. No saint of the Romish Church has ever, perhaps, been more devoted, or, outside a monastery, lived a more reclusely, consecrated life. He was a good man, however lamentably in error; and, though his life and influence have wrought terrible mischief, they

[1] Badeley.   [2] See Ornsby's *Memoirs of Hope-Scott.*

have also been, in some respects, an inspiration for good. Some of his own words may fitly be quoted here: "We should not think," he says in one of his sermons, "the comparative holiness of these men any test as to the truth of any one characteristic doctrine. Holiness (whether produced in the teacher or the taught) proves the presence of some truth, not of the whole truth, nor of the purity of that truth." As with many others, his working faith was better than his teaching. He held doubtless much truth implicitly or unconsciously which he could not, or even would not, have explicitly defined or confessed.

But his praises will be sounded by many writers. His biography sets forth, I will not say unfairly, rather I should say inevitably, a biassed and too favourable view of his whole character and influence. The biographer, from his youth up, was his disciple and intimate friend. He belonged to the same school, and felt for his master the deepest veneration; as was to be expected, accordingly, the biography fails to exhibit features of Pusey's character and influence which in the interest of our national Protestantism, of evangelical truth, of free and manly Christianity, it was necessary to bring fully to the light. It would have been more pleasant to have dwelt chiefly upon the exemplary side of Pusey's character and course. It has been my unwelcome duty, on behalf of the truth, and it will yet again be my duty, to show his errors and faults. It is needful to do this, because the prevalence of Puseyism, rightly so called, the growing influence of that ritualistic and superstitious form of religion, which, though Pusey was never himself a puerile ritualist in matters of ecclesiastical taste and service, has all naturally grown out of principles which he inculcated, is alienating more and more the manly strength of the nation from traditional Christianity, and is increasing the difference and distance, in respect of religious feeling and sympathy, between the majority of the clergy of the nation and the vast majority of its laity. It is now commonly acknowledged by clerical correspondents in Anglican ecclesiastical newspapers that the middle classes refuse to accept the sacramental teaching and the ritualistic opinions and practices of the dominant section of the clergy. This fact, though satisfactory from one point of view, is, on the whole, disquieting. That the congregations should reject the systematic teaching of their clergy is of evil omen for the future of religion in England. Nor can it but be injurious to Christian nobleness of character in the rising generation among the English upper classes, if the principles of priestly rule over the conscience and of sacramental confession are inculcated by those who have a chief hand in the moulding of the character of cultivated Englishmen. These things, it must further be said, exasperate religious schisms and differences; they tend to erect the Church of England into a great social as well as ecclesiastical barrier, which casts its baleful shadow widely over the Christianity of the country, and which is itself the schismatic cause of bitter and uncharitable feelings in the Nonconformist Churches of the land. Already the influence of the causes I have indicated has gone very far towards alienating the mass of English Methodists from the Established Church, and making not a few of them, in effect, throughout a large part of the country, leaders in the movement for its downfall. In truth, as already shown, the effects of Puseyism go to divide the Church of England itself into two, if not three, distinct Churches, as well as to spread religious animosity and controversy through all classes of the community.

NOTE TO PAGE 247.

THE CLAIMS OF ANGLICAN PRIEST-CONFESSORS.

After this chapter was already in print, I met with a passage in *Archdeacon Garbett's Charge to the Clergy of the Archdeaconry of Chichester, August* 1851, which I cannot deny myself the pleasure of quoting, because of the apt confirmation it affords of what I have said in the text.

"We are compelled to acknowledge," says Archdeacon Garbett, "for instance, the insensibility of mankind to the nature of sin—its deadliness, its hatefulness to Almighty God, and its wasting effects upon the soul. We learn by mortifying experience how little men's minds appreciate the dignity and, under whatever light you regard it, the awfulness of our office, and the reverence due to us as the commissioned servants of God. . . . In this mood it strikes us that to be invested with a veritable priesthood, to stand visibly between man and God, and, with the prerogatives of a judge, to hold aloft the keys of heaven and hell, will thrill all hearts with the sense of a real spiritual presence, and alternately shake and support, terrify and attract, as need may be, the souls of sinful men. . . . But, meanwhile, who are we that *we* should clothe *ourselves*, even by delegation, in the awful and eternal priesthood of Christ? Who are we that we should draw men's eyes down from the Lamb that lies bleeding before the throne, and is everlastingly presented and pleaded before Him that sitteth upon it, to men like ourselves, and to a visible mediation? Had God intended us to exercise so tremendous an office as a portion of the normal discipline and inherent attributes of His Church, is it credible, or consistent with the analogy of His dealings, that He would have left us destitute of the faculties which are absolutely indispensable to its discharge? *Has* He given us, *as a matter of fact*, by virtue of our ordination, the power of searching the soul? Can we, indeed, with the penetrating glance of the All-present, see into locked hearts, unravel at a touch the tangled skein of sincerity and self-delusion, and, by an absolute and infallible sentence, anticipate the sentence of the judgment-day? 'I absolve thee, and in heaven my sentence is ratified. O man, thou art unloosed,' or 'Thou art bound, and it is I who have bound thee.' *Can* we try the very hearts and reins? . . . Had He intended His ministers judicially to absolve and condemn, and thus grasp in their hands the keys of heaven and

hell, He would at the same time have bestowed on them the necessary faculties. He would have made us heart-searchers. Men would be forced to recognise in us, by many infallible proofs, not by a mere faith without sight, but as a thing, like every other fact, demonstrated by experience, the possession of this awful and mysterious prerogative."
—*Archdeacon Garbett's Charge to the Clergy of the Archdeaconry of Chichester, August* 5, 1851, pp. 29, 32.

CHAPTER XI.

FULLER DEVELOPMENT OF PUSEY'S DOCTRINE—CONFESSION AND THE EUCHARIST—HIS OWN PENITENTIAL HISTORY AND DISCIPLINE—KEBLE HIS CONFESSOR—BOYS IN THE CONFESSIONAL—COLERIDGE ON THE CONFESSIONAL SYSTEM—THE PRIEST-CONFESSOR—SISTERHOODS AND CELIBACY—PUSEY AND HUMAN NATURE—THE HOUSE OF MERCY AT CLEWER — BISHOP WILBERFORCE AND PUSEY — THE TRUTH LAID BARE—MR. DODSWORTH AND MR. MASKELL—PUSEYISM IN LEEDS—PUSEY AND DR. HOOK.

THE materials of the last chapter were in part derived from the first two volumes of Pusey's biography. The contents of the third volume will furnish a considerable part of the materials for the present chapter.

Whatever expectations may have been formed as to the contents of these volumes of Pusey's Life, I venture to say that, in one respect at anyrate, they have not approached the reality which is presented in the third volume. Such highly-coloured and self-loathing pictures of penitential experience, such confessions of inward sin and guiltiness, are not to be found, so far as I know, in any modern biography, scarcely indeed even in the confessions of such penitents as Bunyan, John Nelson, or Newton of Olney. They are profoundly pathetic, but it almost makes one shudder to read them. They are the confessions, to make the case more extraordinary, not of an unconverted and unchurchly man, but of the Canon of Christ Church, the great University preacher, the guide of forlorn and penitent souls. Besides these startling revelations, there will be found very much else to surprise the student of human nature and of the history of the Church of England. The character of Pusey is seen as under the limelight, and the meaning of Puseyism is revealed, not, indeed, completely and in all aspects, but yet with an authentic and confidential fulness of disclosure not elsewhere to be found in any single work. By the publication of these volumes, taken in connexion with certain other authorities which I shall cite, the means are for the first time available for forming something like a complete judgment on the merits of Pusey as a party organiser and leader. It is a satisfaction to know that Dr. Liddon, by his statement of the case and the history belonging to it, has done all for his revered leader, and for his party, that any good and able man could do; his information, his ability, and his discretion as a disciple and apologist being all that the friends of Pusey could desire. If, with these volumes in our hands, the verdict of public opinion should be adverse to the principles and policy which Pusey spent his life in teaching and promoting, that verdict, it may be believed, is little likely to be reversed.

In the preceding chapter, after tracing Pusey's history and the development of his character up to the period of his settled conversion from liberalism in Church and State to Tractarianism, I dealt with his tract, afterwards expanded to a treatise, on *Baptism*, but yet never completed, and with his "great sermon" on *Sin after Baptism*; then anticipating at this point the contents of the third volume of his Life, I showed how that tract and that sermon were followed up, years afterwards, by the sermon on the "Entire Absolution of the Penitent," preached in the University pulpit in 1845. The tract and the sermons enabled me to draw out pretty fully the principles of Pusey's whole scheme of sacramental doctrine, and especially what he taught as to the relations of private confession to "absolution" and the "Holy Eucharist."[1] Evidence also was adduced from a letter of Pusey's to Mr. Hope-Scott, published in the memoirs of that gentleman, himself a convert, largely through Pusey's influence, to Romanism, as to the terrible lengths to which Pusey was prepared to carry penitential discipline even in the case of women. In the sequel of the biography, as might be expected, we find further and yet more startling developments of Pusey's teaching, both as to the confessional and as to other points of Romanising discipline, with an account of troubles and controversies between himself and his episcopal superiors. It will be necessary, however, in this chapter, as in the preceding, to supplement from other sources the information given in the biography, so as more completely to represent the actual truth as to the character and methods of Pusey, and the operation and influence of Puseyism within the Church of England.

[1] A sermon on the Eucharist, preached in 1843, intended as a sort of sequel to his sermon on "Sin after Baptism," led to his being excluded by the Vice-Chancellor, on the demand of "Six Doctors," from the University pulpit for two years. At the close of this period, his first sermon before the University reasserted the teaching of 1843 more largely. The sermon was that on "Entire Absolution" referred to above. I did not refer in my last chapter to the sermon of 1843, because as to the points under discussion that of 1845 was fuller and more explicit.

Before leading the way to the record of penitential history and discipline, which is the great feature in the earlier portion of the third volume, it will be necessary to set down in order a few points in Pusey's earlier history which must be borne in mind in following, however freely, the lines of his later life-history from 1845 onwards. The fifteen years of the life, from 1845 to 1860, included in the third volume, may be described generally as a period of severe conflict, in which Pusey had more personal difficulties to contend with than at any other period of his history. I have just referred in a Note to his suspension in 1843–1845 from his position as preacher in turn before the University. During those two years the crisis of Newman's career took place. His secession was a terrible blow for Pusey. Whilst he was still staggering under the effects of that blow, the consequences of his undertaking at Leeds, as the founder of St. Saviour's Church and Mission, began to unfold themselves, one after another of the St. Saviour's clergy going over to Rome, while the Bishop of Ripon, Dr. Longley, afterwards Archbishop of Canterbury, was roused to indignation against Pusey and his agents. Almost coincident with Newman's departure from Oxford was the introduction upon the scene, as Pusey's episcopal "father in Christ," of Dr. Wilberforce, who in 1845 was appointed by Sir Robert Peel to the See of Oxford, from which Dr. Bagot was most thankful to be translated to that of Bath and Wells. Wilberforce's relations with Pusey from the first were those of a watchful guardian of old English orthodoxy and Church order, who was filled with suspicions of Pusey's teaching and influence; and soon Pusey, whose period of suspension by the Vice-Chancellor had just come to an end, found himself privately inhibited from preaching within the diocese of Oxford. This inhibition lasted for two years, and was only removed in consideration of certain explanations and pledges the bishop had received from Pusey. It was the immediate consequence of the delivery by Pusey, in 1845, of the sermon on the "Entire Absolution of the Penitent," which was regarded by Pusey as the "fit and natural conclusion" of the sermon condemned in 1843 by the Vice-Chancellor and the Six Doctors. It was the reverse of a recantation of that sermon. Great domestic and personal sorrow and suffering came upon Pusey about the same time. His eldest daughter's death in 1845 was a bereavement second only to the loss of his wife. He himself was prostrated by serious illness, and had to retire for many weeks to Tenby in order to his restoration.

These points being borne in mind, the way will be prepared for some observations on the most salient points in the third volume,—supplementing here and there the information afforded by Dr. Liddon, which does not include all the facts and evidence necessary in order to a complete and true judgment of the character and influence of the "Master of Israel" at whose feet he sat as a student, and whom he regarded with such deep affection.

The third volume of the biography enables us to see what effects the principles which Pusey taught in his sermon on the "Entire Absolution of the Penitent" produced upon his own mind and life. It shows the results of his teaching in his own case. He regarded himself as a penitent who had greatly sinned after baptism, and who could obtain peace only through confession and absolution. His wife's death he regarded as a direct punishment for his sins, and his suspension as a preacher as a providential chastisement for his "secret faults." The death of his daughter also was a punishment for his sins. His illness was another stroke of punishment from the hand of God. He therefore urgently desired to make his private confession to Keble in the church at Hursley, that through his ministry he might receive admonition, strengthening, and comfort. He had begun to press for this as early as 1844, the date of his ominous letter to Mr. Hope-Scott, quoted in the last chapter.

"My dear wife's illness," he writes to Keble, "first brought to me what has since been deepened by the review of my past life, how, amid special mercies and guardianship of God, I am scarred all over and seamed with sin, so that I am a monster to myself; I loathe myself; I can feel of myself only like one covered with leprosy from head to foot; guarded as I have been, there is no one with whom I do not compare myself, and find myself worse than they; and yet, thus wounded and full of sores, I am so shocked at myself, that I dare not lay my wounds bare to anyone: since I have seen the benefit of confession to others, I have looked round whether I could unburden myself to anyone, but there is a reason against everyone. I dare not so shock people; and so I go on, having no such comfort as, in good Bishop Andrewes' words, to confess myself 'an unclean worm, a dead dog, a putrid corpse,' and pray Him to heal my leprosy as He did on earth, and to raise me from the dead: to give me sight, and to forgive me the 10,000 talents; and I must guide myself as best I can, because, as things are, I dare not seek it elsewhere.

"You will almost be surprised that, being such, I

should attempt, as I do, to guide any. I cannot help it. Those whom I in any way guide were brought to me, and by experience or reading, or watching God's guidance of them, I do what I can, and God who loves them has blessed them through me, though unworthy. But I am trying to learn to wish to influence nothing on any great scale; to prefer, I mean, everyone's judgment to my own, and only to act for myself as I best may, and for any souls whom He employs me any way to minister to. When I can, it is a comfort to use words classing myself with other sinners: it is a sort of disowning of what people make of me. I hope all this will not shock you too much, or do you harm; the real testimony to the life of the Church is not in such as me, but in simple people, such as my own dear child. He is working marvels among such; it quite amazes me to see His work with individual souls. So, then, pray be not dismayed at what I write. I have not said so much to anyone for fear of dismaying them. It seemed as if I had no right. But there is abundant, superabundant, proof of God's great grace with people's souls in our Church, though I am a poor miserable leper. . . ."

Keble did not respond to his friend's wish. The feelings, however, expressed in the sermon on Confession and Absolution which Pusey preached in 1845 at Christ Church—a sermon of which parts of the pointed and solemn application had in his own mind a direct and special reference to his own need, as a penitent sinner, of confession and absolution;—his distress arising from Newman's secession; his own long illness; and his seclusion during his convalescence at Tenby,—combined to bring Pusey to a final decision on the subject of personal confession, which Keble found himself unable any longer to resist, much as he shrunk from compliance. Pusey demanded that Keble should put him to severe discipline and self-mortification as a preparation for confession. To this Keble replied : " Mere suffering is the first and simplest thought; but then there are duties to be done. And have we a right to disqualify ourselves for them ? Is it not best to leave it to the Almighty to do so, if He see fit, by sickness ? " No such considerations, however, availed to satisfy or restrain Pusey.

"I am," he wrote, "a great coward about inflicting pain on myself, partly, I hope, from a derangement of my nervous system; haircloth I know not how to make pain: it is only symbolical, except when worn to an extent which seemed to wear me out. I have it on again, by God's mercy. I would try to get some sharper sort. Lying hard I like best, unless it is such as to take away sleep, and that seems to unfit me for duties. Real fasting —*i.e.* going without food—was very little discomfort, except in the head, when the hour of the meal was over, and Dr. W[ooten] said and says, ' It was shortening my life.' Praying with my arms in the form of a cross seemed to distract me, and act upon my head, from this same miserable nervousness. I think I should like to be bid to use the discipline. I cannot even smite on my breast much, because the pressure on my lungs seemed bad. In short, you see I am a mass of infirmities. But I might be able to do something, in faith, if I was bid to do it."

Having in the meantime composed and delivered a sermon in reply to Dr. Jeune, who, in the University pulpit, had attacked Pusey for his sermon on Absolution,

Pusey, on December 1, 1846, went to Hursley and made his confession, sending, before he left, a thank-offering in money for Hursley Church, "from one who feels himself unworthy to offer it himself." A day or two afterwards he wrote the following letter to his father confessor:—

"My dearest Father,—I dare not write much, yet thus much I may say, in comfort for all the sorrow I gave you last week, that I cannot doubt but that through your ministry and the power of the keys, I have received the grace of God, as I know not that I ever did before. I can no more doubt of His mercy vouchsafed to me thus far, than of my own past misery. All indeed is very bad. . . . However, things seem with me other than they ever were before; at least, I seem to hate myself more thoroughly, and bad as my prayers are, still to have a love and hope I never knew before. So although, through my wretchedness, you have seen that what is seeming may be hollow, yet through God's unbounded mercy you will have seen anew that His grace is vouchsafed through His ordinances to penitents, however fallen. You will pray that it be not in vain. You will know, in some little measure, what a hard task is before me. To think of myself as lost in God's sight (had He made me such) would be nothing; but to feel that I have had gifts of nature and drawings above others, and to feel that this wreck is my own making, it is very bitter. . . . May it only be healing. And then I found my late sermon printed. Alas! what a key you have to it. I hardly know how I could have got through it now. Oh that that miserable thing should be I! Yet I trust, by His mercy, it is no more I. It ought to have cut one's heart open to read it. However, do not think (I pray) that I need comfort. It seems to me the most blessed sorrow (when occupation does not take it away) I ever felt. God would not deal thus with me, if He had not pardoned me."

It need hardly be said that "that miserable thing" referred to as being himself, is the unconfessed, unabsolved sinner described in the University sermon of 1845.

Pusey had brought with him a rule of discipline for Keble to sanction. It is portentously voluminous and detailed—it might be the rule of a Middle Age ascetic; it reminds one of the discipline of Oriental ascetics who have never known anything of divine grace, or Christ's mercy, or the liberty of the children of God. Among an infinite number of details, he resolved "to wear haircloth always by day unless ill; to use a hard seat by day and a hard bed by night; not to wear gloves or protect his hands; to eat his food slowly and penitentially, 'making a secret confession of unworthiness to use God's creatures before every meal'"—how unlike the apostle's exhortation, to "eat our food with gladness and singleness of heart"! One of his rules was "never, if I can, to look at the beauty of nature without inward confession of unworthiness"; another, "to make mental acts, from time to time, of being inferior to everyone I see"; another, "to drink cold water at dinner, as only fit to be where there is not a drop to 'cool this flame'"; still another, "to make the fire to me from time to time the type of hell." These are a few selected out of scores of rules. Some, of course, are good rules for useful and lowly living; but most are conceived in a spirit of mechanical self-humiliation, which is most painful to realise, and which ought to open the eyes of all, except those who are completely disciplined and dehumanised ascetic bond-slaves, to the terrible degradation of Christian teaching and principle involved in the doctrines and discipline of "Puseyism."

It would seem that, however reluctantly, Keble let all these rules pass with a general *caveat* and remonstrance. There were some other proposed rules, however, which he absolutely refused to sanction—

"Pusey was very anxious to use 'the discipline' every night with Ps. li. Keble did not advise it. Pusey entreated. 'I still scruple,' wrote Keble, 'about the discipline. I could but allow, not enjoin it, to anyone.' Another rule which Pusey begged to have set him was, 'Not to smile, if I can help it, except with children, or when it seems a matter of love (like one who has just escaped the fire).' But Keble hesitated. 'I should not be honest,' he wrote, 'were I not to confess that I cannot yet reconcile myself to not smiling. Is it not a penalty on others more than on oneself?'"

That Pusey was sincere in what he said and did respecting this question of confession and priestly absolution is, of course, beyond dispute. Nor can we be insensible to the pathetic aspect of his penitential experience. In the "Confessions" which are here in part disclosed we have furnished to us some explanation of the morbid tone of his theology—onesided as it was throughout; we hear the keynote of the minor strain of feeling which dominated all his life-service. But the issue we have to deal with is not affected by the question of personal sincerity and devoutness. Our question is as to the truth and wisdom of his work and counsels; the good or evil of his characteristic aims and influence; and whether he was fit and competent to fill the part of a religious leader and guide. The reply must be that he was in many ways, and on the whole, very unfit. He lived in a private world of his own, which was visited mostly by morbid souls. Of the actual play of life, of the influences which mingle in life's battle, or life's school, and by which character is moulded or marred, he had no true, sober, or practical knowledge. If I could have produced here so much—and, long as it is, it is but a portion—of his voluminous letter to Keble in preparation for his Confession, as is printed by his biographer, we should have had a striking illustration of the infinite multiplicity of mere particulars, many of them quite insignificant, which, in his view, made up the total of conduct, the school of character, the picture of the soul's life and state. The moral principles, of which once and again we catch just a glimpse, are for the most part lost and submerged. Of the grand evangelical truths which make up the gospel revelation as taught by our Lord, as insisted upon and illustrated by the apostles, there seems to be scarcely any recognition. We are in the school, at once Pharisaic and ascetic, of mechanical ordinances —" touch not, taste not, handle not"; we see a soul in bondage, and, it would seem, totally unconscious of the nature or conditions of the true spiritual life and liberty. We are reminded of the petty fanaticism of a mediæval devotee, ignorant of the writings of St. Paul, and with no knowledge, at first hand, of the Gospels. Instead of the pardon of sin to the believing penitent by the Saviour of sinners, we are told of the remission, by the authority of the priest who carries the "keys," of sins confessed to him one by one. It is he who pronounces absolution after having weighed and summed up the items of the confession. The "Great Absolver" is out of sight; the eye of faith is not directed to the "Lamb of God, which taketh away the sin of the world," nor to the one and only Mediator between God and man, who breathes His peace into the soul of the believing penitent.

The Church of England allows confession to be made to the minister of Christ where, for the comfort and relief of the soul, the penitent sinner feels the need of such confession; but the mind of the Church of England, as expounded by her highest authorities, and gathered from her broad and general teaching, is unquestionably opposed to the habitual practice of confession, and especially to any claim on the part of its ministers to require such confession, and to pronounce an authoritative sentence of divine absolution. When this was urged upon Pusey, his stereotyped reply was, as it has been that of his followers to the present time, that he did not enforce confession. What was this but a disingenuous subterfuge? He taught that in the case of wilful sin after baptism there was no means of peace, no provision for the sinner's pardon and absolution, except by the way of auricular confession to the "priest-physician," who is invested with authority to hear the confession, to judge as to the sincerity and sufficiency of the repentance, and to pronounce or withhold absolution. A number of priestly-minded clergymen received Pusey's doctrine on this subject with conviction and enthusiasm. It was whispered with awe and solemnity from lip to lip, it was embraced by women, it was taught to children, and, as the one message of hope to souls awakened to a sense of their sin and the peril of eternal damnation, it became in many quarters the High Church gospel of forgiveness. It had this advantage over the mere formalism of the dry High Church, that it recognised the fact of sin in the depths of human nature, of sin as a barrier between man and God, and the need in order to pardon of conviction and repentance. But, whatever Pusey might pretend, his doctrine did, in effect, enforce confession to the priest on all who received it. It was enforcement by the most stringent method of compulsion. It employed the most potent motives, the most severe spiritual penalties. Whilst Pusey in his correspondence with Dr. Hook and his bishop (Wilberforce) pleaded that he did not teach compulsory confession, that he left it free to his disciples either to confess or to abstain from confessing, he was, in fact, using with all his authority and with terrible solemnity the motives which belong to the eternal world and the dread hereafter, in order to constrain all that came within the scope of his teaching, if they desired peace of conscience and any assurance of pardon, to seek this from the priest by the way of confession. Any other kind of enforcement, any legal compulsion, was, of course, out of the question.[1]

The difference between such a doctrine as this and that of the Church of England, even as understood by a High Churchman like Dr. Hook, is shown by a passage in a letter from Keble to Pusey, given in Pusey's biography as part of the correspondence relating to the case of St. Saviour's Church, Leeds. Keble, who had visited Leeds

[1] The same disgraceful pretence, the same dishonest plea in excuse, is still the parrot-cry of Dr. Pusey's disciples. There is no compulsory confession, is the cry of Lord Halifax and his fellows or followers. Nay, even some bishops speak as if this pretence had some weight as a plea, at least in extenuation of the practice which they dare hardly venture to approve.

at Pusey's request in connexion with that case, reports as follows to Pusey:—

"I called on Hook, and asked him if he objected to the principle or to the way of carrying it out. He said, 'To the principle, for they [*i.e.* Pusey and his followers] taught confession and absolution as a "mean of grace,"' whereas he considered that 'the Prayer-Book allows it only as a "mean of comfort," and that only in "exceptional cases."' I asked him how he reconciled this with what he himself said to me about his opinion of the practice in 1844. He said 'he was of the same mind then as now, that the confession he approved and practised was no more than confession to a Christian friend (quoting St. Jas. v. 16), and that more than that was more than the English Church allowed.'"[1]

Bishop Wilberforce, Pusey's diocesan, held consistently and often insisted on the same view.[2] Hook, in a letter to Bishop Longley, thus states his own feeling and experience on this point: "Often, very often, in my life, God knows, I have required and sought ghostly advice and counsel, but in my early years I sought and opened my grief to a friend who was, and is, a layman; and for the last two-and-twenty years I have obtained it from one who is bound to me by the closest ties which can bind together two human beings, and without whose tender care and affectionate support I should not have been able to endure the hard warfare I have had to sustain during the last fourteen years," etc.[3]

---

[1] *Pusey's Life*, vol. iii. p. 357.
[2] See, especially, *Wilberforce's Life*, vol. iii. pp. 419, 420, and vol. ii. pp. 76–79.
[3] *Hook's Life*, vol. ii. p. 347.

This doctrine of auricular confession and priestly absolution, with all that it involves, its whole depth and mystery, was taught by Pusey through books of Roman Catholic devotion and spiritual discipline, which, with more or less, sometimes with very little, omission or adaptation, he printed and circulated for the use of the priests of his party and the congregations under their charge.[1]

I am not particularly concerned to defend the formularies of the Church of England, in which are to be found some expressions that seem to favour in part the teaching of Pusey. There can also be no doubt that some of its divines and devotional writers have used expressions liable to be interpreted as favouring more or less the views of Pusey and the Anglican Confessionalists of to-day. But there was unquestionably a definite distinction between the principles which underlay Pusey's system of doctrine and those which since the Reformation have ruled in the Church of England, and which give character in general to her formularies. That difference Dr. Hook, in one of his letters printed in the biography, very clearly indicates. He speaks of himself as regarding the Bible and the patristic divines, taken together, as the authorities for the teaching of the Church of England. He intimates that Pusey had dropped the Bible from his basis, and had felt himself at liberty, at his own will, without the authoritative guard

---

[1] One of these was the well-known *Manual for Confessors*, "Adapted for the Use of the English Church." In this he quotes Pope Eugenius to the effect that what a confessor knows through confession he knows as God "ut Deus"; and adds: "I go further still: 'As man he may swear with a clear conscience that he knows not, what he knows only as God.'" I take this passage from Mr. Walsh's volume on the *Secret History of the Oxford Movement*, 6th ed. p. 82. Mr. Walsh gives p. 402 as the place quoted from in the *Manual*.

and correction, if need were, of the Bible, to adopt such opinions as he found and approved in the patristic divines he chose for his authorities.

It seems abundantly clear that the teachings of the Bible, especially of the New Testament, and in particular of St. Paul, scarcely enter into the theology of Pusey except so far as they may have been recognised directly or indirectly,—or, as not seldom is the case, utterly perverted,—by the patristic authorities on whom he relied.[1]

Dr. Pusey insisted on the benefit of confession to children, especially to young boys. This practice of juvenile confession has been characteristic of the whole Puseyite school. No feature of the movement organised and led by Pusey is more painful or deplorable. In the *Life of Archbishop Tait* this subject is dealt with at length, as it formed one of the subjects with which the archbishop was especially called upon to deal. We find him quoting confessional questions addressed to children of six years old, and he gives the following passage from one of several High Church bishops who

[1] Bishop Wilberforce printed in the Appendix to his Charge of 1851 passages from the religious books of devotion borrowed from the Church of Rome which Pusey had reprinted and circulated. He quotes a recent writer of the Romish communion who, referring to "Dr. Pusey's doctrines," says: "For one whom our books of controversy have brought round, twenty at least have yielded to the power of our devotions." The bishop further says: "Even if all direct statement of Roman error were excluded, yet they are alien to the established teaching of the Church of England"; and amongst other passages he gives the following as a sample of the sort of devotional book which Pusey introduced to the congregations of the English Church: "On the second day thou wilt offer homage to the heart of Jesus, lying as an infant in the stable, on the third to His mouth, on the fourth to His eyes, on the fifth to His hands, on the sixth to His feet, on the seventh to His flesh."

condemned the full-blown system of confession which was the direct fruit of Pusey's teaching:—

"Bishop Moberly of Salisbury, as one who had spent most of his life as headmaster of a great public school, expressed his firm conviction that the practice of habitual confession was 'mischievous in the highest degree.' 'I confess,' he added, 'that there is not one thing in all the world which is deeper in my heart and conscience than the corrupting influence of any such system as this getting into our schools. As to little children being taught to go to confession in the manner described, it appears to me to be cruel in the last degree, and not only cruel, but utterly and entirely false.'"[1]

Pusey's heresy on the point of confession and absolution was the tap-root of all the mischievous and fatal influence which he exercised as a leader in his Church, and I cannot refrain from quoting here the words of one who had no sympathy with the views of the Low Church Evangelicals, Samuel Taylor Coleridge. Speaking of the Church of Rome, he uses language which condemns the Puseyism of the Church of England. Having in the first volume of his *Biographia Literaria* set down certain views and considerations which seem to favour the Roman theology at some points, he proceeds as follows:—

"As, at the risk of passing for a secret favourer of superannuated superstitions, I have spoken out my views on the Roman theology, so, at a far more serious risk of being denounced as an intolerant bigot, I will declare what, after a two years' residence in exclusively Popish countries, was the impression left on my mind as to the effect and influence of the Romish religion, as it actually and practically

[1] *Life of Archbishop Tait*, vol. ii. p. 179.

exists. Repeating the answer long since returned to a friend, when I contemplate the whole system as it affects the great fundamental principles of morality, the *terra firma*, as it were, of our humanity; then contrast its operation on the sources and conditions of national strength and well-being; and lastly, consider its woeful influences on the innocence and sanctity of the female mind and imagination, on the faith and happiness, the gentle fragrance and unnoticed ever-present verdure of domestic life,—I can with difficulty avoid applying to it the Rabbin's fable of the fratricide Cain after the curse, that the *firm earth trembled wherever he strode, and the grass turned black beneath his feet.*"

Such has been the effect of that which is the central curse of the Romish system, the practice of sacramental confession and priestly absolution. The same system cannot but directly tend to produce the like results even in England. The influence of the "priest," with his prerogative as confessor and absolver, upon the confidences and the family integrity of the home, is one part of the evil effect to which Coleridge refers, and scarcely less injurious perhaps than the depraving moral influence of the confessional in its secret questions and private answers. The two evils are indissolubly linked together. All the elements of evil, though not as yet, it may be, fully developed, are present in germ in the organised system of Anglican confession and family influence. Indeed, Dr. Pusey himself, in his *Manual for Confessors*, says: "You may pervert this sacrament [of penance] from its legitimate end, into a subtle means of feeding evil passions and sin in your own mind." "It is a sad sight," again he says, "to see confessors giving their whole morning to young women devotees, while they dismiss men or married women, who have, perhaps, left their household affairs with difficulty, to find themselves rejected with 'I am busy, go to someone else!'"[1]

Let me add that, as introduced by Pusey, the system lacked certain provisions which are found in the Church of Rome, and which, though themselves often connected with naturally allied evils, yet at least recognise great dangers and difficulties ignored by the system of confession in the Anglican Church, and against which Pusey would have been powerless to make any provision, even if he had been conscious of the need of such provision. The Church of Rome does not entrust the power of the "keys," the sacramental secrets of the confessional, the minstry of absolution, to utterly unprepared and untrained striplings, fresh in many instances from all that belongs to the secularity and worldliness of university life and English society. Pusey's theory was that even a full-blooded and undisciplined university man, issuing from the midst of his comrades, had no sooner passed through the forms of ordination and under the hands of the bishop, than he was definitely empowered and commissioned to receive secret confessions of sorrow, temptation, and sin; to make what private and privileged inquiries might seem to him to be right; to administer consolation or rebuke according to his best judgment; to pronounce absolution from guilt, and admit into the favour of God and the

---

[1] In 1877, in consequence of the exposure by Lord Redesdale, in the House of Lords, of the infamous manual entitled *The Priest in Absolution*, there was a discussion on the subject in Convocation, when the well-known and highly respected Archdeacon Allen mentioned as a fact, for which he cited very high authority, that three clergymen confessors "had fallen into habits of immorality with women who had come to them for guidance" (Walsh, pp. 120 and 117).

fellowship of the Church, or to repel the unsatisfactory penitent from the sacrament and the Church. The "priest," invested with such an office, ought to have a wisdom more than human; ought to have grace and godliness beyond question, and well approved in the sight of both God and man; ought to be something between a man and an angel. Such, in truth, is the *theory* of the Roman Catholic Church. Their priests have been trained for their office, and are supposed to share the "angelic life." Every priest, moreover, as such, is *not*, in the Church of Rome, entitled to receive confessions. Confessors have a special training and a special licence. How lamentably the Roman Catholic theory breaks down, as practically known and tested, there is no need to say; Liguori himself, indeed, sadly and emphatically laments that in the very training those confessors have sometimes been fatally corrupted and depraved. Coleridge's words describe the result, and the letters of Erasmus, with much literature besides, remain as evidence before the world! But, at least, that Church recognises the monstrous absurdity of investing young men, taken fresh, without training, from the mixed ranks of a seething and promiscuous life, with attributes for which no man can be equal, which, in fact, involve a usurpation of the prerogative of the one and only Priest and Saviour of human kind.

I have intimated that at the bottom even of Pusey's errors there was a truth—the deep truth of man's sinfulness and need for pardon. Let me add that there is truth in what Pusey often says as to the benefit to be derived in certain cases, and especially in the case of the young, from penitent or grievously tempted souls "opening their griefs," their temptations, their besetting sins, their intellectual and moral perplexities, to a wise and good father in Christ, a good man of much experience and approved sympathy and wisdom. But the deadly poison of Pusey's teaching on this subject consists in this, that it is not simply a wise and good man, but it is the priest only—the "priest-physician" of souls—of whom he speaks, the ecclesiastical father-confessor, and that this physician and confessor is, according to his teaching, invested with the power both of searching the heart and of pronouncing or withholding absolution as from God. It is this which turns priestly claims into blasphemy, and depraves spiritual counsel and fellowship into terrible degradation, into demoralising slavery of soul and will.[1]

[1] When the text was sent to press, I had not seen an article on Pusey in the *Month* for October 1882. The article is manifestly well-informed, and is evidently from the pen of an Anglo-Catholic convert to Rome. It is written, of course, from the point of view of one who has completed his career, by exchanging the position of an Oxford Anglo-Romaniser for that of a Roman Catholic. The writer says of Pusey: "He did much to spread the practice of confession among Anglicans. There are strange stories told of his treatment of his penitents; of the severe, not to say cruel, penances he inflicted; of the written confessions he exacted from some, of the unjustifiable promises he forced upon others. This was but the necessary result of an earnest muddle-headed old man, without the grace of the sacraments to help him, untrained and untaught, without Catholic instinct, venturing to practise, unbidden and unsent, the most delicate of all the works entrusted to the priests of God." Elsewhere this Roman Catholic writer says: "Outside the Church, dogmatism is sure to degenerate into self-assertion; the confessional into an organ of clerical despotism; the claim of sacramental powers into a source of superstition and unconscious idolatry; the glorious Catholic ritual into the feeble, effeminate, man-millinery of modern Ritualism." The sting of this censure from the mouth of a full papist, coming down on the Anglo-Catholic quasi-Pope, is the cutting truth of which it is the appropriate expression from the Romish point of view. It is coarse and insolent in tone; but such insolence was, perhaps, not unnatural, however ungraceful, considering the relations

The subject of sisterhoods naturally comes into view in connexion with that of confession. I need not say there was truth in Pusey's general feeling that, when the work of Christ needed to be carried on in society, and especially to be carried into certain classes of society, this could best be accomplished by means of the organised service of devoted women. He was not the first discoverer since the Reformation, and amongst Protestant nations, of the great benefit and need of women's services in the way indicated. German Protestants, as Pusey knew, had organised sisterhoods at an earlier period than Pusey's first movement in the same direction. Sisterhoods, indeed, have been more steadily and effectively organised in connexion with the High Anglican party in the Church of England than with any other section of religious society in England. Too high praise can scarcely be given to the manner in which they have often done their work, especially in hospitals. They have set a high and noble example to the Christian women of all the Churches. And yet this movement has too often been spoiled, sadly marred, even seriously tainted, because of a principle, derived from his patristic authorities, which Pusey associated with it from the very first, as well as by the introduction into many of the Anglican sisterhoods of Pusey's confessional system. That principle was "the superior sanctity of unmarried life."

The doctrine I am now referring to, that of the superior sanctity of the unmarried life, is nothing less than a heresy against the primary and fundamental constitution

of Pusey at once with Rome as his oracle of inspiration, and with the Church of England, whose earnest and penitent children he so fearfully misguided.

See Note at the end of this chapter on "College Guilds."

of humanity, and has in it a taint of heathen Gnosticism. It involves treason against the "honourable" and the divinely-appointed "estate of matrimony." It was a part of the doctrine of celibacy, as taught by mediæval monkery, and incorporated in the popular teaching, the hagiology, and the cherished institutions of the Romish Church. It is possible to conceive of cœnobite institutions, apart from any such doctrine, as founded on high and fine ideals, and as congenial resorts and refuges for sincere devotees, who longed to be separated from the world's corruptions, and consecrated to the service of their fellow-men in all good ways, both in respect to this world and the world to come. Pusey, however, embraced the false and morbid idea just indicated,—an idea which is in direct antagonism to the teaching of the Bible, and which the actual history of the monastic system, regarded in its broad aspect and character, and allowing for happy and eminent exceptions, refutes with a terrible irony of practical contradiction. That consecrated men and women may, in response to a manifest call of combined need and opportunity, and under the highest Christian motives, feel themselves constrained to forego the attractions and comforts, the manifold blessings and means of blessing others, connected with family life, and to give themselves up wholly and solely to sacred missions for many years together, or even in the end for life, no well-informed Christian student of history can doubt. But for men and women to take such a course because a life of celibacy is conceived to be intrinsically holier, more saintly, than any other life, even than the life of a truly Christian wife and mother,—to be a life approaching the angelic,—and, in conformity with this idea, to consecrate themselves by a lifelong vow, this is in reality an antichristian error of the deepest dye, equally opposed to divine doctrine, whether in relation to creation or redemption, to nature or to grace. This, however, was the error which Pusey imbibed, at a comparatively early period of his history, from his patristic guides. In discreetly chosen language his biographer informs us that Pusey's object was not so much to "relieve the misery and ignorance of the great towns," as to "restore the consecrated single life." A "consecrated life" is, of course, the true idea; a consecrated single life may, in some instances, be a noble instance of self-denial and self-sacrifice. But a consecrated married life may be equally noble, equally saintly, not less angelic, if such a word is to be used at all. It may involve even sorer trials and greater self-sacrifice than would, to all human seeming, have been known in a single life, and it may be at least as fruitful in high moral and spiritual results. Here I may quote a few manly and at the same time Christian lines from Dr. Hook's letter of congratulation to Dean Stanley on his marriage. "I look," he says, "upon a good wife as a means of grace intended by God to soften man's heart, and to prepare it for that heavenly joy which is experienced by those over whose heart the love of God is shed by the Holy Ghost through our Lord and Saviour Jesus Christ. How *all* is love when we approach our Lord!"[1]

Pusey's knowledge of human nature was continually at fault, an exemplary illustration of which is afforded by the history of the ill-omened St. Saviour's Church. It would seem, indeed, that at one time his friends dared even to amuse themselves with stories showing his weakness on this point, if we may judge from a

[1] *Dr. Hook's Life*, vol. ii. p. 418.

story which is told in J. B. Mozley's *Letters*, and which may be quoted as a relief to this discussion, as well as an illustration of Pusey's want of insight into character—

"I heard," writes J. B. Mozley to his sister in 1841, "rather an amusing account of a young lady's visit to Oxford last term. The young lady, who had come to Pusey in such deep distress and perplexity, it seems, was flaunting about with young gentlemen a good deal of the time—shopping, going down the river, and amusing herself very pleasantly; dear, good Pusey all the time being full of pity and concern for her painful state of doubt and anxiety. A certain young kid-gloved and scented gentleman of —— college was a particular favourite of the young lady, but she had several others as well, and used to go about quite *comitata catervâ*, as we say in the classics, surrounded by a bodyguard of handsome young gentlemen. . . . Pusey had ventured to suggest that she might dress a little more soberly, but had been answered by her sister: Would he have young ladies to go about like nuns?"[1]

Mozley, it will be remembered, a few years before the date of this letter, had for several years been domesticated within Pusey's house, and knew him better than almost anyone else did. A recluse of such a character was not fitted to organise sisterhoods.

The man who had the clearest knowledge about the sisterhoods which were founded and administered under Pusey's influence was Bishop Wilberforce; and next to him, for distinct and intimate knowledge of the whole matter, must be ranked Archbishop Tait. These two authorities absolutely agreed in their practical judgment and counsel on this question, as may be read in the archbishop's

[1] J. B. Mozley's *Letters*, p. 111.

Life.[1] It was Wilberforce's misfortune to be called to the episcopate just as Pusey's Romeward leading had become conspicuous and prominent. It was his peculiar difficulty and sorrow that by personal association and the closest family ties he was connected, and indeed had been generally identified in public opinion, with the party of which Pusey was the head. Two of his brothers, to whom he was most tenderly attached, were among the most influential supporters of Pusey, and both went over, some years later, to Rome. Under these circumstances, for him to deal with Pusey as his diocesan was a trial and difficulty of extraordinary severity. A dispassionate judge of the case will, I think, admire the bishop's conduct in this matter as much as anything in his life-history. His insight, his patience, his skill in the controversy, and his steadfast firmness and fidelity, maintained during many years, are beyond praise. In this volume of Pusey's biography, as might be expected, an attempt is made to represent Wilberforce as incompetent, for want of patristic learning, to judge or any way deal with Pusey. Let the reader refer to the bishop's Life, and on this point judge for himself. Though not so learned in patristic lore and mediæval theology as Dr. Pusey, Wilberforce was a competently learned prelate : he was not ignorant of the best patristic writers, and he was at pains especially to inform himself as to the views of the standard divines of his own Church. He was moreover incomparably superior to Pusey in theological insight and faculty, as indeed is shown by his acute and able criticism of Pusey's own special views. Not only, however, was it his duty, at the very outset of his episcopate, to deal in the way of discipline with Pusey,

[1] See, in particular, vol. i. p. 452 (cf. 457, 458).

whom he felt compelled privately to inhibit from preaching in the Oxford diocese, but he found it necessary, years afterwards, after long consideration, to remove from Cuddesdon the author of this biography of Pusey, because, with all his learning and excellences, and notwithstanding his self-restraint as a follower of Pusey, Liddon's influence in the college was proved to have been rather Puseyistic than Anglican, to have been the means of imbuing the theological candidates with a Romanising bias, and was increasingly distrusted by loyal Anglican supporters of the college. Dr. Liddon was a great preacher and divine; Christendom owes much to his *Bampton Lectures*; but his Romeward and mediæval bias must have been more extreme than has been generally supposed. The whole tone of this biography, quietly as it is written, tends to show this. He admits no fault in Pusey, except an amiable and over-sanguine confidence in his followers or instruments. He writes throughout as a sedate and discreet partisan, who never forgets himself or uses extreme language, but also, except under the strongest compulsion, makes no concessions to the opposite side. Once, indeed, he forgets his prudence and commits himself. Bishop Longley (then of Ripon) had desired Mr. Macmullen, Pusey's representative and nominee as one of the clergy of St. Saviour's, " to retract the assertion that the Blessed Virgin intercedes." Dr. Liddon hereupon remarks that for such a " retractation it would surely be difficult to allege authority either from Scripture or the formularies of the Church of England " (p. 125). So far Dr. Liddon had gone towards Mariolatry; so unsafe an interpreter was he of the tenets sanctioned by the Reformed Church of England. It is noticeable that, as Liddon holds Wilberforce to have been wrong where he came into collision with Pusey, so he condemns Bishop Longley of Ripon for the part he took, in concert with Dr. Hook, in removing the Romanising clergy from St. Saviour's Church, which Pusey had built and endowed. He couples Bishop Wilberforce and Bishop Longley as having, in their dealings with Pusey and Puseyism, shown a "curious pedantry," and he expresses his belief that if Bishop Longley had exhibited towards St. Saviour's Mission, from which clergyman after clergyman went over to Rome, —till, first and last, the number exceeded a dozen,—the "same discriminating judgment which characterised his gracious sway as Archbishop of Canterbury, much bitterness might have been avoided, and the Church of England might have been spared serious loss" (p. 368). And yet Bishop Longley was the same man as the archbishop, was nearly of the same ripeness in years, and not more infirm or less acute in judgment. It was his fault as Bishop Longley that he differed gravely from Pusey.

The Bishop of Oxford, as might have been expected, was a great friend and zealous promoter of sisterhoods, but not of sisterhoods organised on Pusey's lines. Canon Butler, of Wantage and Worcester, as High a Churchman as is at all compatible with any sort of loyalty to the Church of England,—there was not a little of the Romeward tendency in him,—bore this testimony to the bishop's administration and influence as regards sisterhoods—

"Most tenderly and delicately," he writes, "the bishop enforced his opinions, so that in many delicate and complicated questions we always felt that whether his mind was or was not entirely the same as our own, we should ever be sure of a fair hearing. Nothing could be kinder, wiser, or more large-hearted, than the line which he adopted; and it is certainly not too much to assert that to him our English sisterhoods owe their present position of usefulness and acceptance."

Bishop Wilberforce, however, was totally opposed to the underlying principle of celibacy which to Pusey was of so much importance, and, of course, to the use of confession among the sisterhood. The House of Mercy at Clewer, perhaps the best known of all the sisterhoods, was founded under the direction of Pusey, and was a source of no little anxiety and trouble to the bishop. In regard to that establishment the bishop writes as follows to the Lady Superintendent, a sort of Prioress, who had been placed by Pusey in charge—

"I suppose," he says, " that such a life as that of the Sisters of Clewer is likely specially to attract those who would desire and probably have practised constant confession, who would wish to submit their lives to the direction of the priest, who would crave after books of Roman Catholic devotion, simple or adapted, and who would probably desire to wear and see crucifixes and the like. How, then, are such persons to be treated by us ? (1) We cannot provide for such a life, because we disapprove of it. (2) We cannot suffer it to be led as a part of the common life in sisterhood, so as to give really its colour to our institution. We cannot, *e.g.*, allow the Sisters to practise continual confession to, or elect into directors, the warden or chaplain of our house. Nor can we allow them to use amongst their Sisters, still less to lend to them, Roman Catholic books, or to wear openly, or to exhibit in their rooms, images or representations which the Church of England discourages; nor can we allow them to be visited in the house by other clergy than those of our house, for the carrying out by their means of any system which we do not administer by our clergy."

About the same time, in a letter to the well-known Rev. T. T. Carter, whom Pusey had placed in charge of Clewer, Wilberforce writes as follows :—

"I see plainly that Clewer has a tendency to run into a system with which I can have nothing to do. If sisterhoods cannot be maintained except upon a semi-Romanistic scheme, with its *direction*, with its development of self-conscious and morbid religious affection, with its exaltation of the contemplative life, with its perpetual confession and its un-English tone, I am perfectly convinced that we had better have no sisterhoods. . . . You *must not* let the soft influences of the women's souls with which you have to deal lead you into becoming a director. You must with me distinctly act, and say that Clewer is to be Church of England and *no more*. We must have no *evasions* as to Roman Catholic books, as to the going at stated times to Richards, Pusey, etc. Evasion seems to me to be the very clinging curse of everything Romanistic."[1]

Against the perpetual vow, in particular, the bishop

[1] Canon Carter has gone very far since his bishop wrote to him as I have quoted. Courteous, wary, a favourite "Father" confessor, a man of family, he has worked unweariedly for his sect. He revised for the press the infamous book known as *The Priest in Absolution*, of which Lord Redesdale read portions to the House of Lords, being unable, for decency's sake, to read the worst passages of the book, and which Archbishop Tait spoke of to the assembled bishops and peers as a "disgrace to the community." He has been for many years Superior-General of the Confraternity of the Blessed Sacrament. In that capacity he declared in 1877 that there was no important difference between the Roman and the Anglican doctrine as to eucharistic adoration (Walsh, p. 218). Canon Carter entered into a controversy with me in the columns of the *Times*, on occasion of the publication of this volume. The correspondence is referred to in Appendix B.

never ceased to bear his testimony and assert his authority. To a clergyman of the Puseyite school he wrote in 1850 objecting "absolutely, as un-Christian and savouring of the worst evils of Rome, to the vows involved in such a statement as—'she is for ever consecrated to the service of her Heavenly Spouse.'" "I object," he says, "to the expression itself as unwarranted by God's word, and savouring of one of the most carnal perversions of the Church of Rome." In November 1854, to another clergyman who had written to him on behalf of a young woman who desired to take a vow and enter a sisterhood, he wrote a letter, from which I take the following extract:—

"When you ask me to give her the apostolic benediction 'on her public resolution of chastity and devotion to Christ,' you ask me to do what it is quite impossible for me to do. Such a resolution made publicly, and confirmed by a bishop's act, is really and *bona fide* a vow. Now even a secret resolution of chastity is what I should dissuade. No one has, without God's express appointment, the right, in my judgment, to bind themselves for the future in such matters. Let them follow the guiding hand of God from day to day, and rely for persevering in a course of right or service on His daily gifts of guiding, enlightening, strengthening grace, and not on the strength of any past vow or resolution."

In 1860, Wilberforce had still to contend against the same agitation in favour of perpetual vows. In his Diary, November 30th, he says: "Clewer. Early Communion, and admission of three Sisters—two rejected. Would not consent to alter the rule about no vows." At the Church Congress in 1862 he thus expresses himself: "I believe that the abuses of that life have come (1) from the promises of *perpetuity*, and (2) from the vows connected with the admission of persons having property, and being allowed to give that property up in any moment of excitement to this purpose." He adds a paragraph in regard to the special application of the word "religious" to such a life, which I quote here for a reason which will immediately appear—

"One single word on the use of the term 'religious.' I confess that I have the very deepest objection in any way to apply the word 'religious' to such a life. I think it was adopted at a time when the standard of lay piety was very low; and, at all events, as no good seems to me to be got by the use of a word ambiguous, at least in its meaning, and which seems to imply that God can be better served in the unmarried sisterhood than in the blessed and holy state of matrimony, I think it is a pity that it should be used."

Now, let us compare with what I have quoted a passage in the biography relating to this subject. If we read intelligently and with well-informed minds between the lines, it will, I think, appear to be in effect an admission of the substantial truth of the current charges against Pusey, the same charges which are so distinctly intimated in Bishop Wilberforce's Letters and Diary, as well as a skilful apology on his behalf. It refers to Pusey's tone of feeling and manner of life about the year 1848,—that is, when his work as an organiser of the confessional and of sisterhoods was just beginning—

"Probably he had hardly realised the gravity and intimacy of these questions,—questions often involving delicate family relations,—which he would be called upon to settle, nor the force of prejudice that the religious life would not unnaturally excite, nor the difficulty of guiding and restraining the emotional and sensitive characters with whom he might be brought in contact. It must be remembered that in England and in English families, with the exception of the limited circle of the older Roman Catholics, there had been for centuries literally no experience of the religious life. The special vocation of a Sister of Mercy, the character involved and the claims of such a character, were altogether unknown. That young ladies who were considered 'serious' should object to theatres and dancing was looked upon as a pardonable eccentricity; but that those who were not evangelical should take a stricter view of life, should shrink from society and entertain thoughts of a vow of celibacy in place of an eligible marriage, was almost inconceivable. Besides, there was then, especially amongst religious-minded people, a very high and right sense of filial obligation. There was also a notorious jealousy of interference on the part of a spiritual guide in the private arrangements of family life.

"With his unworldliness and simplicity, his overwhelming sense of divine guidance, the sanctity of the human soul, and the nothingness of all worldly objects and aims, Pusey found himself, almost before he was aware of it, opposed to the wishes and judgments of respected friends, and sometimes thwarting the most cherished aims which they entertained for their children. Again, his small knowledge of the outer world, and his own disciplined disposition, were not the best qualifications for guiding any excitable and emotional temperaments with which he might have to deal; and, in those delicate relations which a gainsaying and censorious world could not rightly appreciate, he laid himself open to misconception and gossip, against which a man more worldly-wise would have been on his guard. . . . In his simplicity Pusey himself was as unconscious of the gossip as he was regardless of the means to avoid it. The fact is, as Keble suggests, that he was so centred on the great spiritual efforts on which his heart was set, that he was too little careful of social conventionalities, the observance of which would have prevented those misinterpretations of his conduct, and relieved his friends of the pain which he could not understand that he was causing them."

So much in general Dr. Liddon has to say by way of explaining, and at the same time explaining away, what he speaks of as exaggerated and distorted stories in relation to Pusey's conduct and deportment as a spiritual director and father, when he had to deal with emotional and excitable women, who came to him for religious counsel and guidance. The tone of the passage is that of one who has himself accepted the views which Pusey held in regard to spiritual direction, to the vow of celibacy, and to what he speaks of as the "religious life," thus laying himself open to the reproof contained in the preceding extract from Bishop Wilberforce.

There are not wanting evidences, indirectly furnished in the biography, of the extent to which Pusey carried the practices of which he was continually accused, but as to which he seemed always to have some evasion to fall back upon. The Rev. Mr. Dodsworth, one of his closest friends and associates for many years, one of his most trusted allies, at length made up his mind to follow Newman and Manning into the Church of Rome. His tongue was then loosed, and being out of patience because Pusey still, as he thought, unfairly and more or less dishonestly, lingered within the Church of England, he wrote a public letter to Pusey, describing the extent to which his former guide had been accustomed to go in the Romanising direction. The date is May 1850, and the subject is "the position which Dr. Pusey had taken in the present crisis."

"You," he said, "have been one of the foremost leaders on to a higher appreciation of that church system of which sacramental grace is the very life and soul, both by precept and example. You have been amongst us the most earnest in maintaining Catholic principles. By your constant communion and practice of administering the sacrament of penance; by encouraging everywhere, if not enjoining, confession and giving special priestly absolution; by teaching the propitiatory sacrifice of the Holy Eucharist as applicatory of the one sacrifice on the Cross, and by the adoring of Christ's real presence on the altar in the form of bread and wine; by your introduction of Roman Catholic books, adapted to the use of our Church; by encouraging the use of rosaries and crucifixes, and special devotions to our Lord—as, *e.g.*, to His five wounds; by adopting language most powerfully expressive of our incorporation into Christ—as, *e.g.*, our being incorporated by the blood of our Lord; by advocating counsels of perfection, and seeking to restore, with more or less fulness, the conventual or monastic life,—I say, by the teaching and practice, of which this enumeration is a sufficient type and indication, you have done much to revive amongst us the system which may be pre-eminently called sacramental. And yet, now, you seem to shrink from the front rank, you seem ready to hide yourself under soft assertions of truths which, it is said, no six men in the Church of England will be found to deny, and behind ambiguous statements which can be subscribed in different senses."

Dr. Liddon seems to have felt it necessary to quote these statements of Mr. Dodsworth, made in a pamphlet too famous to be ignored. But no reply is given or even attempted. Pusey never dealt with them frankly or directly. His biographer has no observation to make. They are fully borne out by the statements of Mr. Maskell, who, like Mr. Dodsworth, had for years been one of Pusey's most influential disciples and helpers, and whose " accomplishments as a liturgical scholar, and position as chaplain to the Bishop of Exeter,"—to borrow Dr. Liddon's own description of the grounds of his importance as a critic of Pusey's conduct and methods,—lend special importance to his assertions. The passages I am about to quote are from a reply by Mr. Maskell to the pamphlet which Pusey, in the form of a letter to his fellow-helper, the Rev. W. Upton Richards, had in 1850 been compelled to write, in consequence of the publication of a joint letter addressed to himself by Mr. Allies, Mr. Dodsworth, and Mr. Maskell, all of whom had then joined the Church of Rome, which letter raised the searching question: " Under what authorisation," to use Dr. Liddon's words, " private confessions were received and absolutions given in the Church of England," thus attacking Pusey at the central point in his confessional system, and showing also how at that point he was personally most vulnerable as an Anglican priest. In Mr. Maskell's reply to Pusey's pamphlet occurs the following passage :—

" In page 6 of your letter to Mr. Richards, you blame Mr. Dodsworth for having said in his published letter to you that you have ' enjoined ' auricular confession, and you say that you could not enjoin it. Suffer me to say that Mr. Dodsworth's use of the word was just and reasonable. He does not use it simply without limitation; he says that you have 'encouraged, if not enjoined,' auricular confession; but it is evident that in the sense of compulsion, he knew, as well as yourself, you could not possibly enjoin auricular confession. And he knew also, as I know, that to say merely that you have encouraged it, would fall as far short of what your actual practice is, as the word enjoin in the sense of compelling would exceed it. He knew that you had done more than encourage confession in very many cases; that you had warned people of the danger of deferring it, have insisted on it as the only remedy, have pointed out the inevitable dangers of the neglect of it, and have promised the highest blessings in the observance, until you have brought penitents in fear and trembling upon their knees before you.

"There are some other parts of your letter to Mr. Richards which have somewhat more than startled me. I have almost begun to doubt the accuracy of my memory, or that I could ever have understood the commonest rules of plain speaking upon very solemn mysteries and duties of the Christian faith. I mean such passages as these: 'We are not to obtrude, nor to offer our services, nor to cause confusion by intruding into the ministry of others. . . . In like manner, when residing elsewhere'; from which, of course, no one would suppose that you go from home into other dioceses for the express purpose of receiving auricular confession . . . 'when any came to me I ministered to them. But not having a parochial cure, I have not led others to confession.' . . . Far be it from me to say you do not believe every word of these sentences to be strictly and verbally true; what I do say is, that so far as I have known it, they do not in any adequate or real way represent your practice. . . . The Bishop of Exeter would repudiate with horror the system of particular and detailed inquiry into every circumstance of sin, which, in correct imitation of Roman Catholic rules, you do not fail to press. . . . What, then, do you conceive that the Bishop of Exeter would say of persons secretly received against the known will of their parents, or confession heard in the houses of common friends, or of clandestine correspondence to arrange meetings under initials, or in envelopes addressed to other persons? and more than this, when such confessions are recommended and urged as a part of the spiritual life, and among religious duties; not in order to quiet the conscience before receiving the communion. I know how heavily the enforced mystery and secret correspondence regarding confession in your communion has weighed down the minds of many to whom you have 'ministered'; I know how bitterly it has eaten, even as a canker, into their very souls; I know how utterly the specious arguments which you have urged have failed to remove their burning sense of shame and deceitfulness."[1]

The reference to the Bishop of Exeter in this extract derives peculiar force and authority from the fact that before he went over to Rome Mr. Maskell had been chaplain to Bishop Philpotts of Exeter, who had done much to shield Pusey from censure, especially in the case of Miss Sellon and the Plymouth Sisterhood.

[1] The foregoing passage is quoted from Maskell's *Letter to Dr. Pusey*, pp. 17-21, by the Rev. Bourchier Wrey Saville in his pamphlet entitled, *Dr. Pusey: an Historic Sketch*.

If we compare Mr. Maskell's statements with the apologetic passage I have quoted from the biography, it will be seen how close the correspondence really is between the positive assertions of the one and the inner meaning—scarcely veiled—of the other. Why Dr. Liddon thought it necessary to quote Mr. Dodsworth, but could not bring himself to quote the more distinct and fuller statement of Mr. Maskell, I shall not try to conjecture. It is evident, however, that in this third volume, as in the volume preceding, the biography omits singularly important and very damaging evidence as to the private influence used and the sort of discipline carried out by Pusey.

The history of the St. Saviour's Church and Mission at Leeds, which was begun in the second volume of the biography, is completed in the third volume. It was the immediate fruit of the penitential sorrow which took hold of Pusey after his wife's death; which deepened during the following years of trouble and grief, when his beloved and devoted daughter was taken from him, and when his sufferings culminated in his illness, compelling him to leave his work and his home, and to seek health on the coast of South Wales; sorrow which knew no relief till he had made his soul's confession to Keble in Hursley Church. During the former part of this period Pusey conceived the thought of making a penitential offering by building and endowing a church and a college for mission priests in Leeds, where his friend, Dr. Hook, was vicar, on whose sympathy and co-operation he thought he could rely. His intention was to apply his system, in full development and force, to a dense and spiritually needy population, consisting chiefly of working men. The parish clergy were to be of his nomination, acting as patron, and they were to be assisted by a college of unmarried priests or deacons. Suspicion, however, was awakened against the project almost from the first, not only in the minds of Dissenters and Evangelicals, but of Dr. Hook and Bishop Longley, neither of whom was in any sense a Low Churchman. The ornaments, the memorial window, and especially the inscription above the porch of the church, asking the prayers of all that entered for the soul of the sinner who built the church,—an inscription standing there to-day, —alike suggested Romish proclivities. The bishop felt it his duty frequently to intervene with objections, all of which did not prevail. He objected strongly to the inscription, but was informed that the unknown benefactor insisted upon that being retained as an absolute condition —without which the whole scheme must be abandoned. Years passed before the church was ready to open. The opening services, in which Pusey took by far the greatest share, did not serve to allay suspicion. Not a word of disclaimer, not a sentence implying at any point a difference from Rome and Romanism, was uttered throughout the twelve services. Pusey, indeed, though by this time his bosom friend, Newman, was known to be determined, and to have made every preparation, to go over to Rome, steadfastly refused his consent to a word being spoken by anyone to reassure those who naturally identified his views with those of Newman. Then came the clergy of the college. Their methods and teaching, and the whole spirit of their administration, savoured of Rome. The books of devotion, the breviary which was recommended for use, the administration of the sacraments, all were, at least to the general view, nothing but popish. Dr. Hook remonstrated. The bishop interfered. Pusey was appealed to, and Pusey called in Marriott and Keble. It was in vain. The clergy, one after another, went over to Rome—till more than a dozen had so gone over. All but one employed during the first five years made their way to that goal.

Dr. Liddon has given a very fair account of this unhappy business, with quotations on both sides, in which he seems to admit that Pusey cannot be acquitted of grave error in administration, although he blames Hook for his vehemence, and—this, I think, is unfair and unreasonable—seeks to make the bishop and Dr. Hook, by their severity of judgment, responsible, at least in part, for the secessions to Rome. Dr. Hook was, indeed, placed in a pitiable condition by the course of events, and certainly in no way and to no degree gave any countenance to the Romanising methods and practices of the offending clergy. The following extract from a letter to Pusey may serve to indicate what his feelings were in the matter:—

"*Knowing* St. Saviour's to be a semi-papal colony, however careful the clergy there may be to keep within the letter of the law, I shall take an early opportunity, and I expect one soon to offer, of speaking of it as I think, and so of disconnecting it in men's minds from Leeds. . . .

"Do not write upon this subject any more, for it is useless. When I compare your defence of St. Saviour's with what goes on there, you only make me the more suspicious. You are either incorrectly informed, or you have got into the habit of defending a cause. I am not going to argue with you. If you are, as you say you are, agreed with me in principle, instead of writing, you will set to work to eradicate Romanism in St. Saviour's. If in your attempt to do so you fail, *then* we shall be in the same boat. I do not care for what men *say*: I look to what they *do*. What you have *done* is to send Romanisers here—one of them the friend of some of the late perverts; if guided or in ignorance, try to prevail upon them to resign. Undo what you have done, or at least attempt it. If you either cannot or will not, do not write any more. All you can say is, that you think that they are not Romanisers; and all I can say is that, as I know them to be Romanisers, I shall warn all men of the danger of touching pitch."

When Charles Marriott, at Pusey's request, went to visit St. Saviour's, he reported to Pusey that "there was more to complain of here than you thought for," and justifies the bishop in removing one of Pusey's trusted agents, whilst he also decides that another, of whom Hook had complained repeatedly and bitterly, was unfit for his post, and ought to be induced to resign. This was in 1846–47. In 1851 things came to a final crisis at St. Saviour's, the result of which is described in a note from Pusey to Keble: "I had a sad visit to St. Saviour's. It has again to be built up from its foundation. The bishop has cleared everything away, and I fear that two at least will come back as Roman priests with a Roman mission." This was in March 1851. All the clergy but one went over. Even Dr. Liddon has to confess that "Hook, if he expressed himself with unguarded vehemence, took the measure of men more accurately than Pusey." The man that led the march Romoward in the first instance was backed up by Pusey to the end of his connexion with St. Saviour's, and it is to this fact in particular that the biographer refers. Besides which, he was sent to the Church, as Pusey had in the end to confess, when he was known by Pusey to "have been seriously shaken as to the English Church."[1] So that there was colourable ground for Hook's charge that Pusey had knowingly sent to St. Saviour's men who were disaffected to the English Church, and Papists at heart— "a colony of Papists," Hook said. Hook's generosity and personal friendship for Pusey, notwithstanding the acuteness of his vexation and his deep indignation, sometimes vehemently expressed, prevented him in his correspondence with Pusey from completely uttering his mind as to the whole character of the movement which Pusey led. But in a letter to his intimate friend Lord Hatherley, written on New Year's Day, 1847, he pours forth freely the bitterness of his grief and vexation: "Out of my family," he says, "my·joy, my happiness was in my parish. I had gained the confidence of my people; my opponents were softened and coming round; I was beginning to feel that Leeds had become a perfect paradise, and now it is a howling wilderness. . . . I have not wept so much for many years as during the last three months. . . . As I have fought for the Church of England against the Puritans, so will I now fight for her against the Romanisers."[2] In *Hook's Life* also, extracts are given from a very strong letter which, thoroughly roused, he sent to the *Guardian* in 1850, and in which he speaks out fully in regard to the Puseyite Movement. He describes the Puseyite party as "calumniators of the Church of England, and vindicators of the Church of Rome; palliating the vices of the Romish system, and magnifying the deficiencies of the Church of England; sneering at everything Anglican, and admiring everything Romish; students of the breviary and missal,

[1] *Letter from Pusey to Hook*, vol. iii. p. 131.
[2] *Life of Lord Hatherley*, vol. ii. p. 197.

disciples of the schoolmen, insinuating Romish sentiments, circulating and republishing Romish works; introducing Romish practices in their private, and infusing a Roman tone into their public devotions; introducing the Romish confessional, enjoining Romish penances, adopting Romish prostrations, recommending Romish litanies; muttering the Romish shibboleth, and rejoicing in the cant of Romish fanaticism; assuming sometimes the garb of the Romish priesthood, and venerating without imitating their celibacy; defending Romish miracles, and receiving as true the lying legends of Rome; almost adoring Romish saints, and complaining that we have no saints in England since we purified our Church; explaining away the idolatry, and pining for the Mariolatry of the Church of Rome; vituperating the English Reformation, and receiving for the truth the false doctrines of the Council of Trent; whispering in the ears of credulous ignorance, in high places as well as low, that the two Churches are in principle the same." [1]

It will be seen that this vivid picture, photographed from the life, tallies closely with the passages already quoted from the letters of Dodsworth and Maskell, and with the statements as to the tactics of Pusey and his coadjutors contained in *Bishop Wilberforce's Life*. The consensus of evidence is indeed conclusive as to the conscientious stealthiness and subtlety with which Pusey used his private counsels and influence in the process of Romanising the Church of England. Very saintly men have indisputably thought, in some instances, that it was their duty to use such means in the prosecution of their religious purposes. The *Tracts for the Times* had given lessons in

[1] *Hook's Life*, vol. ii. pp. 278, 279.

the needful arts. Hook, in his letters, repeatedly describes such tactics as Jesuitism.

NOTE TO PAGES 278-79.
TOWN AND COLLEGE GUILDS—A RECENT DEVELOPMENT OF CONFESSIONALISM.

Dr. Pusey's system of confession, begun in Anglican schools, as in those, for instance, founded by Mr. (Father) Woodard, has naturally developed into a system of guilds and societies, intended to operate especially, though not by any means exclusively, in our colleges and national universities. I take the following paragraphs from a description, furnished to the *Times* (for April 4, 1896) by an Occasional Correspondent, of what is spoken of as a "secret society at Cambridge."

"The full name of the society is 'The Companions of St. John.' It is estimated that at the present time the number of members is considerably in excess of one thousand. It has branches at Oxford, Birmingham, London, and other towns. The year of its foundation was probably about 1886. The leader of the organisation at Cambridge, if not the founder, is the Rev. Ernest John Heriz-Smith, M.A., Fellow of Pembroke College. To his zeal and unbounded energy the rapid growth of the society is chiefly due. Of his unselfish motives no one can entertain a doubt.

. . . .

"Whatever the exact date of the formation of the society, early in the year 1892 its existence was brought to the notice of the Cambridge branch of the Church of England Young Men's Society. An inquiry was instituted by the latter organisation, when the following facts were proved :—That the Society of the Companions of St. John had been in existence for some time, that the Rev. E. J. Heriz-Smith was the head of the society, that there existed a University branch and a town branch. The ceremony of admission to the society was that the candidate for admission should have his hands tied, kneel at a table, have his eyes bandaged, and take a vow, by some described as an oath, to obey the head of the society in all things lawful, and never to mention any matter relating to the society except to a member. After this vow was taken, and not until then, the rules of the society were communicated to the new member—one of these rules being that he should implicitly obey his introducer or sponsor for sixty days, or until he introduced a new member, when such new member would in his turn be bound to obey his introducer or sponsor for the like period, or until he shifted the obligation by obtaining another novice. Further, it was shown that Mr. Heriz-Smith had written a letter to one of the members urging the expediency of confession. The subject of the society was then referred to a Ruridecanal chapter, which reported that it was proved that the society had endeavoured to tamper with the religious convictions of one of its members. The effect of this inquiry was that the majority if not the entire body of townsmen withdrew, although Mr. Heriz-Smith in a letter addressed to them insisted that resignation was inoperative, as once being a member they could not withdraw from companionship of the order.

. . . . . .

"The action of the Ruridecanal chapter had the effect of destroying the society as regards town membership, and it was not until last May that the operations of the association again became a matter of public inquiry. At one of the colleges a complaint was made to the Tutor of an endeavour to obtain recruits. The matter was referred to the Master, who expressed his disapproval, and there is reason to believe that the movement as regarded that particular college was arrested.

"In the month of February of this year the action of the association was again the subject of inquiry. In consequence of this investigation a communication was made to the editor of the *Record*, who was furnished with documentary evidence. A member of Jesus College gives a full account of his introduction to Mr. Heriz-Smith and his admission to the order. Accepting an invitation to luncheon at Mr. Heriz-Smith's rooms in Pembroke, the conversation was led up to the advisability of joining the society. The seductive eloquence of Mr. Heriz-Smith prevailed, and here in his own words is the account of his initiation. 'I was taken into a room, my eyes were bandaged; I knelt down by the side of the table. My hands were tied together, and I took an oath of allegiance to Mr. Heriz-Smith to obey him in all things. I was then shown the rules, and found that I was bound to my sponsor, my brother, who introduced me. I forget some of the things I promised to do, but I remember that I swore never to mention C. St. J. matters to other than C. St. J. members. I also remember that I was bound to my sponsor, that he could punish me if I did anything of which he disapproved, and if I went to any religious meeting which he disapproved of he could fetch me out, and if I refused he could come to my rooms the next day and tie me up to the table leg.'"

Since the facts of the case were published in the *Times* there has been much correspondence on the subject, with the effect of fully establishing the case as stated. A few, indeed, try to treat the whole matter as insignificant. But these persons are interested in minimising the whole affair. " One of the Victims" writes as follows :—

" SIR,—I was very interested in reading in to-day's issue an account of a certain secret society said to be existing at Cambridge. As one who, for a short time, was unfortunately a member of that society, perhaps I may be permitted to write a few of my experiences in connexion therewith.

" Let me begin by saying that exactly the same proceedings were gone through with me as those reported of a certain member of Jesus College, with, perhaps, this difference, that the nature of the society was not fully explained to me *in extenso* until after the mysterious ceremony, and not until it was too late to escape.

" My first introduction to Mr. Heriz-Smith was through a then member of the society and before I had been in Cambridge a month.

" It appears that he treated me in exactly the same way as he did all the others who became members—namely, asked me to his Sunday evening 'At Homes,' and then to various meals, speaking on all these occasions concerning the society and enticing me to become a member.

" After much persuasion, and being a timid freshman, and not having had the experience that three years at a University gives one, I consented.

" It did not take me long to discover the mistake I had made, and with all possible speed I withdrew from the society. It is with the desire to prevent others from being 'caught' in the same way, and with that desire only, that I am troubling you with this letter. A boy, on leaving school, has not usually any very definite religious belief, and it is on entering the somewhat larger sphere of a University, where he is brought in contact with all sorts and conditions of men, with every variety of religious belief, that he forms one for himself; and it is these men, fresh from the public schools, on the threshold of their University career, these are the men whom Mr. Heriz-Smith seduces to become members of the society.

" I do not wish it to be thought that I bear towards Mr. Heriz-Smith any animosity. On the contrary, I fully believe that everything he does is done with the best intention; but my only wish in writing this is to prevent present and future undergraduates from having the same unfortunate experience as happened to myself."

CHAPTER XII.

PUSEY'S DOCTRINE OF THE REAL PRESENCE—CONSUBSTANTIATION AND TRANSUBSTANTIATION — NEWMAN AND PUSEY—PUSEY, BOSSUET, AND NEWMAN—PUSEY AND MANNING—REUNION WITH ROME—PUSEY AND ARCHBISHOP WAKE—HOW PUSEY OUTWENT NEWMAN—GLADSTONE, LORD HALIFAX AND THE POPE — THE ONE HOPE OF THE CHRISTIAN WORLD.

FOR the special purpose of this volume, in what remains to be said as to the action and influence of Pusey as a leader of the Romanising Neo-Anglican Movement, little further help is to be had from his Life. The third volume closes with a chapter on the "Second period of the Eucharistic Controversy," which was connected with the well-known *cause célèbre* of Archdeacon Denison. Into that case, however, there is no need for me to go. But I must needs refer to the huge volume which was Pusey's contribution to the controversy that arose out of that case; and I will at the same time deal with the question generally of his teaching on the subject, as he would have phrased it, of "The Eucharistic Sacrifice." This will form the proper sequel to the subject of confession and absolution already dealt with, and will be found to lead on to that of Pusey's suggestions for reunion with the Church of Rome.

Pusey's doctrine as to baptism, confession, and absolution was rounded and completed by his teaching as to the "Real Presence"—by which he meant the *spirituo-corporeal* presence—of the Lord Jesus in the Sacrament of the Lord's Supper. On this subject, however, not much is learned from the Life. The Denison case in 1854 reopened a question of doctrine, as to which it would seem that Pusey would have been content to say as little as possible. The sermon on that subject, which he had delivered in 1843, and for which he had been suspended from preaching before the University, he had promised to supplement by notes containing patristic evidence in favour of his teaching. He had, however, done nothing in the matter; but the Denison case compelled him to act. He therefore published in 1855 a volume of 722 pages, consisting almost entirely of extracts from the "Fathers" of the centuries succeeding the period of pure and apostolic doctrine in the Church; that is to say, the third, fourth, and fifth centuries, Cyril of Alexandria being his chief authority. The sayings of these imperfectly informed writers,—these, for the most part, altogether un-disciplined thinkers and teachers,—their grossest confusions of thought, their turgid and exaggerated rhetoric, he accepts as if they were the words of profound metaphysical thinkers, of trained and learned theologians, of inspired divines, of men whose most exalted phrases must be taken as equivalent to exact scientific definitions; and insists that they must be swallowed whole by Christians to-day. However learned or devout, however versed in theology, in philosophy, in New Testament exegesis, modern divines may be, they must accept as authoritative the crude and gross language of the men whom Pusey calls the Fathers of the Church, of extracts from whose writings his sermons on this subject were largely composed. The sermons on which we have to rely for a direct statement of his own views are chiefly two, one the University sermon of 1843, already referred to, for preaching which he was suspended for two years; and the other, the sermon preached before the University in 1871 from the text, "This is My body." In the sermon of 1843 he uses the following language: "Receiving Him (the Lord Jesus) into this very body, they who are His receive life which shall pass over to our very decaying flesh," and quotes in support of this language the following passage from Cyril of Alexandria: "As, if one entwineth wax with other wax and melteth them in the fire, there resulteth of both one, ἕν τι (literally, *something that is a unity—one thing*); so through the participation of the body of Christ, and of His precious blood, He in us and we again in Him, are co-united; for in no other way could that which is by nature corruptible be made alive, unless it were bodily entwined with that which is by nature life, the Only-begotten." It is from such crass materialism as this that he derives his doctrine, and by such patristic authority that he supports it. So again he says: "We are members of Him, not by love only, but by very deed; mingled with that flesh, mingled with Him, that we might, in a manner, be one substance with Him." "He is commingled and co-united with us." We have "received into ourselves, bodily and spiritually, Him who is by nature and truly the Son." "He hath united the nature of His own flesh with His eternal nature." In so grossly materialistic a sense as this he says in the same sermon, "Having Christ within him, not only shall he have, but he hath already eternal life"—words which, applied in an evangelical sense, might be joyfully taken home by every true believer, but which he uses in a materialising sense. The Puseyite sense comes out very grossly in the *Devotions for the Holy Communion*, one of the Puseyite text-books of devotion—a book at one time well known, though now, perhaps, partly lost to sight. " Receive, O most loving Father, those thanksgivings which the Blessed Virgin, mother of the only-begotten Son, offered when she conceived and bore in her womb Him whom I now hold in my breast."[1]

Thus the Christian life begun in the soul in baptism was, as he taught, to be nourished and maintained by the " Holy Eucharist." In this way, and in this way only, the flame of the holy life would be fed with its pure, its appropriate, its homogeneous aliment. In this sacrament life was to be replenished by life,—the life of the Spirit of Christ imparted in baptism,—by the very life of Christ Jesus Himself imparted through His real presence, at once corporeal and spiritual, and impregnating the whole humanity of the duly prepared participator. Romanists

[1] I borrow the last quotation from a review of the sermon from which I have taken the preceding quotations, by Archdeacon Garbett, Professor of Poetry at Oxford, a man of the highest qualities and character, who was successful in competition for that office against Isaac Williams, the Puseyite poet, in 1841, and from whom I have already quoted a striking passage on the claims of Anglican Priest-Confessors (pp. 255-6). I will add here that Pusey's volume of 1855 was critically dealt with by the Rev. John Harrison, D.D., in an exceedingly learned and very able volume published by Longmans, and entitled, *Dr. Pusey's Challenge Answered respecting the Doctrine of the Real Presence.* To this masterly work Pusey attempted no reply. All Pusey's quotations are sifted, and the true sense of many of the passages quoted is ascertained from their context, and established in opposition to the gross or perverted sense in which they are taken by Pusey. The whole subject is profoundly and thoroughly argued, the evidence, both from Scripture and from the writings of the Fathers, being clearly adduced and collated. The work is a treasure and mine of learning, such as earnest students will know how to value.

are supposed—and suppose themselves—to believe that what common people would regard as the material substance and properties, what Roman theologians speak of as the *accidents* of bread and wine, are so transubstantiated, under the consecrating energy and efficacy of the priestly invocation, as to be filled and identified with the nature of our risen and glorified Lord, at once human and divine, with His body, soul, spirit, and perfect and absolute divinity. Pusey and his followers believe and teach that the substance and properties, the *accidents*, of bread and wine indeed remain, but that they are interpenetrated with and by the nature and personal presence of the Lord Jesus Christ, as God and man, or, in other words, —though words in truth are altogether incommensurable with propositions so contradictory and unthinkable,— that our Lord, in His perfect fulness, is consubstantiated with every particle of the consecrated bread and wine. Newman declared and maintained that there was only a verbal and apparent difference, but no real distinction, between the two statements of doctrine. Pusey, in his *Eirenicon*, as we shall see, also argues that there is no real difference between what he held and taught on this subject and the Romish doctrine.

The title of the sermon from which I have taken all the preceding quotations, except the last, is "The Holy Eucharist, a Comfort to the Penitent"; it was written and preached as a comforting sequel to the terrible sermon on "Sin after Baptism," and the portentous treatise on Baptism. Pusey's special application of his special doctrine of the real presence, in the way of comfort to the penitent, affords a striking, and also, I venture to say, repulsive illustration of the gross character of his teaching as to sacramental efficacy *ex opere operato*. The specific ground for comfort is that the penitent "drinks his ransom," "drinks his salvation." These are the very words. It is also said that Christ is "the Bread of Life; whoso, then, eateth life cannot die. How should he die whose food is life? how perish who hath a living substance?" These words are borrowed partly from Ambrose. They are applied by Pusey in the gross spirituo-corporeal sense of which we have had so many specimens. *Thus*, the penitent receives the Eucharist, the spirituo-corporeal elements, the divinely-penetrated and consubstantiated elements, for the "remission of sins."

Bishop Wilberforce on a hasty first glance at this sermon, as we learn from a letter contained in his Life, hit one anti-evangelical fault in it, when he says that the sermon "denies the forgiven state of the justified man, and breaks down the one great act of forgiveness into a number of acts of forgiveness, thus contradicting St. Paul"; and he hits another blot when he says that the doctrine of the sermon amounts to teaching the continuation of the atoning sacrifice in every celebration, in direct contradiction to the 31st Article of the Church of England. Later and on fuller thought, when he was resolved to speak out his mind, he went much further and deeper in his condemnation of this and all such teaching, as was shown especially in his address to the rural deans of his diocese, an address not intended for publication, delivered at Winchester House, without notes, three days before his death, and to which reference is made in Dean Burgon's *Lives of Twelve Good Men*, vol. ii. In this address he speaks of "the substitution of a semi-materialistic presence for the actual presence of Christ in the soul of the faithful communicant" as an "abomination."

Pusey's doctrine of consubstantiation—if that be the right word—is not less repulsive or self-contradictory than the Romish teaching as to transubstantiation, and in its effect on faith and worship is identical. Alike on the Puseyite and on the Romanist view, the consecrating lips and hands of the priest work the spell by which so unspeakable a result is effected; and the very Christ Himself is placed in the hands and in the mouth of every participator. If priests are believed able to do this, it is scarcely to be wondered at that, as confessors and absolvers of penitent sinners, the attributes of the Searcher of hearts, the "God of judgment, by whom" both motives and "actions are weighed," are attributed to them. Of course it follows, with the most evident necessity, from such teaching as this, that the communicating congregation cannot but kneel and worship the Saviour, who is both bodily and spiritually with them all and each. The step between such doctrine and worship in Anglican churches, and the celebration of the Mass as in Romish churches, is too short and easy to be appreciable. Pusey's teaching, indeed, leads directly and necessarily to such Romish ritualising as that of the late Father Lowder or Mr. Mackonochie.

The fruits of Dr. Pusey's teaching, in respect of sacramentarian and confessional ritualism, have, since the first edition of this book was published, been shown in excesses outdoing even those of Mr. Mackonochie, as, for example, in the notorious case of "Father Dolling" at Portsmouth.[1]

---

[1] During the month of January 1896 a long correspondence appeared in the *Times* relating to the refusal of the Bishop of Winchester to consecrate a mission church built at Landport by the Rev. Mr. Dolling, who chooses to be styled "Father Dolling," and who had been

I will quote one more passage on this subject from Pusey's writings. It will be found in his sermon, entitled, "This is My Body," preached at St. Mary's, Oxford, in 1871—

"Finding that the words 'Real Presence' were often understood of what is in fact a 'Real Absence,' we added engaged for some years as a mission-priest in that quarter of Portsmouth. The church which the bishop was expected to consecrate had four "altars," and was built and made ready for worship with all suitable provision and arrangements for masses, processions of what Roman Catholics speak of as "the Host," and auricular confession. An account was given by several correspondents—and its truth could not be denied—of the ritualistic services carried on by Mr. Dolling. On the 5th of January he announced from the pulpit of his old mission church that on the last day of his residence there (the following Thursday) there would be exposition of the Blessed Sacrament all day at the high altar—at which he hoped there would be crowds of worshippers—and that the vespers of the Blessed Sacrament would be sung in the evening, with a procession of the Host, followed by Benediction. Vespers of the Blessed Sacrament is the Roman Catholic service appointed for the festival of *Corpus Christi*. In view of the whole case, the Bishop of Winchester declined to consecrate the new church, and pending consecration withheld the necessary licence for the conduct of public worship in the new building. It appears, and must indeed be presumed, that Bishop Thorold, Dr. Davidson's immediate predecessor in the episcopacy, had not been aware of the special Romish features of "Father" Dolling's ritualism—viz., the reservation and exposition of the Blessed Sacrament, presumably in one kind, for the purpose of adoration, processions of the Host, and Benediction, in addition to auricular confession and absolution. It was, at anyrate, high time that episcopal authority should intervene to arrest the course of this Romanising priest who, for years preceding, had been training in the faith and practices of Popery hundreds of spiritually ignorant people, who took him for an authorised Anglican teacher, and were fascinated by his spectacular ritualism and his priestly garb and pretensions.

The following statement appeared in the *Times* on 13th January, the writer signing himself "Conformist":—

"SIR,—Kindly allow me a word or two in vindication of the much-abused Bishop of Winchester.

the word 'Objective,' to express that the Life-giving Body, the *res sacramenti*, is, *by virtue of the consecration*,[1] present without us, to be received by us, in the words of the Fathers, 'for us to lay up Christ in ourselves and place the Saviour in our breasts.' ... I will only add briefly, that the doctrine of the Eucharistic Sacrifice and of Eucharistic Adoration are involved in the doctrine of the Real Presence. ... 'The essence of the Sacrifice of the Eucharist,' Bossuet had said, 'consists precisely in the consecration, whereby, in virtue of the words of Jesus Christ, His Body and precious Blood are placed really on the Holy Table, mystically separated under the species of bread and wine. By this action, taken precisely, and without anything added by the priest, JESUS CHRIST is really offered to His Father, inasmuch as His Body and His Blood are placed before Him, actually clothed with the signs representing His death.'"

That is, of course, Popery. Indeed, Pusey quotes Bossuet, quite simply and naturally, as representing his own views as to the real presence and as to the sacrifice of the Eucharist.

Pusey, as a matter of fact, though he never went

"I was present last Sunday at the High Mass at St. Agatha's. There was a large congregation, but not a single communicant. The Invitation ('Ye that do truly repent'), the Confession, Absolution, and Comfortable Words were all omitted.

"Notice was given that on the following Thursday (the last of Mr. Dolling's stay) there would be exposition of the Blessed Sacrament all day at the high altar. Vespers of the Blessed Sacrament would be sung in the evening, followed by a procession of the Sacred Host round the church, concluding with Benediction of the Blessed Sacrament."[2]

---

[1] The italics are mine.

[2] Mr. Dolling is still a clergyman of the Church of England, and has, or had till lately, a charge in London.

over to Rome, had for forty years before his death been more advanced in his Romanising than was Newman when he found himself compelled, equally by logic and by conscience, to leave Anglican Oxford and to join the Roman communion. In addition to the view already given of Pusey's opinions, the special evidences in proof of what I have now said are to be found chiefly in the Preface which he contributed to an edition of Newman's Tract 90, and in his *Eirenicon*. I shall refer here only to the latter.

When Newman had gone over to the Church of Rome, he wrote as follows, in November 1845, as he tells us in his *Apologia*: "I have felt all along that Bishop Bull's theology was the only theology on which the English Church could stand. I have felt that opposition to the Church of Rome was part of that theology; and that he who could not protest against the Church of Rome was no true divine in the English Church. I have never said, nor attempted to say, that anyone in office in the English Church, whether bishop or incumbent, could be otherwise than in hostility to the Church of Rome." He had written on an earlier page of the *Apologia*: "From the end of 1841 I was on my deathbed as regards my membership with the Anglican Church, though at the time I became aware of it only by degrees."

These statements of Newman's are sufficient of themselves to prove that up to the very eve of his concluding that he could no longer remain in the Church of England, Newman's sentiments were less favourable to the Church of Rome than those of Pusey during the last thirty or forty years of his life. The *Eirenicon*, published in 1865, expounds the views in relation to the Church of Rome which Pusey had held for not less than twenty years. If, as Newman held, so long as he retained his position within the Church of England, he who could not protest against the Church of Rome was "no true divine of the Church of England," Pusey had for many years ceased to be a "true divine" of the English Church. The precise object of the *Eirenicon*, indeed, was to show that no divine of the Church of England was under any necessity whatever of protesting against the Church of Rome. The volume propounds a basis of union between Canterbury and Rome, that basis being nothing else than the very Decrees of the Council of Trent, those decrees being generously and forbearingly interpreted on the part of Rome, and generously and with lowly and loving trustfulness accepted on the part of the English Church.

In his letter to Dr. Jelf, in explanation of Tract 90, Newman sums up the meaning and intent of that famous tract. He desired that "taking away the doctrine of transubstantiation from the Mass, we shall have no dispute about the sacrifice." Pusey, however, not only taught "the sacrifice," but in his *Eirenicon* he takes particular pains to show that his own doctrine of the real presence differs only in the mode of expression from the Romish doctrine of transubstantiation. Newman would, at that time, have left open the point, as he phrases it, of "comprecation with the saints." But Pusey would have gone further, and accepted a determination of the Council of Trent which pronounces the invocation of saints to be "good and useful." In 1841, and for some years afterwards, Newman held that the worship of the Virgin was, at least in principle and tendency, idolatrous, and was very often distinctly idolatrous in practice; whereas, although Pusey had shown in his *Eirenicon*, almost *ad nauseam*, to what frightful lengths of blasphemous superstition this worship had been carried in the Romish Church, he was not prepared to affirm that the Roman Catholic worship of the Virgin was in itself, or in its essential principle, idolatrous.

Pusey was, in fact, about as good a Papist as Bossuet or Dupin. Protestant is a designation which he utterly rejected. Nor could he be classed under any variety or category as receiving the doctrines of the Reformation. He rejected the doctrine of Luther as to faith and justification; he denounced the doctrine of Calvin as to grace and the sacraments; he explained away the doctrines of the Articles and Homilies of the Church of England, as elucidated by the writings of the English Reformers. He can only be described as a mild Romanist, who received the Tridentine Decrees,—these decrees being indeed his proposed basis of union between Rome and the Church of England,—but who would interpret them in the sense least obnoxious to Protestant Christians. Like some of the most eminent Romanist divines, he did not believe in papal infallibility, which, indeed, at the time he wrote his *Eirenicon*, was not yet an article of faith, but he believed in the infallibility of General Councils of the whole Church. The only point as to which, thirty years ago, there was, according to Cardinal Manning, any essential difference between Pusey and himself, was that of the authority of tradition. But, according to Newman, there was no difference at this point between the views of Pusey and of Romanists. In his letter to Pusey, called forth by the *Eirenicon*, Newman declares that the difference "is merely one of words." If so, then was Pusey, thirty years ago, to all intents and purposes a Romanist in faith and doctrine. Almost his last words, in the postscript to his *Eirenicon*, are: "On the terms which Bossuet, we hope, would have sanctioned, we long to see the Church united," and he appeals to all "who now hold with Bossuet to help towards reunion."

Pusey could not indeed go all lengths with the Roman Church, as judged by its vulgar faith and ordinary practices. But neither do Roman Catholics of intelligence and culture. His rejection of papal infallibility would, it may be presumed, preclude him from being accounted a modern Papist. But his faith seems to have strictly coincided with that of the more enlightened Romanist of the naturalised English or of the Gallican school. He was assuredly not an adherent, in any sense, of the Reformed faith. Bishop Wilberforce had ample reason and right when he charged him with doing the work of a Romish priest and confessor within the orders of the Church of England.

He was indeed the main strength of the Romanising conspiracy within the Church of England; he was the arch-priest, the head and chief counsellor, of all the organised subtlety and mischief which were practised throughout the kingdom for enlisting women, for instructing and training boys, for influencing associations of clergy, for taking hold of important centres in the interest of the Romanising propaganda.

Let us clearly understand that Puseyism, indeed, is essentially Popery; not, like the Laudian Movement, Popery revived from its embers in a nation of which the great mass of the people had never really embraced the Reformation, but Popery revived after ages intervening in which England, through all its ranks and classes, had ceased to be popish, and, with whatever shortcomings, had yet been an enlightened and Protestant nation, delivered alike from the gross superstitions and the spiritual despotism of Rome. The two plague-spots of Puseyism—of High Church Catholicism—are its sacramental perversions, whereby the holy seals of the Christian faith and profession are turned into superstitions; and its dehumanising doctrine of the confessional. And these two roots of error being once accepted, there is no tenet either of Tridentine or of modern Popery which may not be received. Those who have learned to regard the priest-confessor as the searcher of hearts, and the healer and absolver of the soul, gifted for his office with corresponding attributes and authority from God, need find no difficulty in addressing prayers to the Virgin Mary, or to perfected saints, and can surely find nothing too hard for them in the doctrine of the Pope's infallibility, when speaking *ex cathedrâ*, as the " Vicar of Christ."

The papal infallibility is, in reality, a less revolting tenet than that which invests the parish priest with the prerogative of confessor. And yet if the priest by his consecrating act can bring to pass the sacramental miracles, what wonder if attributes are imputed to him which are much more than merely superhuman? All the landmarks of truth are confused in such a system; all the perspective of things human and divine is lost and confounded; men are no longer to be sanctified through God's word, which is "the truth," but by participation in theurgic mysteries, wrought by the hands of priests. He who has accepted the main roots of the whole system of error in the sacramental and confessional doctrines, need not stumble even at the doctrine of the Immaculate

Conception of the Virgin. Pusey is said to have declared, that, if the Gorham controversy turned against his party, he should be compelled to go over and accept Popery whole. He did not go, but he need have found no difficulty on the score of doctrine in doing this at any time. Nor was it at any time a real revulsion from the doctrines of Popery which retained him within the Church of England.

Pusey spent more than forty years in carrying out, on a different and a deeper level, the same work of preparing the Church of England for amalgamation with the Romish Church which Newman began but found himself unable to carry through with the consent and co-working of his reason and his conscience. Newman has, in his *Apologia*, laid bare in great part, the working of his mind in this matter. He says of himself in 1840: "I believed that we had the apostolic succession in the Anglican Church and the grace of the sacraments; I was not sure that the difficulty of its isolation might not be overcome. . . . I was not sure that it would not revive into full apostolic purity and strength, and grow into union with Rome herself (Rome explaining her doctrines and guarding against their abuse); that is, if we were but patient and hopeful. I wished for union between the Anglican Church and Rome, if, and when, it was possible." That was his position, consciously and deliberately recognised in 1840. In the following year, 1841, he "was on his deathbed as regarded his membership with the Church of England, though he only became aware of it by degrees"; in 1844 he resigned his offices; in 1845 he went over to Rome. But during the whole interval—nearly half a century—between 1840 and his death, Pusey was steadily and subtly working towards the same end, which now the English Church Union avowedly has in view, the time for silence and privacy having, it seems, passed away. Indeed, in his *Eirenicon*, published thirty years ago in the form of a letter to Keble, Pusey set distinctly forth his method for the consummation of the same end on the basis of the Decrees of the Council of Trent. He argues that there might well be a union between the Roman Catholic and the Anglo-Catholic Churches on the assumption or condition that the decrees of the Roman Catholic Council received a mitigated and minified interpretation; whilst, on the other hand, a relaxed interpretation was allowed on the Thirty-nine Articles. As, however, such an agreement would imply a *maximum* of Romanising expansion and relaxation in the interpretation of the Articles, the contemplated union would leave behind and out of account all ministers and members of the Church of England, doubtless much more than one-half of the whole body of Churchmen, who could not be induced to consent to such an interpretation of the Articles. So that if it could be imagined possible for it to take effect, all true English Churchmen, whether called Evangelical or not, would be left behind in the Anglican limbo,—a point of which Pusey and all Puseyites seem never to have taken account. Pusey pleads the authority of a great name in favour of the idea of the possibility of reunion. He refers to the precedent of Archbishop Wake in his well-known correspondence with Dupin; but it seems never to have occurred to him that there was no real parallel between his proposal and Archbishop Wake's. The archbishop's object was not to attach the

English Church to the Roman communion, but to detach the Gallican Church from the Roman communion, —a proposal which in the early part of the eighteenth century might have seemed not beyond the bounds of possibility. In the Church of Bossuet and Dupin, the Church also of Pascal and Arnauld and Fénélon; in the days of the Gallican liberties, and before the Jesuits had obtained the control of the Royal Court and Council Chamber of France, such a proposal was not altogether Utopian. Archbishop Wake's aim was to foster the latent Protestantism of France in the hope that the French Catholic Church, with the king at its head, might follow, to some extent, the example of the Church of England, and the precedent of Henry VIII. All this was worthy of an ecclesiastical statesman like Archbishop Wake, of whom it must be remembered, moreover, that, in this respect also unlike Pusey, his love of peace and unity was so impartial and comprehensive that he did not merely seek to establish intercommunion between the national Churches of England and France, but frankly admitted the valid ecclesiastical character of Presbyterian and other non-Episcopal Churches in England, and the validity of the ministerial acts performed by the pastors of such Churches.[1] Dr. Pusey, on the other hand, in reply to an appeal from Dr. (afterwards Bishop) Wordsworth, wrote to the *Times*, under date January 2, 1866, that he was not prepared to seek union even with the Scandinavian Episcopal Lutheran Churches, at least until after reunion had been accomplished with Rome and with the Greek Church.

Pusey's proposal, in which he is followed by the

[1] See Maclaine's edition of *Mosheim's Church History*, the last chapter.

Puseyites of to-day, was very different, indeed, from that of Archbishop Wake. Pusey was prepared to accept the Decrees of the Council of Trent with certain explanations. He was prepared to recognise the primacy of the Romish See. His hope was that through the influence and working of himself and his party, the Church of England, as a whole, might be brought eventually to accept his ideas and feelings on this subject. The actual result to-day shows that Pusey was not so absurdly sanguine as was generally supposed at the time. His work has been only too successful. Lord Halifax and the Church Union have for many years been drawing consciously and undisguisedly near the papal centre; nor with the possibility of Church disestablishment in view have we any right to assume that the counsels of the Church Union will prove to be absolutely futile. Let us suppose that the Church being disestablished falls asunder—as every-one expects it will—into at least two, possibly into three, distinct Anglican organisations, — the High Anglican organisation being the Church of Lord Halifax and the Church Union,—what is to prevent that High Anglican section from carrying out the programme of the Church Union, and bringing about an organic union between the Romish Church and itself? Long ago Newman, as we have seen, before he himself went over, had contemplated the possibility of such a union some day taking place. He had intimated, moreover, as we also learn from the *Apologia*, that in order to effect it, certain special conditions might be claimed by the English and conceded by the Romish Church; as, for example, the concession of the cup to the laity, and some explanation of points in the Tridentine Decrees, and of Transubstantiation and Mariolatry.

There is, in fact, an identity and continuity of idea from the time of Newman, more than fifty years ago, to the present hour, which has been kept up by the influence of Newman and Pusey, and of their coadjutors and successors.

Such an idea, however, was, abstractly regarded, less outrageous in 1840 than it is in 1895. In 1840 the Immaculate Conception of the Virgin had not yet been defined as an Article of Faith, the Syllabus-Decree had not yet been issued; above all, the Infallibility-Dogma had not been defined and ratified by a General Council. Ultramontanism, as it has been revived, developed, and reasserted during the last quarter of a century, was hardly as yet thought of. The Primacy of Rome did not imply nearly all that it implies to-day. Sanguine Anglicans and liberal and sanguine Roman Catholics in those days agreed in cherishing the hope that the claim of infallibility had become obsolete and was not likely to be revived, and was least of all likely to be made a dogma by the decree of a General Council; and that Rome itself was accepting and assimilating modern and, up to a certain point, liberal ideas. Such, no doubt, were the cherished hopes of men like Dr. Döllinger and Lord Acton. In such ideas and hopes such Anglicans as Mr. Gladstone undoubtedly sympathised. It is easy to understand, and difficult not to some extent to sympathise with, the feelings which led men, such as those I have named, to cherish the hope that some day the breach in the Western Catholic communion might be healed, at least so far as to reconcile the Church of England to Rome; and that, as a further step towards manifest Christian union throughout the world, a friendly understanding might be brought about between the Western Catholic Church and the Eastern Catholic Church. All such hopes, however, have been rendered unreasonable by the developments of the last quarter of a century. The modern Ultramontanism of Rome has quenched them all.[1]

[1] Mr. Gladstone's feelings in regard to this point are partly indicated in a fine letter to Cardinal Manning.[1] There we see him in his dreams at his best, and see him not without sympathy and admiration. The Vatican Council had not then been summoned, and Mr. Gladstone's *Vaticanism* had not been written. In his letter, on the other hand, sent to the press by the Archbishop of York in May 1896, and which appears, from internal evidence, to have been written in response, direct or indirect, to some communication from Lord Halifax, he is seen at his weakest and worst. He might perhaps be excused on account of his age, although the composition of the letter suggests no decline of mental faculty, but he can hardly, by a clear and sane judgment, be applauded on account of his wisdom. Evidently his hope of reunion with Rome had revived, and had become something like a superstition with him; the question of the ecclesiastical validity of Anglican orders, as regarded from the Romish point of view, is for him a grave and momentous question; the attitude of the Pope, in showing himself willing to appoint a commission to examine this question, was regarded as most condescending and gracious. No wonder that an influential section of Nonconformists, who had charged themselves with the education of Mr. Gladstone in politico-ecclesiastical principles, and had looked upon him as a most promising pupil, and indeed as already a potential leader of their own party, of incomparable distinction and influence, should view this latest development in his amazing history with disappointment not unmixed with disgust. In his last days he went back to his early illusions, to the feelings and views which inspired and coloured his famous book on Church Principles, sixty years ago, and he offered as his contribution to the settlement of the burning ecclesiastical controversy which is disturbing the Church of England to-day, ideas which read like the belated revival of some of his weakest early day-dreams. In the former edition of this volume I had expressed the hope that Mr. Gladstone's paper on *Heresy and Schism* might be taken as evidence that he was looking for a deeper and truer ground of unity among Christians than anything in the nature of organic union or reunion—the basis of Catholic orthodoxy and Christian character. That hope was, it now appears, a vain illusion. He ignores all Nonconformists, all Presbyterians, all Con-

[1] *Life of Manning*, vol. ii. pp. 406–409 (first edition).

Even now, however, and for Evangelical Christians of the free Churches, it is lawful to hope that some time—sooner, perhaps, than we can see our way to calculate—the Ultramontane and *semper eadem* policy of the papal conclave will utterly break down, though in principle it cannot be abandoned by the Pope, as such. That is the one hope,

tinental Protestants in his letter, though it is long enough for a tract. He glances, indeed, at the fact that his "long life had brought him much into contact with those independent religious communities which supply an important religious factor in the religious life of Great Britain," but only to intimate that these communities allow to the Established Church "no inconsiderable hold upon their sympathies." It is certain that those communities had no sympathy with the appeal to Rome for the settlement of the question as to the validity of Anglican orders, but that, like the Duke of Argyll, they regard the whole question as insignificant and as proceeding upon a false and really anti-Christian assumption. They can have nothing but disgust, instead of sympathy, for the feeling which leads Mr. Gladstone in his exuberant gratitude to the Pope to say that "he who bears in mind the cup of cold water administered to 'one of these little ones' will surely regard this effort as stamped in its very inception as alike arduous and blessed," and which prompts him to speak of Leo XIII., not only as the "First Bishop of Christendom, who has the noblest sphere of action," but as one who possesses "an elevation above all the levels of stormy partisanship, and genuineness of love for the whole Christian flock, separate or annexed." Mr. Gladstone fully merited the eulogy pronounced upon him by a Belgian Roman Catholic organ, the *Journal de Bruxelles*, which, in its issue for June 2, 1896, has an article devoted to "an enthusiastic appreciation," to quote the *Times* correspondent, "of Mr. Gladstone's attitude towards the Pope," as contrasted with his tone and temper in 1870, when he wrote his *Vaticanism* pamphlet. "If ever," concludes the article, "the conversion of England becomes an accomplished fact, it may be said that, to a certain extent, her aged statesman collaborated in the glorious work of which another grand old man, Leo XIII., has been the artisan" (*Times*, June 4, 1896). The *Guardian* newspaper agrees with the Brussels journal in its estimate of Mr. Gladstone's action in this matter. "It is Mr. Gladstone's glory," it says, "that he has seen" the merits of the Pope's action "more clearly, and stated it more persuasively than any who have yet dealt with the question on our side."

not only of the Christian world at large, but even of the Western Catholic communion itself, if it can realise its actual position. That the Roman Catholic nationalities of the world will become Protestant, that they will give up the name Catholic, is hardly to be expected. But Popery proper is a priestly growth and usurpation. It is the special creation of the Roman ecclesiastical court; it is no genuine development of the common Christian life of Europe, corrupt and enfeebled although that life was during the dark and middle ages. Many of the developments sanctioned by the Roman Court were resisted, even by a large portion of the clergy, and were odious to such of the laity as were aware of them. Throughout there has been a struggling protest in the body of the Roman Catholic Church itself. Unhappily, the interests of the priests are bound up with the papal policy—so it has been contrived; and the priests and clergy of every order are accepted as such only on condition that they uphold the uttermost claims of the Papacy.

The ecclesiastical claims and official declarations of the Papacy are, indeed, unchanged, except by being enunciated as dogma; they are as presumptuous, as arrogant, as daring and impious as ever; but this is perfectly consistent with the real weakening of the Roman power. The Papacy may have all the more wrath, because of its presentiment that its power is fading away. Pius IX. could summon a so-called Œcumenical Council, but he could not enact the part of a Hildebrand. He could claim for himself and his successors official infallibility, but he could not set his foot upon the neck of princes, or cast the fearful yoke of an interdict over the breadth and body of an empire. He could not even prevent his holy city from being wrested from his hands, and made the capital of a free kingdom. The Pope is now the primate of an aggregate of sects; he could no longer be imagined to be triple-crowned, the great potentate of the world. The next stage in the enfranchisement of the Western Catholic nations must be the development of the national liberties, and of ecclesiastical independency for the nations and their rulers. The Roman Catholic Churches will themselves become truly national in their character and development in proportion as the pulse of national freedom beats more and more powerfully, as true national life works more and more freely in the breasts of the people, nation by nation, citizen by citizen. The concession of the Primacy to Rome by the English Church would be a terribly retrograde step, would tend to rivet spiritual oppression and corruption on the Catholic world. So long as the papal supremacy lasts, in its full Romish sense, the Roman communion is bound to all its traditions, must go encumbered with the weight of all its millennial growth and accumulation of corruptions, impieties, and contradictions. Take this iron-woven swaddling band from off the limbs and the life of the great Western Catholic Church, and she will be able to rise and to move freely. Break up the papal yoke, cast off the papal incubus, throw to the winds the papal supremacy, and national Catholic Churches may grow up in the midst of rising national liberty, and may gradually purge and reform themselves. They would not call themselves Protestant; but they would be national, with their own synods, and with separate governments. In that direction lies the hope alike of liberty and of religious union for Christendom, union—not indeed organic, but moral and practical—for the ends of Christian civilisation.

CHAPTER XIII.

PUSEY'S PERSONAL CHARACTERISTICS—BELIEF IN CONTRADICTIONS — HIS IMMOBILITY—HIS RELATIONS WITH "EVANGELICALS" AND NONCONFORMISTS—PUSEY AND MANNING ON CHURCHMEN AND DISSENTERS — THE CARDINAL AS UMPIRE—PUSEY ON RITUALISM—RITUALISM AND DOCTRINE—ARCHBISHOP BENSON'S JUDGMENT IN THE CASE OF THE BISHOP OF LINCOLN—THE ATTACK ON PROTESTANTISM—ROMANISING ADVANCE—SMALL POPES—SACRAMENTAL LIFE.

PUSEY'S was a character hard to read—he was a man whose meaning was hard to follow. The ordinary man of general intelligence, the mere literary man, the average Churchman, especially the Evangelical Churchman, the average Dissenter or Wesleyan Methodist, or the mere politician,—all alike found his position unintelligible. He seemed to be almost unclassifiable—to be an anomalous specimen of the genus Churchman, and especially to stand apart and alone among modern divines. In 1864 the Protestant and orthodox evangelical section of the nation joined hands with him in his opposition to Broad Church latitudinarianism, and there seemed to be a *rapprochement* between him and his cousin, Lord Shaftesbury. He had earned the thanks, about the same period, of orthodox and anti-rationalistic Christian students by his *Lectures on*

Daniel the Prophet, and his *Commentary on the Minor Prophets*. Yet all the time he had not changed any of his views as to confession, absolution, and sacramental efficacy. It is notable also that in 1865, on the fly-leaf of his misnamed (so it proved to be) *Eirenicon*, there were advertised as "In the Press," besides part iv. of the *Minor Prophets*, and the *fourth thousand* of his *Daniel*, "A preface, chiefly historical, to Tract XC. of the *Tracts for the Times*, together with Tract XC."

The key to his character, given by his old friend in the *Apologia*, explains these seeming inconsistencies. Pusey had a "sanguine, hopeful mind," and was "haunted by no intellectual perplexities." When his own party "had advanced," as Newman witnesses, "a considerable way in the direction of Rome," Pusey was still rejoicing in the confidence and conviction that "among its hopeful peculiarities was its stationariness." This was "his subjective view of it."

Such a man was not likely to be understood. His tactics were naturally denounced as jesuitical. The plain Protestant could not conceive any honourable explanation of his inconsistencies. Nor was his reputation for honesty improved in 1865 by the announcement in the daily papers that he had been visiting two Romish bishops in the south of France, and at Bordeaux had spent his Sunday in the convent of the Dominicans.

Nevertheless, though blinded and doting on more points than one, and though far from being a straightforward or a candid man, Pusey was at bottom an honest-meaning man. His views might be self-contradictory; but that does not affect the question. A man who can believe as Pusey professed in his sermon on the Eucharist to believe, can believe any quantity of self-contradictions. His special doctrine of the real presence, the Puseyite consubstantiation, is yet more uncouthly self-contradictory than even the Romish doctrine of transubstantiation, as to the contradictions and absurdities of which Jeremy Taylor says so many hard and witty things,—things which if a modern Low Churchman or Dissenter had said of Pusey's doctrine, he would have been forthwith charged by the earnest and unhesitating devotee with profanity or even blasphemy.[1] But, notwithstanding its contradictions, which he contrived to get over by means of the verbal distinctions which are mistaken for realities, Pusey for more than forty years believed wholly and absolutely in this doctrine of consubstantiation.

It is scarcely possible to set limits to the power of the human mind to believe in contradictions. A man can, indeed, believe any sort of contradiction except a contradiction in terms. Pusey is essentially one with the Romanists, at least in dogmatic definition, respecting the doctrine of justification by faith. It is inferred from this that, therefore, he can have no sympathy or fellowship with evangelical life or with experimental religion. Hence, when it was found in his Commentary, that he has sympathy with what is spiritual and experimental, with the life of sanctification, with the habitual faith of the Christian saint, readers were confounded, and they know not what to believe. The natural conclusion was that there must have been some exaggeration in reference to his semi-Popery, or that his views when he wrote that Commentary must have materially changed from the time when he published his treatise on Baptism and his sermon on the Eucharist. But, in truth, there had been no change whatever.

[1] See the Preface to Pusey's sermon on the Eucharist (1871).

Newman's *Apologia* compelled his contemporaries to revise the judgment which they had passed upon him. If ever casuistry seemed to be possessed by the spirit of crafty falsehood, "paltering with us" throughout "in a double sense," it was the casuistry of Tract 90. And yet from the *Apologia* it seems to be certain that Newman was never a consciously dishonest man. He was a man whose over-subtlety blinded him. He possessed a highly-trained faculty of mental obliquity,—a faculty which long and skilful culture had developed to a marvellous and pernicious perfection. He had acquired the power of duping himself. But he retained, in an important sense, his moral integrity notwithstanding; he never ceased to be, in the main, an honourable and conscientious English gentleman. There is no doubt some danger lest, in exercising charity towards either Newman or Pusey, or any of their school, we might seem to apologise for what, to the common apprehension, must appear to be dishonest craft.[1] The explanation, however, is, that men trained, as the Tractarians had been trained, and as most Roman theologians are trained, in a school of verbal quibbling and scholastic subtleties, have lost the

---

[1] Newman, indeed, was in his later life dissatisfied with the logic of Tract 90. He admits that "the tract did not carry its object and conditions on its face, and necessarily lay open to interpretations very far from the true one. I considered," he says, "that my interpretation of the Articles would stand, provided the parties imposing them allowed it. When, in the event, the bishops and public opinion did not allow it, I gave up my living, as having no right to retain it." He quotes from his "Loss and Gain" what, though put into the lips of an interlocutor, is his own present judgment respecting his own tract: "The view is specious certainly. But you have no sanction to show me. As it stands, it is a mere theory struck out by individuals."
—*Newman's Letter to Pusey*, pp. 15, 16.

power of appreciating truth. Their theology is mainly a matter of words and phrases. They have not learned to look in the face any fact of life or of nature. A *petitio principii* is always latent in their definitions, or distinctions, or propositions. And so they can believe anything. What student of philosophy knows not that a portentous system of merely verbal metaphysics was *invented* in order to expound and defend the doctrine of transubstantiation, —a system to which there is actually no truth or reality, no fact of nature or life, corresponding? Of course, *on this system* of pseudo-metaphysical quibbling, transubstantiation *may* be defended. This system is borrowed by the Tractarians; and they are able to believe that what Romanists call the accidents—what *they* call the substance —of bread and wine can remain, and yet the bread be the very body, and the wine the very blood, of the Saviour. To all others these are the craziest of absurdities and contradictions. After this, to consubstantiate Protestant evangelical truth, *i.e.* a certain modicum of it, with the Tridentine Articles, or to transubstantiate the Anglican Thirty-nine Articles into a system of quasi-Tridentine theology, is a practicable feat.

These observations are designed to show how Pusey was, almost from the first, consistent with himself in his professions and in his course. As Pascal, and Fénélon, and the Marquis de Renti, although all of them honest "Catholics," and all of them bound by the Decrees of the Tridentine Council, were yet good men who loved and trusted in Christ, and lived to God a life of prayer and faith, in virtue of truths which, however inconsistently, they yet held vitally in connection with a dogmatic adherence to principles altogether contrary; so Pusey contrives, in holding to the mildest interpretation of the Tridentine Canons and Decrees, at the same time to hold fast vitally by such truths of the gospel as suffice to bring him into personal union with his Saviour and into sympathy, at some points, with evangelical Christians.[1]

There are some statements in the *Eirenicon* which bear directly on the point now under consideration. Cardinal Manning, in his tractate on *The Workings of the Holy Spirit in the Church of England*, having spoken of Pusey's co-operation with the Evangelical party as, on his part, "a drifting back from old moorings," the following is Pusey's explanation and defence :—

"Ever since I knew them (which was not in my earliest

---

[1] John Wesley held strong opinions as to Romish doctrine. He says in one place that he has "the same assurance that Jesus is the Christ, and that no Romanist can expect to be saved, *according to the terms of His covenant*." Yet no man exercised a more candid and charitable judgment in regard to individuals. "Persons," he says, "may be quite right in their opinions, and yet have no religion at all; and, on the other hand, persons may be truly religious, who hold many wrong opinions. Can anyone possibly doubt of this, while there are Romanists in the world? For who can deny, not only that many of them formerly have been truly religious, as Thomas à Kempis, Gregory Lopez, and the Marquis de Renti, but that many of them, even at this day, are real inward Christians? And yet what a heap of erroneous opinions do they hold, delivered by tradition from their fathers." "Let us then," he says in another place, "make all that allowance to others which, were we in their place, we would desire for ourselves. Who that knows the amazing power of education can expect a member of the Church of Rome either to think or speak clearly on this subject [justification]? And yet, if he had heard even dying Bellarmine cry out when he was asked,—'Unto which of the saints wilt thou turn?'—'*Fidere meritis Christi tutissimum*'—'It is safest to trust in the merits of Christ,'—would he have affirmed, notwithstanding his wrong opinions, that he had no share in this righteousness?"—*Works*, i. 208; vi. 186, 187; v. 224.

years) I have loved those who are called 'Evangelicals.' I loved them because they loved our Lord. I loved them for their zeal for souls. I often thought them narrow; yet I was often drawn to individuals among them more than to others who held truths in common with myself, which the Evangelicals did not hold, at least explicitly. I believed them to be 'of the truth.' I have ever believed and believe, that their faith was and is, on some points of doctrine, much truer than their words. I believed and believe, that they are often withheld from the clear and full sight of the truth by an inveterate prejudice, that that truth, as held by us, is united with error, or with indistinct acknowledgment of other truths which they themselves hold sacred. Whilst, then, I lived in society, I ever sought them out, both out of love for themselves, and because I believed that nothing (with God's help) so dispels untrue prejudice as personal intercourse, heart to heart, with those against whom that prejudice is entertained. I sought to point out to them our common basis of faith. I formed some lasting friendships with some among them who have finished their course, and with others who still remain. When occasion came, as in some of our struggles at Oxford, we acted together. . . .

"It was not, then, anything new that when, in high places, fundamental truths had been denied, I sought to unite with those, some of whom had often spoken against me, but against whom I had never spoken. It was the pent-up longing of years. I had long felt that common zeal for faith could alone bring together those who are opposed; I hoped that, through that common zeal and love, inveterate prejudices which hindered the reception of truth would be dispelled. . . .

"But while, on the one hand, I profess plainly that love for the Evangelicals which I ever had, I may be, perhaps, the more bound to say, that, in no matter of faith, nor in my thankfulness to God for my faith, have I changed. This was understood on both sides. We united to oppose unbelief, holding each what each believed that God had taught him."—*Eirenicon*, pp. 4–6.

Pusey's *Eirenicon*, indeed, is written in a spirit of charity towards those who differ from him in theological opinions, provided only they hold to the doctrine of the atonement. This charity extends not only to his "evangelical" brethren of the Church of England, but to orthodox and evangelical Nonconformists. And he goes as far in his concessions to such wanderers from the true fold as a Romanising Anglican can be expected to go. But still he unchurches all non-episcopal communities, and claims for the pious votaries of High Church principles, in virtue especially of their sacramental grace and life, a style of piety altogether more saintly and heavenly than that of the best of Nonconformists.

After his *Eirenicon* was published, small popes[1] in different parts of England condescended to express themselves towards Wesleyans and Dissenters in terms borrowed from Pusey's book, denying the validity of their Church orders and ordinances, but at the same time allowing that, individually, their Christian experience may be genuine, and their Christian character high, and that their irregular and unecclesiastical ministrations may be to some the means and channels of personally sanctifying grace. It is consoling, however, to Nonconformists who—with some goodwill, not unmixed with a sense of the ludicrous; with

[1] See Note at the end of the chapter, "Small Popes."

some admiration, not unmixed with disgust—receive these acknowledgments from Anglo-Catholics, to know that precisely the same measure is meted out to Anglo-Catholics themselves which they mete to Protestant Nonconformists. What Pusey says, with embarrassed affability, to me, Archbishop Manning, with a bland smile and with superior grace, says to Pusey.

"God blesseth," says the Anglican doctor, "through the sacraments; and God blesseth through truth. If a Wesleyan minister preaches his naked gospel, that 'we are all sinners,' that 'Christ died to save sinners,' that 'He bids all sinners to come to Him,' and saith, 'whoso cometh unto Me, I will in no wise cast out,' this is, of course, fundamental gospel truth; and when God blesses through it those who know no more, He blesseth them through faithful reception of His truth. So, again, as to the Presbyterians. They deny, in regard to the Holy Communion, what we believe; and their account of their communion is somewhat less than what we mean by a spiritual communion. . . . I do not mean any disparagement to any pious Presbyterians; but, believing the Holy Eucharist to be what we, in common with the whole ancient Church, know it to be, we cannot but know that they who receive it worthily have a much greater closeness of union with our Lord than they who do not. Presbyterians have what *they* believe; we, what *we* believe. But they who have observed pious Presbyterians and pious English Catholics have discerned among our people a spiritual life of a kind which was not among theirs—in a word, a sacramental life."[1]—*Eirenicon*, pp. 272–276.

It was in this manner that Pusey reconciled his exclusive sacramentarian theory with his charity. The Noncon-

[1] See Note at the end of the chapter, "Sacramental Life."

formist may be sanctified and saved, the Spirit co-operating with the truth, the "naked gospel," which is received from the lips of the preacher; but this is only as it may be, for "the Spirit bloweth where it listeth." But the reverent recipient of the consecrated elements at the hand of the priest, whether any gospel has been preached or not, *must* be a partaker of saving grace, and of—what no Nonconformist can enjoy—"sacramental life." Grace and salvation are held in tail by the apostolic and Catholic priesthood. Salvation waits of necessity on their ministrations.

One cannot read such passages as these without pitying these Churchmen in their dire perplexity. Neither can one well avoid thinking of the Apostle Paul and *his* "naked gospel." The Wesleyan minister, I apprehend, is in good company. "I came," says Paul, "not to baptize, but to preach the gospel." "We preach Christ crucified, to the Jews a stumbling-block and to the Greeks foolishness; but to them which are saved, both Jews and Greeks, Christ the power of God and the wisdom of God." This is the very "naked gospel" of the Wesleyan minister.

Leaving aside, however, all questions of doctrine and all comment on the opinions and principles contained in what has been quoted, let us see how Cardinal Manning, on his part, deals with *Anglican* Nonconformists. Pusey might have learnt *his* lesson of charitable exclusiveness from Manning. Before Pusey enacted the part of condescending High Church charity towards Wesleyans and Dissenters, he had had the advantage of seeing how Manning enacted the like part of condescending charity towards schismatics in general, and towards Anglican Churchmen in particular. With high impartial charity the foremost among the prelates of "Catholicism" showed himself indulgent to the involuntary errors of all. But he allows no superiority to Pusey over the "Wesleyan minister"; on the whole, he rather gives the Presbyterian and Dissenter an advantage over the Episcopalian.

"The English people as a body are baptized, and therefore elevated to the order of supernatural grace. Every infant, and also every adult baptized, having the necessary dispositions, is thereby placed in a state of justification; and, if they die without committing any mortal sin, would certainly be saved. They are also, in the sight of the Church, Catholics. St. Augustine says: 'Ecclesia etiam inter eos qui foris sunt per baptismum generat suos.' . . . With perfect confidence of faith we extend the shelter of this truth over the millions of infants and young children who every year pass to their heavenly Father. We extend it also in hope to many more who grow up in their baptismal grace. Catholic missionaries in this country have often assured me of a fact, attested also by my own experience, that they have received into the Church persons grown to adult life, in whom their baptismal grace was still preserved. Now, how can we then be supposed to regard such persons as no better than heathens? To ascribe the good lives of such persons to the power of nature would be Pelagianism. To deny their goodness would be Jansenism. And with such a consciousness, how could anyone regard his past spiritual life in the Church of England as a mockery? I have no deeper conviction than that the grace of the Holy Spirit was with me from my earliest consciousness. Though at the time, perhaps, I knew it not as I know it now, yet I can clearly perceive the order and chain of grace by which God mercifully led me onward from childhood to the age of twenty years. . . .

"We make the largest allowance for all who are in invincible ignorance, always supposing that there is a preparation of heart to embrace the truth when they see it, at any cost, a desire to know it, and a faithful use of the means of knowing it, such as study, docility, prayer, and the like. But I do not now enter into the case of the educated or the learned, or of those who have liberty of mind and means of inquiry. I cannot class them under the above enumeration of those who are inculpably out of the truth. I leave them, therefore, to the only Judge of all men. . . .

"It must not, however, be forgotten for a moment that this applies to the whole English people, of all forms of Christianity, or, as it is called, of all denominations. What I have said does not recognise the grace *of* the Church of England as such. The working of grace *in* the Church of England is a truth we joyfully hold and always teach. But we as joyfully recognise the working of the Holy Spirit among Dissenters of every kind. Ineeed, I must say that I am far more able to assure myself of the invincible ignorance of Dissenters as a mass than of Anglicans as a mass. They are far more deprived of what survived of Catholic truth; far more distant from the idea of a Church; far more traditionally opposed to it by the prejudice of education; I must add, for the most part far more simple in their belief in the person and passion of our divine Lord. Their piety is more like the personal service of disciples to a personal Master than the Anglican piety, which has always been more dim and distant from this central light of souls. Witness Jeremy Taylor's works, much as I have loved them, compared with Baxter's, or even those of Andrewes, compared with Leighton's, who was formed by the Kirk of Scotland. . . .

"To be just, I must say that if the Church of England be a barrier against infidelity, the Dissenters must also be admitted to a share in this office and commendation. And, in truth, I do not know among the Dissenters any works like the *Essays and Reviews*, or any biblical criticism like that of Dr. Colenso. They may not be very dogmatic in their teaching, but they bear their witness for Christianity as a divine revelation, for the Scriptures as an inspired book, and, I must add further, for the personal Christianity of conversion and repentance, with an explicitness and consistency which is not less effectual against infidelity than the testimony of the Church of England. I do not think the Wesleyan Conference or the authorities of the three denominations would accept readily this assumed superiority of the Anglican Church as a witness against unbelief. They would not unjustly point to the doctrinal confusions of the Church of England as causes of scepticism, from which they are comparatively free. And I am bound to say that I think they would have an advantage. I well remember that while I was in the Church of England I used to regard Dissenters from it with a certain, I will not say aversion, but distance and recoil. I never remember to have borne animosity against them, or to have attacked or pursued them with unkindness. I always believed many of them to be very earnest and devoted men. I did not like their theology, and I believed them to be in disobedience to the Church of England; but I respected them, and lived at peace with them. Indeed, I may say that some of the best people I have ever known out of the Church were Dissenters or children of Dissenters. Nevertheless, I had a dislike of their system and of their meeting-houses. They seemed to me to be rivals of the Church of England, and my loyalty to it made me look somewhat impatiently upon them. But I remember, from the hour I submitted to the Catholic Church, all this underwent a sensible change. I had no temptation to animosity towards them; for neither they nor the Church of England could be rivals of the imperishable and immutable Church of God. The only sense, then, in which I could regard the Church of England as a barrier against infidelity I must extend also to the Dissenting bodies." [1]

These are undoubtedly the severest rebukes, from the most authoritative quarter, which Anglican Churchmen have yet received. Pusey's charity looks pale and narrow by the side of the archbishop's; while the setting down, by the *quondam* Oxford man, of exclusive Anglican pretensions, is as just as it is decisive. The petty Romanism of the High Anglican was never so effectually humbled. It was not for Pusey or any High Anglican to deny the orthodoxy, the precedence, the Church authority, of Rome, so long as all Anglican *exaltados* profess to derive their own authority from the same common source and through the same line of priestly succession, and so long as they are willing to admit the theology of Trent and the primacy of the Pope. Their position is utterly untenable, and nothing is so likely to make them feel it as such writing as that which has now been quoted.

The position which Cardinal Manning occupied in regard to Pusey is precisely equivalent with that which Pusey assumed towards Nonconformists. *Mutatis mutandis*, the following propositions, maintained by Cardinal Manning, would be maintained by Pusey. Put

[1] *Workings of the Holy Spirit in the Church of England*, pp. 10-20, 31-33.

Nonconformist Churches for the Church of England, and these propositions will express the High Churchman's position.

"Let me, then, say at once—

"1. That in denying the Church of England to be the Catholic Church, or any part of it, or in any divine and true sense a Church at all, and in denying the validity of its absolutions and its orders, no Catholic ever denies the workings of the Spirit of God or the operations of grace in it.

"2. That in affirming the workings of grace in the Church of England, no Catholic ever thereby affirms that it possesses the character of a Church."[1]

So the Ultramontane prelate qualifies and guards his admissions in regard to the personal godliness and Christianity of many Anglican schismatics; and after just the same manner do the small popes in English parish churches guard and qualify the admissions which they are constrained to make in regard to the true Christian character and experience of many Nonconformists. To a Nonconformist it cannot but be interesting to see the High Churchman put into the corner as excommunicated and schismatic, to see "the engineer hoist with his own petard."

Pusey labours in his effort to come down from his Anglican eminence and meet Nonconformists with a condescending friendliness. The Cardinal with bland and beaming geniality, steps down to meet on terms of easy friendship all non-Catholics, Anglicans, and Dissenters alike on a common platform, placed, to be sure, far below his own. Some Churchmen seem to think it much to say in behalf of Pusey, that, at anyrate, he never left the

[1] *Ibid.*, p. 8.

Church of England; as if on that account he were to be favourably distinguished from Newman or Manning. But is it not, on the contrary, a part of the case against him that he did *not* leave the Church of England? The evil is not so much going over to Rome, as being a Romanist at heart, or a Romaniser within the Church of England. It is the characteristic doctrines and practices, corruptions and superstitions of Rome which constitute the real evil of Romanism,—not the name, but the thing. It is an incomparably more evil and mischievous thing to remain in the Church and make it a business to Romanise it, than even to join the Papal communion; it is far worse to corrupt one-third of the clergy, and through them many of the laity, than to go over to Rome with a few companions. But that is not a complete and frank statement of the case. The Romanising leaven introduced into the Church of England, and remaining there, is in itself a worse thing than the same amount of Anglo-Romanism is after it has found its proper home within the Roman Catholic Church. The confessional, as organised by Pusey, has been in itself a more deadly evil, so far as it took hold, than the practice of confession as used in this country by Roman Catholics. The Romish Church does not teach raw and untrained university men of last evening that to-day they are, by the bishop's hands, made competent to act the part of priest-confessor, of searcher, physician, and judge of souls. The Father Confessors of the Church of Rome are, at anyrate, trained, discreet men, of tested character. In England, so far as can be learned, they are men of high character. Neither does the Church of Rome summon into the confessional boys of six. Not till the period of confirmation do any young people in the Romish Church present themselves for confession and absolution. These two peculiarities of Puseyism, for both of which Pusey personally cannot but be held responsible, are more pernicious and monstrous errors, involve usurpation more terrible and demoralisation more unnatural, than can easily be paralleled even in the Church of Rome. That Pusey was devout, earnest, generous, and was sympathetic with the experience of saintly people—Calvinists and the like—beyond the limits of the "Catholic" Churches, so called, is a fact not to be denied; but this fact cannot avail to annul such other facts as I have referred to, or to redeem the character of Pusey from the reproach of being a "false teacher." That is the phrase which St. Paul would have applied to him, in view of his pernicious doctrine, no less than to the "false teachers" of the Churches in Galatia.

It is not a sufficiently grave view of the case to regard Pusey as, in effect, the father, as he was always the defender, of "ritualism." What I have referred to in the preceding paragraph suggests thoughts deeper and more serious than are generally associated with the word "ritualism." It is, at the same time, true, and it is in itself a grave charge to make, that Pusey's principles lay at the foundation of the ritualism which intelligent Protestants condemn; this is a point by no means to be lost sight of. By "ritualism" is sometimes meant nothing more or worse than an æsthetic and ornate service organised by clergymen who are not disloyal to the Reformation. Of such ritualism I have nothing here to say. Its wisdom or otherwise is a question of taste and degree. Even such ritualism, indeed, though it should conceal underneath its displays no hierarchical pretensions or Romanising corruptions, may nevertheless be excessive, and little conducive to religious solemnity or elevation of feeling. But I refer here only to ritualism which is either symbolic of unscriptural hierarchical pretensions and claims, or is adopted for the sake of what Dr. Littledale has described and strongly recommended as "histrionic" worship,— worship intended to entertain and excite the performers in the true spirit of heathen celebrations. Pusey himself no more used such ritualism than Newman or Keble; he could not well have set it up or maintained it where he was accustomed to worship or to minister, and it was, besides, alien to his natural tastes, which were grave and solemn, and in no way favourable to artistic and imaginative display. Nevertheless, Pusey never failed to use his influence in favour of ritualisers, such as Purchas, for example, at Folkestone, and Mackonochie at St. Alban's. Ritualism is Puseyism adapted to popular acceptance—Puseyism dressed up to suit the tastes and to attract the attendance alike of the gay and frivolous classes on the one hand, and of the mob on the other—Puseyism put on the stage for the public enjoyment. Anyone who doubts the truth of this may refer to the reports of the Ritual Commission, and to the two volumes on *The Church and the World*, for the evidence. When, in 1867, the Archbishop of Armagh asked one of the most distinguished associates and followers of Pusey, Mr. Bennett, then of Frome, in earlier years of St. Barnabas, Pimlico, what doctrine was involved in wearing a chasuble at the celebration of "the Eucharist," Mr. Bennett answered, "the doctrine of sacrifice was involved," and that he himself was "a sacrificing priest," a priest who "offered a propitiatory sacrifice." Mr. Nugée, again, of Wymering, one of the most advanced of ritualists thirty years ago, had embroidered on his altar-cloths, not only I. H. S., but B. V. M.[1] Pusey, while protesting in his *Eirenicon* against the disgusting and even blasphemous excesses of Mariolatry, had yet allowed the lawfulness of the worship of the Virgin. In 1867 a few went to the length of Mr. Nugée; now many do. Pusey sowed the seed whilst protesting against overdoing, and lived to see an abundant crop of English-grown Mass-worship and Mariolatry. Since his death the harvest has become more and more abundant. Burns and Oates, the Roman Catholic publishers, find large custom for their idolatrous hymns to the Virgin among the worshippers in Anglican churches. So long ago as 1867 an article was published in the *Union Review*, in which the name Ritualist was repudiated on behalf of the party so called "as conveying a false impression, and misleading people into supposing that we are mere æsthetes fighting for forms and ceremonies, and nothing more." "'No,' says the writer, 'if we must have a name, call us Catholics.' Our belief is that the Church is Catholic, and that Protestantism in any shape or form has no legal place within her." So in 1889 the President of the English Church Union, recognised for thirty years past as the centre of the Ritualist Propaganda, spoke as follows:—

"The Catholic revival having been so largely concerned with the doctrine of the real presence,—a doctrine which necessarily affects the character of public worship,—how inevitable it was, *since outward acts attract so much more general attention than words spoken or written*, that a contest, if contest there was to be, should take the form of a contest about ritual. At the present moment the attempt to forbid lights, the mixed chalice, the eastward position,

[1] Third Report of the Ritual Commission.

the taking of the ablutions, the singing the *Agnus*, and the use of the sign of the cross in the celebration of the Holy Communion, are an illustration of what I say. Everyone knows that these observances are attacked on account of their connection with doctrine, because they *symbolise the identity in all essentials of our present Communion office in England with the old Communion office* of the English Church as it used to be said in Latin. The attack is on ritual, but the object struck at is the doctrine of the real presence and the eucharistic sacrifice."[1] And in one of the *Essays on the Reunion of Christendom*, a writer whose name is not revealed, but who must, all the more, have been a person

---

[1] Hence the injurious influence of the archbishop's judgment in the case of the Bishop of Lincoln. The things which the archbishop pronounces to be empty of doctrinal significance, and which he accordingly does not disallow, are by the ritualisers regarded as distinctly significant of the doctrine of what they speak of as the Real Presence, while they transform the service of the Holy Supper into a Romish Mass-worship. I will quote here some sentences from an article on that archiepiscopal judgment in the *Times* : "No plain man can doubt that the ritualistic practices have the practical effect of assimilating the administration of the Holy Communion to the celebration of the Mass. . . . It is difficult to look forward without anxiety to the sequel of this memorable judgment. . . . Either the history of this country is a great illusion, or there is a real and vital issue at stake between Roman and Protestant principles, and common sense must allow that a great point is won according as the most solemn and characteristic ceremonies of the Church are made practically to speak one language or the other. . . . The thoughts of every member are free in respect of the teaching of his clergyman ; but if he goes to church at all, he is compelled to participate in the forms of worship adopted. . . . The liberty of the clergyman is the bondage of the congregation. Any country village may suddenly have a priest imposed upon it who will transform its familiar and simple forms of worship into an approximation to that of Rome, and every parishioner must either submit to it or give up his Church altogether" (*Times*, Nov. 25, 1891).

of importance in the party of Reunion with Rome, uses the following language:—

"The marvel is, that Roman Catholics, whatever their views may be, do not see the wisdom of aiding us to the utmost. Admitting that we are but a lay body with no pretensions to the name of a church, we yet, in our belief (however mistaken) that we are one, are doing for England that which they cannot do. We are teaching men to believe that God is to be worshipped under the form of bread, and they are learning the lesson from us which they have refused to learn from the Roman teachers who have been among us for the last three hundred years. We are teaching men to endure willingly the pain of confession, which is an intense trial to the reserved Anglo-Saxon nature, and to believe that a man's 'I absolve thee' is the voice of God. How many English Protestants have Roman priests brought to confession compared with the Anglican clergy? Could they have overcome the English dislike to 'mummery' as we are overcoming it? On any hypothesis, we are '*doing their work.*'"

The attack on Protestantism is skilfully and scientifically, as well as earnestly and daringly, carried on. Even ritualistic displays which are not obviously Romanising, but are often regarded as merely æsthetic and attractive performances, may yet be doing the work of de-Protestantising the nation, as the ritualists themselves explain; while much fashionable ritualism is of such a nature, and is so managed, as to teach the complete system of Puseyite Popery. The mode of operation was thus explained in the *Union Review* long ago (1867):—

"The choirs are properly marshalled outside the cathedral, and then they march in a long procession, each choir preceded by its banners, and sing a processional hymn as they enter. True, these choir festival services are seldom associated with that chief Christian worship, the offering of the Holy Sacrifice. But still they have a great value, as accustoming our people to an external cultus on a grand scale, as well as to the association of that which delights eye and ear with the worship of God. They strike at the root of the old puritanical idea of worship, and that is a great matter. Also, you know the worth of 'hymnology' as a means of spreading the faith. We are wonderfully rich in hymns in England; and the collections issued by the Catholic party are very extensively used even in Protestant congregations, who are thereby unconsciously imbibing the very essence of Catholic truth. It is impossible to overestimate this most important agency at our command." [1]

In this way the suggestions of Dr. Littledale, in an essay on the " Missionary Aspect of Ritualism," contributed in 1866 to the well-known series of essays, entitled, *The Church and the World*, have actually been carried out. He argued for what he justly styled, with an unconscious felicity of satire, " histrionic worship," as the great means of popularising what may be described as Neo-Anglican Popery, of attracting working men to church, and of training them to sympathy with Anglo-Catholic teaching. He compares it to " object-lessons " in an infant school.

In carrying out these methods, the followers of Pusey, with his full sanction, have for more than thirty years past contended—and did contend before the Ritual Commission of 1866—for the use in church of the follow-

[1] For two of the foregoing extracts I am indebted to Mr. Lamb's *A Briton's Birthright* (Nisbet & Co.).

ing ornaments, used formerly in England, although disused since the full establishment of the Reformation in the reign of Elizabeth, viz. for *the church* : " Two Candlesticks, Cense-Pot, Cross for Processions, a lesser Cross for the Dead, Rogation Banners, Images, principal Image of the Saint to whom the church is dedicated, and Lenten Veil"; and for *the minister* the ornaments following : " Amice, Albe and Girdle, Surplice, Stole, Maniple, Sudarium, Chasuble (or principal Vestment), Silk Cope for principal Festivals, and two other Copes for presiding in the Choir at the same, Dalmatic for the Deacon (or Gospeller), Tunicle for the Sub-Deacon (or Epistoler)." They contended for the " Two Lights on the Altar, the Incense, the Mixed Chalice, the Eastward Position in front of the Altar, at the time of the Communion, of the Priest and his Assistants in the Celebration." [1]

What was thus contended for has, in great part, been gained. Pusey ceased not to insist that there could be no peace between the Evangelicals and his own party until the vestments and the eastward position had been conceded.[2] His contention, as we know, has in effect been won. Further, images to the Virgin and to the "saints" are freely introduced; "altars" are multiplied, Mary-altars being conspicuous in some churches, and chapels to suit being also in some cases provided, so that the beautiful and majestic ideal of English Church worship has, in many instances, been exchanged for the garish shows of Romish services. Indeed, by the restoration of such vestments and ornaments as those enumerated, and the lavish use in con-

[1] I have put together these items from *The Church and the World* (Longmans, 1866).
[2] *Archbishop Tait's Life*, ii. p. 291.

nexion with them of music and incense, of ceremony, gesture, and genuflection, a total effect is, in many churches, produced, by far more gaudy, more costly, and more gorgeous, than was ever known in England before the Reformation. Modern splendour of gold and silver, of form and finish; of rich material and radiant dye, green and violet, purple and crimson; modern magnificence in musical effect; the exactness and completeness of modern organisation and discipline,—all combined in the highest degree,—cannot but consummate upon the basis of the ancient ritual a miracle of ecclesiastical artistry, such as to outdo, in luxury of refinement and in sensational effect, all the shows of England except those of the modern theatre or pantomime. The pomp of cathedral ritual in the days of Becket and Wolsey is likely soon to be, if it is not already, outdone in some High Anglican churches. *Thus* religion is to be popularised, and the "masses" are to be made Christian, by means of a gaudy, luxurious, sensational, "histrionic" ritualism. *Thus* the "lust of the eye" and the "pride of life" are made "means of grace" in modern England, and thus "the world" is to be reconciled to "the Father."

What had advanced so far in 1867 has continued steadily to push its way during the years which have intervened. Now reunion with Rome is the public policy of the party. If the English Church Union and the Pope are not on terms of mutual understanding, it is not owing to any want of zeal, goodwill, and explicitness on the part of Lord Halifax, who has paid a personal visit to the Pope, or of the Church Union of which Lord Halifax is chairman. Such reunion has long been prayed for by the Puseyite party; the English cardinals and Roman Catholics, and the

Pope and his counsellors, have long made prayer for the conversion of England their continual exercise ; so, at least, we have often been assured. No wonder that Cardinal Vaughan should see strong grounds for hope and rejoicing in view of the prospect in England. I will quote some of his words ; they are enough to make all who read them deeply serious, they are painfully suggestive and instructive. " The sacramental power of orders," he said in 1890 in his pamphlet on *England's Conversion,* " the need of jurisdiction, the real presence, the daily sacrifice, auricular confession, prayers and offices for the dead, belief in Purgatory, the invocation of the Blessed Virgin and the saints, religious vows, and the institution of monks and nuns,—the very doctrines stamped in the Thirty-nine Articles as fond fables and blasphemous deceits,—all these are now openly taught from a thousand pulpits within the Establishment, and as heartily embraced by as many crowded congregations."

"The Church of England," he further says, "may not be so far off her crisis; pray that, when the State abandons her and the royal supremacy is withdrawn, she may return to the supremacy of the Vicar of Christ."

The one thing now wanting to the consummation of the hopes alike of the cardinal and the English Roman Catholics on the one side, and of Lord Halifax, Mr. Athelstan Riley, Canon Knox Little, and the multitude of English Puseyites on the other, is, it would seem, that the Church of England be disestablished. Then it is expected by the extremists that the Puseyite portion of the Anglican Church will separate from the rest, and go over bodily to Rome. That the bulk of the laity would be a party to such a course is incredible ; but there seems reason to expect that the

Puseyite clergy and the deluded lay leaders who take counsel with them, will complete the results of the Oxford Movement by joining the Romish Church.

Meantime, even High Church correspondents in the *Guardian* are beginning to take alarm at the actual condition of things. The course pursued, indeed, by the *Guardian*—able and scholarly journal as it is—has been open to the gravest censure. Its own chosen writers have made it their business to accept as belonging to the saints of Anglicanism every Roman saint, as such, St. Dominic, to wit, for one, and to whitewash, whenever possible and as far as possible, every Pope, making excuse even for Pope Gregory XIII., "the Pope of St. Bartholomew." [1]

---

[1] In the *Guardian* for March 6, 1895, there is a review of Carpecelatro's *Life of St. Philip Neri*, from which review I take the following extract :—" The counter-Reformation is associated in the minds of Englishmen with so much of questionable politics and doubtful religion, that they are apt to forget altogether that it had a deeper and much more worthy side to it. To most Englishmen Philip II. is the cruel persecutor of the Netherlands and the ambitious lord of the Armada, rather than the sincere and morbidly devout religionist. Pius V. is the author of the Elizabethan bull of deposition, and the instigator of assassination plots, rather than the saintly ascetic ; Gregory XIII. is the Pope of St. Bartholomew, and not the friend and companion of St. Philip Neri. The outward success of the movement appears on the face of history as so largely due to the mundane weapons of fire and sword, persecution and big battalions, that the careless reader is apt to overlook the moral influences at work." That is to say, the Duke of Alva's savage and ruthless massacres, his inhuman tortures, his fire and sword and hellish cruelties, were but a minor auxiliary in the work of extirpating "heresy" in the Netherlands ; the work was mainly accomplished by "moral influences." To couple the Duke of Alva and the Spanish subjugation of the Netherlands with "moral influences at work" is something wonderful. French and English Protestants also, it seems, are to forgive the public rejoicings, the special High Mass and Holy Festival, ordered by Gregory XIII., and the medals struck in commemoration of the

For many years past the main and governing policy of the *Guardian*, with occasional relapses into orthodox Church of England views, has, on the whole, been towards obliterating the distinction between the Church of England and the Romish communion. Now its perplexed correspondents point to the actual condition of things. "Extreme Churches" and "Perplexed Priests" appear in natural conjunction in the index and letter headings of the journal. One correspondent (June 5) wonders if his "bishop has ever been to 'High Mass,' or 'Solemn Evensong and Procession,' at one of the most extreme churches of the so-called Catholic party"; adding, "It is high time that High Churchmen themselves protested against some of the doings of the modern party." Another—a "Perplexed Priest"—says (June 19, 1895): "With the introduction of 'high celebrations,' often without communicants; the revived observance of days which have been excluded from our calendar, such as Corpus Christi, All Souls, the Assumption of the Blessed Virgin; the multiplication of altars in some of our new churches, and so forth, it becomes very per-

massacre of St. Bartholomew's Eve, in consideration that the Pope was the friend of "St. Philip." All these enormities are to be regarded as "questionable politics," or, perhaps, as "doubtful religion." The Duke of Alva's horrible inhumanities are "questionable politics"; Pope Gregory's applause and sacred benediction bestowed on the murderers of Coligny and his fellows are "doubtful religion." What the meaning may be of the reference to Philip's Armada in this connexion is not clear. One is at a loss to discover the "deeper side" of the "counter-Reformation" in Spain. The Armada, no doubt, was an achievement of "questionable politics"; but it is hard to imagine where "moral influences" came in to strengthen the position of the Spanish "counter-Reformation," or where there can have been any "counter-Reformation" with which Philip had to do except in the Netherlands, where surely it was physical and not moral force which crushed and eradicated Protestantism.

plexing to an ordinary Christian, trained up in Prayer-Book principles, to know exactly where he stands, and what is in store for him in the future. If the bishops are not on the alert, the movement will get beyond them, and they will find many of their best supporters falling off from them. . . . We are at present like a ship without a pilot, or rather with everyone taking upon himself the office of pilot." Another, who seems to be a straightforward and practical man, says (June 12), in reference to what another correspondent had said as to " the majority of the laity" being "either evangelical or moderate High Churchmen," who " would not see the work of the Reformation undone," that " they have been seeing it undone for half a century past," and that, in the " utter confusion " of his own mind, he shall be compelled to leave the Church altogether, and " become an ' unsectarian ' believer."

All this lamentable weakness and confusion, this mystery of inconsistency and unfaithfulness, of superstition and manifold schism, all that is included in Puseyism or has grown out of it, is traceable to the principles of ecclesiastical externalism to which the English High Church party have bound themselves. They place the unity of the Church where it is not to be found; they do not understand in what sense its perpetuity is guaranteed by the Lord's promise; they, accordingly, are driven to identify themselves with Rome, and are at their wits' end how to make out the triune identity of the Greek, the Roman, and the Anglican communions, to say nothing of the Armenian, the Coptic, and the Abyssinian Churches. Whereas the true spiritual principle allows those who hold it to acknowledge the good and the truly Christian elements that are to be found in these Churches, and to recognise all true believers in all of them as members of the one true spiritual Church of the Lord Jesus, which is wider than any Church, wider than all the Churches, and yet excludes the unbelieving and the truly evil professing members of every Church. This is the position happily expressed in the daily Liturgy, where Christian believers are virtually defined as those "professing and calling themselves Christians," who maintain the "unity of the Spirit in the bond of peace and in righteousness of life."

From its rise under the joint inspiration of Keble, Froude, and Newman—through the line of Tractarian organisation and influence until Tractarianism was merged in Puseyism—through the development of Puseyism from point to point, from deep to deep, till it combined in itself a confessionalism more exacting and oppressive than that of Rome, with the gaudiest ritualism ever assumed by degenerate and sensuous Christianity as its outward dress; through these stages of transformation the growth of Oxford Neo-Anglican Popery has been traced in the foregoing chapters. The question as to the future remains to disturb and perplex us. Has England seen the worst? Is there reason to hope that a manly and a truly evangelical reaction is at length beginning to make itself felt?

SMALL POPES, p. 335.

In the *Quarterly Review* for October 1878, an article was published, entitled, *Is the Church of England Protestant?* It is an old-fashioned, orthodox, though not illiberal, High Church article. "The effect," it says, "of the new High Church and Roman doctrine is to make a particular succession and order of men indispensable to the administration of the sacraments, and therefore to the reception of the special graces of the gospel. It is evident that, if there be such a class of men, if this be the character of the priesthood and of the episcopacy, Christians in general are at the mercy of priests and bishops. An indispensable caste can make its own terms. Its members are in the position of a king reigning by divine right; and, in short, the only difference between such a system and Roman Catholicism is that it possesses *a corporate Papacy, composed of several thousand clergy*, instead of *a single Pope*. This is the sacerdotalism which the English laity repudiate."

SACRAMENTAL LIFE, p. 336.

The following passage is taken, with some slight alterations, from *An Ordination Charge delivered at the Wesleyan Methodist Conference at its Meeting in Cardiff in* 1893. "The administration of the Lord's Supper, rightly apprehended, is, in truth, only a pre-eminently spiritual way of 'preaching the Word.'[1] It is the Divine Truth, of which the Sacrament is the vehicle, applied by the Holy Spirit, which is the means of quickening the soul. It is not that, by digital contact, divine grace and power—the very life of Christ— have been conveyed through the hands of the priestly celebrant, and are received by the communicant after a mode at once physical and hyperphysical. It is not that as through the working of a spell, under the words and handling of the 'priest,' the bread and wine are transformed into the Body and Blood of the Saviour, thus presented corporeally, as well as spiritually, to the communicants who receive Him, Body, Soul, and Spirit, into their body, soul, and spirit. This, alas! is the superstition that makes union among Christian churches impossible, even in this Christian country; this is the great source of schism in the land. By this superstition, the work of the Reformation is frustrated, and the darkness and narrowness of mediæval popery are brought back. According to the Scriptural view, it is by the manifold truth,—the summary of mutually enfolded sacred truths,—relating to salvation and life in Christ Jesus which the Lord's Supper so vividly presents to the faith of the Christian, it is through this Divine Truth, applied by the Holy Spirit, that the believer's soul is fed, and his life in his Saviour is quickened and replenished. Thus regarded, the Holy Sacrament becomes to the faith of the devout believer transfigured into glorious

---

[1] See Dr. Harrison's *Dr. Pusey's Challenge Answered* (chap. xi. 17–25) for evidence that this was the direct and frequent teaching of Origen, Cyril, Ambrose, and others of the Fathers, as well as in strict harmony with St. Paul's doctrine on the subject.

and divine meaning. Like a gem of many facets, it reflects radiance from every point of view. The Lord Christ is in the Sacrament revealed in all His offices, as our Atonement and our Life, as dying for us, and as living in us while we live in Him, as Brother and Friend, as Master and Redeemer, as going for us to the Father by the way of death, and returning as Judge and King to call us to the feast eternally new in His kingdom. As thus by faith we Realise His Spiritual Presence—

> 'We feed upon him in our hearts,
> And find that heaven and Christ are one.'

Such a divine mystery of death and life, of sanctification and redemption, is the Lord's Supper to the believing communicant."

CHAPTER XIV.

The Outlook—Sources of Pusey's Personal Influence—Signs of Reaction—Forecast.

FOR fifty years the Oxford Movement has continually gained ground, with only one serious check, that which followed the publication of Tract 90. For forty years its progress has been rapid. Its good has been a wide awakening of religious interest and zeal, and the diffusion in many minds of a high ideal of self-denying earnestness. Its evil has been indicated, however inadequately, in the foregoing pages. Both its good and its evil correspond to the good and the evil found in the leader from whom it derived its characteristic moral and ecclesiastical inspiration. It is Pusey's own movement. Newman's inspiration and example would never have taken such hold of the Church of England as Pusey's moral and social power, his preaching and example, have done.

The real truth, however, as to Pusey was never known until his biography was published. His was the life of a recluse; a halo of mystery surrounded the oracle whence issued the counsels of this man of vast learning, of high rank, of awfully sanctified life, who dwelt in unviolated solitude, and scarcely ever visited the outer day. The repulsive hardness of his ghostly counsels was sometimes intimated in whispers; but the secret was darkly kept as to his penitential discipline, his superstitious legalism, the slavery more abject than that of Rome to which he reduced his penitents, and the terrible depths of corporeal mortification and suffering which formed an essential part of his treatment, both for himself and for others. Now, however, his biographer has had no alternative but to disclose so much of the truth as must disenchant most of his readers. He has not told all —not told the worst. The letter to Mr. Hope-Scott was not published by Dr. Liddon, but by the Roman Catholic biographer of the distinguished barrister. Nor do we learn from the biography, what is revealed to us in an article in the *Nineteenth Century* as these pages pass through the press, that, strange as it may seem, chief among those who complained to Bishop Wilberforce of the undue influence exercised by Pusey in sisterhoods, and generally over women and girls, and of his completely popish spirit, was that eminent and ultra-High Anglican "Father," T. T. Carter. Other omissions have been pointed out in this volume. Still, quite enough is disclosed in the biography to show the real character of Pusey's religious teaching and influence. The long-looked-for volumes are not likely to increase the prestige of Pusey or Puseyism. The picture presented by his most distinguished and deeply attached disciple is one more likely to alarm than attract. So long as Pusey was little more than a name and an ideal, an ideal shrouded in secrecy, but known to be worshipped by some eminent and distinguished persons, the element of mystery heightened his influence, and assisted in concealing the actual facts concerning his work and his teaching. His great age also combined with his seclusion to enhance the veneration with which some who were by no means Puseyites regarded him. He was understood to lead a saintly life, apart from all worldly strife or show. His learning was believed to be profound, old world, and complete within its range. He was a man of high family connexions, and of assured social position; and he was not only very wealthy, but very generous. Such a combination of characteristics placed him on a pedestal apart; he was, as Newman said, 'Ο Μέγας—Pusey the Great. But, besides all this, he had spent half a century in magnifying the prerogatives of the "priesthood," and had maintained their claims by all the resources of his learning, all the influence of his urgent and Boanerges-like sermons, and by the unbounded use of his private resources. That Anglican ministers of a priestly temper and of high ecclesiastical claims and pretensions, some of them also, like Pusey, men of marked religiousness of spirit, should use all the means in their power to magnify his fame and bring disciples to his school, was natural and inevitable. He was just the sort of man, also, to influence a certain class of devout, benevolent, and enthusiastic women. Such women have great power over other women sympathetic with themselves. So, not only through sisterhoods, but in many ways besides, the character and influence of Pusey were held up to admiration, and seemed to grow more attractive and potent, from year to year, within a certain zone of church life. Since his death, tradition has risen up to do him reverence, a Pusey-cult has been established, a nimbus of glory and sanctity has gathered about his name and memory. Now, however, that the real facts are brought to light and can be scrutinised closely, now that a deliberate analysis of his character and the elements of his influence is possible, it may be hoped that the process of disillusion will take place speedily and effectually.

Except, indeed, within the ecclesiastical circle which has been indicated, Pusey was never a man of living influence. In the world of literature, in the sphere of intellectual thought, even in the circle of theological science, he has no place; he has made no mark, he has never sent a thrill into the minds of men, or waked an echo in the consciousness of the age through which he lived. He was not in any sense whatever a popular man; nor was he, what some men hardly to be called popular have been, a man of the people. Seldom has any man who attained name and fame been so utterly dead to the nation and the world within ten years after his passing from the world's view, as Dr. Pusey. Since his death, though many years have passed, nothing has been written about him to meet any popular demand. Not so much as a sketch of his life appears to have been published by his followers. At the Christian Knowledge Society's House, in all their pile of booksellers' catalogues, the solitary publication of any sort, the title which could be shown to me, when, for the purpose of this volume, I went there to inquire, was a slight study of his *Life and Life-Work*, published some years before by myself. At Masters', to which ritualistic publishing house I was referred as the most likely to furnish the information I required, I was informed that no sketch of his life was known.

And yet his work lives on, in its effects; his school survives in the congenial errors with which he had it in his power to infect so many clerical minds. What he had absorbed from the darkness of ages, in which so much of heathenism was held in solution by Christianity, what he adopted from the schools and the special devotions of the Roman Church, was readily assimilated by priestly minds prepared to welcome hierarchical or hierurgical ideas, and has become, alas! part of the inheritance of our modern Church of England. Doubtless Pusey, with all his errors and faults of character, was a devoted and self-sacrificing man, who did some good as well as much evil in his life. But in another sense than that which the words were intended to bear in Antony's mouth, it is sometimes true that while "the evil that men do lives after them," "the good is interred with their bones." Is there any reason to hope, now that the real Pusey is known as he was in life, and at the same time public opinion would seem to be stirring itself in anger against the daring strides towards Popery which the *Church Union* is taking before High Heaven, that a real national reaction is about to set in against Puseyism and its ways?

The biography, indeed, would rather intimate that the tide is flowing afresh in favour of Pusey's character and memory. Some words are quoted and attributed to Dr. Hook, which speak of Pusey as the "saint whom England persecuted," and the reader is left to infer that after Dr. Hook's disgust and indignation, because of St. Saviour's Church history, he in later years went back to his former admiration of Pusey. I take leave to altogether distrust this representation. Hook, indeed, always admitted, even in the fiercest heat of his righteous anger, the personal saintliness of Pusey; but that he ever changed his mind as to the evils of his Romanising influence, as to the fatal and terrible mischief of Pusey's teaching on the subject of the confessional, I venture to say there is no evidence;

certainly there is none either in his Life, or in the Life of his brother-in-law and constant correspondent, Lord Hatherley. On the contrary, we find him speaking in 1864 of the High Church party as being damaged by the assumption of its style and title "on the part of those who are grovelling in the lowest depths of Romanism." This was at a period when Dr. Hook had for some years been settled at Chichester as dean, and when many years had passed since the St. Saviour's troubles. Still later, in 1869, when he was much advanced in life, he defined a true High Churchman to be one who "cordially accepted the work of the Reformers; hating Rome as much as Rome hates us." These are not the phrases that would have been employed by Hook if he had changed his mind as to the influence and effects of Puseyism in the English Church. Outside the English Church the effect of the development of Puseyism and its influences has been to render much more intense the antagonism of Nonconformists generally to the Established Church, especially outside of the large towns. In country towns and in villages wherever Dissent, and especially Methodism, has obtained a footing, the Established Church is regarded by an increasing number with an awakened, an alert, an intense feeling of sectarian animosity, such as has not before been known. In London, and some other large towns, the effect of this is seen in the sharp divisions on the School Boards, the like of which were not known in the great towns twenty years ago. Secularism and unorthodoxy make a gain out of the prevalence of High Anglican Romanising claims and superstitions.

The tide, indeed, we may fairly hope, within the Church of England itself, has begun to turn against the

Romanising party. The recent correspondence in the public journals, and especially in the *Times*, on the subject of Anglican Orders is a striking "sign of the times." It arose out of Cardinal Vaughan's attack on the Orders of the Church of England, first in his address on the Reunion of Christendom in 1894, and afterwards in a private letter of explanation published in the *Times* for October 5, 1894. To Cardinal Vaughan, as to Cardinal Manning, Anglican clergymen, from Pusey himself, or the Archbishop of Canterbury downwards, stand in the same category as Nonconformist clergymen; all alike are merely laymen. No Anglican minister can prove his true apostolical succession, or establish any claim to be a "sacrificing priest." In response to the cardinal's challenge, Dr. Taylor of Liverpool, the Archdeacon of Warrington, promptly wrote to the *Times*,[1] blithely consenting to his conclusion. "Cardinal Vaughan," he says, "is quite right. On the basis he assumes the Orders of the Anglican clergy are invalid, and for this simple reason, that the Church of England neither has, nor professes to have, 'a sacrificing priesthood,' which he holds to be the essential character of the Catholic rite of ordination." He proceeds to sum up the evidence in proof that the Church of England, as Reformed, distinctly abandoned (1550–1554) for its clergy the claim and character of a sacrificing priesthood. He closes his letter much as he begins it, disallowing, indeed, the cardinal's contention that the Church of England has "no valid ministry," but earnestly hoping that the cardinal's "authoritative statement will have some effect in dissipating in many minds the idea" that there is in the Church an Order of "sacrificing priests." The Archdeacon of War-

[1] October 9, 1894.

rington thus boldly joins Dean Farrar and Archdeacon Sinclair in their antagonism to such Romanising priestly claims as Dr. Pusey spent most of his life in contending for.[1] After a fortnight's discussion, the leading journal, in its issue of October 20, sums up the case in a remarkable article.

It was the pretence of Pusey and his party—a most audacious pretence—that their system of theology and their priestly claims were founded on the teaching of the "judicious Hooker." The *Times* cites a passage from Hooker—not a few other passages might be quoted—which effectually refutes this claim, and which closes by asking, "what better title could be given" to the clergy than "the reverend name of presbyters or fatherly guides," and by affirming that "the Holy Ghost, throughout the body of the New Testament, making so much mention of them, doth not anywhere call them priests." "Can a Church," says the writer in the *Times*, "which declares in its Articles that the sacrifices of Masses were blasphemous fables and dangerous deceits, be thought to assert for its ministers the sacrificial functions which it thus expressly repudiates?" After intimating that Newman's Tract 90

---

[1] The Archdeacon of Manchester also takes his place publicly with his brother of Warrington in his recognition of Nonconformist ministers. Dean Farrar, whilst still archdeacon, published two trenchant articles in the *Contemporary Review*, in the latter of which ("Undoing the Work of the Reformation," July 1893), he quotes the Archdeacon of Llandaff as to the cause of Welsh popular animosity against the Church of England. "The Welsh cannot," he tells us, "bear with a Church in which the 'Mass' is being made the centre of religious worship; ministers have, in practice, become sacrificing priests; sacerdotalism, with its train of dangerous error, has become the prominent power of our churches; the private confessional is being made the door of full membership."

is the stronghold of the ritualistic innovators, and their only line of defence, from which it has no wish to drive "men of such high personal character and such devotion to their duties as many of them are," the *Times* closes its article with these significant words: "They must not complain if 'An Ordinary Layman' and his like regard their claims and their practices 'sometimes with irritation and always with contempt.'" The last words are quoted from a letter, under the signature "An Ordinary Layman," which is published in the same issue of the paper, and which reflects the prevalent feeling of the laity on the subject. "Among a not inconsiderable acquaintance," says the writer, "I know but a few laymen who would trouble their heads about it at all, and not more than one or two who even profess to believe that either of the miraculous powers claimed by Cardinal Vaughan for the Romish priest are possessed in any degree by our own clergy." This is on one side a reassuring statement; but it suggests alarming questions. What, if this be true, do the laity think of their clergy? And how far are the monstrous, and for most men quite incredible claims, which for nearly half a century have been asserted by a large and often highly-placed section of the religious teachers and guides of the people of England, answerable for the scepticism which during the same period has disturbed the minds and desolated the hearts of so many men of masculine intellect and powerful character? Nevertheless, for the reasons I have intimated, may we not venture to hope that the worst effects of the Romanising conspiracy are over? Forty or fifty years ago Thomas Mozley, at that time one of the innermost circle of the Tractarian school, inspired the *Times* on all ecclesiastical subjects, while the same circle sustained religious reviews and magazines of much apparent learning and of subtly-trained ability, especially in the field of casuistry and special pleading. To-day all this is changed. The balance of learning and ability as writers is no longer on the side of the Anglican Romanisers; there are schools of evangelical training in theology which are no less learned and able than orthodox; while the press teems with volumes of Christian exposition and instruction, to which Nonconformist divines largely contribute, and which are read by students of all Churches. Best of all is the distinct and resolute uprising within the Church of England of a school of teaching at once liberal and orthodox, which is altogether and strenuously opposed to the Romanising and ritualising party in the Church of England. Not only, as I have shown, are deans and archdeacons uniting to arrest the tide of corruption, but there are on the episcopal bench a larger proportion of outspeaking supporters of the Reformation than for many years past. The reaction, indeed, comes late—very late. One cannot but lament that the English Church did not earlier learn the things which belong to its peace. The middle classes distrust Anglican clericalism, even when they go to church. Political power has come to village Methodists and Dissenters coincidently with the development of the irreconcilable spirit of antagonism of which I have spoken. What was officially threatened for Wales they confidently expect, before long, to see consummated not only for Wales, but for England. All that is involved in the question they seldom, indeed, understand. But the situation is not the less serious on that account. I am myself no enemy of the Church of England; but it is not the less a duty to state unpleasant truths on so grave and momentous a subject, and to do my part towards disturbing the clergy in that "fools' paradise," where a large proportion of them, it is evident, continue to dream their dreams in fatal unconsciousness. Ecclesiastical arrogance and intolerance—the intolerance of a curiously ignorant bigotry—coupled with degrading superstitions, weigh, like a sentence of doom, on the Romanising Neo-Anglicanism of modern England.

Few men can have had better opportunities for forming a probable estimate of the effect on the national mind of the full ritualistic and Romanising development of Puseyism, as now disclosed to the people of England, than the late chaplain of the House of Commons. I may therefore fitly quote from Dean Farrar's article in the *Contemporary Review* on "Undoing the Work of the Reformation," the following passage: "Disestablishment will be one of the first consequences of the triumph of Ritualism; and, immediately after Disestablisment, will come the necessity for, and the certainty of, a NEW REFORMATION to re-establish the truths which Ritualism endeavours to overthrow. . . . There are myriads of Englishmen, and not a few even among the clergy, who will not stand a Church of England which shall tend to become Romish in all but name, or perhaps Romish even in name. The days of disruption are being hastened on with giant strides. May God avert the unspeakable evils which they will inevitably bring in their train."[1] If what Dean Farrar forebodes shall come to pass, and the Church of England be in consequence, not disprivileged by graduated stages of reform, with the due unfolding of her intrinsic forces and her liberated faculties, and with ample and kindly

[1] *Contemporary Review*, July 1893.

regard to all the equities involved in the case of a National Church with so grand and, on the whole, till Puseyism arose, so truly national a history, the result will be due to nothing else but the development of Puseyism into the Romanising and superstitious system, of which the Church Union has for thirty years been the representative and the exponent.[1]

[1] In sending the final sheet of this volume [1] to the press, it is not unfitting to refer to the latest official utterance of Cardinal Vaughan on the subject of "Reunion," in his address at Bristol to the "Catholic Truth Society." The cardinal, indeed, has said nothing more or less than he was bound to say, although some have received his words with astonishment at his unyieldingness, while others have been struck with admiration of his sincerity. No prince of the Romish Church —nor even the Sovereign Pontiff himself—can cheapen the terms of admission to the Church, so as to allow Anglicans, even if the whole Church united in the petition, to be excused from accepting every dogma, every decree, of the Church. The cardinal had before insisted on the necessity of reordination for Anglican "priests," now he insists that Roman Mariolatry and the Infallibility Dogma must be distinctly and fully accepted. The multitude waiting at the Gates of Rome can only be received as fellow-citizens of the ecclesiastical imperial State on condition of passing by the appointed way through the Caudine Forks under the yoke of the conquerors. What Newman had to accept must be accepted also by these suitors for the Church's grace.

[1] First edition.

SUPPLEMENTARY CHAPTER.

1895-1899.

THE COURSE OF EVENTS SINCE 1895—NATIONAL AGITATION AND THE CHURCH CRISIS—PENDING QUESTIONS—DISESTABLISHMENT—REFORM IN DISCIPLINE AND ORGANISATION—PERPLEXITIES AND POSSIBILITIES.

WHEN, four years ago, the final pages of this book in its first edition were written, Lord Halifax and his associates, as leaders of the English Church Union, were in eager and intense expectation of the result of their private and informal appeal to the Pope on behalf of the Neo-Anglican section of the clergy for a recognition of the validity of Anglican orders. The Pope had consented to submit the question to his Supreme Council—known in former times of persecuting power as the Holy Office—for re-examination. This step on his part was regarded by the Reunion party as one of encouraging condescension. Even Mr. Gladstone, reverting to the dreams and visions of his early life, was led, in a letter which Lord Halifax was allowed to publish, to speak in strangely unbefitting language, especially as used by the author of *Vaticanism*, of the condescension and benevolence of the Head of the Roman Catholic Church. There was a widespread expectation, to which the *Guardian* thought it not improper or unwise to give sympathetic expression, that by his benignant condescension and his holy zeal for Christ and His Church, the way to reunion would at last be opened, so far at least as to admit the validity of Anglican orders.

The result, however, was, as sober minds had anticipated, that the Pope found himself unable to do anything to comfort or encourage the Ritualist suppliants. To repeat the words used on the last page of the former edition of this book, "the multitude waiting at the Gates of Rome" found that, like all before them who had sought the same distinction, they could only be received as fellow-citizens of the ecclesiastical imperial State " on condition of passing under the yoke of the conquerors." The Papal Bull—or Letter Apostolic—denied absolutely the validity of Anglican orders, the validity of Anglican sacraments, and of all the claims of the ancient Church of England to the style and character of an apostolic Church of Christ, or a branch of the Catholic and apostolic Church. This is one of the notable and memorable facts which have marked the history of the Neo-Anglican controversy, and one of the *momenta* which have contributed to bring about that critical change in the conditions and prospects of the Established Church of this realm of England, which must now be recognised by all who study the "signs of the times" as one of the most important features of English history during these closing years of the nineteenth Christian century.

The question as to the validity of the orders of the Church of England is, indeed, in itself, by no means of the primary and fundamental importance attributed to it by Romish priests and doctors and by Anglican

Episcopal doctrinaires. The lineal succession of ministerial orders is not the source or the condition of Church life. If it were, more than half of the most active and powerful moiety of the professing Christian world would be excommunicated and have to take its place outside the Christian pale. John Wesley was himself a simple presbyter of the Church of England, with no episcopal dignity or prerogative. Yet when thousands of souls in America, "converted" and spiritually renewed through the labours of his preachers, converts scattered through a vast region, mostly wilderness, almost entirely destitute of Christian ministers and without any bishop on the continent to do the work of ordination, or any prospect of the coming of such a bishop, were thus left without any provision for Christian sacramental administrations, without any organised Church or regular Church ordinances, Wesley felt himself compelled, as the minister to whom these thousands looked for help in their sore necessity, to ordain in England, with due solemnity, Dr. Coke, a clergyman of the Church of England, as "Superintendent," that is as Bishop, for America, that he might there ordain Methodist ministers, and, with their help, organise a Christian Church for that vast continent. Thus was founded the largest and most fruitful Protestant communion in the world, from which are derived the sister Methodist Churches of America, North and South, and also in large part the Methodist Church of Canada, although in part also the Canadian Methodist Church has derived its ministers and its ministerial orders directly from the English Methodist Church, the ministers of which Church, again, were, at the beginning, no successionist line, but the itinerant pastors of what was mainly and substantially a self-developed Church, who had been appointed by Wesley his assistant preachers.

So, again, when the irregular offshoot from Methodism, known as the Primitive Methodists, sprang up nearly ninety years ago in Staffordshire, and quickly grew into a distinct Church, the "local preachers" who had founded it were accepted as chief pastors by the "societies" they had organised, and became an order of ministers, from whom has been derived a succession of ordained pastors, ministering to a large and widely spread Church, a Church occupying no mean position in England and its colonies, and doing successful mission work in heathen lands.

With such facts as these in view, it argues no irreverent disregard for Christian orders in Church government and life, if an earnest evangelical statesman like the Duke of Argyll professes something like indifference to the whole controversy, between Rome and the Church of England, as to the validity of Church orders,[1] and if the *Times* in an article on the subject of the Papal Bull on

---

[1] In his pamphlet entitled *Some Words of Warning to the Presbyterians of Scotland*, already referred to on p. 57, the Duke of Argyll speaks of "that extraordinary doctrine of High Anglicanism which makes the whole apparatus of Christianity—sacraments and all—hang on the local preservation of one order in the ministry, for which in the New Testament there is not even a distinctive name." "I am lax enough," he says, "to believe that the Christian Church, as an organised society, with all her divine teaching, and all her sacraments, is independent of both these systems"—meaning successional Episcopacy and Popery. So, also, in a letter to the *Times*, the Duke says, "I have no sympathy with the gushing gratitude with which a few Anglicans have thanked God that the Bishop of Rome has condescended to inquire into what they and he are pleased to call the 'validity' of Anglican orders. The very word implies an assumption which I believe to be irrational" (*Times*, June 12, 1896, in a letter headed "Dr. Parker on Undenominationalism").

Anglican orders says, "The controversy has no meaning for us—and it has never had any."[1]

The most important effect of this controversy, however, is not that it has proved that Anglican clergy can not be recognised as true ministers of Christ by the Papal authorities. That, doubtless, is a very precious lesson for Neo-Anglican High Churchmen to learn and to lay to heart. It cannot but greatly discourage the humiliating and demoralising tendency towards Rome and Romish practices within the Church of England, which brought Mr. Gladstone at the very close of a brilliant historical course, into explicit alliance with Lord Halifax on the subject of reunion with Rome, and which led him to gush with gratitude when he was informed by his lordship with what benevolent wishes and hopes the Pope had taken up the question of Anglican orders and their validity;—expressing the "cordial sentiments of reverence, gratitude, and high appreciation" with which he regarded his action in the matter, and his hope that it might prove to be "a step and even morally a stride" towards reunion.[2]

Much more important must in the end be the effect of this controversy, as thus brought to an issue, in driving home to the mind and consciousness of the English people the unspeakable degradation of Christianity involved in the materialistic superstition which has lain at the bottom of the question as to "orders." What a pitiful spectacle have we in Christendom hopelessly divided, rent asunder, by reason of a ceremonial discontinuity connected with the laying on of the hands of a successional episcopacy! The blasphemy against the spirit and the power of the Saviour's

[1] *Times*, September 21, 1896.
[2] *Times*, September 19, 1896.

atoning work and grace for the world, to save which the Son of God was made man, of His redeeming work for the "Holy Church throughout all the world," which He died and rose again and reigns above to bring into eternal union with Himself,—however unconscious of the blasphemy may be the men that maintain the successional dogma,—is too revolting, when once it is truly realised, for the deliberate acceptance of religiously awakened men and women. The horror of it has been rankling in the minds of serious people more and more for many months past; it has keenly touched the souls of the earnest laity of England. There is a growing and deepening sense of shame and humiliation. Clergy, trained in a superstitious school of hierarchical delusion, may prolong the controversy. Men who seek refuge in the passive acceptance of ritualism from the burden of true moral responsibility and the effort of spiritual faith in an unseen Mediator and Saviour, may conspire with such clergy to keep up the sensuous and materialistic cult which transforms religion into a mixture of Christianity and superstition. But earnest and honest thinkers and truly spiritual seekers after God in Christ must more and more reject perversions of belief and worship, which owe their origin to a heathenish corruption, dating from the later patristic period, a corruption which became continually grosser as the primitive simplicity of the faith came to be increasingly adulterated with the idolatrous materialism of the conquered nations, who passively accepted from their conquerors a form of worship ennobled by the name of Christianity, but only imperfectly imbued with its spirit and power.

Between 1895 and 1898 the process of awakening on this subject was going on in the nation with deepening power. At the same time, however, among the votaries of Romanising practices, after the first rebuff resulting from the Pope's missive, it seemed as if a sort of zeal born of despair in one direction was inspiring wilder lengths of excess in other directions. If they could not be Popish Anglicans—Anglicans in distinct and professed union with Rome—some of the Romanising votaries seemed to be determined that they would be and do within the Church of England all that could be expected of them if they had been in reality earnest Popish missioners. One case which occupied the public attention for many weeks in 1897 may be mentioned by way of illustration. The superstitious excesses of the clergyman in Portsmouth who called himself "Father Dolling," already referred to in a note on p. 311, seem to have surpassed all that had been done before even by such men as Mr. Mackonochie. It became impossible for any bishop who had the least regard for the name of Protestant, or the character of a Reformed Church, to tolerate his transgressions. The Bishop of Winchester, having exhausted all means of instruction and expostulation, felt it to be his duty to bring Mr. Dolling's career in Portsmouth to an end. With steady decision he carried out discipline, and before the close of 1897 "Father Dolling" had to leave the diocese of Winchester. He is now in London, and is very extreme there. He appears, however, to have learnt some lessons of prudence, and the present temper of London compels a certain restraint in his conduct. The bishops, also, have begun to act, and are preparing for more decisive action. The daring lengths to which Mr. Dolling had gone, advancing further and further during several years, and the publicity given to his case in consequence of his bishop's action, did not a little to awaken the public mind to the scandal and the peril involved in the Ritualist movement.[1]

No one of the High Ritualist party had expressed any condemnation of the rank Popery of Mr. Dolling's teaching and ritual. Not only so, but Lord Halifax, while not disguising his disappointment at the result of the Vatican inquiry, did not cease boldly and energetically to urge his party neither to surrender at any point nor to retreat, but boldly to persevere and persist in their Romanising practices. At the same time, Lord Halifax was led into a line of defence against the Roman attitude and judgment, fatal in reality to the pretensions of his own party. In an address to the Church Union he argued, with an almost pathetic earnestness, that, though Rome disowned them, and disallowed their Church orders, God owned them by the seal which He put upon their work. He pointed to their moral and spiritual successes, as evidence that they were, whether acknowledged by Rome or not, in reality a vital part of the Catholic Church of Christ. This was, argumentatively regarded, a fatal shifting of his ground as a High Churchman. The argument he thus used is of the same character, but immensely less powerful, with that which Methodists, Presbyterians, and Evangelical Nonconformists in general, have been accustomed to use against the exclusive pretensions and the virtual excommunication with which High Catholic Anglicans are accustomed to set at naught the claims of all the Protestant Christians of England, and indeed of the world. In his Ordination Charge delivered last summer at Great Queen Street Chapel, to a large company of young Wesleyan ministers, completing their probation, the Rev. H. Price Hughes, referring to this plea against

[1] See Note to p. 311.

Papal exclusiveness put forth by Lord Halifax, said, in his own strong way, that with the sword which Lord Halifax used to cut off the head of the Pope, he himself cut off the head of Lord Halifax. The same sword had been used by others before Mr. Hughes wielded it so mightily. But reason has no effect on infatuated partisans. The Chairman of the English Church Union never condescends to reply to any argument used by a Nonconformist. During the three years which have followed the issue of the Papal Bull he has shown no sign of yielding to either argument or rightful authority. Whether he will be obliged at length to succumb to the joint authority and sentence of the archbishops as now at length pronounced against the Romanising Ritualists is just now the question. Dr. Cobb, a high official of the Church Union, had intimated that nothing would now be left for him and his co-partners to do but to accept Disestablishment. But Dr. Cobb was premature in taking this attitude, and has since found it necessary to submit, however reluctantly. Lord Halifax has delivered himself to the Church Union on the subject. He all but encourages clergymen to resist the decision of the archbishops—their first joint decision—as to incense and lights; if they should resist, he loudly and urgently exhorts the laity of their parishes to back them up strongly. But yet he evidently expects that many of the clergy will not dare to resist, and has no censure for those who may yield. In his personally defiant attitude he has received the public and explicit support of his chosen counsellor, Canon Carter. But in saying this I am anticipating. I was attempting to give a slight sketch of the circumstances, the course of events, and the waves of influence which during the last two or three years have conduced to bring on the present crisis in the history of the Church of England.

During the last eighteen months England has at length given decisive signs of awakening and uprising against the Romanising Movement. Parliament has made its voice heard in good earnest. The House of Commons, indeed, last spring declined by a considerable majority—though the minority was relatively large—to pass the thoroughgoing Church Discipline Bill which the Lancashire Protestants would have enacted, and which would have taken away the bishops' veto on ritualistic prosecutions, but they unanimously adopted the Attorney-General's strong resolution, which gave warning that unless an end were speedily put to Romanising illegalities by other means, Parliament would, without doubt, make an end of them by effective legislation. The bishops, it is now evident, have taken alarm in good earnest—after long-continued supineness, so far as many of them are concerned. The archbishops have given their judgment against the Romanising innovators as to two of the points submitted to them for decision, the points of incense and lights; and they are presently to determine other points,—in particular, and first in order, the point of "Reservation." The principles on which they have condemned the ritualists on the two first points must prevail, as it would seem, to condemn the innovators on most, if not all, the other litigated points. At a private conference of the archbishops and bishops held in November of last year, an agreement was arrived at, as now appears, as to what ritualistic practices must without question be regarded as unlawful, and as to the steps to be taken by the archbishops in order to initiate a course of authoritative prohibition of such practices, to be carried into effect by the bishops in their respective dioceses. This, of course, was before the subject was introduced into the House of Commons, and the Attorney-General's resolution was adopted.

The work done during the last year or two has, it is plain, gone deep; the Protestant reaction against the Romanisers is widespread and exceedingly powerful, notwithstanding Lord Halifax's hardy boasts and daring defiance. The laity of England are beginning to understand the profound importance of the controversy—and that all that belongs to the liberties, the moral greatness and truth, the religious and intellectual honesty and well-being, of the British nation, is involved in the ecclesiastical struggle. It is a fight for life and truth; it is against those whose aims and work would undo all that has made England truly great.

The final closing in of the battle—the gathering of the forces and the clash of the conflict—have come with a swift suddenness which has at last daunted the innovators—has given pause to their boasts—has made them feel that their party has not taken captive the people of England. It is made plain that the nation has never been really with them, and that it is now manifestly against them. Moving and working on surreptitious lines of procedure, and chiefly among the "classes," they knew not that the nation in its depths and its "masses" distrusted and disliked them. The convictions which have now taken such impressive form had slumbered in seeming indifference, the indifference in part of conscious strength and of a contempt that could not bring itself to regard with serious concern claims and pretensions so monstrous as those of the Romanisers. But, when it could no longer be doubted that large numbers had actually, though for the most part and for years together secretly, conspired and combined against the most cherished principles and the most sacred instincts of their race and nation, the loyal adherents of Christian truth and liberty banded themselves together in such force and in such a temper of lofty and severe indignation as could not fail and has not failed to fill the conspirators with alarm.

That the whole of the Oxford Movement, whether known as Tractarian or Puseyite, has in fact been, even from the first, what Hurrell Froude himself, in gay frankness, described it as being, in its earliest inception, sixty years ago, a conspiracy, is a fact that has now been conclusively proved by the volume published by Mr. Walsh, eighteen months ago, on the *Secret History of the Oxford Movement*. That volume, indeed, adds little or nothing to what was previously known as to the Tractarian Movement, as distinguished from the later Puseyite development. But, as respects the work done by Pusey and his coadjutors and disciples during the last fifty years, its disclosures have been to the nation generally nothing less than an appalling revelation. Its author has gained access to the secret archives of the widely ramified conspiracy of which Pusey was the centre, and by which the ends contemplated by the original Tractarian leaders have been for fifty years stealthily promoted and secretly carried into effect. The revelation contained in Mr. Walsh's book supplements the view given in this volume, by bringing to light the carefully hidden plans and aims which underlay the scope and history of the Movement, as known from more or less public sources of information. The result of this revelation has been to kindle a conflagration in the nation.

The *Secret History* discloses a system of un-English methods,—plans and projects suggestive of nothing so much as Jesuitism and its casuistry,—a steady and callous contempt for the traditions of English Protestantism as to religious worship and discipline, as to parental rights and responsibilities, as to family life and relations, as to priestly prerogative, confession, celibacy, monasticism—as to things fit and things unfit for mutual inquiry and conversation between the sexes, and, in particular, between the clergy and the younger members of their flocks. It opens out to view an underworld, created and organised by the Movement, of morbid feelings, of demoralising spiritual scrutiny and investigation carried on by priestly questioners, of debilitating and degrading influences, undermining the sense of personal responsibility and bringing the souls of children, and therefore of men and women, into unholy dependence and subordination to an order of inquisitors, diving and searching in quest of all sins and their motives and possibilities, which may haunt the memory, the senses, the natural affections and passions, and the avenues to these. In a word, it shows an organisation of influences tending to dehumanise those brought under their power, and to make all children, all men, all women, the slaves of the priesthood. It shows us Dr. Pusey as a party to this whole mystery of evil, as in fact the grand master of the entire organisation, which, however, was worked out by many covenanted helpers and agents. It demonstrates that all the results laid bare are a direct consequence of the Oxford Neo-Anglican and Romanising Movement.

Mr. Walsh's *Secret History* has exposed to view the secret motives and designs which, during forty years, governed the conduct and course of the combined bands of conspirators who guided the development of the Movement. The curtain was drawn up, and an astonished and indignant public beheld the long-drawn-out history of plans and projects, for so many years successfully concealed, but also successfully carried out, infinitely more deadly in their aim and more pernicious in their secret operation than any conspiracy which the national history has disclosed to the student of its secret records.

The vast extent of the conspiracy, in its various ramifications, was amazing and alarming. It was proved to embrace thousands of clergy, to have entangled in its coils hundreds of the laity, to have numbered among its leaders not a few dignitaries of the Church, to have cast its net over thousands of women and children, bringing them under an oppressive and degrading yoke of bondage. There had long been more than suspicions of what was going on, but, so effectually was the seal of secrecy enforced, that it was all but impossible to obtain evidence for the public eye.

Once, indeed, as long ago as 1877, Lord Redesdale, in the House of Lords, had obtained information which enabled and constrained him, High Churchman as he was, to describe and, by quotations, partly to expose, and to hold up to national condemnation, a grossly indecent book, secretly prepared and in secret use, entitled *The Priest in Absolution*. This public exposure alarmed the nation and, for a time, gave some check to the Puseyite Movement. Lord Redesdale could not expose the whole depth or iniquity of the evil of the confessional system and practice. Some portions of the book, indeed, were too grossly indecent to read in Parliament, or to print in the newspaper press. But what he read and said made a profound impression.

His lordship, however, was not in a position to make known to the country that that famous and favourite Puseyite confessor, Canon Carter, the model organiser of Sisterhoods, had read and revised the proof-sheets of the infamous book from which he quoted. We learn this from Mr. Walsh's volume, and also that "he had recommended the author," as he himself stated, "to publish it in Latin." This was the book in regard to which an address was forwarded to the Archbishop (Tait) of Canterbury signed by a multitude of noblemen, the most illustrious names in the peerages of England, Ireland, and Scotland, in which they expressed their "deep sorrow and indignation at the extreme delicacy and impropriety of the questions therein put to married and unmarried women and children." This volume was published by the Society of the Holy Cross (the S.S.C.), who, notwithstanding its public exposure and Parliamentary censure, refused to condemn the book. The well-known Rev. A. H. Mackonochie took a leading part in defence of the volume; and finally, with the consent of Canon Carter, in opposition to a motion for condemnation proposed by the Rev. F. N. Oxenham, a resolution was adopted, "repudiating the unfair criticisms passed on the book," and "without intending to imply ANY condemnation of it, yet in deference to the desire expressed by the Archbishop of Canterbury," consenting "that no further copies of it be supplied." The transactions relating to this book took place in a secret conclave of the Society. The sale of the volume had been very strictly guarded, but one volume had fallen into wrong hands, and thus the secret came to be divulged. Mr. Mackonochie, after the exposure of the book, wrote to another clergyman that—"Its principles are those which govern, I believe, all confessors among ourselves." He declared his belief that "the bishops had got up the attack" upon the book.

Dr. Pusey appears in Mr. Walsh's volume as the author or editor of the *Manual for Confessors*, a book largely adapted from the French. In this book he prescribes for Sisters of Mercy, as a penance, and "for mortifications, the Discipline for about a quarter of an hour a day," the discipline meaning a severe whipping by a scourge of knotted cords on the bare back. He printed also and secretly circulated for thirty years *Hints for a First Confession*, which has been published since his death, and which insists particularly on the need in a first confession of an absolutely complete enumeration of all the sins committed by the penitent during his whole life. In the *Manual for Confessors*, moreover, he insists that father confessors should remember the canonical warning, "What I know through confession, I know less than what I do not know." He quotes Pope Eugenius as saying, "What a confessor knows in this way he knows as God—'ut Deus'; while out of confession he is only speaking as man—'ut homo.'" But he goes further still and adds, "As man he may swear with a clear conscience that he knows not, what he knows only as God."

No wonder that the system and movement known as Puseyism has a "secret history," without which its real character cannot be known. But in this "mystery of iniquity" is a system of "wheels within wheels," and Mr. Walsh's volume contains, besides a general view of the "secret history of the movement," an outline of the history of the secret societies—the secrecy of which has been most sacredly and rigidly kept—the societies by which the movement has been inspired and guided from within. Such are:—" The Society of the Holy Cross," " The Order of Corporate Reunion," " The Confraternity of the Blessed Sacrament," a " Purgatorial Society," the " Guilds of All Souls," " The Secret Order of the Holy Redeemer,"—in which there is an " Inner Circle,"—the " Brotherhood of the Holy Cross,"—" The Order of the Holy Redeemer,"—which recognises the Pope as " the Pastor and Teacher of the Church,"—" The Secret Order of St. John the Divine," " The Society of St. Osmond "—the Alcuin Club—a " Laymen's Ritual Institute," with a " Secret Oath," —and a number of local " Secret Guilds." The " Romeward Movement" is followed and described in detail, and in an Appendix a summary view is given of the special teaching of the Ritualist organisation.

By the time this *Secret History* was published the country was well prepared to receive and appreciate its disclosures. In addition to the materials of instruction used in the earlier part of this volume, among which, in particular, Dr. Pusey's *Life* was painfully suggestive of depths of Romanising policy and perversion only partially revealed, there was the humiliating history of the appeal to the Pope on the question of " orders," already referred to—the appeal to an authority so deeply discredited in England and in English history, with its ignominious issue, on a question so merely technical and externalist, and in a controversy so unspiritual and unapostolic. But there was more than this.

The revelations contained in Pusey's *Life* as to the subject of the confessional, of penance, of absolution, supplemented as they had been by the information contained in the Memoirs of Hope-Scott as to his commission to inquire on the Continent on behalf of Dr. Pusey about the "discipline" and its proper use in the case of women, especially delicately-nurtured women, had brought home to English Protestants what the haircloth and the scourge, what fasting and bodily torture, in the hands of fanatical English Romanising priests, might mean for English women and girls—what, in fact, they did mean. A zealous and fervid Protestant bookseller in Paternoster Row, having had his attention led to these subjects, and, as it happened, having for his neighbour a Roman Catholic bookseller who dealt in articles used for purposes of "discipline," made it his business to inquire into the facts of the case as to the use of such articles, and to discover who were the bookseller's chief customers. The results were published to the world in one of the ablest, and most influential politically, "Liberal" evening newspapers.

On the evening of September 9th, 1896—a date nearly synchronising with that of the Papal Bull on orders—the *Westminster Gazette* contained an article on this subject, from which I quote a few lines. "John Kensit, 'the Protestant Bookseller,' has given Paternoster Row a new sensation this week. For some days a large part of his window has been used for the exhibition of a large sheet displaying half a dozen 'instruments of torture,' *said to be used and recommended by members of the Church of England*. Whoever they are used by—and it is certain they are not mere ornaments or playthings—these 'instruments of torture' by no means belie the name Mr. Kensit has bestowed upon them."

A description follows—of a "broad stomacher of horsehair," to be used next the skin—the mildest sort of "discipline"; of the "severer penance" of the Barbed Heart

—from which barbs project, "finer than the ends of the barbed fences of our fields"; of wristlets and anklets and the broad band of netted barbs—"equally fiendish in purpose"—which the penitent fastens around his or her leg; and of the two knotted scourges applied to the bare skin, "of which one is of knotted ropes, half a dozen ends attached to a pliant handle, the other of well-hardened and polished steel, each end of the five chains neatly finished with a steel rowel." Naturally enough, passers-by refused to believe in the reality and genuineness of these instruments of torture. Mr. Kensit directed the incredulous to inquire about them at the Popish bookshop next door where he bought them. One such sceptic having inquired, returned to Mr. Kensit and said, "If you believe me, the shopman said that for every one he sold to a Catholic he sold three to Church of England people." "I not only believe it," replied Mr. Kensit, "but I know it."

Such is, in brief, the account given by the *Westminster Gazette* in the article which Mr. Walsh quotes in his volume. It is little wonder that Mr. Kensit has, during the last year or two, taken a leading part in the agitation against the Anglican Romanisers for which the last year has become a historical year. If his zeal has sometimes seemed to border on the fanatical, his error may have been grave but not unpardonable. On the whole, he conducts his literary crusade with great efficiency, and his shop is a focus of effective Protestant agitation and a depôt of cheap and popular anti-ritualistic publications, including cartoons, as well as tracts and handsheets, and contributions from able and truly Protestant high dignitaries in the Church. The Bishop of London little knew what he was doing when, in reply to a respectful complaint from

Mr. Kensit as to the nature of the advanced and sensational services in his church, the church of St. Ethelburga, he replied not uncivilly, but unworthily, by advising him, if he did not approve of them, to go to worship at another church, where the services were such as he approved. The success of Mr. Kensit's appeal to the Chancellor of the Diocese against the services in question has been a sharp blow for the bishop. Mr. Kensit is now recognised as a zealous Protestant Churchman, loyal to the Establishment, though intensely opposed to Romanising doctrine and practices, and as a formidable factor in the agitation against the Romanisers who carry on a disloyal conspiracy in opposition to the principles of the Church of England.

There can be no doubt that Mr. Kensit's lectures and publications have touched deeply the popular feeling, and that they helped to prepare a welcome for Mr. Walsh's volume, of which tens of thousands of copies have been circulated. Since Mrs. Stowe's *Uncle Tom's Cabin* it may be doubted whether any work has so swiftly gained so large a circulation in England as this plain, matter-of-fact disclosure of the "secret history of the Oxford Movement" in the direction of Rome.

The result from all the forces that have been enumerated has been a truly national agitation, in the face of which ritualistic contempt has given place to alarm, passive bishops have been stimulated to serious inquiry, lukewarm statesmen have been stirred into earnest study of the "signs of the times," the House of Commons has, with impressive unanimity, shown its determination to put down the Romanising plot and party, and the House of Lords has in its own dignified way indicated its deep feeling on the great question involved.

At first the Government were lukewarm. Mr. Balfour, taking his tone from the archbishops and, perhaps, from some of his political associates, refused to believe that there was any really powerful or widespread conspiracy against Protestantism. Lord Salisbury would not at first deal explicitly with the subject, though, after a while, he found it necessary to admit that there was a grave want of discipline in the Church of England, and that, if the clergy would not, of themselves, be amenable to the bishops and the Prayer-Book, it would be necessary to compel them to be so. But all is now changed. That leading statesmen could have been so ill-informed as they appeared to be, that so many bishops should have minimised the terrible evil, is sufficiently surprising. Mr. Balfour, indeed, as a Scotch laird and a Presbyterian, was, no doubt, inadequately informed on the subject. But as to those who should have kept him better informed, it is impossible not to be reminded of the old adage, that "none are so blind as those who will not see." For archbishops and leading bishops, and for leading statesmen and members of Parliament, to persist, as they did, till six months ago, in saying that the number of extreme and Romanising ritualists was small and insignificant, is very extraordinary. At the same time, it must be remembered that the chief offenders were, for the most part, to be found either in the villages of rural and sparsely-peopled counties, or in the metropolis. In such villages the means of publicity were hardly to be had, the inhabitants were practically helpless, the clergy could work their own will, and the squires would not be disposed publicly to complain of their doings, while it must also be remembered that concealment and not publicity was a settled principle in the policy of the innovators. In the manufacturing villages of the North there has been comparatively little of organised Romanising, and attempts to bring it in have been mostly failures. On the other hand, in the metropolis, where, in certain districts, extreme ritualism abounds and is most extreme, little notice, till lately, has been taken of such excesses. Londoners are immersed in business, employers and employed seldom live in the same vicinity, or have any but business relations, mutual tolerance or indifference prevails as to most things, especially religion, and, besides, as the Bishop of Hereford said in a letter to the *Times* last year (April 26, 1898), "sensational, morbid, and superstitious forms of worship seem to fascinate and mislead many people, especially women, in the artificial and luxurious atmosphere of our wealthier classes," and may almost be accounted the "inevitable accompaniment of an artificial, luxurious, sensation-loving city-life." Fashionable watering-places in this respect closely resemble London. In Liverpool, where quasi-metropolitan influences and the hard-headed intelligence of manufacturers, commercial men, and the working classes meet each other at every turn, where Irish Protestants and Irish Catholics combine to make the religious instincts and temperament keen, sensitive, and combative, the controversy has been kept alive for years past, and the strong and able, though now aged, bishop has powerfully instructed and manfully led Protestant Anglicanism in its contest with Romanising ritualism, and has been loyally and effectively helped in his struggle not only by Archdeacon Taylor but by many others, laymen as well as clergy. The issue of a parliamentary bye-election at Southport has shown that in West Lancashire the ritualist question is regarded as more important than even party politics.

Nor have Protestant leaders been wanting among the London clergy. Dean Farrar, before he went not long ago to Canterbury, was Archdeacon of Westminster, and no one has more powerfully withstood or more wakefully noted and exposed the advances of the ritualists. Archdeacon Sinclair, also, though standing nearly, if not quite, alone in the Chapter of St Paul's, has, with equal intelligence and courage, taken his position as a Protestant champion in the struggle. None of the men I have referred to—and not a few others among the clergy might have been mentioned—would have agreed with the Archbishop of Canterbury or Lord Salisbury that the number of Romanising ritualists among the clergy was comparatively insignificant. Nor is it possible for a well-informed Protestant, however tolerant and liberal, to approve of what the *Times* in May of last year (May 11) spoke of as " the somewhat contemptuous indifference with which the Bishop of London treated " the ecclesiastical controversies in the City of London. " The public, when questions of Church order arose," had a right to " expect something more from the heads of the Church than masterly inactivity relieved by epigrams."

At last, however, the day of indifference is over. Mr. Kensit's organised public protests were violent, and could not but be offensive to many. But they compelled public attention, they did not a little to rouse the latent indignation of the people, they sounded an alarm, like a tocsin-bell, that resounded through London, was re-echoed in Liverpool, sent an awakening thrill through the land. Canon Fleming was moved to write a strong and stirring letter to the *Times*. The Canon has a respected name both in London, where as an evangelical clergyman he ministers to one of the largest and most influential and generous congregations of the West End, and in the country, where as Canon of York he has held fast his evangelical integrity in the midst of strong High Church influences. With his letter to the *Times* began that remarkable correspondence on "Lawlessness in the Church," or "The Crisis in the Church," which has run its course for eighteen months. His letter seems to have immediately followed Mr. Kensit's public protest, and to have been almost coincident with the publication of Mr. Walsh's book.

In the *Times* correspondence, Sir W. V. Harcourt has done signal service to the Protestant cause. His first letter was dated July 16, 1898. The masterly ability, and the wise limits of discussion, by which his letters have been distinguished, have, of course, excited the bitter animosity of those who are leagued against the principles of the English Reformation. But the nation is more grateful to him for this work than for anything he has done in Parliament. Old politicians may be reminded of the articles of *Historicus* in the *Times* on some principles of international jurisprudence involved in our relations with America during the Anti-Slavery civil war of 1862–64, articles which first established the fame of the rising barrister who was soon to become a distinguished political force in Parliament. It is satisfactory to note that, having withheld his hand for some months, he has resumed his pen to comment on the hearing and judgment of the archbishops on the subject of incense and lights, and on the effect of their judgment on Lord Halifax and his associates. Very much, indeed, depends on the vigilance, acuteness, and determination with which the judgments of the archbishops are analysed and scrutinised by competent critics, and the fidelity and competent learning and ability with which the process of hearing and judgment continues to be carried on by the archbishops who have made so hopeful a beginning in their great and most responsible work. The position won in Parliament, by which the House of Commons has decisively committed itself in opposition to the ritualisers, under strong pressure from the nation, was due not a little to Sir W. Harcourt's controversial acuteness and to his courage and force as a public correspondent. If the good beginning is to be carried to an effective conclusion, "all hands" must continue their work, and Sir W. Harcourt must on no account stay his hand or abate his discriminating zeal.

It is noteworthy that the first formal discussion by the bishops of the critical situation into which matters had drifted in the Church, took place in the Convocation of Canterbury, on occasion of the presentation by the Bishop of London of a petition from Mr. John Kensit, on Tuesday, May 10, 1898. The archbishop, after the Bishop of London had presented the petition, spoke of it "as one of the gravest importance." He "wanted severely to censure those men against whom Mr. Kensit was protesting," though he "regretted" the course Mr. Kensit had taken in his public agitation.

After an inadequate attempt, on the part of the archbishop, to compose the rising agitation by proposing to restrain and regulate by episcopal authority new and additional services and ceremonies in the churches, the bishops began their charges, in the autumn of 1898, during the course of delivery of which the sense of the far-reaching scope of the questions raised and of the gravity of the still growing agitation continually deepened. The Charge of the Archbishop of Canterbury, although on not a few points satisfactory, and throughout clear and able, was weak on the subject of private confession, and comes very near the sanction, or at least the official allowance, of false doctrine when dealing with the subject of the Real Presence at the Eucharist.[1] The Charge was delivered in sections early in the autumn of last year. The Charge of the Northern Archbishop, which followed after a few weeks, was unexpectedly clear and sound, as if his strong High Anglican leanings had received a salutary check. Somewhat later, but before Christmas, the archbishops and bishops met in secret council to consider what course should be agreed upon to stay the plague of Romanising on the one hand and disaffection on the other. Of that private episcopal meeting, one result, as already intimated, has been the procedure in the way of hearing complaints as to unlawful usages or services by the two archbishops, of which the first-fruit has been the prohibition of the ceremonial use of incense and lights; while as to the question of the Reservation of the Holy Sacrament, the decision of the primates has not yet been declared. Doubtless the discussions in Parliament and the strong resolution adopted unanimously in the Lower House—together with the general rousing of all classes in the nation on behalf of the principles of Protestantism—have had a powerful effect on the archbishops and bishops. I ventured to intimate in the last chapter of the first edition of this volume that there were some signs of a rising Protestant feeling—that was four years ago—on the part of the episcopal leaders of the Church. With this view many did not agree, and the apparent supineness of the bishops

[1] See Appendix A.

during a great part of the interval since then did not seem to support my intimation. Yet it now appears that I was not far wrong. There has been a natural reluctance to be the first to stir questions which were likely to lead to a Church convulsion, or at least a "crisis." The influences of society and fashionable Churchmanship, especially in London—and also the undoubted religious zeal and generous self-sacrifice of many of the advanced ritualists—operated powerfully as a deterrent against official episcopal resistance to the innovators in the "high places of the field," and fears of what a ritualistic and doctrinal war might bring forth contributed strongly to inaction. But now that war is proclaimed, and battle joined, bishop after bishop is declaring himself clearly and decisively on the side of Protestantism and the English Reformation. The Church and nation have always known where the aged Bishop of Liverpool stood, but now they see his coeval, the learned and venerable Bishop of Gloucester, declaring himself full-heartedly on the same side. The Bishop of Worcester has always been clear and strong on the side of the Reformation; with him stands no less boldly his neighbour of Hereford. The broad-minded and philosophic Bishop of Manchester is on the same side. The scholarly and able Bishop of Southwell (Dr. Ridding, formerly headmaster of Winchester) has done great service to the cause of gospel truth and freedom by his letters on the confessional in the *Times*. The Bishops of Exeter and Peterborough are known to be earnest and true-hearted Evangelicals. The Bishop of Bath and Wells declared himself on the right side comparatively early. In short, in both provinces a clear majority of the bishops are known to be earnest on the side of the Reformation. But especially, and perhaps of more importance than almost any other of the prelates, the Bishop of Winchester, in a Charge of equal discrimination and distinctness, as decisive as it is calm, as truly Protestant as it is judicial and comprehensive, has given his judgment against every principal innovation on the Romanising side. His thoroughgoing condemnation of the practice of private confession, and his distinct defence of the liberty within the Church of England of evening communion, show how fearless and how radical is his condemnation of Puseyite Romanising. This uprising of the bishops against Romanising Neo-Anglicanism may well give heart and hope to the Protestant Anglicanism of our nation.

Among the grounds for encouragement also ought to be specially mentioned the Conference of Churchmen which met last April, under the presidency of the Bishop of Hereford. That Conference adopted an admirable series of truly Protestant resolutions, which have been very numerously and impressively signed. The number of signatures amounts to nearly 3000, and includes men of the greatest distinction in science, literature, society, and public life, as well as Church dignitaries, University professors, and beneficed clergymen. Indeed, since the rise of the Oxford Movement, no such array of signatures on a Church question has been seen. The effect of this manifesto has been very marked. Great thanks are due to the Hon. and Rev. W. E. Bowen for the part he has taken in this matter, as well as for his masterly controversial letters in the *Times* and the *Guardian*.

Meantime, the final issue seems hardly likely to be Disestablishment. The nation appears to have learnt that Disestablishment is no more a remedy for Romanising ritualism, than mere force for Irish discontent.

In America, where it is ages since Episcopalianism was established in any part of the territory, ritualism, alike in its histrionic excesses, and in its sectarian narrowness and bigotry, follows in the wake of English fashions among the leaders of society, as all English fashions are copied in Boston and New York.[1] If Disestablishment is to take place, moreover, its conditions and equities will need to be dispassionately studied; and the disestablishing legislation will have something other and much more to do than simply to confiscate revenues and leave the Church of England as a clergy-Church to help and please itself.

As to the ultimate result of the present conflict of ideas and convictions, it would be rash to hazard a judgment. That the liberal and guarded Protestantism of the Established Church will be destroyed or set aside is not indeed to be imagined; not for a moment to be feared. But a place within the Church, no doubt, must still be left for some sort of High Anglicanism in a form consistent with the principles of the Reformation. Ancient tendencies —habits of thought and feeling centuries old—die hard, if they die at all. Even politico-ecclesiastical errors, founded in old-fashioned sentiments of loyalty, and sustained by much in Church history and literature which is attractive and which appeals to the dainty culture and exclusive ideas of the leisurely and privileged classes, will, for a long time to come, retain more or less hold on an influential class of the population, including many persons of devout mind and of artistic tastes. The present controversy is, in fact, a very old one. In its

[1] For evidence of this the author may refer to his volume on *Church Organisations*, 3rd ed., pp. 108–109.

essentials it existed and held great sway among many minds of the higher and middle classes more than three centuries ago. From England the elements of the conflict were carried by emigrants for conscience' sake across the Atlantic, and in the American continent at this moment the controversy still maintains its ground here and there. Even in Scotland, Knox's Presbyterianism did not utterly extirpate the seeds of High Sacramentarian Prelacy, of which the principles and fruit are found in patches to this day. Charles I. and Laud went a long way in their time towards putting down Protestantism in England; in return, Cromwell and his Parliament trampled down, though they could not extirpate, prelacy and Romanising ritualism. With the Restoration came a settlement which was intended as a compromise, and on which the Church of England founds itself to-day. But the conflict was suspended only for a brief season. Papal proclivities and sacramentarian superstition survived and revived in the Church of England, especially during the reign of the open and confessed Papist James II., who was franker in his religious partiality than the sensualist, at heart a Papist so far as he had any religion, whom he succeeded. Then came the revolution of 1688 and the reign of the Dutch Protestant William, after which High Churchmanship gradually withered away, its last living remnant being found among the Nonjurors, who, as they died down in the country, left scarcely a root behind, and yet did leave some feeble fibres in the soil during the half-century which preceded the Oxford Revival. During that icy period, when Methodism was the one religious force, the one element of religious inspiration and initiative in the nation, it seemed as if at anyrate the Protestantism of England was unassailable. But at

length, sixty years ago, the Church principles of Laud,
the old leaven of the Nonjurors, reappeared at Oxford, and
the reaction which then set in having attained its culmination during the last few years has bid defiance to the
principles of the Reformation, and has once again reverted
in sympathy and idea to the High and narrow Anglicanism
of Laud, coming indeed nearer to Rome than Laud ever
came. Thus the struggle of centuries is renewed, with less
of provocation, less of reason, than ever before, but with
the utmost advantage for the High Anglican party which
genius, culture, fashion, could combine to give, and with the
zeal and courage inspired by the dread of finally losing
from the Church of England—and from the social caste
which has made itself one with the clergy for the mainten-
ance, on the lines of a High Clerical Renaissance, of an
English monopoly as old as the nation—that predominance
in the education and the social life of the country which
even Cromwell could not destroy and could only interrupt
for a little while.

Times, however, have changed too far, and too deeply,
for the party of old privilege and predominance to gain
more for themselves, even on religious lines, than kindly
consideration and equal liberty. Half England is now
Nonconformist, and Nonconformity, not seeking for more
than justice, will know how to maintain its right even in
the face of ancient prescription. In Great Britain,
Scotland, by its learning, its political force, its moral
influence, and its national history, must be in radical
reality at one with the Nonconformity of England in its
intellectual and moral opposition to the claims of High
Anglican exclusiveness. We neither anticipate nor desire
the root and branch destruction of High Churchmanship,

with its distinguished history and its refining and civilising influences. But it must be purged of its Popish flavour and influence, its bigotry must be abandoned, it must be more than content to own as its complement and co-equal the Evangelical Protestantism of the Established Church, and to respect the position and just claims of Christian Nonconformity.

The struggle may yet be protracted a while, and will no doubt be stubborn, but to this issue it must come before very long. If, through the folly of the extreme Neo-Anglican party, the way to the end of the conflict should have to be hewed through the rocky process of Disestablishment and, together with it, of Disendowment—for if that road must be taken the two things must be faced together—the blame of such an untoward and unscientific ending must rest with the party of obsolete pretensions and High Church bigotry, who have refused to listen to either common justice or common sense, and have defied alike the teachings of Christianity and of politico-ecclesiastical wisdom.

After all, it may not be denied that it is possible, and friends of the Church who, though sanguine, are fully alive to the difficulties of the situation, are not to be scoffed at for hoping, that, without any legislation at the present time, the Church of England, under the guidance of its primates and bishops, may be saved from its present imminent and terrible peril by accepting, with virtual unanimity, and by obeying, the directions and counsels of the two archbishops as to the lawful meaning and requirements of the Prayer-Book in matters of doctrinal teaching, of services, and of ritual. Should this result be thus brought about, as Sir W. Harcourt has all along insisted that it might be and ought to be, without the creation of any new court, and without any special legislation whatever, there will be gained a "season of fair weather"—a fresh opportunity—during which the all-important underlying and finally critical questions may be studied and in the end dealt with—relating to the unification of the Church in respect of its Convocation, the equitable and adequate representation in Convocation of the whole body of clergy, and especially of those who serve the urban populations of the country; and, most essential and fundamental—perhaps also most difficult—question of all, the definition and creation of a representative Church laity, for parochial service in the first place, but also to furnish members competent to occupy seats in a lay or mixed representative Assembly, which would co-operate with Convocation, in its Upper and its Lower Houses. If, on these questions, the Church of England was well and effectively united, Parliament might perhaps agree to such proposals as I have hinted at.

Upon some such re-organisation being carried out depends the effective future of the Church of England. Possibly, even if all this be accomplished, it may but pave the way towards Disestablishment. But even so, it would make it possible to carry into effect such a disestablishment as would not mean the rending of the Church into two or three sections, or the confiscation of her endowments, or the entire and absolute separation of the Government of the realm from all religious observances and all national acknowledgment of Divine Providence in human affairs. This is a matter beyond the limits of discussion proper to the present volume, and I can only bespeak the indulgence of the reader for venturing to approach it. My politico-ecclesiastical creed does not include the Disestablishment dogma. The Church, when first the nation accepted the Christian faith, was of necessity established nationally and also endowed. In the beginnings of national organised existence it could not be otherwise. Even in our own modern mission field, when there has been a real tribal parallel, similar circumstances have not seldom produced similar effects, notwithstanding the financial support rendered by the " parent Society."

How best to effect a passage from the conditions entailed at the first creation of national Churches, when Voluntaryism in its modern sense could have no existence, to a settlement of all Churches on a voluntary basis without any recognised national Church whatever, is a problem of which the satisfactory solution has not yet been discovered. Those who have closely studied American history will hardly be of opinion that England can find in that history the solution of its own difficulties. But we may surely trust that if, from point to point, the wise and equitable thing is God-fearingly carried out, the true solution will one day be effected.[1]

[1] For note on "Lord Halifax and the Church Congress, 1899," see p. 416.

APPENDIX A.

The Primate on Consubstantiation as taught in the Church of England.

THE Archbishop of Canterbury in his Visitation Charge or Charges last year (October 1898) dealt with the chief points in controversy with the ritualistic party. The Charge, as a whole, was marked by great ability and equitable calmness of judgment. His treatment, however, of two questions created widespread alarm. One of these is the customary use of private confession, as to which he is more than tolerant. As to that point, however, it does not seem necessary to add to what has been said in the body of this volume. The other is the Eucharist. The Primate's treatment of this subject is such as seems to call for special notice in an Appendix in order to make the present volume complete. The position taken by the Primate of All England on this cardinal question is one which was hardly to be expected, and must be regarded as peculiarly unfortunate. He appears to teach that the findings of the Privy Council in the Bennett Judgment—on appeal from the Court of Arches—extend the comprehensive character of the teachings allowed within the Church of England so as to include consubstantiation as lawful doctrine to be held and taught by a minister of the Established Church. The correspondence on this subject, however, in the *Times* seems to have made good some important objections to this finding of the archbishop. The letters of Archdeacon Taylor of Liverpool, of Canon Birch, and others, show that as to this point of consubstantiation Mr. Bennett was compelled, in the course of his trial, to qualify and amend his definition of doctrine, and that, even as so modified and amended, his teaching was not sanctioned by the Privy Council, though, by a majority of one in the Court, it escaped direct condemnation. Canon Birch cites the words of the judgment of the Privy Council as follows: "Their lordships, not without doubts and division of opinions, have come to the conclusion, that the charge is not as clearly made out as the rules which govern penal proceedings require." "Even in their maturer form Mr. Bennett's words are rash and ill-judged, and are perilously near a violation of the law." Their lordships further explain that if it had been charged and proved that Mr. Bennett "had performed an outward act of adoration," he would have been condemned. As "the proceedings" were "highly penal," they concluded "to give him the benefit of the doubt that had been raised." Sir W. Harcourt, writing to the *Times* on this subject, has no difficulty in showing that the Neo-Anglican doctrine of consubstantiation is in direct contradiction to the rubric on the subject of kneeling at the Holy Communion, and that which rejects "any corporal presence of Christ's natural flesh and blood."

It can hardly be doubted that by the "tolerance" which he bespeaks for the doctrine of consubstantiation in connexion with the "Real Presence" of the Saviour at the Holy Supper, the archbishop has himself gone "perilously near" to allowing a cardinal heresy in the system of Anglican doctrine. Archdeacon Taylor, of Liverpool, in a very able letter to the *Times* (October 17, 1898), justly says: "If consubstantiation be admitted, as the archbishop defines it, as 'a presence attached somehow to the elements *by the act of consecration*' and not dependent on the faith of the recipient, these other things will logically follow— the Reservation of the Blessed Sacrament, the Adoration of the Host, the Eucharistic Sacrifice, and, in due time, the Sacrifice of the Mass." The archbishop's sincere admirers will many of them feel that the only thing to be fitly said of his action in this case is to endorse the opinion of another correspondent of the *Times*—a "Layman"— that, in his intense desire to maintain the "comprehensive" character of his Church, he has been betrayed into "a rash *obiter dictum*."

Our English Reformers, it is certain, denied alike transubstantiation and consubstantiation. It must also be remembered that Lutheran divines, while professing to hold a certain metaphysical doctrine of consubstantiation, have so taught that doctrine as not to involve the consequences stated, and justly stated, by Archdeacon Taylor, as necessarily flowing from the Neo-Anglican doctrine of consubstantiation. Canon Birch, in one of his able letters on this subject to the *Times* (October 31, 1898), explains that the Lutheran statement of doctrine on the subject of consubstantiation contains some very important guards and limitations. It teaches that the presence of the body and blood of Christ in the Lord's Supper "does not come by virtue of any priestly consecration, and is not attached to the bread and wine lying on the table before or after consecration. It is only communicated by Christ at the time at which the bread is being eaten and the wine is being drunk by the communicants." The Lutheran teaching "distinctly denies the idea of a sacrifice being made in the Lord's Supper. It denounces the sacrifice of the Mass in its entirety. It opposes the notion of eucharistical adoration, or of any veneration being paid to the consecrated bread and wine." It excludes "all reservation of the elements." This definitive statement rests on the authority of the late learned Dr. Wright, of the British and Foreign Bible Society, author of a standard work entitled *Service of the Mass in the Greek and Roman Churches.*

The peculiar *virus* of the Romish and Romanising doctrine of the sacramental efficacy in the Lord's Supper is that the divine and saving Presence, the Real Presence, of the Lord Jesus Christ with His believing disciples in the Supper, is made to depend directly on the mediatorial office and action of the duly ordained priest, on the form of words he officially uses and the manual acts he officially performs, so that apart from these priestly rites and their due performance there is no flow of spiritual life from the Saviour to the penitent and believing recipient—to the believer trusting and adoring with his whole soul the Saviour spiritually present. It is this limitation of the saving virtue of the Lord Jesus within the priestly official channel—this relic of priestly paganism—this taint of materialistic fetichism—which infects the Neo-Anglican sacramentarianism with a sort of pagan-priestly character of anti-Christian superstition.

A singularly wise letter—a letter full of spiritual discernment—which Dr. Llewellyn Davies addressed to the *Times* (17th October 1898), in connexion with the controversy on the Primate's Charge, contains the following passages, which it is a great pleasure for an old friend to quote, who has not always agreed with the able and accomplished writer. "All the language" (as to the presence of the Lord Jesus in the Holy Supper) "that the archbishop quotes from our Anglican documents has been used freely, and could still be used, by Nonconformists as well as by Protestant Churchmen. Nor need these holders of doctrine hesitate to adopt the terms 'real' and 'objective' presence, except that Englishmen cannot easily get out of their heads the notion that these terms cannot be used, if they do not mean something corporeal. They assuredly hold that Christ is present in the Eucharist, and that He is present, whether communicants are thinking of Him or not. . . .

"The archbishop is satisfied and optimistic, and bids us trust the bishops and be tolerant. But his Charge is likely to increase the alarm and misgivings of those who are convinced that the belief of a corporeal presence embodied in the elements of bread and wine is a superstition, and that auricular confession is contrary to the spiritual freedom which St. Paul asserted so vehemently; and that the Church of England by its teaching and system rejects both consubstantiation and the confessional."

The last words quoted refer, of course, to the too indulgent manner in which the archbishop has dealt with the subject of confession as well as consubstantiation.

APPENDIX B.

CORRESPONDENCE RELATING CHIEFLY TO NEWMAN,
PUSEY, AND MANNING.

NOT long after the publication of the first edition of this volume, I received several letters relating to it from my old friend Canon Jenkins, of Lyminge, one of the most learned of ecclesiastical students and antiquarians, whose learning also was absolutely at his command, as if it referred to the things of yesterday. I corresponded with him as to the publication of his letters, which seemed to me to be of great interest and value, and obtained some directions as to what I was at liberty to publish, and what, as too merely personal, should be omitted. What I am about to quote is selected for publication in conformity with his suggestions as expressed not long before his death.

"LYMINGE RECTORY, 15th November 1895.

"MY DEAR DR. RIGG,—I am reading with the deepest interest your *Oxford High Anglicanism*, and with entire concurrence. My knowledge of the leaders of the Movement, for I enjoyed the intimate friendship of Newman and Manning, and was well acquainted (through correspondence at various periods) with Dr. Pusey, constitutes me a kind of *testis oculatus*; and I was (as it were) behind the whole Movement from the beginning. My knowledge of the Movement began in 1836, when Cardinal Wiseman gave his memorable Lectures at Moorfields. You have not, I think, mentioned this movement in the Roman camp, which really was one of the great factors in the reaction against the old Evangelical school of Oxford. The conversions which followed these Lectures, and the new position which Rome was beginning to fill in England, rendered it necessary then to produce a form of Anglicanism which should give it a clear position between Rome and Nonconformity, such as Newman drew in his *Romanism and Popular Protestantism.* In (I think) 1836 I published my *Defence of the Eucharistical Doctrine of the Church of England,* in opposition to Wiseman, whom some years after I knew personally, and for whom I had a sincere regard. His peculiar grace and gentleness of manner attracted more converts to Rome than even Newman or Manning.

"I think that your view of Pusey is just and accurate. His religion was the product of the bitter Calvinism of his ancestors, which was in a manner petrified into sacramentarianism. The morbid ideas of the sinfulness of the merest trifles of daily life, and revolting pictures of the state of the sinner, are well illustrated in the history of Thomas Papillon of Acrosse Place in 1666, lately published by his descendant, Major Papillon. The whole system of the Huguenot theology is drawn out in this interesting biography, and the letters of the young daughter describing her irremissible guilt and ideal ruin are very well illustrated. It is to this theology we must look for the source of Pusey's horrible delusions. It was qualified by his Germanising influences, but these soon passed away. He became morose and embittered.

"I have seen and read a correspondence he had with a man who afterwards joined the Roman Church, but who had followed him till he could follow him no longer. It came into the hands of my friend, Mr. ———, one of the chamberlains of the present Pope. . . . Dr. Pusey had forced his pupil to the edge of the precipice, and then reviled him for falling over. Nevertheless, I had friendly correspondence with him from time to time, his little fragmentary letters sometimes giving an idea that he possessed some sympathy. . . .

"Passing on to Newman, what a contrast! Keen controversialist, though, like Pusey, dishonest in his quotations, he was nevertheless so gentle and so lovable. I shall never forget the day I spent with him at Edgbaston. . . . Oh, the charm!

"We got on many controversial subjects; but what amazed me most was his absolute ignorance of the history of the Papacy in its later stages. When I dwelt upon the horrors of the Carafa, the Ghislieri, the Pamfili papacies, not to speak of the Borgia, he seemed to draw back in a kind of shudder. Manning had the same ignorance and the same terror. He said to me once when I brought the horrors of the Vatican before him, 'My only comfort is that I believe in the Holy Catholic Church,' to which I rejoined, 'But what if it is *not* holy?'

. . . . . .

"When I was at Edgbaston, I had some talk with Newman on his Development doctrine, and alleged that it was the only possible ground on which the Protean changes of the Roman Church could enable it to build any argument at all. But the Council of Trent has shut it out altogether, as the Council of Florence did a century before.

"Manning's conversion is less traceable to any special influences than those of his friends. Its suddenness and the violence of the impulse forced him into excesses,[1] which shocked his more learned colleague, Newman, who told me in one of his letters that it surprised him how anyone claiming to be a theologian could have written some of the passages of his more recent works. But he had got together a number of fragments, and wanted the Pope to give them a setting.

"The idea of the necessity of a human headship seemed

[1] This was written before the Cardinal's *Life* had been published, which explained the mystery, whilst not doing away with the scandal to the general view, of the *apparent* suddenness.

to predominate in both their minds. Newman wrote to me in 1877 in his own amusing vein: 'The Pope is the keynote, the bishops the third, the priests the fifth, and the Protestant the flat seventh, which needs resolving.'

"Manning had in his heart a grand hierarchical ideal, and admired greatly the 'Celestial Hierarchy' of the pseudo-Dionysius the Areopagite. But the enlargement and enlightenment of his views as he came towards the close of his life was very beautiful to witness. In one of his last letters to me he wrote that he was weary of controversy, and added, 'Peace be with all those who love the Lord Jesus Christ in sincerity. . . .'"

"17th November 1895.

"It occurred to me, after writing my letter to you, that I had not mentioned an amusing fact in regard to Dr. Pusey, which came to me from the same authority as the letters I described excommunicating the unfortunate convert. The strange way in which the last years of Dr. P.'s life were spent, and his semi-Benedictine household, you are doubtless aware of. The victim of the denunciation called upon the Doctor to know (as he was going on the Continent) how he could keep up his duties as a communicant in the Church of England. He was recommended to carry the reserved Sacrament with him, for which he was to call at the Doctor's, who gave him some pieces of bread or wafer wrapped in a most unseemly manner in a piece (I think) of common brown paper. This rather shocked the inquirer, who went to a jeweller's shop to see whether he could find any worthier shrine for so precious a treasure, but all that he could find was a jewelled snuff-box, which was at once employed as a kind of casket for these souvenirs of the Doctor and his doctrine of eucharistical reservation. Lord Grimthorpe was much amused when I told him this story, which came direct to Mr. —— from the excommunicated man. Neither Newman nor Manning could have possibly done anything so *gauche*."

Canon Jenkins in both the letters from which I have quoted, and also in a third, written shortly afterwards, gives instances to prove Dr. Pusey's ignorance both of ecclesiastical history and of Scripture exegesis, which there is no need for me to quote. His suggestion in his first letter as to the real, though remote, origin of Pusey's morbid views respecting sin and penance is very noticeable. In some letters which Canon Carter sent to the *Times* by way of criticism on the first edition of this volume, he suggested that the reason why Dr. Pusey remained in the Church which Newman quitted was that, whereas Newman was brought up as a Calvinistic Evangelical, Pusey was brought up as a High Churchman of the ancient English type. By his mother, as the *Life* shows, Pusey was trained as a child in the plain and homely way in which the children of devout Churchmen were brought up at the beginning of this century, at a time when the High Church of Laud and the Nonjurors had died out—all but that antique survival, Dr. Routh—while of the modern High Church school there was as yet no trace. Through his father, and through his aunts on his father's side, he was linked in hereditary connexion with the Huguenot family to which Canon Jenkins refers, a Calvinistic strain far more intense, in its peculiar tone, than any belonging to Newman's family. Canon Carter's hypothesis as to the distinction in tone and character between the Churchmanship of Newman and that of Pusey is in fact—I will not say mere invention—but pure imagination, like so much which passes for fact in Canon Carter's school of ecclesiastical assumptions.

I may be permitted to quote here the first paragraph of Canon Carter's first letter to the *Times* relating to this book (a letter written but a few days after the publication of the book, a review of which had appeared in the *Times* on the day of publication) as an illustration of the licence which a Neo-Anglican leader feels at liberty to take in referring to a volume dealing with the Church school to which he belongs. His letter is headed, "A Wesleyan View of the Oxford Movement." Canon Carter begins: "To very many, as to Dr. Rigg, that eventful Movement has appeared as an unnatural intrusion into the orderly tenor of the Church of England life, without ground or precedent in its former history, and deeply tinged with Romanism." And then he proceeds to assign its origin to the Nonjuring and Divine Right school of the seventeenth century. If he had but looked over the table of contents, he would have seen that I begin my history by explaining,—if he had looked into the early pages of the book, he would have found that I explain with particular care and at considerable length,—the relation of the Tractarian ideas to the Nonjuring prototypes of the Oxford High Church school. Before the correspondence in the *Times* was brought to an end, he had to confess that he knew nothing whatever of my book. He had only seen the notice in the *Times*. He had presumed that, being only a Wesleyan Methodist, I was of course utterly ignorant of the early and inner history of the Church of England, and he thought it desirable to lose no time in writing a letter to the *Times* calculated to convey that impression. He headed his letter "A Wesleyan View of the Oxford Movement"; the view which he describes as "Wesleyan," and represents as mine, being in direct contradiction to the actual view given in my book.

It is painful to see a clergyman who, for his age, ought to be venerable, cultivating to the end of his life faculties and habits the reverse of venerable. Even in the case of a newspaper criticism—to speak correctly, a pretended criticism—of a volume on the history of the Oxford Movement, he practises disingenuous subtlety, and writes what is so far from fair and frank, that it is not even straightforward.

NOTE TO PAGE 404.

LORD HALIFAX AND THE CHURCH CONGRESS, 1899.

Whilst the last chapter of this book has been passing through the press, the Church Congress has been held (October 9-14). Held in London, it was looked for with anxiety, but has passed over without any explosion. The speakers and essay-writers, with scarcely an exception, kept warily at a distance from the mouth of the volcano; and, though there were smoulderings and rumblings, there was no eruption. At the preliminary meeting of the Church Union, indeed, Lord Halifax was more defiant than ever; 'his goal now is clearly visible—it is nothing else than disestablishment and undisguised revolution. But Canon Gore and Canon Body refused to follow his lead. Of course unbridled licence of ritualistic practice and of ultra-sacerdotal doctrine, such as Lord Halifax claims so daringly, is incompatible with the position of a Church nationally established and endowed. Such a Church can no more escape from State supremacy than a bird, whether lark or eagle, or even the giant condor of the Cordilleras, can rise above the atmosphere on which he floats, and without which he could not live. Lord Halifax is a transcendental sacerdotalist, and talks like a fanatic. He seems to be beside himself in his misguided enthusiasm. But he has not yet found the $\pi o\hat{u}$ $\sigma\tau\hat{\omega}$ from which he can move the world. He addressed the public meeting of the Congress on the Friday night on the subject of Ritual, and, passing curtly and superciliously by the teaching of the New Testament and the precedents of truly primitive antiquity, he found his ideal of ritual and worship in the earlier mediæval period—in the thirteenth century. To this standard of the dark ages, before the Bible was in the hands of the people, he would carry back the Reformed Church of England. Fortunately, the other speakers on this occasion were more than usually well-informed and reasonable, especially in referring to Nonconformist Churches.

INDEX.

A

ABBOTT DR., work on Newman by, preface xi.
ACT of UNIFORMITY (1662), rudiments of High Church system in teaching of some divines connected with passing of, 24.
ACTON, LORD, a passing hope of, as to reunion, 323.
ALEXANDER, ARCHBISHOP, criticism of *Christian Year*, by, 31 *Note*.
ANGLICAN CHURCH, errors and schisms within the, 49, 50; two, if not three, parties within the, 205–208, 322; "extreme churches" and "perplexed priests" within the, 354; the present crisis in the history of, 380.
Apologia, NEWMAN'S, basis of material for historical view of Oxford Movement, preface iv; consummate skill of, preface viii, 2 *Note*; influence of, on Keble's reputation, 6.
APOSTOLICAL SUCCESSION, Newman's *Tract* on, 53; Anglicanism and, 54; invention of doctrine of, 55; revival of argument of, by Newman, 56; Duke of Argyll on, 57; "a fable," 196.
Appendices: A. "The Primate on Consubstantiation as taught in the Church of England," 405–409; B.

"Correspondence relating chiefly to Newman, Pusey, and Manning," 410–416.
ARGYLL, DUKE OF, on Apostolical Succession, 57; the validity of "orders," 374.
ARNOLD, DR., friendship of J. T. Coleridge and Keble with, 7; influence of Maurice on, 40; Fellow of Oriel, 220.
ARTICLES, THIRTY-NINE, irreconcilability of Tractarian teaching with, 25.
ASHLEY, LORD (EARL OF SHAFTESBURY), Pusey declines to read for lectures with, at Oxford, 215.

B

BOWDEN, JOHN, Newman's letter to, on the introduction of Newman to Keble, 12.
British Critic, The, 36, 61.
British Magazine, The, 36.
British Quarterly Review, The, Mr. Gladstone's article in, on the Evangelical Movement, 1.
BURGON, DEAN, his account of Hugh James Rose, 37; representation of Oxford Movement in *Twelve Good Men*, 97.
BUTLER, CANON, a High Church testimony to Bp. Wilberforce, 285.

C

CANTERBURY, ARCHBISHOP, Visitation Charge of (1898). *See* Appendix A. pp. 405-409.

CARTER, CANON, OR, "FATHER," T. T., placed by Pusey in charge of Clewer, 287; letter from Bishop Wilberforce to, 287; approval of *The Priest in Absolution* by, 287, 385 *Note*; complaint by, to Bishop Wilberforce concerning Pusey's popish spirit, 360; support of Lord Halifax's contentions, 379. *See* Appendix B.

CHRISTIAN YEAR, THE, criticism of, by *Spectator*, 5; earliest poems of, 11; publication of (1827), 17; theology of, 19-23; estimate of poetry, and popularity of, 28-32; tribute of a Nonconformist critic to, 29; Archbishop Alexander's criticism of, 31 *Note*.

CHURCH CONGRESS, THE, Lord Halifax and (1899), 416 *Note*.

CHURCH, DEAN, history of the Oxford Movement, 2 *Note*, 43, 93, 97, 98; ecclesiastical position of, 94-97; relation of, to Newman, 99; where he stopped short, 100, 101; position of (in 1840-45), 102, 103, 105; what Newman owed to, 107; description of Keble, 108; remarks on Hurrell Froude, 110; lecture on Bishop Andrewes by, 130 *Note*.

CHURCH UNION, THE, 207, 208; its preparation of the Anglican Church for amalgamation with Rome, 320 -322; President of, quoted, 346; exertion of, for the "conversion" of England, 351, 352; Romanising and superstitious, 370; appeal to the Pope on the validity of Anglican "orders," 371.

CLAYTON, THE JACOBITE METHODIST, relationship to the Wesleys; influence on Keble and others, 3.

CLEWER, House of Mercy at, 286, 287.

CLOSE, DEAN, 244.

COBB, DR., a Romanising ritualist willing to accept Disestablishment, 379.

COBBETT, WILLIAM, an unwilling compliment to, by John Parker of Sweeney Hall, 215.

COLERIDGE, S. T., politico-ecclesiastical speculations of, 39; opinion of, as to baneful effects of the confessional, 274, 275.

COLONIAL CHURCHES, ritualistic developments in, 208.

CONFERENCE OF CHURCHMEN (April 1899), Protestant resolutions of, 398.

CONFESSIONAL, THE. *See* "Pusey."

CONSUBSTANTIATION. *See* Appendix A. pp. 404-409.

Contemporary Review, The, article by Dean Farrar, 366 *Note*, 369.

CONVOCATION OF CANTERBURY, *The Crisis in the Church* and, 395; Charges of the Archbishops, 396.

COPLESTON, BISHOP, opinion of, on Newman, 14; Provost of Oriel, 220, 225.

CRISIS, THE, IN THE CHURCH, first formal discussion of, 395; deterrent influences in relation to, 397; opinions of Bishops on, 397; future possibilities of, 399; the present controversy three centuries old, 399; review of events leading up to, 400, 401; critical questions underlying, 402; the solution of, 403, 404.

D

DENISON, ARCHDEACON, controversy with Pusey (1854) on the Eucharist, 305, 306.

DISESTABLISHMENT, Card. Vaughan on, quoted, 352; Dean Farrar on, quoted, 369; not a remedy for

Romanising ritualism, 398; the "rocky process" of, 402; even re-organisation may pave the way for, 403.
DODSWORTH, REV. MR., an exposure of Pusey by, 291, 293.
DOLLING, "FATHER," ritualistic practices of, 311 *Note*; obliged to leave diocese of Winchester, 377.
DÖLLINGER, DR., Cardinal Newman and, 160; passing hope of, as to reunion, 323.

E

Evangelical Magazine, The, Mr. Gladstone's article on the Oxford Movement, 1.

F

FABER, perversion of, to Rome, 200.
FARRAR, DEAN, antagonism of, to Romanising claims: articles in *Contemporary Review*, 366 *Note*, 369, 393.
FLEMING, CANON, letter of, to *Times*, on *The Crisis in the Church*, 393.
FROUDE, HURRELL, intercourse of Newman with, 2; source of Anglican indoctrination of, 3; Newman introduced to Keble by, 12, 13; affinities and animosities of, 15; editorship of the *Remains*, 17 *Note*; presence of, at Rose's rectory (1833), 36; impetus given by, to Oxford Movement, 43, 49.

G

GARBETT, ARCHDEACON, the claims of Anglican priest-confessors, 255 *Note*; criticism of Pusey, 308 *Note*.
GLADSTONE, MR., honours the memory of Pusey, preface viii; article of, on "The Evangelical Movement," in *British Quarterly Review*, 1; on reunion with Rome, 323; a communication from Lord Halifax to, 324 *Note*, 371, 375.
Guardian, The, 206, 207, 233, 353, 371.
GUILDS, TOWN AND COLLEGE; a recent development of Confessionalism, 302-304 *Note*.

H

HALIFAX, LORD, influence of Pusey on, 202; official head of Church Union, 207, 208, 251 *Note*; denial of "compulsory" confession, 270 *Note*; approach of, to the papal centre, 322; a communication of, to Mr. Gladstone, 324 *Note*, 375; personal visit of, to the Pope, 351; probable wish of, as to Disestablishment, 352; the Pope, and Anglican orders, 371; shifting of ground of, as a High Churchman after Vatican pronouncement, 378; counsel of, to Anglican clergymen, 379; defiance of, but reality of Protestant reaction, 381; the Church Congress (1899) and, 416 *Note*.
HALL, ROBERT, sermon of, on the "Sentiments proper to the present crisis," 21 *Note*.
HARCOURT, SIR W. V., letters of, to the *Times*, 394, 395, 402.
HARE, ARCHDEACON, witness of the writings of, 39.
HARRISON, DR., criticism of *Pusey's Challenge Answered*, 357 *Note*.
HATHERLEY, LORD, correspondence of, with Dean Hook, 364.
HAWKINS, DR., Fellow and Provost of Oriel, 53 *Note*, 220, 225.
HERBERT, LADY HENRY, sister-in-law of Pusey, 219, 220.
HEREFORD, BISHOP OF, on the Romanising Movement, 393, 398.

Historicus, letters of, to *Times*, 394.
HOLY CROSS, SOCIETY OF, publication of *The Priest in Absolution* by, 385.
HOOK, DR., correspondence of, with Pusey, on Confession, 270; a criticism of Pusey by, 272; congratulation on Dean Stanley's marriage, 281; remonstrance and letters of, as to St. Saviour's Church, Leeds, 297, 301; opinion of, as to Pusey's teaching, 363.
HOOKER, RICHARD, Puseyite pretence to follow, 233, 366.
HOPE-SCOTT, MR., perversion of, to Rome, 200; influence of Pusey upon, 250, 251, 360.
HUGHES, REV. HUGH PRICE, reference to "orders" in Ordination Charge of, 378.

J

JELF, DR. R. W., early friendship of, with Pusey, 216, 221; Fellow of Oriel, 220; Newman's letter to, on Tract 90, 315.
JUSTIFICATION BY FAITH, the teaching of Hooker and Barrow on the doctrine of, irreconcilable with Tractarian teaching, 25.

K

KEBLE, JOHN, preface viii, 2; Sir J. T. Coleridge's life of, 2 *Note*; Lock's biography of, 2 *Note*, 3; ecclesiastical exclusiveness and intolerance of Dissent, 4, 23, 25; volume of sermons of (1847), rendered notable by Newman, 4; death of, universally lamented, 4-6; character and influence of, 5, 7; influence of, in relation to Tract 90, 5, 25; secluded life of, 6; friendship of, with Arnold and Coleridge, 7;

home education of, 8, 10; elected Fellow of Oriel, 9; success of, at Oxford, 10; ordination and curacies, 11; introduction of, to Newman, 11, 12; distaste of, for Newman, 13; feminine vein in character of, 14, 32 *Note*; union of, with Newman, 17; *Assize Sermon*, 20, 51; support of Tractarian movement: tribute to, by Newman, 20; earlier and later theology of, 19-23; *Lyra Apostolica*, 19; *Lyra Innocentium*, 19, 23; perplexities of, as a Churchman, 25, 26; a remark of, on hearing of Newman's secession, 26 *Note*; a remark of, on the defection of Robert Wilberforce, 27; elected Professor of Poetry at Oxford (1831), 27; accepted vicarage of Hursley (1835), 27; death of, 28; estimate of, and popularity as a poet, 28-32; doctrinal sympathies of, 50; description of, by Dean Church, 108-110; rejected as Provost of Oriel, 225; appeal of Pusey to, concerning St. Saviour's Church, Leeds, 298.
KEN, BISHOP, 3.
KENSIT, MR. JOHN, exposure of "instruments of torture" by, 388; his Protestant zeal, 389, 390; appeals of, to Bishop of London and Chancellor of the Diocese, 390; protests of, 393, 395.
KINGSLEY, CHARLES, criticism of, as to lack of virility in Tractarian leaders, 214.
KNOX, ALEXANDER, his doctrine of faith, 234.
KNOX-LITTLE, CANON, probable wish of, as to Disestablishment, 352.

L

LAW, WILLIAM, 3.
LIDDON, CANON, wide influence of, preface viii; biography of Pusey by,

210, 222, 231, 233, 236, 258; Romeward and mediæval bias of, 284; admissions in Biography of Pusey, 289, 296.
LINCOLN JUDGMENT, THE, criticism of, 347 *Note*.
LIVERPOOL, BISHOP OF, Protestant Anglicanism of, 392, 397.
LLOYD, DR., influence of, on Pusey, 223, 224.
LONDON, BISHOP OF, the reply of, to Mr. Kensit, 389, 390; criticism of, by *Times*, 393.
London Quarterly Review, The, reference to article in, on "Religion in Germany," 228 *Note*.
LONGLEY, BISHOP, 284, 297.

M

MACKONOCHIE, REV. A. H., his defence of *The Priest in Absolution*, 385.
MANNING, CARDINAL, the "charitable exclusiveness" of, 337; on Churchmen and Dissenters, 338; attitude of, in regard to Pusey, 341. (*See also* Appendix B. pp. 410–416.)
MANUAL FOR CONFESSORS, 386.
MARRIOTT, REV. CHARLES, appeal of Pusey to, as to St. Saviour's Church, Leeds, 298, 299.
MASKELL, REV. MR., an exposure of Pusey by, 293, 295.
MAURICE, the mysticism of, 37; his *Kingdom of Christ*, 40.
Metaphysical Society, The, W. G. Ward, President of, 171.
MOBERLY, BISHOP, 274.
Modern Anglican Theology, pref. iii, iv.
Month, The, quotation from, 278.
MOZLEY, JAMES B., a pupil of Pusey, 231; a story from the *Letters* of, 282.

MOZLEY, THOMAS, reference of, to Pusey's sermon on "Sin after Baptism," 237; Tractarian influence of, on the *Times*, 367.

N

NELSON, ROBERT, 3.
NEWMAN, CARDINAL, preface iv, viii; "conversion" of, 1, 2; relationship of, to Keble, 2, 3; to Froude, 3, 16; elected Fellow of Oriel (1822), 11; introduction of, to Keble, 11, 12; feminine vein in character of, 14; union of, with Keble, 17; casuistry of Tract 90, 25, 53; *Tracts for the Times*, 25, 36, 51–54; *British Critic*, organ of, 36; relations of, with Rose, 37, 42–44; perversion of, to Rome, 37; association of Froude with, and Tractarian Movement, 43; early development of, 45; influence upon, of Thomas Scott and Dr. Hawkins, 45; first inspiration of, Romewards, 47; characteristic work of, 48–50; publication and subsequent retractation of *Romanism and Popular Protestantism*, 57, 58; retractation of criticisms of Rome, 58, 59 *Note*; joined the Church of Rome, 60, 62; some mental characteristics of, 68; contrast of, with Ward, 69; essay of, on the development of Christian doctrine, 103; indebtedness to Dean Church, 106–108; Oxford life and influence, 118–120; reserve and austerity, 121; development theory, 122; weakness in character of, 124–126; Ward's influence over, 126–128; Ward's witness against, 129; extravagant eulogies of, 131; Mr. R. H. Hutton's monograph on, 133–142; Mr. Arthur Hutton on, 134 *Note*, 135; Mr. James Macdonell on his

Grammar of Assent, 143; philosophical scepticism of, 145; pursuit of infallibility, 147; view of faith, 149; remarks of Archdeacon Hare on, 148, 149; views of religion in Catholic and in Protestant countries, 151; defects of teaching as to faith, 153; confusion of black and white, 154, 155; on Roman Catholic and Protestant morality, 156, 157; denial of persecution by the popes, 158, 159; Dr. Döllinger and, 160; estimate of character of, 161-164; last years of, at the Oratory, 165-167; some lessons from the life of, 196-198; association of, with Hawkins at Oriel, 225; Pusey and, coalesce, 231; important letter of, to Pusey, 250 *Note*—comparison of, with Pusey, 314; quotation from *Apologia*, 319. (*See also* Appendix B. pp. 410-416.)

Nineteenth Century, The, incidental light on Pusey's career in, 360.

O

OAKELEY, joins the Church of Rome, 62, 200.

OXENHAM, Rev. F. N., motion of, to condemn *The Priest in Absolution*, 385.

Oxford High Anglicanism, recent literature upon, preface iv; the only Nonconformist history of, preface v; the taint of error in, preface ix.

P

PALMER, REV. WILLIAM, his narrative of the *Tracts for the Times*, 36 *Note*.

PALMER, WILLIAM, the brother of Lord Selborne, the case of, 202 *Note*.

PARKER, JOHN, attempt of, to influence Pusey, 215.

PARLIAMENT, the voice of, as to the Romanising Movement, 380, 390, 391, 395.

PATTISON, MARK, effect on, of residence with Pusey, 231.

PRIMITIVE METHODISTS, 374.

PROTESTANT REACTION, signs of a, 381.

PUSEY (AND PUSEYISM), pref. viii, 2 *Note*; defence of German Protestantism, 40; share of, in the inspiration of Tractarian Movement, 54; transition from Tractarianism to, 199-202; seeds of Romanising Movement, 208; responsibility for the present schism, 209; Newman's remarks on, 209; Liddon's life of, 210; biographical facts, 211, 212; at school, college, university, 213-216; *Theology in Germany*, 215; engagement and marriage, 216, 224, 225; a tour in Switzerland, 217; a challenge of speculative unbelief, 218; passing influence of Byron and Scott on, 217-219; brother's marriage to Lady Emily Herbert, 219; fellowship at Oriel, 220-222; visit to Germany as a student, 223; controversy with Rose, 224-227; *Character and Life Work of*, 226 *Note*; his Churchmanship (1830), 227; he becomes a High Anglican, 228, 229; *Tract on Baptism*, 228, 235; the spell of Newman over, 229; Newman and, coalesce, 231; development as a Churchman, 234; "Sin after Baptism," 237, 243; *Doctrine of Holy Baptism*, 238-241; infant baptism, 242; teaching of, on Confession and Absolution, 244-247; re-baptism of Mrs., by Newman, 249; death of Mrs. 249; extreme views on penance, 251, 257; general remarks on, and his influence, 252; temporary exclusion of, from University pulpit, 259 *Note*; brief review of earlier history of, 260; penitential and disciplinary practices, 261; Keble asked to be confessor of, 262; confession of, to Keble in

INDEX

Hursley Church, 296 ; self-loathing confessions, 264-267 ; Was, a fit religious leader ? 267 ; confession in the English Church, 269 ; auricular confession and priestly absolution, 271-274 ; young boys in the confessional, 273; the priest-confessor, 276, 279; also *Note* on College Guilds, 302-304 ; criticism of, by a Romanist, 278 ; teaching of, on sisterhoods and celibacy, 279 ; his views of human nature, 281 ; Bishop Wilberforce and, 282 ; *House of Mercy* at Clewer and, 286 ; sisterhoods and perpetual vows, 287·; St. Saviour's Church and Mission, Leeds, 296-301 ; doctrine of the Real Presence, 305 ; sermon on the Holy Eucharist, 307 ; consubstantiation and transubstantiation, 309-313 ; agreement with Bossuet, 313, 316, 317 ; a comparison of, with Newman, 314 ; not Protestant but Papist, 316 ; reference to Manning and, 316 ; on reunion with Rome, 318 ; how, outwent Newman, 321-324 ; peculiarities in the character of, 328 ; belief of, in contradictions, 329, 330 ; letter from Newman to, 331 *Note* ; love of, for Evangelicals, and "charitable exclusiveness," 333-335 ; the "naked Gospel" and "Sacramental Life," 336 ; comparison with Manning's "charity," 343 ; position of, in Church of England, 343 ; his "ritualism" and doctrine, 344-347 ; the attack on Protestantism, 348; the Romanising advance, 350-356 ; the secret of the influence of, and some limitations, 360-362 ; signs of healthy reaction against, 364, 367 ; responsibility of, for present crisis, 383 ; "secret history" of Puseyism, 386. (*See also* Appendix B. pp. 410-416.)

R

REDESDALE, LORD, exposure by, of *The Priest in Absolution*, 384.
REFORM BILL (1832), influence of, upon Church of England, 34, 35.
REUNION, conditions, of, 372.
RICHARDS, REV. W. UPTON, Pusey's pamphlet letter to, 293.
RILEY, ATHELSTAN, MR., probable wish of, as to Disestablishment, 352.
ROSE, HUGH JAMES, tribute to, by Newman, 35 ; *British Magazine*, edited by, 36 ; important gathering at Hadleigh Rectory, 36 ; Dean Burgon's account of, 37 ; association of, with Newman, 37, 38 ; early death of (1838), 37 ; remarks on, in relation to the Oxford Movement, 42-44 ; *The State of Protestantism in Germany*, 223 ; controversy with Pusey, 224-227, 248.
ROUTH, DR., influence of, upon Keble and Hurrell Froude, 3.

S

"SACRAMENTAL LIFE," THE, Pusey's theory of, 336, 357 *Note*.
St. *Saviour's Church, Leeds*, Romanising clergy removed from, 285, 296 ; tell-tale inscription above porch of, 297 ; popish character of services at, 297 ; perversion of clergy of, to Rome, 298 ; Hook's strong letter to Pusey as to, 298 ; Marriott's visit to, 299 ; further notes as to, 299-301, 363.
SALISBURY, LORD, the memory of Pusey honoured by, preface viii.
SAVILLE, REV. BOURCHIER WREY, quotation from pamphlet on Dr. Pusey, 295 *Note*.
SELLON, MISS, the case of, and the Plymouth Sisterhood, 295.
SIMEONITE EVANGELICALS, THE, 39.

SINCLAIR, ARCHDEACON, remarks of, on the Church Union, 205; antagonism of, to Romanising claims, 366, 393.
SISTERHOODS AND CELIBACY, 279.
"SMALL POPES," 335, 342, 356 *Note.*
SOUTHPORT, Parliamentary bye-election at, and Romanising Movement, 392.
Spectator, The, criticism of the *Christian Year* in, 5, 30.

T

TAIT, ARCHBISHOP, familiarity of, with, and grief at Puseyite practices, 228, 273, 282, 287 *Note*; address to, concerning *The Priest in Absolution,* 385.
TAYLOR, ARCHDEACON, Protestant Anglicanism of, 392.
Times, The, correspondence in, on Town and College Guilds, a development of Confessionalism, 302 *sq.*; on Anglican orders, 365, 374, 375; letter of Bishop of Hereford to, 392; criticism by, of Bishop of London, 393; Canon Fleming's letter to, on *The Crisis in the Church,* 393; Sir W. V. Harcourt's letters to, 394; letters of *Historicus* to, 394; letters of Bishop of Southwell to, 397.
Tracts for the Times, The, Keble's counsel to Newman respecting, 25; first issue of (1833), 36, 52; William Palmer's narrative of, 36 *Note*; object, teaching, and general effect of, 52-54; the chief three of, 53; Pusey in, on "Baptism," 53, 54; Dean Church's remarks on, 110-114.
TRACTARIAN COTERIE, THE, in Oxford, 114-118.
TRACTARIAN MOVEMENT, THE, first inspiration of, from union of Keble,

Newman, Hurrell Froude, 18; the start of the, attributed by Newman to Keble's *Assize Sermon,* 20; Newman and Pusey's influence on, 54; a momentous change in, 123; some lessons from, 196-198; transition from, to Puseyism, 199 *sq.*
TRACT 90, Keble and Newman jointly responsible for, 5; the casuistry of, 25; the condemnation of, 90.

U

UNITED STATES, ritualistic development in the, 208.
UNITY, CHURCH, true and false views of, 40-42.
UNIVERSITIES, different schools at Oxford and Cambridge, 39.

V

VAUGHAN, CARDINAL, an address by, at Bristol, on reunion, 370 *Note.*

W

WAKE, ARCHBISHOP, 320.
WALSH, MR., his *Secret History of the Oxford Movement,* pref. vii, viii, 272 *Note,* 276 *Note,* 382, 383, 385, 386, 390.
WARD, W. G., incidental references to, preface iv *Note,* xi, xii; friendship of, with Newman, 58; ecclesiastical point of view of, 59; joined the Roman communion, 60, 62, 90; biography of, by his son (vol. i.), 60; *Ideal of a Christian Church* published, 61; examined, 73-76; unique identity of, 63; early life of, 65; a disciple of Newman, 66; thoroughgoing boldness of, 67; contrast of, with Newman, 69, 70; intrepid logic of, 71; intellectual scepticism of,

75; family history of, 77; as a schoolboy, 78-80; characteristics and eccentricities of, 81-84; how, became Newman's disciple, 85-87; burlesque jocoseness of, 88; marriage of, and residence at Ware, 91; biography of (vol. ii.), 168; brief review of English Romanising, 169; President of Metaphysical Society, 171; an Ultramontane idealist, 172-174; Theism and Popery of, 175; faith of, and its grounds, 177; daily routine of life of, 179; mania of, for the sensational drama, 181; contrasted phases of character of, 183; association of, with Faber, 185; unique character of, 187; real earnestness of, 189; relations of, to Liberal Catholicism, 191; originality and eccentricities of, 193; the merits of, 195; Tennyson's tribute to, 195; some lessons from the life of, 196-198.

WARRINGTON, ARCHDEACON OF, letter to the *Times* on Anglican orders, 365.

WESLEY, JOHN, opinion of, as to Romish doctrine, 333; ordination of Coke by, 373.

Westminster Gazette, The, article in, on instruments of torture, 388, 389.

WHATELY, 220.

WILBERFORCE, ROBERT, pupil of Keble, 3; defection to Rome, 27, 200, 235.

WILBERFORCE, SAMUEL, alienation of, from High Anglican party, 235; protest of, against Romanist books of devotion, 273 *Note*; relations with Pusey (Sisterhoods), 282, 285, 286; skill and competency of, 283; Canon Butler's testimony to, 285; objection of, to the perpetual vow, 288.

WILLIAMS, ISAAC, pupil of Keble, 3.

WORLD, THE CHRISTIAN, the one hope of the, 325-327.

PRESS NOTICES OF THE FIRST EDITION.

OXFORD HIGH ANGLICANISM AND ITS CHIEF LEADERS.

Demy 8vo, 7s. 6d.

Dr. Rigg is perhaps the best known member of his communion in this country—known for his moderation of view, his wide reading, and his excellent literary style. . . . It is the only history of the Movement that is primarily critical, not to say hostile, if we except Pattison's Memoirs. Dr. Rigg strives to be fair; he lets his personages speak for themselves; and only here and there, and in his general summing up, does he allow himself the pleasure of denunciation. When this comes, however, it is done with a will.—*Times.*

The book is eloquently written; it presents a case which deserves and will repay attention, and is undeniably interesting.—*Manchester Guardian.*

It is an admirable piece of work, and can be cordially recommended to all who wish to have a readable and adequate account of Oxford High Anglicanism and its chief leaders.—*Glasgow Herald.*

Eminently fair. . . . No one who desires to understand some of the more important chapters in the religious life of the England of this century can afford to pass by the volume.—*Critical Review.*

Exceedingly interesting in itself, and marked by eminent ability and full competence to deal with the Oxford Movement from an external point of view.—*Record.*

Dr. Rigg is always strong, and, in our opinion, he is scrupulously just. His position is somewhat peculiar, if not altogether unique. He tells us he is "not a political Dissenter." There is certainly no trace of bitterness even in the force and cogency with which he combats the arguments and condemns many of the practices of the Oxford school. His estimate of the result of Newman's teaching and influence is singularly outspoken and essentially just. The comparison between Hugh James Rose and the great Tractarian leader is marked by true critical acumen. . . . For ourselves, we detect none of the omens for good which Dr. Rigg finds. . . . Of the literary and historic value of Dr. Rigg's book we cannot well speak too highly.—*Independent and Nonconformist.*

A somewhat conspicuous gap in the literature of the Oxford Movement has been filled by the publication of Dr. Rigg's work on Oxford High Anglicanism. . . . What gives the book its special value is the view it offers, impressive and even startling in its connected sequence, of the mental and moral characteristics, as well as of the doctrinal prepossessions, of the men who during the last half century have been endeavouring to revolutionise the religion of England.—*Christian World.*

Dr. Rigg examines High Anglicanism with great acumen and breadth. No student of the period can afford to neglect this important volume.—*Irish Times.*

We need a history of this crusade in the interests of mediævalism, and we could not have it from a better pen. The book is graphically written, and shows evidence on every page of a wide acquaintance with all that has been written upon the subject.—*Christian Leader.*

A real and valuable and permanent contribution to the religious history of our time. . . . It fills admirably a great gap, and is an invaluable guide to the issues of the day.—*Bristol Mercury.*

The whole book is full of interest.—*Lincoln Mercury.*

BY THE SAME AUTHOR.

A Comparative View of Church Organizations, Primitive and Protestant. With a Supplement on Methodist Secessions and Methodist Union. Third Edition, Revised and Enlarged. Demy 8vo, 7s. 6d.

"The work is more than ever worthy of its place in ecclesiastical literature."—*Scotsman.*

Modern Anglican Theology: Chapters on COLERIDGE, HARE, MAURICE, KINGSLEY, and JOWETT; and on the Doctrine of Sacrifice and Atonement. Third Edition, to which is prefixed a Memoir of Canon KINGSLEY, with Personal Reminiscences. Crown 8vo, 7s. 6d.

"Exceedingly cultured essays on the various aspects of Anglican theology. . . . Dr. Rigg has added an extremely interesting and valuable memoir of Canon Kingsley."—*Nonconformist and Independent.*

The Living Wesley. New Edition. Much Enlarged, including a Chapter on the Progress of Universal Methodism since the death of Wesley. Crown 8vo, with Portrait, 2s. 6d.

"A strong, sound, mature book, written by a Christian statesman who knows his subject to its last recesses."—*British Weekly.*

The Churchmanship of John Wesley, and the Relations of Wesleyan Methodism to the Church of England. New and Revised Edition. Crown 8vo, 2s. 6d.

"Dr. Rigg is a clear and precise writer, and in a few brief chapters he has not only admirably portrayed this phase of Wesley's character, but he has been successful in clearly defining the position of Methodism with regard to the Establishment."—*The Christian.*

National Education in its Social Conditions and Aspects, and Public Elementary School Education, English and Foreign. Crown 8vo, 6s.

"We know of no book in which the reader will find the educational schemes of the Continent and America laid before him in a manner so concise and yet so sufficient for practical purposes. . . . As a clear description and acute comparison of the different national schemes of education, Dr. Rigg's book leaves nothing to be desired."—*Times.*

"History outlasts polemics; judgment is longer lived than partisan advocacy; and we therefore believe that Dr. Rigg's homelier but steadier light will remain when Mr. Morley's clever fireworks have gone out."—*Guardian.*

Discourses and Addresses on Leading Truths of Religion and Philosophy. Demy 8vo, 468 pp., 10s.

"Dr. Rigg writes in a generous, earnest, and evangelical spirit; and no one will be able to read this vigorous, warm, and eloquent presentation of his views without deriving moral, spiritual, and intellectual benefit."—*Leeds Mercury.*

The Connexional Economy of Wesleyan Methodism in its Ecclesiastical and Spiritual Aspects. Crown 8vo, 3s. 6d.

"Able, weighty, and powerful. . . . This invaluable treatise."—*Methodist Recorder.*

The Sabbath and the Sabbath Law before and after Christ. Second Edition. Crown 8vo, 2s.

"It is characterised by great fairness, and is clear and dispassionate."—*Christian Age.*

LONDON: CHARLES H. KELLY, 2, CASTLE STREET, CITY ROAD, E.C.;
AND 26, PATERNOSTER ROW, E.C.

CHARLES H. KELLY'S RECENT BOOKS.

The Fernley Lecture of 1896.

The Theology of Modern Fiction. By THOMAS G. SELBY. Third Thousand. Demy 8vo, paper covers, 2s. ; cloth, gilt lettered, 3s.

"Mr. Selby brings to the treatment of his subject extensive and accurate knowledge and a fine literary taste. His exposition of the teachings of the writers with whom he deals is done with remarkable care, whilst his lucidity of style and felicity of illustration are everywhere conspicuous."—*Leeds Mercury.*

The Fernley Lecture of 1897.

The Spiritual Principle of the Atonement as a Satisfaction made to God for the Sins of the World. By J. SCOTT LIDGETT, M.A., Warden of the Bermondsey Settlement. Second Edition. Demy 8vo, xxiii, 498 pp., 5s.

"For the total impression made upon us by this work is that of a performance which in its grasp of the subject, its research, and its critical ability is fitted to rank with the ablest treatises on its theme that have appeared in this generation."—*Christian World.*

By Professor Davison.

The Christian Interpretation of Life, and Other Essays. By WILLIAM T. DAVISON, M.A., D.D., Author of "The Praises of Israel," "The Christian Conscience," etc. Post 8vo, 4s. 6d.

"An exceedingly able and instructive criticism from the orthodox standpoint. He brings to his topics not only a thorough grasp of the points in discussion, but a general literary culture and an epigrammatic force of expression which make it a real pleasure to read him."
—*Christian World.*

"Helps Heavenward."—Second Series.

Saints of Christ. By T. F. LOCKYER, B.A., Author of "The Inspirations of the Christian Life," "The Gospel of St. John: An Exposition," etc. Crown 12mo, art linen, gilt top, 1s. 6d.

"Thorough, practical, and stimulating."—*Sunday School Chronicle.*

"The treatment of the subject is clear and sensible. Mr. Lockyer's idea of saintship is thoroughly biblical, and therefore human."—*Hastings and St Leonards Times.*

"Books for Bible Students."

Studies in Comparative Religion. By ALFRED S. GEDEN, M.A., Author of "Exercises for Translation into Hebrew." Small crown 8vo, 2s. 6d.

"The author writes with a very full knowledge of the literature of his subject, and presents the results of wide research in a readable and attractive form. The book is remarkably well informed, and it cannot fail to be useful as an introduction to this wide and growing subject."—*Glasgow Herald.*

The Church of the West in the Middle Ages. By HERBERT B. WORKMAN, M.A. Small crown 8vo, 2s. 6d.

"Intent on Pleasing Thee." A Manual for Would-be Christians. By A. R. KELLEY, Author of "Following Christ." Crown 12mo, art linen, gilt top, 1s. 6d.

"Devout and practical, and for those beginning the Christian life nothing could be more admirable. This little book is calculated to do much good."—*Christian Leader.*

Creed and Conduct. A Series of Readings for Each Week of the Year from Dr. ALEXANDER MACLAREN. Selected and Arranged by Rev. GEORGE COATES. Second Thousand. With Portrait. Crown 8vo, 3s. 6d.

"I cannot imagine a more serviceable aid to private devotion or a more valuable help to those who . . . need suggestions for the exposition, illustration, and application of the Word of God. It is a perfect mine of evangelical and spiritual truth."—*Great Thoughts.*

LONDON: CHARLES H. KELLY, 2, CASTLE STREET, CITY ROAD, E.C.;
AND 26, PATERNOSTER ROW, E.C.

CHARLES H. KELLY'S RECENT BOOKS.

A Young Man's Bookshelf. By Rev. GEORGE JACKSON, B.A. Second Thousand. Crown 12mo, art linen, gilt top, 2s. 6d.

"A model handbook. The style, which is lucid and flowing, would of itself enchant intelligent readers. It is wonderful how much information he compresses into a narrow space, and how helpful towards the purpose in view every detail becomes."—*Methodist Recorder.*

Beckside Lights. By JOHN ACKWORTH, Author of "Clog Shop Chronicles." Fifth Thousand. Crown 8vo, art linen, gilt top, 3s. 6d.

"Mr. Ackworth can set the springs of human sympathy flowing in the most barren ground. . . . To this keen and humorous observer of village life there are ever new phases of the old to describe."—*Manchester Guardian.*

Lectures and Sermons of Peter Mackenzie. Edited by Rev. JOSEPH DAWSON. Fifth Thousand. With Two new Portraits. Crown 8vo, 3s. 6d.

"A choice volume, and one which will be sure to receive a cordial welcome. . . . It is astonishing how much of the popular personality of the humorous preacher and lecturer is introduced."—*Lincolnshire Free Press.*

Great Britain and her Queen. An Account of the Queen's Reign, 1837-1897, with a Chapter on Methodist History of the Period. By ANNE E. KEELING. Illustrated with more than 150 Portraits of Public Persons, including Presidents of the Conference; also views of the chief Public Buildings of Methodism. Crown 8vo, 2s.; gilt edges, 2s. 6d.

The Tendencies of Modern Theology. By Rev. J. SHAW BANKS, Headingley College. Post 8vo, 3s. 6d.

"A volume of great interest. The most important theological works of recent years are reviewed with a skill and competence beyond all question. Mr. Banks' wide knowledge and forceful style make his book of the highest value to every student of theology."—*Christian World.*

Creed and Conduct. A Series of Readings for each Week of the Year from Dr. ALEXANDER MACLAREN. Selected and Arranged by Rev. GEORGE COATES. With Portrait. Crown 8vo, 3s. 6d.

"I cannot imagine a more serviceable aid to private devotion, or a more valuable help to those who . . . need suggestions for the exposition, illustration, and application of the Word of God. It is a perfect mine of evangelical and spiritual truth."—*Great Thoughts.*

COPYRIGHT SERIES OF "AMERICAN AUTHORS."—NEW VOLUME.

Overruled. By "PANSY." Crown 8vo, 2s. 6d.

Parables and Pictures from MARK GUY PEARSE. Selected and Arranged by Mrs. HAMLY. Royal 16mo, red lines round page, art linen, gilt top, 2s. 6d.

"Probably no religious writer of the present day has the gift of parable more strongly developed than Mr. Pearse. They are clean cut, concise, pre-eminently to the point, and always readable."—*The Presbyterian.*

Irish Methodism. A History for the People. By Rev. RANDALL C. PHILLIPS. Crown 8vo, paper covers, 4d.; cloth boards, 9d.; cloth, gilt lettered, 1s.

Modern Thoughts on Ancient Stories. By Rev. JOSEPH BUSH. Post 8vo, 2s. 6d.

The Scripture Way of Salvation. By Rev. JOHN WESLEY, M.A. With Preface and Notes by Professor J. AGAR BEET, D.D. Crown 12mo, cloth, gilt top, 8d.

The Treasures of the Snow, and other Talks with Children. By Rev. THOMAS HIND. Illustrated. Crown 8vo, 1s. 6d.

Barbara Heck. A Story of Early Methodism in America. By W. H. WITHROW, M.A. Fifteen Illustrations. Crown 8vo, 2s. 6d.

Clog Shop Chronicles. By JOHN ACKWORTH. Tenth Thousand. Crown 8vo, art linen, gilt top, 3s. 6d.

"The book is distinctly a work of genius, the author is not only saturated with his subject, but has the power to convey his impressions vividly and distinctly. Humour, pathos, tragedy, abound. . . . From first to last presents feasts of good things."—*Birmingham Daily Gazette.*

LONDON: CHARLES H. KELLY, 2, CASTLE STREET, CITY ROAD, E.C.;
AND 26, PATERNOSTER ROW, E.C.

CHARLES H. KELLY'S RECENT BOOKS.

A String of Chinese Peach Stones. Being a Collection of the Tales and Folk-lore of the Hankow District, which eventually becomes a story of the Tai-ping Rebellion in Central China. By Rev. W. ARTHUR CORNABY. More than 100 Original Illustrations. 496 pp. Demy 8vo, cloth extra, gilt top, 10s. 6d.

"This book might be best characterised by a string of epithets—charming, instructive enthralling, romantic, picturesque, tragic, kaleidoscopic in its shifting scenes and adventures . . . There may be little in a name, but there is no doubt that the charm is in the book."—*Scottish Geographical Magazine.*

In the Banqueting House. A Series of Meditations on the Lord's Supper. By MARK GUY PEARSE. Second Thousand. Printed in Two Colours. Large crown 8vo, art linen, gilt top, 3s. 6d.

"These charmingly written and beautifully printed chapters. They are both spiritual and literary ; the fruit of long mastery of the English language and of long fellowship with God."—*Expository Times.*

THE FERNLEY LECTURE OF 1896.

The Theology of Modern Fiction. By Rev. T. G. SELBY. Third Thousand. Demy 8vo, paper covers, 2s. ; cloth, gilt lettered, 3s.

"Mr. Selby brings to the treatment of his subject extensive and accurate knowledge and a fine literary taste. His exposition of the teachings of the writers with whom he deals is done with remarkable care, whilst his lucidity of style and felicity of illustration are everywhere conspicuous."—*Leeds Mercury.*

Across Siberia on the Great Post Road. By CHARLES WENYON, M.D. Third Thousand. With Portrait, Map, and Twenty-seven Illustrations. Imperial 16mo, 3s. 6d.

"One of the pleasantest books of travel we have read for some time. It is the chatty record of a cultured and genially-minded man, of a journey across the vast Siberian steppes. One lays it down with the feeling of parting from a congenial fellow-traveller on a long and memorable journey."—*Sheffield Independent.*

Peter Mackenzie : His Life and Labours. By Rev. JOSEPH DAWSON. Thirty-fifth Thousand. Three Portraits and Eighteen other Illustrations. Crown 8vo, 3s. 6d.

"Mr. Dawson has collected his materials with praiseworthy industry, and he has woven them together in a skilful and artistic manner. . . . Those who wish to know something more of the extraordinary nature of Peter Mackenzie's life and work, we can only advise to obtain Mr. Dawson's admirable memoir, and to read the remarkable record for themselves."—*Leeds Mercury.*

Bryan Roe : A Soldier of the Cross. Sketches of Missionary Life and Adventure in West Central Africa. By Rev. C. R. JOHNSON. Second Thousand. Numerous Illustrations. Crown 8vo, 2s. 6d.

"His life was full of stimulus to others ; and the little book which tells the story breathes the same excellent spirit. It should be put into the hands of all friends of missions, young and old."—*Christian.*

Gleanings in the Gospels. By Rev. HENRY BURTON, M.A., Author of St. Luke in "The Expositor's Bible." Demy 8vo, 3s. 6d.

"Seventeen exquisite chapters on the 'Sweet Story of Old' in its varied beauties of aspect. Cultured and devout Christians will find in this book a storehouse of saintly reflections and holy thoughts to delight the soul."—*Joyful News.*

Digging Ditches, and Other Sermons to Boys and Girls. By Rev. FREDERIC B. COWL. Second Thousand. Small crown 8vo, 1s. 6d.

"Short, simply worded, charged with moral lessons of moment, and as full of interest as an egg is full of meat ; . . . might be taken as models of their kind."—*Christian Age.*

The Popular History of Methodism. By Rev. JOHN TELFORD, B.A. Ninetieth Thousand. 64 pp. Crown 8vo, 1d. ; or 6d. per 100 net.

A Pioneer of Social Christianity : Count Zinzendorf. By FELIX BOVET. Translated, Abridged, and Adapted by Rev. T. A. SEED. With Portrait, and several rare and curious Illustrations. Crown 8vo, 1s. 6d.

"Mr. Seed is to be greatly congratulated upon having produced a most fascinating volume, which, once begun, will not be laid aside until the last page is read."—*Methodist Times.*

LONDON: CHARLES H. KELLY, 2, CASTLE STREET, CITY ROAD, E.C. ;
AND 26, PATERNOSTER ROW, E.C.

SOME RECENT FERNLEY LECTURES.

Jesus Christ and the Present Age. The Twenty-fifth Fernley Lecture, delivered in Plymouth, August 2, 1895. By JAMES CHAPMAN. Demy 8vo, paper covers, 1s. 6d.; cloth, gilt lettered, 2s. 6d.

"A book well worth reading; full of careful thought on every page, often in every sentence. . . . Vigorous, manly, scholarly, an excellent specimen of Methodism at its best."
—*Manchester Courier.*

Christian Doctrine and Morals viewed in their Connexion. The Twenty-fourth Fernley Lecture, delivered in Carr's Lane Chapel, Birmingham, July 27, 1894. By GEORGE G. FINDLAY, B.A. Demy 8vo, paper covers, 2s.; cloth, gilt lettered, 3s.

"It is a thoroughly able, devout, and well-balanced presentation of Christian doctrine."—*British Weekly.*

"It is fresh and full and living, more than all, it is prophetic. Let our readers read themselves into its spirit, into its philosophy, and into its gospel, without a day's delay."—*Free Methodist.*

Christianity and Socialism. By WILLIAM NICHOLAS, M.A., D.D. Demy 8vo, paper covers, 2s.; cloth, 3s.

"With admirable clearness and fairness he has traced the rise and development of the various theories of Socialism. . . . With equal clearness and ability Dr. Nicholas shows that Socialism is unnecessary, that Christianity is sufficient for our needs, and that, were its principles applied, the evils which curse modern society would disappear."—*Christian Age.*

The Design and Use of Holy Scripture. By MARSHALL RANDLES, D.D. Demy 8vo, paper covers, 2s.; cloth, 3s.

"A weighty and sober contribution to Christian apologia."—*Thinker.*

"Abounds with evidences of wide reading, and contains much that cannot fail to be helpful in the culture of the Christian life."—*Christian World.*

The Credentials of the Gospel. A Statement of the Reason of the Christian Hope. By JOSEPH AGAR BEET, D.D. Fifth Thousand. Demy 8vo, paper covers, 1s. 6d.; cloth, gilt lettered, 2s. 6d.

"However well read in apologetic literature any one is, he will find much to interest and much to convince in the chapters which deal with the resurrection and the miraculous. At this point Professor Beet makes a distinct advance in the argument, and deserves the thanks of all who are interested in the defence of Christianity. The book is throughout written in an admirable style."—Dr. MARCUS DODS in the *Expositor.*

The Christian Conscience. A Contribution to Christian Ethics. By WILLIAM T. DAVISON, M.A., D.D. Fifth Thousand. Demy 8vo, paper covers, 2s.; cloth, 3s.

"Acute, forcible, and interesting. . . . Treats a large subject entirely without superficiality, and yet in a popular style."—*Scotsman.*

"Unquestionably one of the finest and most timely deliverances that has ever emanated from the Fernley chair."—*Lincolnshire Free Press.*

The Creator, and What we may Know of the Method of Creation. By WILLIAM H. DALLINGER, D.D., LL.D., D.Sc., F.R.S. Tenth Thousand. Paper covers, 1s. 6d; cloth, 2s. 6d.

"A most carefully written discourse, and will unquestionably be read with profit by the thoughtful reader."—*Scientific Enquirer.*

"Contains as much real thought, sound philosophy, logical reasoning, and solid instruction as are found only in large treatises."—*Oldham Chronicle.*

The Influence of Scepticism on Character. By WILLIAM L. WATKINSON. Eighth Thousand. 8vo, paper covers, 1s. 6d.; cloth, 2s. 6d.

"Demonstrates very ably and clearly the demoralising effects of scepticism."—*Record.*

"Outspoken and ably written."—*Leeds Mercury.*

"It enters very thoroughly into the subject, and numerous examples are given of the deteriorating effect of unbelief in the human character."—*Daily Chronicle.*

LONDON : CHARLES H. KELLY, 2, CASTLE STREET, CITY ROAD, E.C.;
AND 26, PATERNOSTER ROW, E.C.

www.ingramcontent.com/pod-product-compliance
Lightning Source LLC
Chambersburg PA
CBHW022141300426
44115CB00006B/293